The American Community College

Fifth Edition

Arthur M. Cohen
Florence B. Brawer

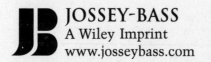
JOSSEY-BASS
A Wiley Imprint
www.josseybass.com

Published by Jossey-Bass
A Wiley Imprint
989 Market Street, San Francisco, CA 94103-1741—www.josseybass.com

Readers should be aware that Internet Web sites offered as citations and/or sources for further information may have changed or disappeared between the time this was written and when it is read.

Jossey-Bass books and products are available through most bookstores.
To contact Jossey-Bass directly call our Customer Care Department within the U.S.
at 800-956-7739, outside the U.S. at 317-572-3986, or fax 317-572-4002.

Jossey-Bass also publishes its books in a variety of electronic formats. Some content that appears in print may not be available in electronic books.

Library of Congress Cataloging-in-Publication Data

Cohen, Arthur M.
    The American community college/Arthur M. Cohen and Florence B. Brawer.—5th ed.
      p. cm.
    Includes bibliographical references and index.
    ISBN 978-0-470-17468-5 (cloth)
      1. Community colleges—United States.   I. Brawer, Florence B., 1922-   II. Title.
LB2328.C55   2008
378.1'5430973—dc22
                                              2008018498

Printed in the United States of America
FIFTH EDITION
HB Printing 10 9 8 7 6 5 4 3 2 1

The Jossey-Bass
Higher and Adult Education Series

Contents

Foreword to the First Edition

This book appears at a time of great significance to the community college. The decade of the 1980s will mark a turning point in its history. It is already evident that the community college is experiencing the effects of lean years, following an unusually long succession of fat years when a new college appeared each week and double-digit enrollment increases were announced annually. Especially threatening are the public's efforts to curtail spending by propositions such as 13 (California) and 2½ (Massachusetts) and by caps on enrollment. Significant for the future may be the end of the campaign to transmute the community college into a new kind of institution, neither college nor high school—an idea espoused by Edmund J. Gleazer, who recently retired as president of the American Association of Community and Junior Colleges. These developments and many others mentioned by Cohen and Brawer may denote for the community college maturity, as well as the end of the Golden Age.

Cohen and Brawer's book will take its place alongside books by such community college giants as Koos, Eells, Bogue, and Medsker. Their comprehensive, incisive, interpretive analysis of the community colleges covers nearly all facets of the college. They start with a historical analysis of the origins and development of the college and end with a critique of the college's critics. In between, chapters are devoted to administrators, students, and faculty. Four chapters, almost one-third of the book, are devoted to the curriculum functions. Chapter One offers the rationale used throughout most of the book. The authors state that their function is to present information and examine the many viewpoints that have been advanced. From this approach, they do not expect to find ultimate answers but hope that better questions will result.

Those acquainted with the authors will not be surprised that they undertook this formidable task. They know that Cohen and Brawer have been immersed in community college research for more than two decades. During that time they have visited hundreds of community colleges, associated with nearly all those who have written on the college, reviewed thousands of documents sent for inclusion in the collection of the ERIC Clearinghouse for Junior Colleges since it was organized in 1966, edited the quarterly *New Directions for Community Colleges* series from its origin in 1973, and conducted major research in the humanities and sciences through the Center for the Study of Community Colleges. There is hardly a subject or topic on community college education that does not appear in one or more publications that have been written by them or produced under their guidance. Their book is a distillation of this vast experience and knowledge and is a capstone to the many articles and books they have written individually and as coauthors.

The [original] thirteen chapters describe, probe, and dissect every facet of the institution, sometimes sympathetically, at other times critically, although seldom superficially. Despite the kaleidoscopic nature of the community college, the authors' comprehensive, incisive treatment brings into focus the changes it has undergone since its modest beginnings as a liberal arts junior college to the multifaceted giant community college of the 1960s and 1970s. Now, the incipient reform movement calls into question the sacrosanct principles of the open door and equal opportunity. Instead of the new institution, neither high school nor college, the authors see a return to an expanded version of the college of the postwar era of the 1940s and 1950s.

In chapter after chapter the authors make clear that research as often as not raises more questions than answers. In the areas of teaching and especially learning, the profession has made very little progress in evaluating its efforts. A historical survey of the research in these two areas would, if presented graphically, look much like graphs depicting the course of the economy, with cyclical changes representing the rise and fall of particular theories. One would like to see the trend line in community college learning slope upward, but as Cohen and Brawer intimate, the trend line here, as in nearly all segments of education, would have a downward slope. Despite all the labors, the results, except as reported by those in charge of the experiments, are of minor significance unless one gains some comfort that the educators have learned which ideas and theories do not produce results.

Although the authors modestly assert that answers to current problems will not be found, one wonders whether it is possible for two of the most prominent students of the community college, with strong convictions expressed in many publications, to submerge those convictions in questions in such a comprehensive, wide-ranging book. Their strategy of wondering, offering information, and examining many viewpoints has enabled them to range further afield speculatively, seemingly without committing themselves. Yet questions, no matter how carefully worded, often suggest the answers the authors would have given if they had been taking the test instead of administering it. It is noteworthy that in the four curriculum chapters, the authors dispense with questions; they substitute their convictions. How could it be otherwise with authors who have been immersed in the study of the community college for two decades?

The reader will be confronted with the many paradoxes surrounding the community college. The most nettlesome is, as the authors point out, that it is called a college, but elementary-grade subjects—arithmetic, reading, writing—rank high in terms of courses offered and students enrolled. Another: although it has been the fastest-growing segment of education, it seems to be the least known. After seventy-five years it has yet to adopt a name that describes its functions. "Identity" or "image" remains one of the most serious concerns of community college educators—a concern that has been with them almost from the beginning. It will, the authors imply, remain with them as long as the community college remains for students a second or lower choice rather than an equal choice with other higher education institutions and as long as educators and leaders of their professional organizations continue to emulate chameleons in adopting and dropping one educational fad after another, all in the name of innovation.

One of the most intriguing chapters is "The Social Role." The reader will find here the arguments of the leading critics that the community college has failed to provide upward mobility or access to higher education. Briefly, the authors describe the criticisms and, at times, raise questions about their validity. They resist the temptation to be apologists, pointing out that the persistence of doubts concerning the community college's role in furthering upward mobility derives "from a gap in perception" of the educators.

In the chapter "Collegiate Function," the authors make a strong plea for "liberal education for the informed citizen." The community colleges, they maintain, must "provide some portions of the education for the masses that tends toward encouraging exercise of the intellect." They offer a "model for effecting general education for a free people in a free society."

Because this book records the many changes that affect the community college and, more important, the way educational leaders react to them, it will appeal to those who seek only the "facts." How many? What courses and curricula? Where from? At the other extreme it will help those seeking to understand the philosophy—philosophies perhaps—that has propelled this institution to its present status. The critics—the community college personnel and the authors' colleagues who are involved in research on the institution—will find much to applaud and probably more to contend with. Although the authors will welcome the plaudits, they will not be disappointed if they elicit disagreement. They have strong beliefs and they are critics. So they will welcome the opportunity to be on the receiving end for the sake of starting a dialogue that they believe is urgently needed as educational leaders struggle to find solutions in the new, unfamiliar environment of zero growth and fiscal retrenchment.

September 1981   *John Lombardi*
                                                     Former President
                                               Los Angeles City College

Preface

This is the fifth edition of a book published originally in 1982. It is about American community colleges, institutions that offer associate degrees and occupational certificates to their students and a variety of other services to the communities in which they are located. These 1,285 colleges range in size from fewer than one hundred to more than forty thousand students. Around one-tenth of them, mostly the smaller institutions, are privately supported. The others, the larger, comprehensive structures, are found in every state.

Audience

In this edition, as with the previous editions, our purpose is to present a comprehensive, one-volume text useful for everyone concerned with higher education: college staff members, graduate students, trustees, and state-level officials. The descriptions and analyses of each of the institution's functions can be used by administrators who want to learn about practices that have proved effective in other colleges, curriculum planners involved in program revision, faculty members seeking ideas for modifying their courses, and trustees and officials concerned with college policies regarding curriculum and student flow.

The book focuses mainly on the period since 1960, when the community colleges underwent several major changes. Since that time, the number of public two-year institutions has increased by 200 percent and their enrollments by 800 percent. The relations between administrators and faculty changed as multicampus districts were formed and as contracts negotiated through collective bargaining became common. Institutional financing was affected by both tax limitations and a continuing trend toward state-level funding. The proportion of students transferring to universities fell, and those transferring from universities rose. The collegiate function was shaken as vocational and community education made tremendous strides and as the colleges grappled with problems of teaching the functionally illiterate.

The book is written as an interpretive analysis. It provides data summaries on students, faculty, curriculum, and many other quantifiable dimensions of the institutions. It explores the inversion of institutional purpose that resulted in the vocational programs serving as a major preliminary for transfer and the transfer programs losing their preeminence. It explains how students' patterns of college attendance forced a conversion from a linear to a lateral curriculum pattern, from students taking courses in sequence to students dropping into and out of classes almost at will. It shows how the vocational, developmental, community, and collegiate education functions are interrelated and how counseling and other auxiliary services can be integrated into the instructional program. It examines some of the criticism that has been leveled at the community college by those who feel it is doing a disservice to most of its matriculants, especially ethnic minorities. And it concludes with a look at the future development of these institutions.

A revised edition of our work is warranted now because several changes have occurred since the fourth edition appeared. In the colleges, faculty power has consolidated, only to be met by countervailing power concentrated at the state level. Mandatory testing and placing of students has spread. Developmental education has become more prominent, taking its place as a curriculum function second only to vocational and collegiate education. Administrators have had to become more attentive to state-level directives regarding institutional functioning and funding.

Yet many things have remained the same. Few new public colleges have been formed in the past twenty-five years, and the ratio of full-time students to part-time students and of full-time faculty to part-time faculty has changed very little. College organization, instruction, and institutional purpose are not different. The colleges are still concerned with providing relevant educational services to their clients, who attend for various reasons. Most of the issues that we noted at the end of each chapter in the earlier editions are repeated here; the most intractable problems are never solved. As I. F. Stone said in *The Trial of Socrates*, "Change is a constant but so is identity. The whole truth can only be achieved by taking both into consideration" (1987, p. 69).

We have made several changes in the book from the previous edition. The chapter organization remains the same, and each chapter reviews the antecedents of practices and policies purposely to show that all have a history underlying contemporary activities and perceptions. But within each chapter, we have updated the tables and figures to depict the most recent data, and we have incorporated new examples of the services that the colleges provide. We have expanded our discussions of student flow, institutional finance, instruction, student services, and curricular functions by providing recent information in these areas. We have traced the spread of online instruction and the intractable need for developmental education. We have documented the demographically influenced increase in baccalaureate-bound students and its effect on curriculum. We have made a case for revising general education to emphasize service learning and sustainability. And we have criticized some of the economic impact studies and reviewed the outcomes indicator reports that have been produced in response to legislative demands for accountability.

Overview of the Contents

Chapter One recounts the social forces that contributed to the expansion and contemporary development of the community colleges. It examines the ever-evolving institutional purposes, showing how their changes sometimes conflict with funding patterns and often lag behind public perceptions. It traces the reasons that local funding and control have given way to state-level management, and it questions what the shape of American higher education would be if there were no community colleges.

Chapter Two displays the changing patterns of student demographics and explores the reasons for part-time attendance patterns. The chapter also examines attrition, showing that the concept is an institutional artifact that masks students' true achievements, and it reviews the most recent data on student transfer rates.

Chapter Three draws on national data to show how the full-time and part-time faculty differ. It examines tenure, salary, workload, modes of faculty evaluation, professional associations, and faculty preparation. It discusses satisfaction, professionalism, and the conflict between instructors' desires for better students and the realities of the institutions in which they work.

Chapter Four reviews the modifications in college management that have resulted from changes in institutional size, the advent of collective bargaining, reductions in available funds, and changes in the locus of control. Examples of varying modes of college organization and the role of each administrator within them are presented.

Chapter Five describes the various funding patterns, showing how they have followed shifts in mode of organization. Relations between tuition and student aid are explored. The chapter details the effects of fiscal limitation measures and shows how various cost-saving practices have been installed. It also considers the often incredulous attempts to assess the colleges' impact on the economy of their local communities.

Chapter Six reviews the stability in instructional forms that have been maintained in the colleges. It discusses instructional technology and such instructional techniques as television, computers, writing across the curriculum, supplemental instruction, and mastery learning. Notes on learning resource centers, the idea of the learning college, and online and competency-based instruction precede a discussion of the assessment of instructional effects.

Chapter Seven traces the student personnel functions, including counseling and guidance, student recruitment and retention, orientation, and extracurricular activities. It also considers financial aid and the shifting patterns of articulation, detailing efforts to enhance student flow from community colleges to senior institutions.

Chapter Eight considers the rise of occupational education as it has moved from a peripheral to a central position in the institutions. No longer a terminal function for a few students, vocational education now serves people seeking new jobs and upgrading in jobs they already have, students gaining the first two years of a career-oriented bachelor's degree program, and candidates for relicensing. The chapter also discusses the contributions that vocational education makes to the community.

Chapter Nine traces the decline in student literacy at all levels of education and shows how community colleges are bearing the brunt of students' ill-preparedness. It reviews specific college programs designed to strengthen students' basic skills, examines the controversies surrounding student mainstreaming and restrictive programming, and explores the options of screening students at entry on a course-by-course basis or, instead, allowing students to enter any course of their choice but requiring simultaneous remedial assistance. The chapter details the rise of developmental education to a level of importance second only to that of collegiate and career studies.

Chapter Ten considers adult and continuing education, lifelong learning, and community services. It recounts numerous examples of cooperative arrangements between colleges and community agencies, asks how funding can be maintained for this function, and explores how the major institutional associations continue to promote community education. The chapter also considers the assessment of effects and the validation of services that fall outside traditional collegiate offerings.

Chapter Eleven considers the rise, fall, and subsequent stabilization of the liberal arts. How collegiate studies affect student transfer to senior institutions is included, as are discussions of the academic disciplines, the idea of general education, the faculty as a liberal arts support group, transfer rates, reverse transfers, and assessment of student learning in the liberal arts.

Chapter Twelve discusses research in and about the community colleges, an area that until recently has received little acknowledgment from sources outside the colleges. It reviews the groups that conduct research, the types of research they report, the external mandates that affect their studies, and some of their findings.

Chapter Thirteen examines the philosophical and practical questions that have been raised about the community college's role in leveling the social class structure in America in general and in enhancing student progress toward higher degrees in particular. It shows how the same data can be used to reach different conclusions when the critics do not properly consider the differences between social equalization and equal access for individuals. The chapter poses alternative organizational forms within existing community colleges so that the colleges can provide equity, access, and an avenue for individuals to attain higher degrees.

Chapter Fourteen projects trends in student and faculty demographics and indicates the areas where change will occur in college organization, curriculum, instruction, and student services. It also comments on the ascendant role of developmental education and projects the future of moves toward assessing college outcomes.

Sources

The information included in this book derives from many sources but predominantly from published observations and findings. Major books and journals and the Educational Resources Information

Center (ERIC) files have been searched for documents pertaining to each topic. We have also relied on our own surveys, conducted since 1974 through the Center for the Study of Community Colleges.

This attention to the extant literature has both positive and negative features. On the plus side, it enables us to plot trends in curriculum, faculty functioning, patterns of student attendance, and college organization. On the other side, it limits our sources of information to surveys and written material. Surveys necessarily condense unique activities into percentages, thereby muting some of the vibrancy that colleges and their offerings manifest. Researching just the available literature limits our awareness of college practices to a view of institutions where staff have written descriptions for general distribution.

Although we have relied primarily on printed sources and our own research studies, we have also sought counsel from the many community college staff members around the country whom we met at conferences and during our visits to their own institutions. Although we have drawn on all these sources and tried to present an even-handed treatment, we must admit that we have our prejudices. We are advocates for community colleges, believing that they have an essential role to play in the fabric of American education. We are advocates for their educative dimension, the aspect of their efforts that affects human learning. And we favor especially the collegiate function, feeling that it must be maintained if community colleges are to continue as comprehensive institutions and if students are to be prepared for life in an ever-changing world.

Above all, we are critical analysts, concerned more with examining the ideas undergirding the community colleges' functions than with describing the operations themselves. We wonder about the interrelations of funding, management, curriculum, and teaching. And we are concerned about the shape that the institutions have taken as they continually seek to modify their functions.

The last point deserves elaboration. Which college serves best? One with ten thousand students, each taking one class? One with five thousand students, each taking two classes? Or one with twenty-five hundred students, each taking four classes? In all cases, the cost is about the same, but the institutions are quite different. In the first example, the college has a broad base of clients, and its curriculum has a lateral form composed of disparate courses, such as those offered through university extension or adult education centers. In the second, the curriculum has taken a more linear shape, and the implication is that students are expected to progress toward a certificate or degree. The third type of college has apparently restricted admission to those who can attend full time, and its courses are arrayed in sequential fashion, each of them demanding prerequisites. The recent moves toward offering the baccalaureate and toward creating early college initiatives are the most notable contemporary examples of that. When state regulations authorize such vertical expansion, some college-level policymakers eagerly accept the opportunity to change their institutions, whereas others shun it. Those who open bachelor's degree programs argue they are satisfying demand and relish the four-year college status. Those who erect collaborative grades 11 to 14 structures that reduce dropout and enhance college-going assert they are mitigating social problems. The point is that either of these modifications can be made by officials operating colleges within the same state and under the same statutes.

Numerous changes in American society and in public outlook have occurred in recent years, but the colleges have been affected hardly at all. The federal budgetary surplus, a short-lived phenomenon of the 1990s, has given way once again to deficit financing. The number of homeless people and immigrants, documented and undocumented, has grown substantially. Drug abuse, white-collar crime, gangs armed with automatic weapons, terrorism, and antigovernmental sects have become national threats. Yet the colleges continue as always, adjusting only slightly to the cosmic issues noted above. What can they do? They are schools, able only to minister to their clients. They cannot directly resolve any of the major issues confronting society. Broad-scale social forces swirl about them, but the colleges are propelled mainly by their internal dynamics—a point that can be readily recognized by viewing the differences between institutions in the same types of communities.

Acknowledgments

No long-sustained project of this kind ever operates in isolation, nor is it the work of its authors alone. For this book and the research on which it is based, many agencies provided assistance: National Endowment for the Humanities, National Science Foundation, the Andrew W. Mellon Foundation, the Ford Foundation, the Carnegie Foundation for the Advancement of Teaching, and the E. M. Kauffman Foundation's Center for Entrepreneurial Leadership. We are indebted also to the National Center for Education Statistics, whose numerous studies provide baseline data regarding all sectors of education.

We have included in this edition the foreword to the first edition, by the late John Lombardi, because we continue to value his insights. He dedicated his professional life to the community colleges. His writings, several of which we cite in this book, reveal his analytical approach to every issue concerning the institutions.

Among the people who helped put the edition together were several students in UCLA's higher education program, including Rozana Carducci, Ed Ryan, and Pam Schuetz, who updated tables and obtained bibliographic citations, and Kristin Angiulo, who prepared the first draft of the chapter on student services. Ed Ryan and longtime associate Elaine Howell typed the final manuscript.

We anticipate that all of them will find their careers as personally rewarding and professionally beneficial as we have found ours.

Los Angeles, California   *Arthur M. Cohen*
June 2008   *Florence B. Brawer*

The Authors

Arthur M. Cohen has been professor of higher education at the University of California, Los Angeles (UCLA), since 1964; he became emeritus in 2004. He received his B.A. (1949) and M.A. (1955) degrees in history from the University of Miami. He received his Ph.D. degree (1964) in higher education from The Florida State University. He was director of the ERIC Clearinghouse for Community Colleges from 1966 to 2003 and president of the Center for the Study of Community College from 1974 to 2007. Cohen has served on the editorial boards of numerous journals and has written extensively about community colleges. His first book was *Dateline '79: Heretical Concepts for the Community College* (1969).

Florence B. Brawer was research director of the Center for the Study of Community Colleges. A former research educationist at UCLA, psychometrist, and counselor, she received her B.A. degree (1944) from the University of Michigan in psychology and her M.A. (1962) and Ed.D. (1967) degrees from UCLA in educational psychology. She is the author of *New Perspectives on Personality Development in College Students* (1973) and the coeditor of *Developments in the Rorschach Technique*, vol. 3 (1970).

Cohen and Brawer together wrote *Confronting Identity: The Community College Instructor* (1972), *The Two-Year College*

Instructor Today (1977), and *The Collegiate Function of Community Colleges* (1987). Together with other ERIC staff members, they also wrote *A Constant Variable: New Perspectives on the Community College* (1971) and *College Responses to Community Demands* (1975). Cohen and Brawer have edited several series of monographs published by the Center for the Study of Community Colleges and the ERIC Clearinghouse for Community Colleges. They initiated the Jossey-Bass quarterly series *New Directions for Community Colleges* in 1973.

1

Background

Evolving Priorities and Expectations
of the Community College

The American community college dates from the early years of the twentieth century. Among the social forces that contributed to its rise, most prominent were the need for workers trained to operate the nation's expanding industries; the lengthened period of adolescence, which mandated custodial care of the young for a longer time; and the drive for social equality, which supposedly would be enhanced if more people had access to higher education. Community colleges seemed also to reflect the growing power of external authority over everyone's life, the peculiarly American belief that people cannot be legitimately educated, employed, religiously observant, ill, or healthy unless some institution sanctions that aspect of their being.

The ideas permeating higher education early in the century fostered the development of these new colleges across the country. Science was seen as contributing to progress; the more people who would learn its principles, the more rapid the development of the society would be. New technologies demanded skilled operators, and training them could be done by the schools. Individual mobility was held in the highest esteem, and the notion was widespread that those people who applied themselves most diligently would advance most rapidly. Social institutions of practical value to society were being formed. This was the era of the Chautauqua, the settlement house, the Populists. And in the colleges, the question, "What knowledge is of most worth?" was rarely asked; the more likely question was, "What knowledge yields the greatest tangible benefit to individuals or to society?" The public perceived schooling as an avenue of upward mobility and a contributor to the community's wealth. The diatribes of Veblen (1918) and Sinclair ([1923] 1976) against domination of the universities by industrialists were ineffectual outcries against what had become a reality.

Publicly supported universities, given impetus by the Morrill Acts of 1862 and 1890, had been established in every state. Although many were agricultural institutes or teacher-training colleges little resembling modern universities, they did provide a lower-cost alternative to private colleges. The universities were also pioneering the idea of service to the broader community through their agricultural and general extension divisions. Access for a wider range of the population was increasing as programs to teach an ever-increasing number of subjects and occupations were introduced. Schools of business, forestry, journalism, and social work became widespread. People with more diverse goals demanded more diverse programs; the newer programs attracted greater varieties of people.

Probably the simplest overarching reason for the growth of community colleges was that an increasing number of demands were being placed on schools at every level. Whatever the social or personal problem, schools were supposed to solve it. As a society, we have looked to the schools for racial integration. The courts and legislatures have insisted that schools mitigate discrimination by merging students across ethnic lines in their various programs. The schools are expected to solve problems of unemployment by preparing students for jobs. Subsidies awarded to businesses that train their own workers might be a more direct approach, but we have preferred paying public funds to support vocational education in the schools. The list could be extended to show that the responsibility for doing something about drug abuse, alcoholism, teenage pregnancy, inequitable incomes, and other individual and societal ills has been assigned to schools soon after the problems have been identified. Schools were even supposed to ameliorate the long-standing problem of highway deaths. Instead of reducing speed limits and requiring seat belts in the 1960s, many states enacted laws requiring schools to provide driver education courses. And recently, instead of imposing automobile mileage standards similar to those that have been in place in Europe for decades, we are installing "green" curriculums in an effort to teach young people to conserve energy.

Despite periodic disillusionment with the schools, the pervasive belief has been that education, defined as more years of schooling, is beneficial. It was not always that way. In earlier centuries and in other societies, people did not ascribe such power to or make such demands on their schools. Instead the family, the workplace, and various social institutions acculturated and trained the young. But the easily accessible, publicly supported school became an article of American faith, first in the nineteenth century, when responsibility for educating the individual began shifting to the school, and then in the twentieth, when the schools were unwarrantedly expected to relieve society's ills. The community colleges thrived on the new responsibilities because they had no traditions to defend, no alumni to question their role, no autonomous professional staff to be moved aside, no statements of philosophy that would militate against their taking on responsibility for everything.

Institutional Definitions

Two generic names have been applied to two-year colleges. From their beginnings until the 1940s, they were known most commonly as junior colleges. Eells's definition (1931) of the junior college included university branch campuses offering lower-division work either on the parent campus or in separate facilities; state junior colleges supported by state funds and controlled by state boards; college-level courses offered by secondary schools; and local colleges formed by groups acting without legal authority. At the second annual meeting of the American Association of Junior Colleges, in 1922, a junior college was defined as "an institution offering two years of instruction of strictly collegiate grade" (Bogue, 1950, p. xvii). In 1925, the definition was modified slightly to include this statement: "The junior college may, and is likely to, develop a different type of curriculum suited to the larger and ever-changing civic, social, religious, and vocational needs of the entire community in which the college is located. It is understood that in this case, also, the work offered shall be on a level appropriate for high-school graduates" (p. xvii). But the instruction was still expected to be "of strictly collegiate grade"; that is, if such a college had courses usually offered in the first two years by a senior institution, "these courses must be identical, in scope and thoroughness, with corresponding courses of the standard four-year college" (p. xvii). Skill training alone was not considered sufficient to qualify an institution for the appellation *junior college*. A general education component must be included in the occupational programs: "General-education and vocation training make the soundest and most stable progress toward personal competence when they are thoroughly integrated" (p. 22).

During the 1950s and 1960s, the term *junior college* was applied more often to the lower-division branches of private universities and to two-year colleges supported by churches or organized independently, while *community college* came gradually to be used for the comprehensive, publicly supported institutions. By the 1970s, *community college* was usually applied to both types.

Several names in addition to *community college* and *junior college* have been used. Sometimes these names refer to the college's sponsor: *city college, county college,* and *branch campus* are still in use. Other appellations signify the institutions' emphases: *technical institute* and *vocational, technical, and adult education center* have had some currency. The colleges have also been nicknamed *people's college, democracy's college, contradictory college, opportunity college*, and *anti-university college*—the last by Jencks and Riesman (1968), who saw them as negating the principles of scholarship on which the universities had been founded.

Sometimes deliberate attempts have been made to blur the definition. For example, during the 1970s, the American Association of Community and Junior Colleges (AACJC) sought to identify the institutions as community education centers standing entirely outside the mainstream of graded education. In 1980, the AACJC began listing "regionally accredited proprietary institutions" in addition to the nonprofit colleges in its annual *Community, Junior, and Technical College Directory*. Since the 1990s, a few states have authorized their community colleges to offer bachelor's degrees, thus further blurring the definition. The Carnegie Foundation's 2006 reclassification of institutions of higher education created a new category, "baccalaureate/associate colleges," into which it placed associate degree-granting colleges that awarded as many as 10 percent of their degrees at the bachelor's level. And the National Center for Education Statistics (NCES), the major national data compiler, moved the institutions that were awarding bachelor's degrees to its "Four-year Public" category, a decision that accounts for its losing twenty-five community colleges between 2004 and 2005. But as of 2006, the states reporting fiscal appropriations for the annual "Grapevine" tabulations were still listing as community colleges even those institutions that had begun offering bachelor's degrees, as were the National Association of College and University Business Officers and the College Board.

We define the community college as *any institution regionally accredited to award the associate in arts or the associate in science as its highest degree.* That definition includes the comprehensive two-year college as well as many technical institutes, both public and private. It eliminates many of the publicly supported area vocational schools and adult education centers and most of the proprietary business and trade colleges that are accredited by the National Association of Trade and Technical Schools but not by the regional accrediting associations. However, numerous institutions in the latter group, the fastest-growing sector of post-secondary education in the 1980s and 1990s, are being accredited to award associate degrees; hence, some lists include them in the two-year college category. By 1985, "half of the private two-year institutions were organized as profit-making entities," according to the U.S. Department of Education's National Center for Education Statistics (NCES), which had begun counting them as part of the group (Adelman, 1987, p. 5); by 2003, this proportion had risen to more than 90 percent.

Figures reported in this book generally refer to institutions in the public two-year college sector. However, some information related to independent and proprietary institutions is included in areas where data are available.

Development of Community Colleges

The development of community colleges should be placed in the context of the growth of all higher education in the twentieth century. As secondary school enrollments expanded rapidly in the early 1900s, the demand for access to college grew apace. The percentage of those graduating from high school grew from 30 percent in 1924 to 75 percent by 1960, and 60 percent of the high school graduates entered college in the latter year. Put another way, 45 percent of eighteen year olds entered college in 1960, up from 5 percent in 1910. Rubinson has contended that the growth of schooling in the United States can be predicted by a "model in which the proportional change in enrollments at any given level of schooling is a simple function of the numbers of people in the relevant age group and in the previous level of schooling" (1986, p. 521). Green (1980) put it more simply, saying that one of the major benefits of a year of schooling is a ticket to advance to the next level. As high school graduation rates stabilized at 72 to 75 percent in the 1970s, the rate of college going leveled off as well, but turned up again in the 1990s.

The states could have accommodated most of the people seeking college attendance simply by expanding their universities' capacity, as indeed was the practice in a few states. Why community colleges? A major reason is that several prominent nineteenth- and early-twentieth-century educators wanted the universities to abandon their freshman and sophomore classes and relegate the function of teaching adolescents to a new set of institutions, to be called junior colleges. Proposals that the junior college should relieve the university of the burden of providing general education for young people were made in 1851 by Henry Tappan, president of the University of Michigan; in 1859 by William Mitchell, a University of Georgia trustee; and in 1869 by William Folwell, president of the University of Minnesota. All insisted that the universities would not become true research and professional development centers until they relinquished their lower-division preparatory work. Other educators—such as William Rainey Harper, of the University of Chicago; Edmund J. James, of the University of Illinois; Stanford's president, David Starr Jordan; and University of California professor and member of the State Board of Education Alexis Lange— suggested emulating the system followed in European universities and secondary schools. That is, the universities would be responsible for the higher-order scholarship, while the lower schools would provide general and vocational education to students through age nineteen or twenty. Folwell argued for a strong system of secondary schools with "upward extension to include the first two college years," because "a few feeble colleges, an isolated university, cannot educate the people" (cited in Koos, 1947a, p. 138). Harper also contended that the weaker four-year colleges might better become junior colleges rather than wasting money by doing superficial work. In fact, by 1940, of 203 colleges with enrollments in 1900 of 150 or fewer students, 40 percent had perished, but 15 percent had become junior colleges (Eells, 1941a).

In California, it probably would have been feasible to limit
Stanford and the University of California to upper-division and
graduate and professional studies because of the early, widespread
development of junior colleges in that state (nearly two opening
every year between 1910 and 1960). Such proposals were made
several times, especially by Stanford's President Jordan, but were
never successfully implemented. Grades 13 and 14 were not given
over exclusively to community colleges in any state. Instead, the
colleges developed outside the channel of graded education that
reaches from kindergarten to graduate school. The organization of
formal education in America had been undertaken originally from
both ends of the continuum. Dating from the eighteenth century,
four-year colleges and elementary schools were established; during the nineteenth century, the middle years were accommodated
as colleges organized their own preparatory schools and as public
secondary schools were built. By the beginning of the twentieth century, the gap had been filled. If the universities had shut down their
lower divisions and surrendered their freshmen and sophomores to
the two-year colleges, these newly formed institutions would have
been part of the mainstream. But they did not, and the community
colleges remained adjunctive well into the middle of the century.

Their standing outside the tradition of higher education—first
with its exclusivity of students, then with its scholarship and academic freedom for professors—was both good and bad for the
community colleges. Initially, it gained support for them from
influential university leaders who welcomed a buffer institution
that would cull the poorly prepared students and send only the best
on to the upper division. Later, it enabled them to capitalize on
the sizable amounts of money available for programs in vocational
education, accept the less-well-prepared students who nonetheless
sought further education, and organize continuing-education activities for people of all ages. But it also doomed community colleges
to the status of alternative institutions. In some states—notably
Florida, Texas, and Illinois—upper-division universities were built

so that the community colleges could feed students through at the junior level, but few of those innovative structures survived.

Organizationally, most of the early public community colleges developed as upward extensions of secondary schools. Diener has compiled several nineteenth- and early-twentieth-century papers promoting that idea. Included are statements by Henry Barnard, the first U.S. commissioner of education; John W. Burgess, a professor at Columbia College; William Rainey Harper; and Alexis Lange. In 1871, Barnard proposed that the schools in the District of Columbia be divided into five sectors, one of which would be "Superior and Special Schools, embracing a continuation of the studies of the Secondary School, and while giving the facilities of general literacy and scientific culture as far as is now reached in the second year of our best colleges" (Diener, 1986, p. 37). In 1884, Burgess recommended that high schools add two or three years to their curriculum to prepare students for the work of the university. Harper also proposed that high schools extend their programs to the collegiate level: "Today only 10 percent of those who finish high school continue the work in college. If the high schools were to provide work for two additional years, at least 40 percent of those finishing the first four years would continue until the end of the sophomore year" (Diener, 1986, pp. 57–58). Lange regarded the junior college as the culmination of schooling for most students, with the high school and junior college together forming the domain of secondary education. But in his view, the junior college would do more than prepare young people for college; it would also train for "the vocations occupying the middle ground between those of the artisan type and the professions" (Diener, 1986, p. 71). Increasing access to postsecondary education was also an important aspect of Lange's plans.

Rationalizing the New Form

Reasons for the growth of community colleges in their early years have been stated by numerous commentators, each with an argument that has some appeal. The idea that rapid growth in the high school population in the early years of the twentieth century led to student demand for additional years of schooling could be rationalized, but so can many others. The claim that business-people supported the institutions so that they would have a ready supply of workers trained at public expense has some adherents; this seems more valid in the light of contemporary events as states put forth low-cost funding and education projects in attempts to attract industry, with the community colleges as central elements in their presentations. And the literature certainly supports the idea that community leaders saw the formation of a college as an avenue to community prestige. Even the notion of a grand scheme to keep poor people in their place by diverting them to programs leading to low-pay occupational positions has found some accep-tance, particularly among those who perceive a capitalist conspir-acy behind all societal events.

Which belief has the most credibility? Each has its adherents. But why can't they all be true? There certainly does not need to be one reason above others for any major shift in institutional forms. Each year of schooling does give rise to a desire for an additional year. School superintendents may want to be college presidents, and teachers to be college professors. Communities erect signs pointing to their local college and announce its presence in all their displays. Industries and professions need skilled practitioners. All the reasons mentioned can be justified as contributing to the opening of one thousand public community colleges in not much more than fifty years. Why must one argument be more valid than the others?

Harder to reconcile is the fact that the other developed nations, especially those of Western Europe from which most of the American ideas of education were imported, did not develop community colleges of their own. They all faced the same phenomena of rising populations, changing technologies, different expectations for child rearing, and a shifting pattern of preparation for the workforce. However, they built adult education centers and vocational schools separate from each other and rarely founded institutions that would enable people to transfer credit to baccalaureate programs. Were their school superintendents less eager to become college presidents? Were their high school populations more docile in accepting the decision that they would never have a chance for a baccalaureate? Were their communities less eager to enjoy the prestige that goes with a local college? Were they more subject to conspiracies to keep the lower classes in their place, hence to keep poor people out of school entirely?

The best answer might be that since its founding, the United States has been more dedicated to the belief that all individuals should have the opportunity to rise to their greatest potential. Accordingly, all barriers to individual development should be broken down. Institutions that enhance human growth should be created and supported. Talent is potentially to be found in every social stratum and at any age. People who fail to achieve in their youth should be given successive chances. And perhaps most crucial—absent a national ministry of education or even, until recently, much state control or oversight—the local school districts could act on their own.

Much recent scholarship (Dougherty, 1994; Frye, 1992; Gallagher, 1994; Pedersen, 1987, 1988, 2000) has documented the influence of local officials in forming the colleges. Pedersen especially challenges community college historiographies that emphasize the emergence of junior colleges as a reflection of a "national movement intent on fundamentally transforming an elitist higher education into a democratic and socially efficient system of advanced learning" (2000, p. 124). Through an examination of primary sources such as local school records, newspaper reports, community histories, state surveys, and dissertations, he attributes the development of the early public community colleges to local community conditions and interests. Frequently operating in high school facilities, the colleges were local institutions, and much civic pride surrounded their development. As they were formed, schoolteachers became college professors and school superintendents became college presidents, a significant force for building an institution that would accord prestige to its staff and its township.

Prior to midcentury, the notion of statewide systems or a national agenda hardly existed. But by then, according to Meier, the American Association of Junior Colleges had become a major presence, promoting "an educational social movement combining evangelism, moderate liberalism, and civic nationalism," to accelerate college growth in every state. The association's leaders from the 1950s through the 1970s did not hesitate to conflate "Christianity, education and democracy" in furthering the spiritual dimensions and social purposes of the movement, including reference to Scripture: "Behold, I have set before thee an open door," and employing "the rhetoric and organizing techniques of evangelical religion" to further their agenda (2008, pp. 8–10).

Historical Development of the New Form

The thesis attributing the rise of two-year colleges to the efforts of local, civic, and professional leaders has merit. For one, it provides an explanation for the two-year colleges as a twentieth-century phenomenon, although calls for their development had been made by university leaders decades earlier. The need for trained manpower had been apparent too, but apprenticeships were the dominant way into the workforce. Until the 1900s, two essential components were not yet in place: sizable numbers of students graduating from high school, and public school districts managing secondary schools to which they could readily append two more years of curriculum, with or without special legal sanction.

Much of the discussion about junior colleges in the 1920s and 1930s had to do with whether they were expanded secondary schools or truncated colleges. The school district with three types of institutions (elementary schools with grades 1–6, junior highs with grades 7–10, and combined high schools and junior colleges with grades 11–14) was set forth as one model. This 6–4–4 plan had much appeal: curriculum articulation between grades 12 and 13 would be smoothed; the need for a separate physical plant would be mitigated; instructors could teach in both high school and junior college under the same contract; superior students could go through the program rapidly; vocational education could be extended from secondary school into the higher grades; and small communities that could not support self-standing junior colleges would be helped by appending the college to their secondary schools. The 6–4–4 plan also allowed students to change schools or leave the system just when they reached the age limit of compulsory school attendance. Most students did (and do) complete the tenth grade at age sixteen. A high school that continues through grade 12 suggests that students would stay beyond the compulsory age.

Would a four-year junior college beginning at grade 11 enhance schooling for most students? Those who completed the tenth grade and chose to go beyond the compulsory age would enter a school in their home area that could take them through the senior year and on to grades 13 and 14 or through a vocational program. But hardly any public school districts organized themselves into a 6–4–4 system, possibly because, as Eells (1931) suggested, this system did not seem to lead to a true undergraduate college, complete with school spirit. He also mentioned the ambition of junior college organizers to have their institutions elevated to the status of senior institutions. And as Kisker (2006) has argued, the 6–4–4 plan was antithetical to most community college laws enacted by state legislators who were focused on governing and funding two-year colleges as institutions of higher education, separate from the high schools from which they emerged.

However, the idea did not die. In 1974, educators at LaGuardia Community College in New York established Middle College High School, a secondary school within a community college (described by Cullen and Moed, 1988) and eventually facilitated over thirty middle college replications across the country. The idea of integrating high school and community college also gained some traction in recent years. Funded by over $120 million in grants primarily from the Bill and Melinda Gates Foundation, 130 Early College High Schools (small, autonomous institutions that combine high school and the first two years of college into a coherent education program) were established in twenty-three states between 2002 and 2006.

Arguments in favor of a new institution to accommodate students through their freshman and sophomore years were fueled by the belief that the transition from adolescence to adulthood typically occurred at the end of a person's teens. William Folwell contended that youths should be permitted to reside in their homes until they had "reached a point, say, somewhere near the end of the sophomore year" (quoted in Koos, 1924, p. 343). Eells posited that the junior colleges allowed students who were not capable of taking the higher work to stop "naturally and honorably at the end of the sophomore year" (1931, p. 91). "As a matter of record, the end of the second year of college marks the completion of formal education for the majority of students who continue post–high school studies" (p. 84). They would be better off remaining in their home communities until greater maturity enabled a few of them to go to the university in a distant region; the pretense of higher learning for all could be set aside. Harvard president James Bryant Conant viewed the community college as a terminal education institution: "By and large, the educational road should fork at the end of the high school, though an occasional transfer of a student from a two-year college to a university should not be barred" (quoted in Bogue, 1950, p. 32).

The federal government provided impetus in 1947 when the President's Commission on Higher Education articulated the value of a populace with free access to two years of study more than the secondary schools could provide. As the commission put it, because around half of the young people can benefit from formal studies through grade 14, the community colleges have an important role. That idea had lasting appeal; fifty years later President Clinton (1998) underscored the importance of making education through grades 13 and 14 as universal as a high school diploma.

Expansion of Two-Year Colleges

Junior colleges were widespread in their early years. Koos (1924) reported only 20 in 1909 but 170 ten years later. By 1922, thirty-seven of the forty-eight states contained junior colleges, this within two decades of their founding. Of the 207 institutions operating in that year, 137 were privately supported. Private colleges were most likely to be in the southern states, publicly supported institutions in the West and Midwest. Most of the colleges were quite small, although even in that era, public colleges tended to be larger than private colleges. In 1922, the total enrollment for all institutions was around twenty thousand; the average was around 150 students in the public colleges and 60 in the private. California had twenty private junior colleges in 1936. But those institutions together enrolled fewer than two thousand students, and by 1964, all but three of them had disappeared (Winter, 1964).

By 1930, there were 440 junior colleges, found in all but five states. Total enrollment was around 70,000, an average of about 160 students per institution. California had one-fifth of the public institutions and one-third of the students, and although the percentages have dropped, California has never relinquished this early lead; in 2004, its full-time student equivalent enrollment was well over double that of the next largest state. Other states with a large number of public junior colleges were Illinois, Texas, and Missouri; Texas and Missouri also had sizable numbers of private junior colleges. By 1940, there were 610 colleges, still small, averaging about 400 students each. One third of them were separate units, almost two-thirds were high school extensions, and but ten were in 6–4–4 systems (Koos, 1947a).

The high point for the private junior colleges came in 1949, when there were 322 privately controlled two-year colleges, 180 of them affiliated with churches, 108 independent nonprofit, and 34 proprietary. As Table 1.1 shows, they began a steady decline, merging with senior institutions or closing their doors. No new independent nonprofit schools have been organized since the mid-1970s. Never large, the median-sized private, nonprofit college had fewer than 500 students by the late 1980s. By contrast, the median public college enrolled nearly 3,000 students. The sources of information on the number of colleges vary because they may or may not include community colleges' branch campuses, the two-year branches of universities such as those in New Mexico, South Carolina, and Wisconsin, and various categories of technical institutes such as those in Indiana, where not until 2005 did the state legislature mandate their offering transferable courses and two-year degree programs. Not only do the data vary among the directories, but because of revised survey procedures or definitions, they are not consistent from year to year within the same directories.

Although the number of colleges has changed little recently, enrollments have grown. Even so, this has not changed the median college size, because most of the growth has taken place in the larger institutions. In 2004, one-third of the public community colleges had enrollments of 2,440 or fewer, one-third enrolled between 2,441 and 5,855, and one-third were from 5,856 on up to 40,000 or more (Carnegie Foundation, 2006). This is essentially the same breakout of small, medium, and large-size colleges as was apparent in the early 1980s. In the 1990s, more than one million students were enrolled in colleges that had over twenty thousand students each.

More than any other single factor, access depends on proximity. Public universities, even highly selective ones that are located in urban areas, draw most of their entering freshmen from within a short radius. Hence, the advent of the community college as a neighborhood institution did more to open higher education to

Table 1.1.   Numbers of Public and Private Nonprofit Two-Year Colleges, 1915–2005

Year	Total	Public		Private Nonprofit	
		Number	Percentage	Number	Percentage
1915–16	74	19	26	55	74
1921–22	207	70	34	137	66
1925–26	325	136	42	189	58
1929–30	436	178	41	258	59
1933–34	521	219	42	302	58
1938–39	575	258	45	317	55
1947–48	650	328	50	322	50
1952–53	594	327	55	267	45
1956–57	652	377	58	275	42
1960–61	678	405	60	273	40
1964–65	719	452	63	267	37
1968–69	993	739	74	254	26
1972–73	1,141	910	80	231	20
1976–77	1,233	1,030	84	203	16
1980–81	1,231	1,049	85	182	15
1984–85	1,222	1,067	87	155	13
1988–89	1,231	1,056	86	175	14
1992–94	1,236	1,082	88	154	12
1996–97	1,239	1,080	87	159	13
1998–99	1,244	1,075	86	169	14
2000–01	1,220	1,076	88	144	12
2003–04	1,204	1,086	90	118	10
2004–05	1,173	1,061	90	112	10

Sources: American Association of Community and Junior Colleges, *Community, Junior, and Technical College Directory*, 1992; Palmer, 1987b, National Center for Education Statistics *Digest*, 1993–2006.

a broader population than did its policy of accepting even students who had not done well in high school. Pederson (2000) notes that community colleges in rural and suburban areas were given a great impetus in the 1920s when federally funded highways were built allowing students to drive to campus. The interstate freeways that followed federal funding beginning in the late 1950s had a similar effect, as community colleges were built along the beltways that ringed the major cities. Throughout the nation, in city after city, as community colleges opened their doors, the percentage of students beginning college expanded dramatically. During the 1950s and 1960s, whenever a community college was established in a locale where there had been no publicly supported college, the proportion of high school graduates in that area who began college immediately increased, sometimes by as much as 50 percent. The pattern has not changed: 96 percent of the two-year-college matriculants nationwide are in-state residents; the distance from their home to the campus is a median of ten miles (Horn, Nevill, and Griffith, 2006).

Fueled by the high birthrates of the 1940s, this rapid expansion of community colleges led their advocates to take an obsessive view of growth. Obviously, though, the number of new institutions could not continue expanding forever. In 1972, M. J. Cohen studied the relationship among the number of community colleges in a state, the state's population density, and its area. He found that community colleges tended to be built so that 90 to 95 percent of the state's population lived within reasonable commuting distance, about twenty-five miles. When the colleges reached this ratio, the state had a mature community college system, and few additional colleges were built. As that state's population grew larger, the colleges expanded in enrollments, but it was no longer necessary to add new campuses. In the early 1970s, seven states had mature systems: California, Florida, Illinois, New York, Ohio, Michigan, and Washington. In these states, the denser the population, the smaller the area served by each college and the higher the per campus enrollment. Applying his formula of the relationship between number of colleges, state population, and population density, Cohen (1972) showed that 1,074 public community colleges would effectively serve the nation. In 2001, 1,076 such colleges were in operation; thus, after three decades, the formula has been proven valid and the resultant figure incredibly precise.

Diversity marked the organization, control, and financing of colleges in the various states. Like the original four-year colleges and universities, junior colleges grew without being coordinated at the state level. Decapitation was one impetus. Four-year private colleges struggling to maintain their accreditation, student body, and fiscal support might abandon their upper-division specialized classes to concentrate on freshman and sophomore work and thus become junior colleges. The University of Missouri helped several struggling four-year colleges in that state to become private junior colleges. In southern states where weak four-year colleges were prevalent, this dropping of the upper division also took place, helping to account for the sizable number of private junior colleges in that region. Originally, over half the private colleges were single-sex institutions, with colleges for women found most widely in New England, the Midwest, and the South.

The public sector grew in various ways. A few junior colleges opened in the 1930s under the auspices of the federal government. More often, colleges were organized by public universities wanting to expand their feeder institutions. The first two-year colleges in Pennsylvania were established as branch campuses of the Pennsylvania State College. The state universities of Kentucky, Alaska, and Hawaii also organized community colleges under their aegis. Some public universities established two-year colleges on their own campuses. A University Center System gave rise to several two-year institutions in Wisconsin, and the University of South Carolina founded several regional campuses.

Although community colleges now operate in every state and enroll half of the students who begin college in the United States, they found their most compatible climate early on in the West, most notably in California. One reason may have been that many of the ideals of democracy first took form in the western states, where women's suffrage and other major reforms in the electoral process were first seen. But the expansion of the community college in the West must also be attributed to the fact that during the eighteenth century and the first half of the nineteenth, while colleges sponsored by religious institutions and private philanthropists grew strong elsewhere, the West had not yet been populated. In the twentieth century, it was much easier for publicly supported institutions to advance where there was little competition from the private sector. California became the leader in community college development because of support from the University of California and Stanford University, a paucity of small denominational colleges, and strong support for public education at all levels. Even now, more than half of the college students in Arizona, Washington, and Wyoming, as well as California, are in community colleges.

A 1907 California law authorizing secondary school boards to offer postgraduate courses "which shall approximate the studies prescribed in the first two years of university courses," together with several subsequent amendments, served as a model for enabling legislation in numerous states. Anthony Caminetti, the senator who introduced the legislation, had been responsible twenty years earlier for an act authorizing the establishment of high schools as upward extensions of grammar schools. Actually, the law sanctioned a practice in which many of the high schools in California were already engaged. Those located at some distance from the state university had been offering lower-division studies to assist students who could not readily leave their home towns at the completion of high school. When Fresno took advantage of the law to establish a junior college in 1910, one of its presenting arguments was that there was no institution of higher education within nearly two hundred miles of the city. (Such justifications for two-year colleges have been used throughout the history of the development of these institutions.) Subsequent laws in California authorized junior college districts to be organized entirely independent of the secondary schools, and this form of parallel development continued for decades. Indicative of the inchoate nature of the institution in its early years, in 1927 California had sixteen colleges organized as appendages of the local secondary schools, six as junior college departments of state colleges, and nine organized as separate junior college districts. In 1936, the number operated by the high schools had increased to twenty-three and those by separate junior college districts to eighteen, but the junior college departments of state universities had declined to just one. By 1980, nearly all the junior college districts had been separated from the lower-school districts.

The beginnings of the two-year college in other states that now have well-developed systems followed similar patterns but with some variations. Arizona in 1927 authorized local school districts to organize junior colleges. In Mississippi, they were spawned by county agricultural high schools. In 1917, a Kansas law allowed local elections to establish junior colleges and create special taxing districts to support them. Michigan's authorizing legislation was passed the same year. Public junior colleges had already begun in Minnesota before a law was passed in 1925 providing for local elections to organize districts. Missouri's legislation permitting secondary schools to offer junior college courses dates from 1927, although junior colleges were established there earlier. Most of the community colleges in New York followed a 1949 state appropriation to establish a system of colleges to "provide two-year programs of post-high-school nature combining general education with technical education, special courses in extension work, and general education that would enable students to transfer" (Bogue, 1950, p. 34). Each state's laws were amended numerous times, usually to accommodate changed funding formulas and patterns of governance.

But these patterns are not uniform. Many aspects of college operations continue as they were when the institutions were under the local control of school boards; faculty evaluation procedures and funds awarded on the basis of student attendance are prime examples. And sometimes, just as one characteristic of the college changes in the direction of higher education, another moves toward the lower schools. In 1988, the California legislature passed a comprehensive reform bill that made many community college management practices correspond with those in the state's universities, but in the same year, a proposition that was passed by public initiative placed college funding under guarantees similar to those enjoyed by the K–12 system.

Curricular Functions

The various curricular functions noted in each state's legislation usually include academic transfer preparation, vocational-technical education, continuing education, developmental education, and community service. All have been present in public colleges from the beginning. In 1936, Hollinshead wrote that "the junior college should be a community college meeting community needs" (p. 111), providing adult education and educational, recreational, and vocational activities and placing its cultural facilities at the disposal of the community. Every book written about the institution since then has also articulated these elements, and recently, the definition of community has been broadened to include foreign nationals and a global workplace (Levin, 2001).

Academic Transfer

Academic transfer, or collegiate, studies were meant to fulfill several institutional purposes: a popularizing role, a democratizing pursuit, and a function of conducting lower-division general education courses for the universities. The popularizing role was to have the effect of advertising higher education, showing what it could do for the individual, and encouraging people to attend. The democratizing pursuit was realized as the community colleges became the point of first access for people entering higher education; by the late

1970s, 40 percent of all first-time-in-college, full-time freshmen were in the two-year institutions. The function of relieving the universities from having to deal with freshmen and sophomores was less pronounced because the universities would not relinquish their lower divisions. Instead, community colleges made it possible for them to maintain selective admissions requirements and thus to take only those freshmen and sophomores they wanted.

In 1930, Eells surveyed 279 junior colleges to determine, among other things, the types of curricula offered (Eells, 1931). He found that 69 percent of the semester hours were presented in academic subjects, with modern foreign languages, social sciences, and natural sciences predominating. The 31 percent left for nonacademic subjects included sizable offerings in music, education, and home economics and courses similar to those offered in extension divisions. At that time, there was little difference between the curricula presented in public colleges, whether state controlled or locally controlled, and in private denominational or independent institutions; but the older the institution was, the more likely it was to be engaged in building a set of nonacademic studies. The universities accepted the collegiate function and readily admitted transferring students to advanced standing, most universities granting credit on an hour-for-hour basis for freshman and sophomore courses. Bogue reported that "60 percent of the students in the upper division of the University of California at Berkeley, according to the registrar, are graduates of other institutions, largely junior colleges" (1950, p. 73).

Vocational-Technical

Vocational-technical education was written into the plans in most states from the earliest days. The first act providing state funding for community college in North Carolina, passed in 1957, specified that "most of the programs offered within the Community College System are designed to prepare individuals for entry level technical positions in business and industry with an associate of applied science degree (North Carolina Community College System, 2007a, I, 6). In the 1970s, the U.S. Office of Education popularized *career education*, which is still widely used. However, it never replaced *vocational education*, the phrase used throughout this book as a collective term for all occupational, career, and technical studies. Originally conceived as an essential component of terminal study—education for students who would not go on to further studies—vocational education in the two-year colleges was designed to teach skills more complicated than those taught in high schools. Whereas secondary schools in the 1930s were teaching agriculture, bookkeeping, automobile repair, and printing, for example, junior colleges taught radio repair, secretarial services, and laboratory technical work. Teacher preparation, a function of the junior college in the 1920s, died out as the baccalaureate became the requirement for teaching, although it reappeared in the 1990s, as in Maryland where a transferable Associate of Arts in Teaching degree was formulated (McDonough, 2003). But a sizable proportion of the occupational curriculum in the 1930s was still preprofessional training: prelaw, premedicine, preengineering. According to Eells (1931), in 1929 the proportional enrollment in California public junior colleges was 80 to 20 in favor of the collegiate; in Texas municipal junior colleges, it was 77 to 23. By the 1970s, the percentage of students in vocational education had reached parity with that in the collegiate programs.

Continuing Education

The continuing education function arose early, and the percentage of adults enrolled increased dramatically in the 1940s. The 1947 President's Commission on Higher Education emphasized the importance of this function, and Bogue noted with approval a Texas college's slogan: "We will teach anyone, anywhere, anything, at any time whenever there are enough people interested in the program to justify its offering" (1950, p. 215). He reported also that "out of the 500,536 students reported in the 1949 [AACJC]

Directory, nearly 185,000 are specials or adults" (p. 35). The open-end nature of continuing education fit well with the idea that the colleges were not to be confined to particular curricular patterns or levels of graded education but were to operate in an unbounded universe of lifelong learning, which would, not incidentally, enhance public support.

Developmental Education

Developmental education—also known as *remedial, compensatory, preparatory,* or *basic skills* studies—grew as the percentage of students poorly prepared in secondary schools swelled community college rolls. Although some remedial work had been offered early on, the disparity in ability between students entering community colleges and those in the senior institutions was not nearly as great in the 1920s as in recent years. Koos (1924) reported only slightly higher entering test scores by the senior college matriculants. The apparent breakdown of basic academic education in secondary schools in the 1960s, coupled with the expanded percentage of people entering college, brought developmental education to the fore.

Community Service

The community service function was pioneered by private junior colleges and by rural colleges, which often served as the cultural centers for their communities. Early books on two-year colleges display a wide range of cultural and recreational events that institutions of the time were presenting for the enlightenment of their communities. Public two-year colleges adopted the idea as a useful aspect of their relations with the public, and special funds were set aside in some states for this function. By 1980, the AACJC *Directory* listed nearly four million community education participants, predominantly people enrolled in short courses, workshops, and noncredit courses. The community service function also included spectator events sponsored by the colleges but open to the public as well as to students.

Intertwined Functions

This book presents separate chapters on each of the curricular functions: collegiate (academic transfer and general education), vocational (technical, occupational), and developmental (remedial) education. Community service and continuing education are merged, and student guidance, often mentioned as a major function, is covered in the chapter on student services. Yet all the functions overlap because education is rarely discrete. Community college programs do not stay in neat categories when the concepts underlying them and the purposes for which students enroll in them are scrutinized. Although courses in the sciences are almost always listed as part of the collegiate program, they are career education for students who will work in hospitals or medical laboratories. A course in auto mechanics is for the general education of students who learn to repair their own cars, even though it is part of the offerings in a career program. Collegiate, vocational, and continuing education are all intertwined. Who can say when one or another is being provided?

Such definitions are pertinent primarily for funding agents and accreditation associations and for those who need categories and classification systems as a way of understanding events. "Vocational" education is that which is supported by especially earmarked funds or is supposed to lead to direct employment. When a course or program is approved for transfer credit to a senior institution, it becomes part of the "collegiate" function. When it cannot be used for associate degree credit, it is "developmental" or "community" education. That is why community college presidents may honestly say that their institutions perform all tasks with great facility. When confronted with the charge that their school is not doing enough in one or another curriculum area, they can counter that it is, if only the courses and students were examined more closely. All education is general education. All education is potentially career enhancing. All education is for the sake of the broader community.

Colleges in Other Countries

All nations face similar issues of workforce development, societal cohesion, and providing avenues of individual mobility, and every nation with a formal education system has institutions that serve people between the years of compulsory schooling and various adult pursuits, especially transition into the workforce. Whether named a school, college, or institute, two-thirds of the institutions listed in Table 1.2 have *vocational* or *technical* in their title. No other countries but the United States (and to some extent Canada) have formed comprehensive community colleges. The primary reason is that compulsory schooling continues for a greater number of years for America's young people than it does in any other nation, a phenomenon seeding the desire for more schooling. The second reason is that Americans seem more determined to allow individual options to remain open for as long as each person's motivations and the community's budget allow. Placing prebaccalaureate, vocational, and developmental education within the same institution enables students to move from one to the other more readily than if they had to change schools.

Changing Emphases

Community colleges have led to notable changes in American education, especially by expanding access. Well into the middle of the twentieth century, higher education had elements of mystery within it. Only one young person in seven went to college, and most students were from the middle and upper classes. To the public at large, which really had little idea of what went on behind the walls, higher education was a clandestine process, steeped in

Table 1.2. Sample Listing of Institutions Providing Community College Functions in Other Countries

Country	Institution
Australia	Technical and Further Education (TAFE) College
Austria	Regional or District College
	Fachhochschule (Institute of Technical/Vocational Higher Education)
Belgium (French)	Haute Ecole (Higher School)
Canada	Collège Communautaire (Community College)
	Collège d'enseignement Général et Professionnel (CEGEP)
People's Republic of China	Dazhuan (Upper-level Specialized College)
	Gaodeng Zhiye Jishe Xueyuan (Vocational-Technical College)
	Zhiye Jiaoyu Zhongxin (County-level Vocational Education Centre)
Croatia	Veleučilište (Polytechnic)
	Visoka Škola (School of Professional Higher Education)
Czech Republic	Střední Odborné Učiliště (Upper Secondary Vocational School)
	Vysoká Škola (College)
Denmark	Korte Videregående Uddanelser (Short-Cycle Higher Education Institution)
	Voksenuddannelsescenter (VUC) (County Adult Education Centre)
Finland	Aikuiskoulutuskeskus (Adult Education Centre)
	Avoin Ammattikorkeakoulu (Open Polytechnic)
France	Lycée Professionnel (Vocational College)
	Institut Universitaire de Technologie (IUT) (Technology Institute)

Germany	Fachhochschule (Institute of Technical/Vocational Higher Education)
	Berufsakademie (Vocational Academy)
Greece	Institouta Epagelmatikis Katartisis (IEK) (Vocational Training Institute)
Hungary	Szakiskola (Vocational School)
Iceland	Idnskólar (Vocational School)
	Sérskólar (Specialized Vocational School)
Ireland	Institute of Technology
Israel	Vocational Training Centres
	National Institute for Technical Training
Italy	Istituto Tecnici (Technical School)
	Istituto Professionale (Vocational School)
Japan	Tanki-Daigaku (Junior College)
	Koutou-Senmon-gakko (College of Technology)
	Special Training School
Luxembourg	Lycée Technique (Technical Secondary School)
Mexico	Colegio Nacional de Educación Profesional Técnica (CONALEP)
	Universidad Tecnológica (Public Technological University)

(Continued)

Table 1.2. (*Continued*)

Country	Institution
Netherlands	Regionaal Opleidingscentrum (ROC) (Regional Training Centre)
	Vakschool (Specialized Vocational College)
Norway	Videregående skole (Upper Secondary School)
	Teknisk fagskole (Technical schools)
Poland	Technikum Uzupełniające (Supplementary Technical Secondary School)
	Szkoły Policealne (Postsecondary School)
Portugal	Centro de Formação Profisional (Vocational Training Centres)
	Reconhecimento, Validação e Certificação de Competências (RVCC) (Centre for the Recognition, Validation and Certification of Competencies)
South Korea	Vocational Junior College
Spain	Institutos de Educación Secundaria (Secondary Education Institutes)
Sweden	Upper Secondary School
Switzerland	Höhere Fachschule/Ecole Professionnelle supérieure (Advanced Vocational College)
Turkey	Mesleki ve Teknik Lise (Vocational and Technical High School)
United Kingdom	Further Education College
	Community Consortia for Education and Training (CCETs)

Sources: Cohen, 1994; Raby, 2001; Philips, 2007.

ritual. The demystification of higher education, occasioned by the democratization of access, has taken place steadily. After World War II, as a result of the GI Bill, which made available the first large-scale financial aid packages and made it possible for people to be reimbursed not only for their tuition but also for their living expenses while attending college, the number of people going to college increased rapidly. By 2005, 37 percent of all American adults had completed four years of college (OECD, 2006).

The increase in enrollments was accompanied by a major change in the composition of the student body. No longer were colleges sequestered enclaves operated apparently for the sons of the wealthy and educated, who were on their way to positions in the professions, and for the daughters of the same groups, who would be marked with the manners of a cultured class; now colleges were opened to ethnic minorities, lower-income groups, and those whose prior academic performance had been marginal. Of all the higher education institutions, the community colleges contributed most to opening the system. Established in every metropolitan area, they were available to all comers, attracting the "new students": minorities, women, people who had done poorly in high school, those who would otherwise never have considered further education.

During this same era, community colleges contributed also to certain shifts in institutional emphasis. They had always been an avenue of individual mobility; that purpose became highlighted as greater percentages of the populace began using college as a way of moving up in class. The emphasis in higher education on providing trained personnel for the professions, business, and industry also became more distinct. Admittedly, it is difficult to identify the students who sought learning for its own sake or who went to college to acquire the manners that would mark them as ladies or gentlemen; perhaps students whose purposes were purely nonvocational were rare even before 1900. But by the last third of the twentieth century, few commentators on higher education were even articulating those purposes. Vocationalism had gained the day. College going was for job getting, job certifying, job training. The old value of a liberal education became supplemental, an adjunct to be picked up incidentally, if at all, along the way to higher-paying employment.

Other shifts in institutional emphasis have been dictated not by the pronouncements of educational philosophers but by the exigencies of financing, state-level coordinating bodies, the availability of new media, and new groups of students. There has been a steady increase in the public funds available to all types of educational institutions, but the community colleges have been most profoundly affected by sizable increases in federal appropriations for vocational education. Beginning with the Smith-Hughes Act in 1917 and continuing through the Vocational Education Acts of the 1960s and later, federal dollars have poured into the education sector. Community colleges have not been remiss in obtaining their share. Their national lobbyists have worked diligently to have the community college named in set-asides, and the colleges have obtained funds for special occupational programs. The vocational education cast of contemporary colleges is due in no small measure to the availability of these funds.

State-level coordinating agencies have affected institutional roles. Coordinating councils and postsecondary education commissions, along with boards of regents for all higher education in some states, have attempted to assign programs to the different types of institutions. These bodies may restrict lower-division offerings in community colleges. In some states, continuing education has been assigned; in others, it has been taken away from the colleges.

The new media have had their own effect. Electronic gadgetry has been adopted, and elaborate learning resource centers have been opened on campus. Because learning laboratories can be made available at any time, it becomes less necessary for students to attend courses in sequence or at fixed times of day.

The new media, originally radio, then television, and more recently computers, have made it possible for institutions to present sizable proportions of their offerings over open circuits. The colleges have burst their campus bounds.

But the new students have had the most pronounced effect. The community colleges reached out to attract those who were not being served by traditional higher education: those who could not afford the tuition; who could not take the time to attend a college full time; whose ethnic background had constrained them from participating; who had inadequate preparation in the lower schools; whose educational progress had been interrupted by some temporary condition; who had become obsolete in their jobs or had never been trained to work at any job; who needed a connection to obtain a job; who were confined in prisons, physically disabled, or otherwise unable to attend classes on a campus; or who were faced with a need to fill increased leisure time meaningfully. The colleges' success in enrolling these new students has affected what they can offer. Students who are unable to read, write, and compute at a level that would enable them to pursue a collegiate program satisfactorily must be provided with different curricula. As these students become a sizable minority—or, indeed, a majority—the college's philosophy is affected. Gradually, the institution's spokespersons stop talking about its collegiate character and speak more of the developmental work in which it engages. Gradually, faculty stop demanding the same standards of student achievement. Part-time students similarly affect the colleges as new rules of attendance are adopted to accommodate students who drop in and out. And new types of support systems and learning laboratories are installed for those who do not respond to traditional classroom-centered instruction.

Overall, the community colleges have suffered less from goal displacement than have most other higher education institutions. They had less to displace; their goals were to serve the people with whatever the people wanted. Standing outside the tradition, they offered access. They had to instruct; they could not offer the excuse that they were advancing the frontiers of scholarship. Because they had expanded rapidly, their permanent staffs had not been in place so long that they had become fixed. As an example, they could quite easily convert their libraries to learning resource centers because the libraries did not have a heritage of the elaborate routines accompanying maintenance and preservation of large collections. They could be adapted to the instructional programs.

In 1924, Koos was sanguine about the role of the junior college in clarifying and differentiating the aims of both the universities and the secondary schools. He anticipated an allocation of function "that would be certain to bring order out of the current educational chaos. . . . By extending the acknowledged period of secondary education to include two more years . . . allocation of purpose to each unit and differentiation among them should take care of themselves" (p. 374). Koos believed that most of the aims and functions of the secondary school would rise to the new level, so that the first two years of college work would take on a new significance. These aims included occupational efficiency, civic and social responsibility, and the recreational and aesthetic aspects of life. The universities would be freed for research and professional training. Furthermore, the college entrance controversy would be reduced, and preprofessional training could be better defined. Duplication of offerings between secondary schools and universities would also be reduced by the expansion of a system of junior colleges.

Clearly, not many of Koos's expectations were borne out. He could not have anticipated the massive increase in enrollments, the growth of universities and colleges and the competition among them, or the breakdown in curriculum fostered, on the one hand, by part-time students who dropped in and out of college and, on the other, by the institutions' eagerness to offer short courses, workshops, and spectator events. His scheme did not allow for students who demanded higher degrees as a right, crying that the colleges had discriminated against them when degrees were not awarded as a matter of form. And he was unaware of the importance that students and educators alike would place on programs related to job attainment.

Current Issues

The revolution in American education, in which the two-year college played a leading role, is almost over. Two years of postsecondary education are within the reach—financially, geographically, practically—of virtually every American. Three generations have passed since President Truman's Commission on Higher Education recommended that the door to higher education be swung open. Now community colleges are everywhere. There are systems with branches in inner cities and rural districts and with programs in prisons and on military bases. Classes are offered through online instruction, twenty-four hours a day, every day. Open-admissions policies and programs for everyone ensure that no member of the community need miss the chance to attend.

Riding the demographics of the World War II baby boom, the fiscal largesse resulting from an expanding economy, and a wave of public support for education, community colleges had been organized in every state by the 1960s. By the mid-1970s, when the colleges enrolled 34 percent of all students in U.S. higher education, there were nearly eleven hundred institutions; this mature system has taken its place as a central element in the fabric of American postcompulsory education.

This maturity has not changed the colleges' perennial problems of funding, public perception, relative emphasis, purposes, and value. To Bogue in 1950, the critical problems of the community colleges were devising a consistent type of organization, maintaining local or state control, developing an adequate general education program integrated with the occupational, finding the right kinds of teachers, maintaining adequate student guidance services, and getting the states to appropriate sufficient funds. These problems have never been satisfactorily resolved.

Recent changes in both intra- and extramural perceptions of community colleges have led to other issues. Some of these shifts are due to educational leadership at the state and the institutional level, but more are due to changing demographic patterns and public perceptions of institutional purposes.

First, there has been a blending in the uses of vocational and collegiate education. Vocational education was formerly considered terminal. Students were expected to complete their formal schooling by learning a trade and going to work. Students who entered vocational programs and failed to complete them or failed to work in the field for which they were trained were considered to have been misguided. Collegiate programs were designed to serve as a bridge between secondary school and baccalaureate studies. Students who entered the programs and failed to progress to the level of the baccalaureate were considered dropouts.

Since the 1970s, however, high proportions of students who complete vocational programs have been transferring to universities. Vocational programs typically maintain curricula in which the courses are sequential. Many of these programs, especially those in the technologies and the health fields, articulate well with baccalaureate programs. Most have selective admissions policies. Students are forced to make an early commitment, satisfy admissions requirements, maintain continual attendance, and make satisfactory progress. This pattern of schooling reinforces the serious students, leading them to enroll in further studies at a university. The collegiate courses, in contrast, are now frequently taken by students who have not made a commitment to a definite line of study, who already have degrees and are taking courses for personal interest, or who are trying to build up their prerequisites or grade point averages so that they can enter a selective-admissions program at the community college or another institution.

Thus, for many students enrolled in them, the collegiate courses have become the catchall, the vestibule program.

A second issue is that by the 1970s, the linear aspect of community colleges—the idea that the institution assists students in bridging the freshman and sophomore years—had been severely reduced as a proportion of the community colleges' total effort. The number of students transferring was reasonably constant, but most of the expansion in community college enrollments was in the areas of vocational and continuing education. The collegiate programs remained in the catalogues, but students used them for completely different purposes. They dropped in and out, taking the courses at will. Among California community college students, Hunter and Sheldon (1980) found that the mean number of credit hours completed per term was between seven and eight, but the mode was three—in other words, one course. The course array in the collegiate programs was more accurately viewed as lateral rather than linear. Not more than one in ten course sections enforced course prerequisites; not more than one course in ten was a sophomore-level course. What had happened was that the students were using the institution in one way, whereas the institution's patterns of functioning suggested another. Catalogues displayed recommended courses, semester by semester, for students planning to major in one or another of a hundred fields. But the students took those courses that were offered at a preferred time of day or those that seemed potentially useful. In the 1980s, many colleges took deliberate steps to quell that pattern of course attendance, but requirements regarding sequence proved difficult to enforce until the recent growth in the number of eighteen-year-olds brought higher proportions of baccalaureate-bound students into the community colleges.

Third, a trend toward less-than-college-level instruction has accelerated. In addition to the increased number of remedial courses as a proportion of the curriculum, expectations in collegiate courses have changed. To take one example, students in community college English literature courses in 1977 were expected to read 560 pages per term, on average, whereas, according to Koos (1924), the average was three times that in *high school* literature courses in 1922. These figures are offered not to derogate community colleges, but only to point out that the institutions cannot be understood in traditional terms. They are struggling to find ways of educating students whose prior learning has been dominated by nonprint images. The belief that a person unschooled in the classics was not sufficiently educated died hard in the nineteenth century; the ability to read anything as a criterion of adequate education has been questioned in an era when most messages are carried by wires and waves.

Fourth, external demands for *achievement indicators* have not been uniformly well received. Introducing finite concepts such as graduation, transfer, and job-getting rates into an enterprise that has at bottom the open-ended goal of leading people to a better life has had a jarring effect, which explains much of the antagonism to contemporary moves toward judging, comparing, and in some cases funding, community colleges on the basis of their products or outcomes. Statements such as "The value of education becomes apparent only years after the students have left college" (sometimes expressed as "The things we teach can't be measured") have been made for decades by staff members whose focus is on process. In sum, an unbridgeable gulf exists between concentrating exclusively on individual progress and assessing institutional accomplishments.

But all questions of curriculum, students, and institutional mission pale in the light of funding issues. Are the community colleges—or any other schools—worth what they cost? Have the colleges overextended themselves? Do their outcomes justify the public resources they consume? Can they, should they, be called to account for their outcomes? These questions have appeared with increasing frequency as public disaffection with elementary and secondary schools has grown. Whether the community colleges stand alone or whether they are cast with the higher or lower schools, their advocates will be forced to respond.

Several other current issues may also be phrased as questions. How much more than access and illusory benefits of credits and degrees without concomitant learning do the colleges provide? Are they in or out of higher education? How much of their effort is dedicated to higher learning, to developing rationality and advancing knowledge through the disciplines? How much leads students to form habits of reflection? How much tends toward public and private virtue?

Is it moral to sort and grade students, sending the more capable to the university while encouraging the rest to follow other pursuits? Commenting on the terminal programs—the commercial and general education courses that did not transfer to the universities—Eells noted, "Students cannot be forced to take them, it is true, but perhaps they can be led, enticed, attracted" (1931, p. 310). And in his chapter on the guidance function, he stressed, "It is essential that many students be guided into terminal curricula" (p. 330). Koos also contended that "the great majority will be best served by terminal programs" (1941b, p. 327).

What would the shape of American education be if the community colleges had never been established? Where would people be learning the trades and occupations? Apprenticeships were the mode in earlier times. Would they still dominate, as they do in Europe? Would the less-than-college-level regional occupational centers and area vocational and technical schools be larger and more handsomely funded? Would different configurations have developed?

What would have happened to the collegiate function? How many fewer students would be attending college? Would the universities have expanded to accommodate all who sought entry? Community colleges certainly performed an essential service in the 1960s and 1970s when masses of high school graduates, the first wave of baby boomers, demanded access. By offering an inexpensive, accessible alternative, these colleges allowed the universities to maintain at least a semblance of their own integrity. How many universities would have been shattered if community colleges to which the petitioners could be shunted had not been available? Similar issues arose in the 1990s, when the second wave arrived and a steady increase in the number of high school graduates brought access forward once again as a major issue.

If there were no community colleges, what agencies would be performing their community service? How many of the services they provide would be missed? Would secondary schools better maintain their own curricular and instructional integrity if community colleges were not there to grant students absolution for all past educational sins? Would other institutions assume the developmental function?

Although such questions have been asked from time to time, they have rarely been examined, mainly because during most of its history, the community college has been unnoticed, ignored by writers about higher education. Books on higher education published from the turn of the century, when the first community colleges appeared, through the 1980s rarely gave even a nod to the community college; one searches in vain for a reference to them in indexes. In 1950, Bogue deplored the lack of attention paid to the junior colleges, saying that he had examined twenty-seven authoritative histories of American education and found only superficial treatment of junior colleges or none at all. Rudolph's major history of the higher education curriculum, published in 1977, gave them a scant two pages. Pascarella and Terenzini's massive review, *How College Affects Students* (1991), offered little more. Recently, however, their 2005 update and a small body of literature, noted in Chapter Twelve on research, have been filling in some of the gaps.

Perhaps community colleges should merely be characterized as untraditional. They do not follow the central themes of higher education as it developed from the colonial colleges through the universities. They do not typically provide students with new value structures, as residential liberal arts colleges aspire to do. Nor do they further the frontiers of knowledge through scholarship and research training, as in the finest traditions of the universities. Community colleges do not even follow their own traditions. They change frequently, seeking new programs and new clients. Community colleges are indeed untraditional, but they are truly American because at their best, they represent the United States at its best. Never satisfied with resting on what has been done before, they try new approaches to old problems. They maintain open channels for individuals, enhancing the social mobility that has characterized America, and they accept the idea that society can be better, just as individuals can better their lot within it.

2

Students

Diverse Backgrounds, Purposes, and Outcomes

Two words sum up the students: number and variety. To college leaders, the spectacular growth in student population, sometimes as much as 15 percent a year, has been the most impressive feature of community colleges. The numbers are notable: enrollment increased from just over five hundred thousand in 1960 to more than two million by 1970, four million by 1980, nearly 5.5 million by the end of the 1990s, and over six million by 2005 (NCES *Digest*, 2001, 2006). During the 1960s, much of the increase was due to the expanded proportion of eighteen- to twenty-four-year-olds in the population—the result of the World War II baby boom. More people were in the college age cohort, and more of them were going to college. A similar phenomenon was apparent in the 2000s.

Table 2.1 shows the number of undergraduates in all types of colleges relative to the number of eighteen- to twenty-four-year-olds in the American population for each decade from 1900 to 1970. The table accurately depicts the proportion of the age group attending college for those years, but because many undergraduates—nearly half the community college population currently—are older than twenty-three, it is not reasonable to extend the table. A more accurate depiction of the rate of college going now is to divide the number of eighteen- to twenty-four-year-olds enrolled in college by the number of that age group in the population; the figure equaled 38 percent in 2004. From the

Table 2.1.   Undergraduate Enrollment in U.S. Colleges and
Universities as Compared to Eighteen- to Twenty-Four-Year-Old
Population, 1900 to 1970

Year	College-Age Population (in thousands)	Undergraduate Enrollment (in thousands)	Percentage
1900	10,357	232	2.2
1910	12,300	346	2.8
1920	12,830	582	4.5
1930	15,280	1,054	6.9
1940	16,458	1,389	8.4
1950	16,120	2,421	15.0
1960	15,677	2,874	18.3
1970	24,712	6,274	25.4

Source: NCES *Digest*, 1970.

early 1960s through the 1980s, between 50 and 55 percent of high
school graduates were entering some postsecondary school within
a year of leaving high school. In 1999, that figure had climbed
to 63 percent and by 2005 it reached 67 percent (NCES *Digest*,
2001, 2006).

This chapter reports data on the numbers and types of students
attending community colleges, including reasons for the different
enrollment patterns, college effects on various student groups, and
student goal attainment and dropout. Student transfer rates are
examined, but information on jobs subsequently attained appears
in Chapter Eight, on vocational education.

Reasons for the Increase in Numbers

The increase in community college enrollments may be attributed
to several conditions in addition to general population expansion:
older students' participation; financial aid; part-time attendance;
the reclassification of institutions; the redefinition of students and
courses; and high attendance by women, low-ability, and minority

students. Community colleges also recruited students aggressively; to an institution that tries to offer something for everyone in the community, everyone is potentially a student.

Demography has a profound effect on college enrollments. The number of eighteen-year-olds in the American population peaked in 1979, declined steadily throughout the 1980s, and was 23 percent lower in 1992, when it began increasing again. Overall enrollments in public two-year colleges doubled during the 1970s, then slowed to a 15 percent increase during the 1980s. This growth in a period of decline in the eighteen-year-old population indicates the influence of other factors on community college enrollments. However, it pales in comparison with the surge of students entering in the 1970s.

In order to make up for the shortfall in potential younger students, the colleges expanded programs attractive to older students. Numbers of working adults seeking skills that would enable them to change or upgrade their jobs or activities to satisfy their personal interests enrolled because they could attend part time. Older students swelled the roster. According to the *AACJC Directory*, the mean age of students enrolled for credit in 1980 was twenty-seven, the median age was twenty-three, and the modal age was nineteen. A national survey conducted by the Center for the Study of Community Colleges found that by 1986, the mean had gone up to twenty-nine, the median had increased to twenty-five, and the mode had remained at nineteen. But the percentage of students younger than age 24 has increased steadily in recent years, from 43 in 1995–96 to 47 in 2003–2004; 26 percent were under age 20 (NCES *Digest*, 2006). Advanced placement and similar collaborations with high schools have led to a 5 percent population of students who are younger than age eighteen; in 2005, 8 percent of the full-time equivalent enrollment in Washington community colleges was generated by dual-enrollment high school students (Washington State Board for Community and Technical Colleges, 2006). Overall, the national mean age was 27.7 years, the median 23.6, and the mode just under age nineteen.

Note the discrepancy among these three measures. The mean is the most sensitive to extremes; hence, a program for even a few senior citizens affects that measure dramatically. The median suggests that the students just out of high school and those in their early twenties who either delayed beginning college or entered community colleges after dropping out of other institutions accounted for half the student population. This 50 percent of the student body that was composed of students aged eighteen to twenty-three was matched on the other side of the median by students ranging in age all the way out to their sixties and seventies. The mode reflects the greatest number; nineteen-year-olds continued as the dominant single age group in the institutions. Thus, a graph depicting the age of community college students would show a bulge at the low end of the scale, a peak at age nineteen, and a long tail reaching out toward the high end.

The availability of financial aid brought additional students as state and federal payments, loans, and work-study grants rose markedly. From the 1940s through the early 1970s, nearly all the types of aid were categorical, designed to assist particular groups of students. The largest group of beneficiaries was war veterans; in California in 1973, veterans made up more than 13 percent of the total enrollment. Students from economically disadvantaged and minority groups were also large beneficiaries of financial aid; more than thirty thousand such students in Illinois received state and local funds in 1974. Since the mid-1970s, more of the funds have been unrestricted. Overall, 62 percent of full-time students and 44 percent of the part-timers attending public two-year institutions received some form of financial aid during the 2003–04 academic year. Total aid averaged $2,300 per aid-receiving student (NCES *Digest*, 2006).

As the age of the students went up, the number of credit hours each student attempted went down. In the early 1970s, half of the students were full-timers; by the mid-1980s, only one-third were (see Table 2.2). And these figures do not include noncredit students enrolled in community or continuing education, high

Table 2.2.   Part-Time Enrollment as a Percentage of Total Enrollment in Public Two-Year Institutions of Higher Education, 1970–2004

Year	Total Fall Enrollment	Part-Time Enrollment	Percentage
1970	2,195,412	1,066,247	49%
1975	3,836,366	2,173,745	57%
1980	4,328,782	2,733,289	63%
1985	4,269,733	2,772,828	65%
1990	4,996,475	3,279,632	66%
1995	5,277,829	3,437,239	65%
2000	5,697,388	3,697,380	65%
2001	5,996,701	3,841,205	64%
2002	6,270,380	3,937,068	63%
2003	6,207,618	3,806,637	61%
2004	6,243,576	3,817,955	61%

Source: NCES *Digest*, 2006.

school completion courses, and short-cycle occupational studies. The pattern was consistent throughout the country; in nearly all states with community college enrollments greater than fifty thousand, part-time students far outnumbered full-timers. In Illinois, part-timers outnumbered full-timers, sometimes by as much as three to one.

The rise in the number of part-time students between 1980 and 2002 can be attributed to many factors: the opening of non-campus colleges that enroll few full-timers; an increase in the number of students combining work and study; and an increase in the number of reverse transfers, people who may already have baccalaureate and higher degrees; to name but a few. As examples of the latter group, over 48 percent of the 92,594 graduates receiving bachelor's degrees from the University of California and the California State University systems in 2001 took one or more classes at California community colleges in the ensuing three years. Nearly all were credit courses. The colleges made deliberate efforts to attract part-timers by making it easy for them to attend. Senior citizens' institutes; weekend colleges; courses offered at off-campus centers, in workplaces, and in rented and donated housing around the district; and countless other stratagems have been employed. Notable, however, is that even though the recent increase in younger students has decreased the ratio of part-timers, it is still above 60 percent: 64 percent in Illinois, 63 percent in Florida and Washington, 65 percent in Texas and North Carolina, and 87 percent in California. And nearly four of five of all students were employed, with 40 percent working full-time (Horn, Nevill, and Griffith, 2006). The Community College of the Air Force claims 231,098 students, but because it automatically enrolls and awards credit for training to all enlistees, these "students" are not included in the overall national figures (*Community College of the Air Force Fact Sheet*, 2007).

The community colleges play a role in educating international students. Fifteen percent of the more than half million international students in U.S. higher education are in community colleges; Santa Monica College (California) and Houston Community College (Texas) each enrolls more international students than any other institution in the nation. Most need to study English before attempting particular college programs. In the community colleges, even though they pay $6,500 tuition on average, they find English as a Second Language courses offered at lower cost than in senior institutions and they are less likely to have to qualify for admission (Redden, July 26, 2007). More than three-fourths of them are between the ages of twenty and thirty-four; most are enrolled full-time, often a qualification set by the conditions of their visas, and they stay enrolled for an average of more than six semesters (Hagedorn and Lee, 2005). The majority are from Asia.

The growth in total enrollments did not result alone from the colleges' attracting students who might not otherwise have participated in education beyond high school. Two other factors played a part: the different ways of classifying institutions and a redefinition of the term *student*.

Changes in the classification of colleges are common. Private colleges become public; two-year colleges become four-year (and vice versa); adult education centers and proprietary trade schools enter the category, especially as they begin awarding degrees. The universe of community and junior colleges is especially fluid. From time to time, entire sets of institutions, such as trade and vocational schools and adult education centers, have been added to the list. As examples, in the mid-1960s, four vocational-technical schools became the first colleges in the University of Hawaii community college system, and in the mid-1970s, the community colleges in Iowa became area schools responsible for adult education in their districts. Indiana's Ivy Tech became a set of comprehensive colleges in 1999. Sometimes institutional reclassification is made by an agency that gathers statistics; in the 1990s, the NCES and the Carnegie Foundation for the Advancement of Teaching began adding accredited proprietary schools to their community college databases. And in 2005 both removed the community colleges that had begun offering bachelor's degrees. All these changes modify the number of students tabulated each year.

Reclassification of students within colleges has had an even greater effect on enrollment figures. As an example, when the category "defined adult" was removed from the California system, students of all ages could be counted as equivalents for funding purposes. In most states, the trend has been toward including college-sponsored events (whether or not such activities demand evidence of learning attained) as "courses" and hence the people attending them as "students." The boundaries among the categories "degree-credit," "nondegree credit," "noncredit," and "community service" are permeable; student tallies shift about as courses are reclassified. Furthermore, the community colleges have taken under their aegis numerous instructional programs formerly offered by public and private agencies, including police and fire academies, hospitals, banks, and religious centers. These practices swell the enrollment figures and blur the definition of student, making it possible for community college leaders to point with pride to larger enrollments and to gain augmented funding when enrollments are used as the basis for accounting. They also heighten imprecision in counting students and make it difficult to compare enrollments from one year to another.

Nonetheless, the proportion of Americans attending college increased steadily through the twentieth century, and the availability of community colleges contributed notably to this growth. In 2003, 43 percent of all students beginning postsecondary education enrolled first in a two-year college (NCES *Digest*, 2006). Of the students who delayed entry until they were age thirty or older, nearly 60 percent began in a community college. As the following sections detail, the colleges have been essential especially to the educational progress of people of lower academic ability, lower income, and other characteristics that had limited their opportunity for postsecondary enrollment.

Student Ability

Classification of students by academic ability revealed increasing numbers of lower-ability students among community college entrants. As Cross (1971) pointed out, three major philosophies about who should go to college have dominated the history of higher education in this country: the aristocratic, suggesting that white males from the upper socioeconomic classes would attend; the meritocratic, holding that college admission should be based on ability; and the egalitarian, which "means that everyone should have equality of access to educational opportunities, regardless of socioeconomic background, race, sex, or ability" (p. 6). By the time the community colleges were developed, most young people from the higher socioeconomic groups and most of the high-aptitude aspirants were going to college. Cross concluded, "The majority of students entering open-door community colleges come from the lower half of the high school classes, academically and socioeconomically" (p. 7).

Various data sets reveal the lower academic skill level of the entrants. The College Board's Scholastic Aptitude Test (SAT) means for community colleges have been considerably lower than the norm for all college students. In 2004–2005 the average national SAT composite score was 841 (420 Verbal, 421 Math) for students who indicated a two-year college degree as their objective whereas it was 968 (481 Verbal, 487 Math) for students with bachelor's degree aspirations (NCES *Digest*, 2006). Since the SAT scores are highly correlated with annual family income (Michaels, 2006), these norms reflect not only the college's lower entrance requirements but also the socioeconomic status of their students.

Like most other institutions of higher education, the community colleges have also sought out high-ability students and made special benefits available to them. For example, in 1979, Miami-Dade Community College began giving full tuition waivers to all students graduating in the top 10 percent of their local high school class, and in 1991 it extended that offer to the top 20 percent. Students in that group were eligible to apply for the Academic Achievement Award, which provided $3,200 to cover in-state tuition and fees for two years. Those individuals graduating in the top 5 percent received $5,000 for two years, which essentially covered not only tuition and fees but also textbook costs. This program has since evolved into an Honors College (Miami Dade College, 2007).

The growth of honors programs evidences the colleges' welcoming the better-prepared students. White (1975) surveyed 225 colleges in the North-Central region and found that about 10 percent had formalized honors programs. Twenty years later, *Peterson's Guide to Two-Year Colleges, 1995* (1994) listed honors programs in over 25 percent of the institutions, and by 2005 they had been established in more than one-third (Wyner, 2006). Outcalt and Kisker (2003) found over 9 percent of the faculty reporting they had taught at least one honors course in the previous two years. Often, universities get involved; UCLA has assisted colleges throughout Southern California in building honors programs and linking them with transfer opportunities (Kane, 2001). The students in honors programs often receive priority registration, special academic advisors, and tuition discounts, in addition to intensive courses. Montgomery College (Maryland) has honors programs on each of its three campuses. Its Montgomery Scholars enrolls students directly from high school and pays their tuition and fees for two years, including the cost of a summer studying in England. More than 80 percent graduate and most transfer. A Sophomore Business Honors Program is open to second-year students. Two additional programs are designed for part-time, working adults at the college's branch campuses (Ashburn, 2006).

Gender

Probably because it is easier to sort students by gender than by any other variable, differences between male and female college students have long been documented. Historically, among students of questionable ability, fewer women than men attended college. When funds were limited, more male than female high-ability students from low-income families entered college. Furthermore, the women who went to college were more likely to be dependent on their families for support. Not until 1978 did the number of women attending college in the United States exceed the number of men. By 2003, women were ahead, 58 to 42 percent. Overall, in each year since 1978, more women than men have earned associate degrees; in 2005–06, 62.7 percent of the degrees went to women (NCES *Digest*, 2006).

Some slight change has occurred in the types of programs that community college students enter, although the traditionally gender-differentiated fields persist. The associate degrees awarded reveal these differences. In 2003–04, women earned 87 percent of the degrees in the health professions; 82 percent in education, and 66 percent in business. Men dominated in mechanics and repairers with 94 percent of the degrees; engineering technology, 85 percent; and computer and information science, 69 percent. Women had a slight edge in liberal arts degrees, men in security and protective services. Interestingly, the degrees awarded in physical sciences were about equally divided (NCES *Digest*, 2006).

Ethnic Minorities

The community colleges' diligence in recruiting students from segments of the population that had not previously attended college yielded sizable increases in the college attendance of ethnic minorities. By 1997, community colleges, with 38 percent of the total enrollment in American higher education, were enrolling 46 percent of the ethnic minority students. In 2004, minority students constituted 36.5 percent of all community college enrollments nationwide, up from 20 percent in 1976 (NCES *Digest*, 2005). Naturally, the pattern differed from state to state depending on the minority population. Hawaii, with 77 percent, and California and New Mexico, with over 50 percent, had the highest percentages of minorities among their community college students. Minorities were also enrolled in significant numbers in other states that had well-developed community college systems: Texas, Mississippi, Georgia, Maryland, and Florida were above the national norms (American Association of Community Colleges, 2003).

When the enrollment figures are disaggregated by ethnic groups, they are even more revealing of the community colleges' contributions to access for minority students: African American, 13.8 percent; Hispanic, 14.8 percent; Asian American, 6.5 percent; Native American, 1.2 percent. As shown in Table 2.3, the African American proportion of community college

Table 2.3.   Percentages of African American and Hispanic Population by State, Compared with Ethnic Enrollments in Two-Year Colleges

	African American		Hispanic	
	State Population	Two-Year College Enrollment	State Population	Two-Year College Enrollment
Alabama	25.5%	25.5%	0.8%	0.8%
Alaska	4.1	3.1	4.6	3.1
Arizona	3.1	3.6	22.3	19.3
Arkansas	15.5	16.7	1.3	1.7
California	6.6	7.5	32.7	26.2
Colorado	4.3	4.7	14.3	14.0
Connecticut	8.9	14.2	8.7	11.1
Delaware	18.6	19.9	3.3	3.9
Florida	14.2	15.9	15.7	17.7
Georgia	28.7	32.8	2.4	2.1
Hawaii	2.1	1.6	8.6	2.6
Idaho	0.5	0.4	7.2	3.5
Illinois	15.0	14.3	10.5	16.1
Indiana	8.2	10.3	2.3	2.3
Iowa	2.1	2.7	1.8	1.8
Kansas	6.3	6.4	5.2	4.4
Kentucky	7.1	9.1	0.8	1.1
Louisiana	32.5	31.5	2.7	2.5
Maine	0.4	0.6	0.7	0.4
Maryland	27.7	28.1	4.1	4.0
Massachusetts	5.3	9.3	7.0	8.6
Michigan	14.6	11.1	2.7	2.3
Minnesota	3.1	4.5	2.0	1.2
Mississippi	35.9	36.4	0.8	0.6
Missouri	11.2	11.7	1.6	1.5
Montana	0.4	0.4	2.2	1.2
Nebraska	4.1	4.5	3.5	3.3
Nevada	6.8	7.0	14.7	13.5

New Hampshire	0.6	1.3	1.4	1.6
New Jersey	13.5	14.7	12.8	13.6
New Mexico	1.8	2.3	39.6	37.2
New York	14.7	14.3	15.5	11.8
North Carolina	22.2	23.7	1.5	2.0
North Dakota	0.7	1.3	1.1	0.8
Ohio	11.5	13.0	1.6	1.9
Oklahoma	8.2	8.5	3.7	3.3
Oregon	1.8	2.2	5.7	4.0
Pennsylvania	9.7	14.2	2.7	2.9
Rhode Island	4.1	5.8	7.6	7.8
South Carolina	29.8	31.3	1.1	1.4
South Dakota	0.6	0.4	1.1	0.5
Tennessee	16.4	17.8	1.0	1.1
Texas	12.0	11.8	29.2	27.6
Utah	0.8	0.7	6.2	4.1
Vermont	0.5	1.4	1.0	1.1
Virginia	19.9	19.3	3.8	4.0
Washington	3.1	4.5	6.1	4.9
West Virginia	3.1	4.7	0.7	0.5
Wisconsin	6.0	5.7	2.5	2.5
Wyoming	0.8	0.9	6.5	3.7

Source: American Association of Community Colleges (2003).

enrollment in 2003 *exceeds* the African American proportion of the eighteen- to forty-four-year-old population in thirty-six states, up from eighteen states in 1999. Comparable figures for Hispanic enrollments are found in seventeen states, up from eleven states four years earlier.

More so than in the universities, the community college student population tends to reflect the ethnic composition of the institution's locale. Community colleges in cities with high proportions of minorities—Chicago, El Paso, Los Angeles, Miami, New York, Phoenix—enroll sizable numbers of minority students. Ninety-four percent of the students at Laredo Community College

(Texas) were Hispanic; 82 percent of the students at Lawson State Community College (Alabama) were African American. The evidence of neighborhood attendance is revealed when the community college has several campuses in the same city. At East Los Angeles College in 2000, 70 percent of the students were Hispanic; at Los Angeles Southwest College, 72 percent were black; at Los Angeles Pierce College, 42 percent were white and 19 percent Asian. More than thirty community colleges enrolling around 20,000 students have been established especially to serve Native Americans; Oglala Lakota College (North Dakota), Haskell Indian Junior College (Kansas), Navajo Community College (Arizona), and Bacone Community College (Oklahoma) are notable examples. The federal Tribally Controlled Community College Assistance Act of 1978, and the grants awarded by Congress beginning in 1980, gave a great impetus to the development of these colleges, now functioning in thirteen states.

Because the issue of minority students' progress in college has been so charged politically, the question of whether the community colleges have enhanced or retarded progress for minority students has been debated at length (see, for example, Astin, 1982; Richardson and Bender, 1987; Richardson and de los Santos, 1988). Those who say that the community colleges have assisted minority students point to ease of access, low tuition, and minimal entrance requirements. They note the numerous programs that provide special services to minority students and applaud efforts made to recruit them. Their most telling argument is that a sizable percentage of those students would not be in college at all were it not for the community colleges.

Several analysts have charged that minority students who begin their college education at a community college will do less well than those of equal ability who enroll at the senior institution and that this differential is greater for them than it is for the majority of students. These detractors have taken the position that because students who begin at a community college are less likely to obtain degrees, minorities are actually harmed by two-year institutions. What is the evidence? The best estimates suggest that white students, who comprise 62.5 percent of community college enrollment, obtain 68.5 percent of the associate degrees; African American students, 13.3 percent of enrollment, obtain 12.2 percent of the associate degrees; Hispanic students, 14.8 percent of enrollment, obtain 10.9 percent of the degrees; Asian students, 6.7 percent of enrollment, obtain 5.0 percent of the degrees (NCES *Digest,* 2006). These figures suggest not only differential achievement but also the imprecision of the term *minority student.*

It is difficult to disaggregate the effects of community colleges from the characteristics of the students who enter them. In general, students who enter community colleges instead of universities have lower academic ability and aspirations and are from a lower socioeconomic class. The various studies that have attempted to control for those variables frequently also attempt to control for the fact that minority students are more likely to attend school part-time, and the community colleges encourage part-time attendance. However, as Adelman (2005) noted, "The studies often highlight variables over which the community college has but modest control—gender, race and ethnicity, first-generation college status, SES, second language background, marital and parental status" (p. 118). He concluded that the colleges can do little to change them but must work with the students they have.

The question of whether community colleges are beneficial to minority students is thus unresolved. If sizable percentages of minority students would not attend any college if no community college were available, and if the act of attending college to take even a few classes is beneficial, then community colleges have certainly helped in the education of minority students. But if the presence of a convenient community college discourages minority students from attending senior institutions and reduces the probability of their completing the baccalaureate, then for those students who wanted degrees, the college has been detrimental. However, the latter contention is tempered by the numbers of minority students who enter community colleges and subsequently transfer to selective senior institutions where they would not be admissible as freshmen.

The question is not whether minority students tend to be concentrated in two-year colleges; they do. The question is not whether they tend to go through to the level of the associate degree and then transfer to the university; as a group, they do not. The question is what effect the community colleges have on *all* their students. And the answer is that they have a similar effect on everyone, minority and majority. As an example, the transfer rate nationwide is higher for white and Asian students than it is for African American and Hispanic students. However, in colleges that have a transfer rate substantially higher than the national norm, the transfer rate for African American and Hispanic students is higher than the national norm for *all* students (ERIC Clearinghouse for Community Colleges, 2001). The colleges are not designed exclusively for the purpose of passing students through to the baccalaureate. The issue must be seen in its total context; it does not merely affect the minorities.

Whom do the community colleges best serve? Egalitarians would say that the institutions should maintain parity in the percentage of each ethnic group attaining each of the following goals: entering college, enrolling in transfer-credit courses, persisting in any courses, gaining the associate degree, gaining admittance to a high-level technological program, graduating from such a program, transferring to the university at any point, and transferring to the university at the junior level. In practice, however, this level of equivalence is impossible to attain, short of imposing strict quotas at every step. For the minorities as for any other identifiable student group, the question should be put more broadly: "The community college or what alternative?" For most students in two-year institutions, *the choice is not between the community college and a senior residential institution; it is between the community college and nothing.*

Classifying the Students

The classification of students into special groups is more politically inspired than educationally pertinent. Women, ethnic minorities, and the disabled were able to have their concerns translated into special programs only after they became politically astute. From the college perspective, the temptation to place courses or students in separate categories was always present. The mature woman with a bachelor's degree, taking an art class for credit because it was taught by someone she admired and was scheduled at a time of day that was convenient for her, was not deserving of the special treatment accorded to "returning women," "the aged," or "students intending to transfer." She was there for her personal interest. Yet because of politically and institutionally inspired definitions, she would be counted each time the institution reported its numbers of women, aged, and transfer students.

Classifying students takes other forms as well. Assessments of community college students have been made from perspectives that span the social sciences: psychological, sociological, economic, and political. To the psychologist, community college students are pragmatic, little concerned with learning for its own sake. They are not self-directed or self-motivated; they need to be instructed. To the sociologist, the students are struggling to escape from their lower-class backgrounds; some do, but many are inhibited by a bias against leaving family and friends that a move in class would engender. To the economist, students from low-income families pay more in the form of forgone earnings as a percentage of total family income than their counterparts from higher-income groups, a differential that more than offsets the savings gained by attending a low-tuition institution. To the political scientist, students attending community colleges are given short shrift because the institutions are funded at a lower per capita level than the universities, and hence the students do not have equivalent libraries, laboratories, or faculty-student ratios available to them.

But determining the reasons that students attend college is not an exact exercise. They come for a variety of purposes, and the same person may have a half-dozen reasons for attending. As an example, when the National Postsecondary Student Aid Study offered students the opportunity to cite their reasons, 52 percent chose "transfer," 43 percent, "complete associate's degree," 17 percent, "complete certificate," 42 percent, "job skills," and 46 percent, "personal interest" (Horn, Nevill, and Griffith, 2006). Much depends on the way the questions are asked and the interpretations that the respondents make. There can be little doubt that although most students attend community colleges to better themselves financially, a sizable percentage are there for reasons of personal interest having nothing to do with direct fiscal benefit. In 1986 the Center for the Study of Community Colleges (CSCC) asked students their primary reason for attending and found 36 percent seeking transfer, 34 percent job entry skills, 16 percent job upgrading, and 15 percent personal interest. Voorhees and Zhou (2000) found comparable figures: 66 percent of the students were seeking either a certificate or degree or transfer credit, 21 percent enrolled in order to improve job skills, and 12 percent were enrolled for personal interest. Hoachlander, Sikora, and Horn (2003) reported 59 percent seeking transfer, degree, or certificate; 23 percent job skills; and 16 percent personal interest.

The conventional belief is that community college students—in contrast to students in four-year colleges—are less interested in academic studies and in learning for its own sake; instead, they are interested primarily in the practical, which to them means earning more money. Although some research evidence supports that belief, the perception that higher education is to be used particularly for occupational training seems pervasive among students in all types of institutions.

Whether these characterizations are correct, they mean little to institutional planners. Certainly, community college students are realistic in the sense that they use the institutions for their own purposes. But what students do not, in schools where attendance is not mandated? Certainly, more are from lower social classes than those attending the universities, but their class base is higher than that represented by the sizable percentage of Americans who do not attend college at all. Certainly, many are from the lower-income groups, but their attendance usually leads to higher earnings. Certainly, they welcome an instantly responsive institution, but the effects of nonpunitive grading and of forgiveness for past educational sins on their proclivities for learning have not yet been traced.

Unaware of all these analyses, the students continue attending the community colleges for their own purposes. Those just out of high school may matriculate merely because they have been conditioned to go to school every time September appears on the calendar. Students of any age wanting a better job may attend because career programs are connected to employers. Those who have jobs but want additional skills may hope to find a short-term program that will teach them to use new equipment introduced in their industry. Many begin at the introductory level and learn complete sets of job skills enabling them to qualify for trades that they might have known nothing about before entering the programs. Some students seek out special-interest courses, ranging from "The Great Books" to "Poodle Grooming," taking a course or two whenever one that strikes their fancy appears in the class schedule. Some use the community colleges as stepping-stones to other schools, finding them convenient and economical entry points to higher education and the professions.

The community college certainly serves a broader sector of the local population than does any other higher education institution. In 2003, the community colleges in thirteen states enrolled 6 percent or more of the population aged eighteen to forty-four (five states, all in the West, enrolled 8 percent or more), up from nine states in 1999 (Table 2.4). Much depends on demography—the percentage of population that is over age seventeen—but more relates to the overall college-going rate in the state, the

Table 2.4.   Estimated Percentage of State Population Aged Eighteen to Forty-Four Attending Community College, 2003

State	Estimated Percentage
Alabama	4.8
Alaska	0.5
Arizona	9.1
Arkansas	4.4
California	9.5
Colorado	4.5
Connecticut	3.5
Delaware	4.2
Florida	4.7
Georgia	3.6
Hawaii	5.6
Idaho	2.3
Illinois	7.3
Indiana	2.7
Iowa	7.1
Kansas	7.2
Kentucky	5.0
Louisiana	3.0
Maine	2.4
Maryland	5.5
Massachusetts	3.4
Michigan	5.5
Minnesota	5.6
Mississippi	6.0
Missouri	4.0
Montana	2.6
Nebraska	6.0
Nevada	5.6
New Hampshire	2.9
New Jersey	4.5
New Mexico	9.1
New York	3.5

North Carolina	6.0
North Dakota	4.0
Ohio	4.3
Oklahoma	5.2
Oregon	6.2
Pennsylvania	2.8
Rhode Island	3.9
South Carolina	5.0
South Dakota	1.9
Tennessee	3.3
Texas	6.1
Utah	3.3
Vermont	2.3
Virginia	5.2
Washington	8.0
West Virginia	1.7
Wisconsin	5.5
Wyoming	10.0
Total	5.5

Source: NCES *Digest,* 2006; U.S. Census Bureau, 2004.

availability of other postsecondary forms, and the accessibility of community colleges.

The socioeconomic status of dependent students attending two-year colleges tends to be lower than that of dependent students attending four-year institutions. Of the students entering public four-year institutions in 1995–96, 23 percent came from the bottom socioeconomic quartile and 27 percent from the top quartile. For those entering the public two-year colleges, comparable ratios were 28 and 19 (NCES, 1998). In 2003–04, 26 percent of community college students and 20 percent of four-year college students were from the lowest quartile (Horn, Nevill, and Griffith, 2006).

Transfer Rates

Five students in junior standing at a university are asked about their educational background. The first one explains that he did his first two years in a community college and the university concurrently, that he took all his general education courses in the community college while he was taking major-field courses in the university. The second replies that he started in the university as a freshman, dropped out to spend his next term in the community college, and then came back to the university and has been there ever since. The third says that she took two courses at a community college in the summer after her high school graduation and then matriculated at the university. The fourth studied for one year at a community college ten years earlier and when she decided to come back to school, entered the university as a sophomore. The fifth finished her first two years at the community college and transferred as a junior in mid-year. How many of the five are "transfer students"? *None*, according to some reports; *all*, according to others.

In 1989, the Center for the Study of Community Colleges began collecting data on transfer, using the definition: *all students entering the community college in a given year who have no prior college experience, and who complete at least twelve college credit units within four years of entry, divided into the number of that group who take one or more classes at an in-state, public university within four years.* By collecting data from individual colleges and state agencies, the Center published national transfer rates for students entering in each year, beginning in 1984. Table 2.5 displays those findings.

Figures for the 1995 entrants were corroborated by the NCES, which found over 22 percent of the students entering two-year institutions transferring within three years (Bailey, Jenkins, and Leinbach, 2005a, 2005b). Different rates obtain when students transferring to private or out-of-state institutions are included.

Table 2.5.   Transfer Rates for Students Entering in 1984–1995

Entering Year	Percentage Receiving Twelve or More Credits Within Four Years	Percentage Transferring Within Four Years	Number of Colleges in Sample
1984	50.5	23.7	48
1985	46.7	23.6	114
1986	46.7	23.4	155
1987	46.9	22.6	366
1988	45.5	22.1	395
1989	44.3	21.5	416
1990	47.1	21.8	417
1991	47.3	22.1	424
1993	50.7	23.4	345
1995	52.5	25.2	538

Source: ERIC Clearinghouse for Community Colleges, 2001.

The transfer rates certainly would be further inflated if more than four years were allowed before tabulating the transfers. Doyle (2006) used data from the Beginning Postsecondary Students Survey to show that 66 percent of the students who declared bachelor's degree intent at entry had transferred within six years. The transfer rates range as high as 63 percent when only the associate in arts degree recipients are tabulated (Townsend, 2002). Since community college matriculants arguably are potential transfers until they either show up at a university or die, the transfer rate calculations can never be fully reflective of student performance.

The transfer rates for community college students can be modified by adding in different types of information. For example, how many entering students aspire to further education? The way that the question is asked is key. When students in degree-credit classes were asked their primary reason for attending, as in several state-wide and one national study reported in the 1980s, the proportion of bachelor's degree aspirants approximated one-third (Center for the Study of Community Colleges, 1986). A compilation of data from several NCES studies regarding purposes for attending found 37 percent of the students beginning in community colleges citing transfer intentions (Hoachlander, Sikora, and Horn, 2003). But subsequent NCES reports found that in response to the question "What is the highest level of education you ever expect to complete?" 71 percent in 2000 and over 75 percent in 2004 indicated "bachelor's degree or higher" (Bradburn and Hurst, 2001; Horn, Nevill, and Griffith, 2006). And when Hagedorn and Maxwell (2002) asked a smaller sample, "If there were no obstacles, what is the highest degree you would like to obtain in your life?" 88 percent aspired to bachelor's or beyond. The American College Testing Program's 2006 survey found only a slightly higher percentage of the students enrolled for credit anticipating transfer than those who sought preparation for employment (American Association of Community Colleges, 2006). Retrospective studies, examining the transcripts of baccalaureate recipients to see how many transferred credits from community colleges, usually report that from 40 to 65 percent of the people obtaining bachelor's degrees from public universities have some community college courses on their record.

Interestingly, although the transfer rate in most of the states with comprehensive college systems clusters around the 25 percent national mark, the range between states is from 11 to 40 percent. Some of the reasons for this wide interstate disparity are obviously related to the structure of higher education within a state. Where the two-year colleges are organized as branch campuses of the state university, the transfer rates are high; where they function as technical institutes that emphasize trade and industry programs, the transfer rates are low. Deviations from the norm appear also in states where transfer to independent universities is a prominent feature of the higher education system or policies related to enrollment have been effected. For example, state-mandated limitations on college growth eventually elevate the transfer rate because the community colleges tend to react to enrollment caps by cutting the programs that attract adult, part-time students, that is, those least likely to transfer. Transfer rates among colleges in the same state similarly show wide variations, undoubtedly because of local conditions, community demographics, college proximity to a university campus, and employment or economic conditions in the district (Cohen and Brawer, 1996). Nonetheless, for the analyst seeking evidence of the role of the community college in assisting people toward the baccalaureate, the data that have been collected uniformly across the states are indispensable.

Dropout

To transfer to a senior institution, enter the job market, get a better job, or merely learn for one's own purposes: these are students' chief reasons for attending community colleges. How do they fare? The community colleges pride themselves on open access, which translates into ease of entry. In general, this means that students may register with little advance commitment and enroll in classes without completing a plan of study. Part-time attendance is not discouraged, and withdrawing from classes without penalty and reenrolling is considerably more typical student behavior than that found at the universities. The colleges have made numerous efforts in recent years to tighten requirements by demanding advance registration, preenrollment counseling, filing of matriculation plans, and mandatory testing and advisement. But the attendance patterns that were encouraged during an era of laissez-faire, open-access policies still dominate.

Which students persist? Who drops out, and when? Who completes the programs, transfers, or satisfies the reasons for entry? More studies of student attendance patterns have been conducted than of any other area within the institutions. Students are tracked, transcripts are analyzed, the dropouts are surveyed, and grade point averages earned by transferring students are reviewed, all in an attempt to learn how and why students stay or leave. The presenting reason is to determine how the college can better serve its matriculants; the result is a wealth of research tracking community college students into and out of the institutions.

Most studies of dropout rely on surveys of nonreturning students (Joliet Junior College, 2005; Nitzke and Wacker, 2001; Northern Virginia Community College, 2000; Salt Lake Community College, 2006; Scoggin and Styron, 2006; Zhai and Monzon, 2001). The reasons that students drop out are quite varied, but in general, most of them are related to situations beyond the college's control. A change in work schedule is often cited, along with such personal reasons as health problems, difficulty in obtaining child care, family conflicts, financial burdens, change in residence, or attendance at another institution. Many of the early leavers have already attained the objective for which they attended; they wanted only to take a course or two. Hence, their leaving had nothing to do with college policies or procedures; they got what they wanted and then withdrew. And in studies that asked students whether they intended to return, a majority of the respondents indicated that they would be back one day. The availability of the institution seemed quite popular and may even have contributed to the lack of persistence: Why not leave when other demands interfere? You can always return.

Although most of the reasons for leaving school are beyond the institution's ability to amend, some of the reasons suggest that institutional intervention might be helpful. One discovery is that decisions to drop out are usually made early on. As an example, Kangas (1991) interviewed students who withdrew and found that 71 percent of them thought about leaving in the first four weeks; 85 percent did not talk to their instructor about withdrawing. And although he found that only around one student in six offered reasons related to the classroom, the instructor, or the college, the students who withdrew indicated that they had never really gotten involved with the college; most of them studied alone, and most were working forty or more hours per week outside school. Nationally, of the students entering community colleges in fall 1989 and leaving by the end of their first year, 39 percent indicated they had never participated in a study group, 34 percent had never socialized with faculty or advisers, and 45 percent had never spoken with faculty outside class (NCES, 1994c). Lucas and Meltesen (1991) found that only 8 percent of the students indicated the college was in any way responsible for their decision to withdraw; nearly half of the dropouts had never consulted a counselor. Involvement aside, NCES data (1998) demonstrate that among students in public two-year colleges, risk factors for attrition prevail. These students are more likely than students from other institutional types to be first-generation students, have delayed entry into higher education, attend part-time, work full-time, be financially independent with dependents, and be single parents.

Retention can be enhanced if actions are taken to integrate the students with the college. This must be started early, even before the instructional term begins. Programs of early start and summer involvements have been tried and have been demonstrably successful. Adelman examined several large-scale data sets and concluded that summer-term credits "held a consistently positive relationship to degree completion" (2006b, p. xx). The National Science Foundation funds summer bridge programs to increase the number of secondary school, community college, and four-year college students entering science, mathematics, and engineering curriculums. But these reach only a few students, those who in the main are already committed. The rest of the beginning students need to be alerted to the availability of advising and, more important, to the campus services that can help them in making the transition from their life in the community to life as a student. Child care facilities, now found in most colleges, are essential. Interestingly, few colleges have created sizable numbers of on-campus jobs for aides, paraprofessionals, peer tutors, teaching assistants, clerical workers, or custodial assistants, all jobs that might bring the students into closer association with the institution and thereby allow them to work fewer hours away from the campus. And few have installed early-alert systems, arrangements whereby if a student has missed more than two classes, a staff member seeks out the student to find out if there are any problems with which the college can help.

Determining the intra-institutional procedures that affect dropout tells only part of the story. The colleges' efforts to recruit and enroll sizable numbers of students must also be considered. As open-door, noncompulsory institutions, community colleges have made tremendous efforts to bring in sizable numbers of students. They have established off-campus recruitment centers and sent vans staffed with counselors into shopping centers and parks. They have advertised in newspapers and on billboards and conducted telephone solicitations. Some of the advertising campaigns were planned as carefully as sophisticated marketing plans used by private businesses.

Johnson (1979) defined marketing as an integration of promotional activities with programs designed particularly for certain population segments and offered at times and places convenient to those groups. He considered it important for college managers to understand marketing, put all elements of the college into a marketing stance, and organize marketing task forces to work with instructors and other staff members in devising and promoting new programs. By 1988, a sizable percentage of the nation's community colleges had organized marketing divisions (Bogart and Galbraith, 1988). These efforts shifted subsequently as budget reductions made it more difficult to provide noncredit activities for special groups. But attracting students to degree-credit programs remained a high priority in institutions where fiscal survival was tied directly to the number of people in classrooms. These efforts certainly contributed to maintaining enrollments, but they also tended to attract students with only a casual commitment to college-level studies. And they still continue, even in an era of enrollment caps.

The admissions procedures alone, which allowed students to enter classes almost at will, certainly contributed to the dropout rate. Studies of the reasons that students drop out of college rarely consider the strength of their initial commitment, but it seems likely that a student who petitions for admission, takes a battery of entrance tests, and signs up for classes six months in advance of the term is more genuinely committed to attending than one who appears on the first day of classes with little preliminary planning. Data on students' ethnicity, prior academic achievement, and degree aspirations pale in comparison with the essential component: the degree of their personal commitment. Tinto has asserted that any valid study of dropout must consider the intensity of the student's "educational goal commitment . . . because it helps specify the psychological orientations the individual brings with him into the college setting" (1975, p. 93). The NCES defined "more committed" students as those enrolled for at least half time and reporting that transferring or earning a credential were reasons for attending (Horn, Nevill, and Griffith, 2006, p. 25). The "more committed" were less likely to drop out, a finding corroborated in several studies such as in North Carolina (North Carolina Community College System, 2007a, 2007b). This group also tended to be younger.

Studies of student dropout may be only marginally relevant to an institution that regards accessibility as its greatest virtue. The community colleges have organized themselves around the theme of ease in entrance, exit, and reentry. Having made a considerable effort to recruit students and offer them something useful, most faculty members and administrators do want to keep them enrolled, at least until degree or program objectives have been fulfilled. But it is difficult for an institution built on the theme of easy access to limit easy exit.

Goal Attainment

Goal attainment takes many forms, with transfer and job getting leading the list. Numerous studies have been made of the students who transfer from community colleges to baccalaureate-granting institutions. Once the students arrive, they seem to do as well eventually as the native juniors, although they may take longer overall to obtain the bachelor's degree. Other consistent findings are that students who transfer with greater numbers of community college credits do better than those with fewer, especially if they have received an associate's degree; and continuous enrollment, even part time, increases the probability of degree completion (Adelman, 2006b, p. xxi). The phenomenon of transfer shock, the first-term decline in grade point average that has been observed for decades, is still apparent, evidenced by studies done in Virginia (Tidewater Community College, 2005), Iowa (Breja, 2006), Hawaii (University of Hawaii, 2005), North Carolina (Glass and Harrington, 2002), and Maryland (Filipp, 2004).

The reasons that students transferring to universities may have difficulties are not fully understood. Possibly the native students were tied into an informal network that advised them on which professors and courses were most likely to yield favorable results. Students transferring to research universities have said the competitive environment differed markedly from the cooperative relationships they had enjoyed at their community colleges (Chang, 2006; Townsend and Wilson, 2006). Transfers may have satisfactorily completed their distribution requirements at the community colleges but could not do as well when they entered the specialized courses at the universities. Community colleges may have been passing students who would have failed or dropped out of the freshman and sophomore classes in the senior institutions. And as a group, the community college students were undoubtedly less able at the beginning. All these variables probably operate to some degree and tend to confound the reasons for junior-level dropout and failure.

Astin has said that for those who begin at a community college, "even after controlling for the student's social background [and] ability and motivation at college entrance, the chances of persisting to the baccalaureate degree are substantially reduced" (1977, p. 234). He found several factors leading to the attainment of a degree: residence on campus, a high degree of interaction with the peer group, the presence of good students on the campus, and full-time-student status. These factors are rarely found in community colleges. Except for the colleges serving rural areas, hardly any have residence halls; in most states, the community college students are of lesser ability; most are part-timers; and most have jobs off campus. Thus, the combination of individual and institutional factors at the community college level operates distinctly to reduce the probability that a student will complete the two years and transfer to a baccalaureate-granting institution.

However, the situation is not as bleak as some commentators have made it. Pascarella and Terenzini's (2005) meta-analysis showed that initial attendance at a two-year institution reduces the likelihood of bachelor's degree completion by 15 to 20 percent. But two-year college students "who make the transfer are as likely as four-year matriculants to persist overall (76 percent versus 78 percent)" (p. 376). "Net of other relevant variables, former community college students were as likely as their four-year counterparts to graduate from a baccalaureate degree-granting institution, to aspire to attend graduate school, and to enroll in graduate school" (p. 377). Furthermore, students who began at community colleges typically transferred to four-year institutions that have students with considerably higher SAT scores. Put another way, "students are able to attend more selective four-year institutions if they first attend community colleges" (Pascarella and Terenzini, 2005, p. 495). This benefit is largest for community college students who come from poor families, are of low ability, or performed poorly in high school. Low socioeconomic status (SES) students who transfer to elite universities are more likely to graduate than their counterparts who start at four-year schools. And "starting postsecondary education at a community college, versus a four-year institution, had only a small and statistically nonsignificant effect" on subsequent earnings (p. 494).

As confirmed in the studies of dropouts, most students seem to attain at least their short-term goals. Students usually have more than one reason for attending, and the importance of one or another may shift over time. The students who attend for only a short time and then transfer or go to work without receiving a degree or certificate of completion may be the pragmatic ones. The associate degree itself has had little value in the marketplace, a fact acknowledged by the AACJC, which organized a short-lived "Associate Degree Preferred" campaign (Parnell, 1985) to encourage students to obtain degrees and employers to give preference to those who have them. The proponents of program completion policies must continually battle not only the students' and employers' perceptions but also the universities that readily accept transfers without associate degrees and the colleges' own managers who may want to maintain the institutions as passive environments providing ad hoc studies for anyone at any time. Still, there is an earnings premium of $7,300 for associate degree holders aged twenty-five to thirty-four relative to those in that age group who hold high school diplomas only (College Board, 2006a, p. 3). This premium is a result largely of the credentials (lab technician, paralegal, medical assistant) that many graduates possess.

Assessment and Tracking

Curriculum tracking within the colleges has risen and fallen with the times. Throughout their early years, the community colleges typically administered achievement tests to matriculants and attempted to place students in courses presumed to be consonant with their abilities. Students were shunted from transfer to remedial or occupational programs, a practice that gave rise to the "cooling-out" thesis postulated by Clark in 1960. Most institutions also maintained academic probation, F grades, one-term dismissal of students not making satisfactory progress, transcripts required for admission, entrance tests, midterm grades, penalties for dropping classes after the eighth week, mandatory exit interviews, required class attendance, and mandatory orientation courses. However, during the early 1970s, these practices fell into disfavor as many students demanded the right to enter courses of their own choosing. Furthermore, measuring students' abilities has never been an exact science; a student deficient in one area of knowledge may be well qualified in another, and stories of abuses in program tracking are common. Educators rationalized their inability to assess their students accurately by saying that anyone had the right to try anything, even if it meant failure. The 1970s saw an erosion of course prerequisites as surely as dress codes had been abandoned in an earlier day.

By the end of the decade, the pendulum had swung back, propelled more by the students than by changes in institutional philosophy. The vocational programs were being reserved for the favored few, while the transfer curricula were entered by those unqualified for the technologies or uncertain of their direction. This use of the collegiate courses by the less able, those waiting for billets in the more desirable programs to open, and those trying to make up deficiencies in prior preparation may have contributed to high dropout rates. Subtly but decisively, the collegiate programs were being transformed into catchalls for unable and uncommitted students.

During the 1980s, the community colleges groped for a middle ground between linear, forced-choice, sequential curricula and the lateral, laissez-faire approach of letting students drop in and take any course they wanted. Recognizing that neither of the extremes was tolerable and that neither best served the clients, the staff in most institutions attempted to maintain some semblance of counseling, orientation, and testing to determine why students had appeared and how they could best be helped. But students were using the college for purposes other than those anticipated by program planners. Except for those enrolled in the selective-admissions, high-technology, and allied health fields, few students attended courses in the sequence envisaged by program planners.

Moves toward encouraging students to matriculate in and to complete programs gained momentum during the 1980s. One of the first requirements was to test the students at entry, place them in programs commensurate with their aspirations and abilities, and demand that they make steady progress toward completing the program. For example, Miami-Dade Community College established a policy of assessing students, mandating certain courses, and placing on probation or suspending students who were not making satisfactory progress toward completing a program—in short, reinstating the policies under which most institutions had operated fifteen years earlier (Middleton, 1981). During the first two years that the policy was in effect, several thousand students were dropped from the rolls, but enrollments eventually stabilized and student attendance patterns increasingly reflected the changed policy.

The practice of requiring testing and program placement spread, often prodded by legislators who were appalled at the dropout rates. Florida, Georgia, New Jersey, Tennessee, and Texas mandated that all entering students or students seeking degrees or transfer take tests in the basic skills. And numerous community colleges in states where testing had not been mandated were beginning to require testing on their own. The Southern Regional Education Board (Abraham, 1987) found that twice as many two-year colleges as four-year colleges in its region had policies governing testing and placement. A national survey found that although the majority of the two-year colleges accepted all persons over age eighteen who had earned a high school diploma, almost 90 percent of them used tests to place first-time students (Woods, 1985).

The move was not without its detractors. Some felt that state-mandated testing would lead to a reduction in institutional ability to serve various types of clients. In 1988, a group of Latino rights organizations sued a California college on the grounds of discrimination in access. This led to a state mandate that entrance tests be validated in relation to student achievement. (See Chapter Nine on developmental education.) Others deplored the tests' effects on curriculum; students take the courses that teach them to pass the tests, and mandated exit tests invariably are built on generalized content.

Still, any institution needs to demonstrate its usefulness to society if it is to continue to be supported. When a school that people are not obligated to attend continues to enroll greater segments of the population, its administrators can argue that it must be offering something of value to those who are investing their own time and money. They can also argue that enrolling ever greater percentages of the population is a social good because the more people who are exposed to schooling, the more likely it is that intellectual leaders will emerge from among them. If intellectual ability in the population is distributed on a probability basis, intelligent people will come forth if more are given access to schooling. By that line of reasoning, any restricted educational system runs counter to social policy, whether the restriction is by wealth, sex, race, or scholastic test.

Questions of program completion pale in that light. The better question to ask is, "Of what value is the community college even to those people who do not graduate or transfer to a baccalaureate-degree-granting institution?" By their nature, by deliberate intent, the community colleges sought to become open-access institutions. They vigorously recruited part-timers, commuting students, and students who were working off campus. To attract these students, they abandoned most of the punitive grading, academic probation, class attendance requirements, and other policies designed for the more traditional students. Who can estimate the extent of the social need they were fulfilling?

In summation, if the purpose of the collegiate enterprise is to pass most students through to the baccalaureate degree, then the community college is a failure by design. Its place in the total scheme of higher education ensures that a small percentage of its matriculants will transfer to universities and obtain the baccalaureate. It accepts poorly prepared students and encourages part-time and commuter status. Its students perceive the institution as being readily accessible for dropping in and out without penalty. They know they need not complete a program soon after leaving secondary school; the institution will be there to accept them later.

Issues

Institutional planners will continue to face questions about the numbers and types of students properly enrolled in community colleges. For example, which groups have first claim on the institution? If enrollment limitations mean that some students must be turned away, who shall they be? Those of lesser ability? Those with indistinct goals? Those who already have baccalaureate degrees? Lists placing the categories of potential students in order from highest to lowest priority may have to be developed.

Classifying students is due for an update. Historically, age, gender, ethnicity, and some measure of competence such as high school standing or test scores have been dominant. But socioeconomic status could well be brought forward. The definition of an *adult student* could be modified to include anyone who is at least eighteen years old and working at least twenty-five hours per week, raising a child or children while enrolled, or both (Schuetz, 1999). Thus, the students' life conditions become more important than chronological age.

Up to a point, colleges can influence the types of students they attract by expanding or contracting off-campus classes and enforcing student probation and suspension procedures more or less stringently, to name but two obvious means. Who should decide on the policies and hence the student types, the colleges or the state?

Historically, the community college student has been defined as one who is enrolled in a course. But it may be time to modify the definition of *student* to include only those who are enrolled past the first census week. Counting everyone who registers, even those who take no classes or who drop out after the first couple of sessions, distorts the data on student success.

How will the recent moves toward assessing students at entry and demanding that they make continual progress toward completing a program affect enrollments of various groups? How will they affect retention and program completion?

And the broadest questions of all: Which people benefit most from, and which are harmed by, an institution that allows all to attend at their pleasure? For which students should society pay full fare? The personal and social implications of these questions give way rapidly to the political and fiscal as soon as they are put to the test.

3

Faculty

Building a Professional Identity

As arbiters of the curriculum, the faculty transmit concepts and ideas, decide on course content and level, select textbooks, prepare and evaluate examinations, and generally structure learning conditions for the students. In common with nearly all other teachers, they are not independent practitioners. They work in institutions and are subject to the rules thereof; the workplace shapes their behavior. At the same time, they communicate with their colleagues and take on the mores of the profession.

This chapter views many aspects of the faculty: their demography, preparation, and salary; their working conditions, including tenure, workload, and evaluation; and the less tangible concerns of faculty satisfaction, desires, and professionalism. Unless otherwise noted, data regarding the contemporary faculty are drawn from three sources: "A Profile of the Community College Professoriate, 1975–2000" (Outcalt, 2002), *National Study of Postsecondary Faculty* (Cataldi, Bradburn, and Fahimi, 2005), and the NCES *Digest of Education Statistics* (2005).

The Workplace

Community college instructors rarely write for publication; when they do and when they speak at conferences or respond to surveys, they often reveal persistent concerns about their workplace. One concern is the low academic achievement of sizable numbers of their students. The faculty whose first job after graduate school is in a community college suddenly are in a milieu where high achievement, dedication to study, and academic goal directedness are not the norm. They may feel they have little control over the criteria for determining who enters their classes and deplore the institutional policies that attempt to retain on the rolls students who fail to keep up with their course work. Those committed to the traditional academic disciplines are often likely to feel out of place because of their institutions' commitment to students and to curricula with which they have little affinity. Eventually, most of them find the community college a personally satisfying environment, welcoming their role and becoming highly involved with their teaching, but the early years can be difficult.

People willingly endure incredible levels of discomfort when they believe that they are striving for a higher cause. The history of saints and soldiers, monks and missionaries reveals that when superordinate goals are dominant, participants relinquish the tangible rewards that they might otherwise think are their due. But when faith or patriotism wanes, demands for more immediate benefits increase, and the group must provide extrinsic incentives to sustain its members' allegiance. Eventually, a formal organization evolves, with ever stricter rules of conduct guiding the lives of its people, who themselves have since been transformed from participants into workers.

Many two-year colleges began as small adjuncts to public secondary schools, and their organizational forms resembled the lower schools more than they did the universities. Their work rules and curricula stemmed from state education codes. Mandated on-campus hours for faculty members, assigned teaching schedules, textbooks selected by committees, and obligatory attendance at college events were common. Institutional size fostered close contact among instructors and administrators. The administrators held the power, but at least they were accessible, and face-to-face bargains could be struck regarding teaching and committee assignments. And as long as the institution enrolled students fresh from high school, the faculty could maintain consistent expectations.

The major transformation in the community college as a workplace came when it increased in size and scope. Size led to distance between staff members; rules begat rules; layers of bureaucracy insulated people between levels. Decision making shifted from the person to the collectivity, decisions made by committees diffusing responsibility for the results. The staff became isolates— faculty members in their academic freedom–protected classrooms, administrators behind their rulebook-adorned desks.

As the colleges broadened their scope, the transformation continued: first vocational education, then developmental programs, and—unkindest of all from the faculty viewpoint—the drive to recruit and retain apathetic students. Numerous instructors—who may have regarded themselves as members of a noble calling, contributing to society by assisting the development of its young— reacted first with dismay, then with withdrawal or antagonism, to the new missions articulated by the college spokespersons. Feeling betrayed by an organization that had shifted its priorities, they shrank from participation, choosing instead to form collectivities that would protect their right to maintain their own goals. The *Gemeinschaft* had become a *Gesellschaft*.

Whether collective bargaining in community colleges resulted from this transformation, it did contribute to faculty well-being, although not nearly as much as its proponents had hoped nor as much as its detractors had feared. The working conditions most obviously affected were class size, the number of hours instructors must spend on campus, the out-of-class responsibilities that may be assigned to them, the number of students they must teach each week, and the funds available for professional development opportunities. Because all of these elements were associated with contractual requirements, informal agreements between instructors and administrators about switching classes, trading certain tasks for others, and released time in one term in return for an additional class in another were rendered more difficult to effect. Work rules often specified the time that could be spent on committee service, media development, and preparing new courses. In brief, the contracts solidified the activities associated with teaching, binding them by rules that had to be consulted each time a staff member considered any change; hence, they impinged on the instructors as though they had been mandated by an autocratic administration.

Levin, Kater, and Wagoner trace several broader assaults on the workplace: extramurally mandated formulas for accountability; institutional entrepreneurialism, especially contract training for industry; and "the ideology of neo-liberalism and the process of economic globalization" (2006, p. 2). These have led to a focus on "economic matters as opposed to more social or cultural endeavors" (p. 3) and by converting the college to bureaucratic businesses have changed faculty roles to those of participants in a "labor force that is shaped by both a managerial class and corporate elites" (p. 15).

The People

Although it is possible to generalize in only the grossest way when one is describing 300,000 people, demographically the community college faculty differ from instructors in other types of schools. The proportion of men is lower than in universities and higher than in secondary schools. Most of the faculty members hold a master's degree or have equivalent experience in the occupations they teach; they are less likely to hold advanced graduate degrees than university professors. Their primary responsibility is to teach; they rarely conduct research or scholarly inquiry. They are more concerned with subject matter than are their counterparts in the secondary schools, less so than university professors. On a full-time basis, they conduct four or five classes each term. Well over half are part-time employees at their colleges, teaching only one or two classes. Many, both full- and part-timers, sustain other jobs in addition to their teaching.

There have been recent increases in minorities and women. In 1987, 9 percent of the full-time faculty in two-year public colleges were classified as Native Americans, Asians, African Americans, or Hispanics; a proportion that rose to 15 percent during the 1990s, and nearly 20 percent by 2003. The ratio of women climbed from 38 to 48 percent during the same period. The faculty overall have been aging: between 1975 and 2003, the median age increased from just over forty to just under fifty years; the modal age went from thirty-three to fifty-five.

Preparation

When the size and number of community colleges were increasing rapidly, the question of proper training and experience for instructors was frequently debated. Should instructors have prior experience in the lower schools? Should they hold the doctorate? What qualities are needed? The answers varied, but the flow of instructors into the community colleges can be readily traced.

Beginning with the earliest two-year colleges and continuing well into the 1960s, instructors tended to have prior teaching experience in the secondary schools. Eells (1931) reported a study done in the 1920s showing that 80 percent of junior college instructors had previous high school experience. In the 1950s, Medsker (1960) found 64 percent with previous secondary or elementary school experience. Around 44 percent of new teachers of academic subjects entering two-year colleges in California in 1963 moved in directly from secondary schools, and others had had prior experience with them (California State Department of Education, 1963). In 1973, Bushnell reported that 70 percent of the two-year college faculty nationally had previously taught in public high schools. However, as the number of newly employed instructors declined in the 1970s, the proportion of instructors with prior secondary school experience declined with it. More were coming from graduate programs, the trades, and other community colleges.

Preservice Training

The master's degree obtained in a traditional academic department has been the typical preparation. The doctorate has never been considered the most desirable degree; arguments against it may be found from Eells in 1931 to Cohen and Brawer in 1977. The major objections are that most doctorate holders have been prepared as researchers, not teachers, and that they expect fewer teaching hours and higher salaries. During the 1920s, fewer than 4 percent of the instructors at two-year colleges held the doctorate. By the 1950s, the proportion had climbed to between 6 and 10 percent, and there it remained for two decades; Blocker (1965–1966) reported 7 percent, Bayer (1973) 6.5 percent, and Medsker and Tillery (1971) 9 percent. By the mid-1970s, it had reached 14 percent, as fewer new instructors without the degree were being employed. In the early 1980s, the proportion exceeded 20 percent, largely because of the relatively stable employment scene, coupled with the tendency for instructors already in the colleges to obtain doctoral degrees and concomitant salary increases.

Table 3.1 shows the proportions of instructors holding bachelor's, master's, and doctorate degrees from 1930 through 2003. Graduate degrees were rarely found among teachers in career programs, where experience in the occupations along with some pedagogical training was considered the best preparation; but among the liberal arts instructors in many colleges, the proportion with the doctorate surpassed 25 percent and were considerably less likely to be concurrently employed outside higher education (Palmer, 2002).

Table 3.1. Highest Degree Held by Instructors at Two-Year Colleges

Year and Source	Less Than Bachelor's	Bachelor's	Master's	Doctorate
1930 (Wahlquist, cited in Eells)	7	29	59	5
1941 (Koos, cited in Monroe)	3	27	64	6
1957 (Medsker, cited in Monroe; includes administrators)	7	17	65	10
1969 (National Center for Education Statistics)	17 (includes both)		75	7
1972 (National Center for Education Statistics)	3	13	74	10
1979 (Brawer and Friedlander)	3	8	74	15
1984 (Carnegie Faculty Study, cited in Ottinger)	5	10	63	22
1989 (Astin, Korn, and Dey)	11	10	61	18
1998 (National Center for Education Statistics)	26 (includes both)		60	14
2000 (Outcalt)	6	15	63	16
2003 (Cataldi, Bradburn, Fahimi)	18 (includes both)		63	19

Sources: Eells, 1941a; Monroe, 1972; NCES, 1970, 1980; Brawer and Friedlander, 1979; Ottinger, 1987; Astin, Korn, and Dey, 1991; Zimbler, 2001; Outcalt, 2002; Cataldi, Bradburn, and Fahimi, 2005.

Regardless of the degree titles and types of programs, an emphasis on breadth of preparation and sensitivity to the goals of the community colleges and the concerns of their students has been a standard recommendation. Calls for these types of people have been made not only by community college administrators but also by major professional associations. But few community college instructors were prepared in programs especially designed for that level of teaching. Few had even taken a single course describing the institution before they assumed responsibilities in it. And although Eells (1931) had recommended that people entering two-year college instruction after having secondary school experience take intervening work at the university, not many followed that route.

Several well-integrated graduate school–based programs for preparing community college instructors have been established, and specially tailored degrees have been introduced on numerous occasions. The master of arts in teaching received some support during the late 1960s when colleges were expanding rapidly and seeking well-qualified staff, and the doctor of arts was promoted by the Council of Graduate Schools and the Carnegie Commission on Higher Education. These programs usually include a base of subject matter preparation in an academic department, some pedagogical preparation, and a period of practice teaching or internship. They are offered in a limited number of subject fields at only a few universities. None, including the specially sponsored programs for instructors in areas of short supply, has ever developed as a major source of community college instructors.

The drive to attract minority-group instructors has led to various special efforts. Some colleges recruit minority students enrolled in neighboring university graduate programs, offering part-time teaching or internship opportunities with the expectation that students in these programs will be employed as full-time instructors when they graduate. Many have developed pre-education courses for students during their associate degree experience, guiding them toward academic discipline–centered teacher preparation programs at baccalaureate-granting institutions, with the hope that at least some of them will become community college instructors. An internship program sponsored by two community college districts near San Diego selects thirty to forty interns annually from among 150 applicants, mostly Hispanic. Around 60 percent of them obtain full- or part-time positions after completing the program (Piland, McFarlin, and Murillo, 1999).

In-Service Training

Calls for expanding formal in-service training, a feature of the community colleges throughout their history, reached a peak as institutional expansion subsided and relatively few new staff members were employed. Who would teach the new students and handle the different technologies? Faculty members already there had their own priorities, based on their expectations when they entered the college and their subsequent experience within it. Administrators had found it much easier to employ new instructors to perform different functions than to retrain old instructors, a procedure that worked well as long as expansion was rapid. But when the rate of change exceeded the rate of expansion, when new priorities were enunciated more quickly than new funds could be found, the residue of out-of-phase staff members became greater and calls for staff development increased. Added to the perennial challenges of working with underprepared students were the new demands for reliable coordinated assessment of student learning.

Several types of in-service preparation programs have been established. The most popular have been discipline-based institutes, release time, and tuition reimbursements for instructors to spend time in a university-based program, as well as short courses or workshops on pedagogy sponsored by single institutions or institutional consortia. Although sabbatical leave options are in effect in around half the colleges, they have never become as widespread as those available to faculty in universities. And according to Wallin (2003), hardly any college presidents consider them important. Instructors have sought courses and programs in their teaching field, offered by universities close at hand, so that they could gain further knowledge in their sphere of interest, degrees and credits that would enable them to rise on the salary schedule, and time off from their teaching responsibilities.

Many colleges have developed elaborate, continuing professional development activities and nearly all have some sort of new faculty orientation program. At St. Louis Community College, new faculty development starts with awarding "a one credit-hour payment to each faculty member who participates in the weeklong program in August" (Welch, 2002, p. 13) and continues with three credit hours of release time during the fall term. The college also pays for program costs. Newly employed part-time faculty members are brought into a faculty development program at Johnson County Community College (Kansas) where they are assigned to facilitators and reviewed throughout the year (Burnstad, 2002). The institution attempts to bring them into the staff culture by involving them on committees and providing continuing orientation throughout the year. The College of DuPage (Illinois) also provides institutionwide incentives integrated with its staff and faculty development programs (Troller, 2002). The Community College of Baltimore County (Maryland) developed an extended orientation program based on the principles of learning communities (Ebersole, 2003). Nearly all the presidents in a survey conducted by Wallin (2003) saw new faculty orientation as a high priority.

Organizing continuing faculty developments has become more formalized. Eddy (2007) reported that urban colleges were more likely to have dedicated resources and centralized structures, whereas rural institutions had administrator-led committees to plan the activities. Some states—for example, Florida in the 1970s and California in the 1980s—appropriated sizable funds to be used for staff development at the college's discretion. However, the form of in-service preparation most preferred by the faculty has been that which they themselves initiate. Consistently over the years, between 15 and 20 percent of instructors have been enrolled in graduate programs in universities. Miami Dade College and Florida International University are among several institutional pairings that give tuition discounts to staff enrolled in doctoral programs (Lukenbill, 2004).

Workload, Salary, and Tenure

Faculty workload. The term usually connotes the hours spent in the classroom each week times the number of students enrolled, occasionally with a nod to committee service. No one speaks of the community college professor's research load, scholarship load, or consulting load. Teaching is the ponderous portion of the profession, the burden to be carried.

Prior to the 1970s, the community colleges operated under work rules much like those in the secondary schools. The principal, president, or governing board set the hours and the working conditions and hired and fired the staff. When rules authorizing public employee bargaining units were passed, collective bargaining spread until it formed the basis of contractual negotiations for around 60 percent of the community college instructors. Even so, although faculty workload varies among teaching fields and types of courses, over time, it has been remarkably consistent. Koos (1924) reported 13.5 hours taught weekly by full-time faculty in the public colleges of the 1920s. Numerous studies since have found 13 to 15 classroom hours per week to be the norm.

Class size is also quite variable. Many negotiated contracts specify the maximum number of students that can be assigned to a class, but student dropout invariably reduces class size before the end of the term. Instructors of physical education, studio courses in music and the arts, and courses in laboratory sections usually have the highest number of teaching hours but the smallest class sizes. Smaller classes are also seen in upper-tier or advanced courses. In introductory classes, the norm is from the low twenties in English and foreign languages to the high twenties in history and the social sciences (Brawer, 1999).

There is little difference in faculty workload in states where a majority of the faculty are covered under collective bargaining agreements (California, Illinois, Michigan, New York) and those where the faculty are not so covered (Texas, Arizona, Utah). Salaries are about 10 percent higher in colleges with collective bargaining, but this is more related to the median income level in those states than to the presence or absence of bargaining agreements, as evidenced by the comparable salaries in colleges in the same state regardless of union representation. Also, salaries differ by institutional locale, averaging $59,960 in suburban colleges and $46,534 in rural colleges (Roessler, 2006). The major contrast is in administrative involvement in setting the working conditions for the faculty. The negotiations yield contracts that move nearly all decisions to the level of the negotiators, that is, the board and the faculty unit representatives. Attorneys for both groups are involved in interpreting the contracts and arbitrating the disputes. The choice for the administrators is not whether they approve of such contracts but of how they learn to live with them. Many of the administrators in states where bargaining began were slow to realize that. It is difficult for people who grew up with a perception of their professional role as one of closely managing staff behavior to realize that the rules have shifted: the contract negotiated with the staff has become the dominant force. Years after the faculty won the right to bargain collectively, this perception seems quaint, but as the unions were growing, it was high on the list of administrators' concerns.

The relationships between administrators and instructors head the list of changes occasioned by collective bargaining.

The contracts spell out the details of class size, hours that the instructors are to spend on campus, conditions of sabbatical leaves, and numerous other aspects of faculty life. But the number of teaching hours and the size of the classes have not changed much in decades. Nor have faculty concerns about workload and committee service changed. Instructors may fight continually for reduced hours in the classroom, but they are reluctant to give up the chance to teach additional hours for extra pay. In California, 36 percent of the full-time instructors teach at least one additional class per year (California Community Colleges, 1999).

Instructors who are active in their disciplinary associations often call for reduced teaching loads. The pages of the journal *Teaching English in the Two-Year College* and various disciplinary association newsletters carry articles commenting on how community college instructors teach liberal arts classes to freshmen and sophomores just as the university professors do. And they say that community college instructors have a more difficult job because their students are less well prepared. Why, the argument goes, should they teach twice as many hours? Still, few sustained practices are being introduced that would have students taught by paraprofessional aides or through reproducible media that would reduce live-contact hours.

Except for the part-timers paid at an hourly rate, salary ranges for community college instructors have tended to be higher than in secondary schools and lower than in universities. Eells (1931) reported that the median salary of the best-paid instructors in the 1920s was about the same as that of starting professors in the universities. But most community college instructors were able to reach the top of the salary scale in twelve or fifteen years whereas in the universities, although a higher ceiling was available, more steps intervened. The ratio shifted somewhat when collective bargaining made deep inroads and the tops of the salary schedules were lifted, but the university ranges remained greater. The difference between community college and university base pay rates widened from less than 7 percent at the beginning of the 1980s to nearly 10 percent in 1985–86, 15 percent in 1992–93, and 29 percent in 2006–07. Nationwide, overload teaching adds around 10 percent to community college faculty salaries.

Tenure patterns in community colleges more closely resemble those in the lower schools than they do the procedures in universities. Tenure is awarded after a single year or, in many cases, after a probation of two to three years; the practice rarely approximates the seven-year standard common in universities. Although tenure rules vary from state to state, in some states tenure is awarded simultaneously with a full-time teaching contract. That is, after a one-year contract has been tendered and the instructors have fulfilled their responsibilities, contracts for the succeeding year can be demanded unless the institution can show cause that the instructors are not deserving of them. Often, unless it is included in the state laws governing community colleges, tenure becomes a negotiable item in contract bargaining.

Part-Time Faculty

More so than in the universities, less so than in the for-profit sector, community colleges depend on a part-time workforce. The reasons part-timers continue to be employed in sizable numbers are that they cost less; they may have special capabilities not available among the full-time instructors; and they can be employed, dismissed, and reemployed as needed.

The ratio of part-time to full-time instructors has changed during various stages of community college development. In the early years, sizable percentages of the instructors were part-timers, often from local high schools. As the colleges matured, they were more able to support a corps of full-time instructors; in the late 1960s, almost two-thirds were so employed. Then the ratio of part-timers increased, and by 2003, 63 percent of the faculty were part-timers. (Note how the figures on part-time faculty detailed in

Table 3.2.   Numbers of Full-Time and Part-Time Instructors in Public Two-Year Colleges, 1953–2003

Year	Total Instructors	Full-Time Instructors		Part-Time Instructors	
		Number	Percentage	Number	Percentage
1953	23,762	12,473	52	11,289	48
1958	33,396	20,003	60	13,394	40
1963	44,405	25,438	57	18,967	43
1968	97,443	63,864	66	33,579	34
1973	151,947	89,958	59	61,989	41
1978	213,712	95,461	45	118,251	55
1983	251,606	109,436	43	142,170	57
1988	254,449	106,868	42	147,580	58
1993	276,661	110,111	41	166,550	60
1998	301,000	113,176	38	187,824	62
2003	378,700	138,300	37	240,400	63

Sources: American Association of Community and Junior Colleges, 1955–1988; NCES, 1994e; NCES *Digest*, 2001–2006.

Table 3.2 track those of part-time students as shown in Table 2.2.) These ratios depend on growth and decline in various areas of the curriculum, state and accrediting association guidelines, workforce availability, and numerous other factors. Overall, though, the colleges have come to depend on low-cost labor to balance the budget. As long as the law or collective bargaining agreements do not stop them, administrators will continue to employ lower-paid part-time instructors. Part-time instructors are to the community colleges what migrant workers are to the farms.

Pay rates are the key to employment of part-timers. On a strictly per class basis, they cost considerably less. In California in 2006, their hourly pay averaged $62.86, or around $3,000 for a sixteen-week, three-unit course. The full-timers were earning $78,498 plus fringe benefits for teaching ten classes per year, that is, $9,000 per course, or three times as much (California

Community Colleges, 2006). Other states showed similar patterns. The nine-month salary for full-time faculty in Illinois in 2005 was $58,300 plus $16,900 in retirement compensation and other benefits, roughly $7,200 per course, while the part-timers were being paid $2,900 per course (Illinois Community College Board, 2005). The sizable gains in compensation made by community college instructors during the 1980s were granted to the full-timers, whose average basic nine-month salary nationally in 2007 was more than $50,000 (American Association of University Professors, 2007).

The sources of part-timers have shifted. The early junior colleges sought secondary school instructors because they were qualified teachers, and they sought university professors because they lent an aura of prestige. By the mid-1970s, those two sources had diminished, and most of the part-timers were referred to as "volunteers" (retired teachers, business or professional people, or other citizens) or "captives" (graduate students or teachers with no other source of income, most of whom aspired to full-time employment). Community colleges in rural locations face greater staffing challenges than those in urban areas because of a limited pool of applicants.

Are the part-time instructors qualified? Do they teach as well as full-timers? Numerous studies have found that students learn as much in their classes, but one recent study reported that institutions with higher percentages of full-time faculty have higher overall completion rates (Jaschik, Oct. 16, 2006). The part-timers are less likely to be professionally involved, but they are generally satisfied with most aspects of their jobs (see Table 3.3). They certainly seem to present few problems; their student ratings and the grades they award are comparable to those displayed by the full-time instructors. Still, they occupy a different status. They are chosen less carefully, the rationale being that because the institution is making no long-term commitment to them, there is no need to spend a great deal of time and money in selection.

Table 3.3. Significant Differences Between Full-Time and
Part-Time Faculty, 2000

	Full Time (n = 1064)	Part Time (n = 467)
Instructional activities		
Revised syllabus in past three years	95%	86%
Taught jointly with colleagues outside own department	24	15
Received award for teaching	39	23
Taught honors course	10	5
Organized extracurricular activities for students	72	59
Professional involvement overall	23	19
Traveled off campus to conference	87	65
Belonged to education associations		
Any type	74	48
General educational association	45	28
Community college association	29	11
Disciplinary association	52	33
Sources of teaching advice		
Department chairs useful	74	82
Colleagues useful	94	86
Education journals read regularly		
General education	48	40
Community college specific	28	18
Disciplinary	<2	<2
Satisfaction overall	32	31
Current position seen as attractive in five years	79	77
Good or excellent relations with colleagues	92	88
Desire more interactions with colleagues	38	42
University position seen as attractive	30	47
Experience considerable stress in job	53	27

Source: Outcalt, 2002.

The most positive aspects of the part-timers are seen where they are business or professional people conversant with the latest developments in their field by virtue of their concurrent involvement with it—for example, when the local minister teaches a course in religious studies or a realtor teaches courses in real estate. They may be more directly connected to the practical aspects of their work, and they may have a greater fund of knowledge than most full-time instructors. They also enable small colleges to offer courses for which a full-time load could not be mounted: an esoteric foreign language or religious studies course, for example. And they allow the colleges to meet last-minute demands for an extra section of a popular course. The worst features of their use are when the college brings in two or more part-timers to teach similar courses as a way of avoiding employing a full-timer, or when they are overrepresented in classes that the full-timers prefer not to teach, such as developmental or those offered at night or on weekends. But the noncampus colleges thrive on them; Rio Salado College (Arizona), with 46,506 (FTE: 13,332) students and only thirty-one full time instructors, is a notable example.

A broader issue is related to the part-timers' effect on community college teaching as a profession. Clark deplores the widespread use of part-timers, saying, "Nothing deprofessionalizes an occupation faster and more thoroughly than the transformation of full-time posts into part-time labor" (1988, p. 9). Nonetheless, the colleges' reliance on part-timers has been consonant with developments in most other areas of the American workforce, where the tendency has been to convert as many jobs as possible to positions for which the employer has minimal responsibility for staff continuity or fringe benefits. Periodically, the part-timers have petitioned for pay-per-course and health and retirement benefits equal to those earned by the full-time faculty, but these efforts have borne scant fruit. As more part-timers gain bargaining rights (see Chapter Four), the likelihood of pro-rata pay and benefits increases.

The issue of pay and benefits for part-time faculty is often reviewed at the state level, but the cost of providing pro-rata pay is so great that little change is made. As an example, the California Bureau of State Audits released a report showing that between 1995 and 2000, "the percentage of credit teaching conducted by part-time faculty has grown from 40 percent to 47 percent" and that if that group were to teach a full course load, they would receive 31 percent less in annual wages than full-timers receive (California State Auditor, 2000, p. 1). The report acknowledged that the condition exists because of the large number of people "willing to work for less pay." However, if the legislature were to eliminate the pay difference, it would cost the state "about $144 million annually." The report concluded, "The unequal compensation of part-time faculty either creates problems that should be addressed or *reflects an appropriate balance of market conditions at the local level that should not be tampered with*" (emphasis added, p. 2).

Evaluation

The how and why of faculty evaluation have been considered since the community colleges began. Because of the colleges' roots in the lower schools, early evaluations were often conducted by administrators who visited classrooms and recorded their perceptions of instructors' mannerisms, appearance, attitude, and performance. As the colleges broke away from the lower schools and faculty gained more power, evaluation plans became more complex. Peers and students were brought into the process, and guidelines were established for every step. These procedures often gained labyrinthine complexity; rules specified how often evaluations would be made, how much time they would take, who was to be involved, at what point the instructors would be notified of the results, which people or committees would notify them, how long an instructor's file would be maintained, who would have access to the file, and what steps would be involved in the appeal process.

Superficially, the procedures gave the appearance of attempting to improve instruction. Practically, they had little effect. If an instructor were to be censured, dismissed, or rewarded for exceptional merit, the evaluation records provided essential documentation. But only a minuscule percentage of the staff was affected. Instructors who wanted to improve could act on the commentary of peers, administrators, and students. Those who chose instead to ignore the feedback could do so. Only instructors who were far distant from any semblance of good teaching—for example, those who failed to meet their classes regularly—could be called to task. In general, the most minimal evidence of classroom performance or student achievement satisfied evaluators.

Faculty associations' intrusion into the evaluation process proved a mixed blessing. Frequently, the contracts mandated that the whole faculty be involved in evaluation at every stage. This involvement would be a step toward professionalization because, by definition, a profession should police its own ranks, set standards of conduct, and exercise sanctions. However, faculty bargaining units leaned considerably more in the direction of protecting their members from judgments made by administrators than toward enhancing professional performance. The types of faculty evaluation in vogue at the time the contracts were negotiated tended to be written into the rules. The forms, checklists, and observations remained the same.

Still, faculty evaluation persists because it suggests that the institution and the profession are concerned with improvement. Nearly all institutions engage in it on some basis, from pro forma procedures to satisfy a set of rules to more genuine attempts to affect the person. Evaluations related to instructional practices can be useful in enhancing perceived effectiveness; however, evaluations conducted for the primary purpose of satisfying external agencies have little effect, and the staff tend to be dissatisfied with them. Attempts to link faculty evaluation with merit pay have been tried numerous times, with limited success. Seniority remains dominant as a determinant of salary level.

The best faculty evaluation plans are those built for the purpose of improving teaching rather than for determining who receives tenure or a salary increment. Although the two reasons are usually linked, a primary focus on instruction, staff integration, colleagueship, and instructors' goal attainment—in short, a formative development process—is considerably more likely to be welcomed by the faculty and lead to better instruction overall. Such programs often employ combinations of workshops, portfolio generation, mentoring, and similarly tested practices. They rely on perceptions of peers, students, and self (the person who is the subject of the effort). They are idiosyncratic, not normative or comparative, designed to assist, not to reward or punish.

Satisfaction

Faculty satisfaction and dissatisfaction have been traced for some time. For the first half-century of community college history, when most faculty members were recruited from the secondary schools, positive attitudes among the faculty were the norm. Moving from a secondary school to a college faculty position offered both higher status and a reduced teaching load. Consequently, most studies of faculty satisfaction found that it was related to the conditions under which the person entered the institution. Older faculty members—those who were appointed from secondary school positions, entered teaching after retiring from a different type of job, had made a midlife career change, or were teaching in career programs after being affiliated with an occupation—showed up as the more satisfied group. The younger instructors—who may not have thought of themselves as career teachers but found themselves performing the same tasks year after year with little opportunity for the revitalization that accompanies a new challenge—were the dissatisfied ones.

The term *burnout* was used often in the 1980s and 1990s to connote faculty members who felt so overwhelmed or depressed that they could no longer function effectively. Many articles about how to confront that problem pervaded the literature. However, Bok noted that professors who did not want to teach anymore "probably suffer from deeper problems of motivation beyond the reach of crude incentives such as money or loss of tenure" (1993, p. 172). In short, people who instruct try to do a reasonable job because it is satisfying for them. If they are so disaffected as to be characterized as burned out, nothing short of a major shift in responsibilities, a career change, or a modification in their personal life will help.

Many of the institutional changes that have occurred since most faculty members were employed might have been expected to lead to dissatisfaction. An increase in the number of ill-prepared students made it more difficult for instructors to find satisfaction in effecting student achievement. A reduction in the number of specialized courses made it less likely that an instructor would be able to teach in an area of special interest. More students tended to be part-timers, dropping in and out of school; as a result, faculty could not sustain relationships with these students beyond one term. The percentage of students completing courses fell sharply, so that instructor satisfaction in seeing individual students through even a single course was reduced. More formal requests for measures of productivity were installed, along with demands that instructors present evidence of student achievement. And the feasibility of moving from community college to university teaching, never great, has become even less likely.

Recent national faculty studies have traced characteristics of the people and the workplace that relate to satisfaction and dissatisfaction. Compared with university faculty, community college instructors are more satisfied with their salaries, the reputation of their departments and their institutions, the time they can spend with their family, and their social relations with other faculty. They are less satisfied with the quality of their students, teaching load, rigidity of their work schedule, and opportunities for scholarly pursuits and professional recognition. When asked about sources of stress, they are understandably less likely to indicate the institution's review or promotion process or its demands that they conduct research, and they are also more likely to feel that they are working in a collegial environment.

Institutionally supported practices have a significant effect on faculty satisfaction. Dee (2004) found a strong relationship between support for innovation and faculty intentions to remain at the college. Other studies have pointed up faculty affinity for developmental activities related to their disciplines and a decided dislike of generic "teaching tips" (Lail, 2005). Professional development opportunities, especially sabbaticals and funds for travel to conferences, always receive high marks on satisfaction indices (Cohen and Brawer, 1987; Mounfield, 2005).

Desires

Like members of any other professional group, most instructors would like to improve their working conditions. They want more professional development opportunities, sabbatical leaves, grants for summer study, provisions for released time, and allowances for travel. They would like better students too, more highly motivated and with stronger academic backgrounds. They would like better instructional materials. Many of them are not satisfied with the textbooks, laboratory materials, or collections of readings that they are using in their classes. Many want more and better laboratory facilities. Brawer and Friedlander (1979) reported similar findings, and Seidman (1985) and Outcalt (2002) corroborated them.

Thus, faculty desires seem to have stabilized. Despite the rhetoric surrounding collective bargaining and contract negotiations, instructors are generally satisfied. They want to better their working conditions, but they tend not to aspire to positions at other levels of schooling. Some of their desires are much like those articulated by employees in other enterprises: security and a living wage. Continuity of employment and periodic salary increases are the minimum. The faculty feel threatened when enrollment declines or declining budgets bode to strike at those essentials.

But beyond the basics, the instructors seem unrealistic. They want better working conditions, but that translates into shorter working hours, better-prepared students, and smaller classes. Desirable as these might be, they are difficult to obtain because they run counter to community college policies and budgetary realities. As long as colleges are reimbursed on the basis of the number of students attending, instructors will have a difficult time achieving more pay for fewer student contact hours. As long as colleges are pledged to maintain a door open to all regardless of prior academic achievement or innate ability, instructors will be unable to satisfy their desire for students who are better prepared.

Even when the desired changes in the workplace are more realistic, one goal is often in conflict with another. To illustrate, faculty members in general want more participation in institutional decision making, but they dislike administrative work. They do not aspire to be administrators; they may resent the time spent on committees; they see their classroom activities and their meeting with students outside class as the portion of their workday that brings the greatest satisfaction. But administrative decisions are made in the context of committees, memoranda, and persuasion—a context similar to a political arena. Instructors will not easily attain their goal of participation in decision making as long as they shun the mechanisms through which decisions are made.

The matter of support services offers a second illustration of conflict between instructors' desires. Relatively few instructors have paraprofessional aides or instructional assistants available to them, and few express a desire for more of these types of assistants.

The ideal of the instructor in proximity to the students remains a paramount virtue. Instructors seem unable to perceive themselves as professional practitioners functioning with a corps of aides. They want to do it all: interact with students, dispense information, stimulate, inspire, tutor—all the elements of teaching—through personal interaction. They do not realize the magnification of influence that they might obtain through relinquishing some portion of their work to paraprofessionals or assistants.

Through contracts or agreements otherwise negotiated, instructors have tried to mitigate the untoward conditions of the environment and attendant feelings of dissatisfaction. These agreements may make it possible for instructors to be relieved of routine responsibilities and to change their milieu. Provisions for released time to work on course revisions or other projects related to teaching are often established, and institutional support for innovation does seem to relate to faculty's intentions to stay on the job (Dee, 2004). Some contracts allow the faculty-student ratio to be spread across the academic department, making it possible to compensate for low enrollments in specialized courses with high enrollments in the department's introductory classes. Funds for travel and for sabbatical leave have also been negotiated.

The agreements, however, may not offer enough. No contract can substitute for the feelings of self-worth engendered by the knowledge that one can always escape the current workplace by moving to a different institution. Nor can they ameliorate the faculty's feeling that students are poorly prepared and that traditional programs, in which the instructors taught when they entered the institutions, are on the decline. The contracts' provisions for job protection through tenure and elaborate procedures for due process are of minimal value to people who find themselves forced to teach subjects not of their choosing. The attempts to recruit students to the institution ring like false coin on the ears of instructors, who suspect, with good reason, that these students will be even less interested in affairs of the mind than those with whom they are already confronted. Administrative pleas for retaining students are hardly welcomed by instructors who feel that students have a responsibility either to pursue the course work satisfactorily or leave.

Professionalism

To what degree are the faculty professionalized? Professionalization is multidimensional; it relates to public perception, training, work responsibilities, degree of organization, codes of ethics, and licensure. Progress on a continuum of professionalization has to be measured with a variety of benchmarks. Some data are available. On the dimension of teaching, the faculty's core responsibility, there seems little change. Teaching still is generally regarded as a solo performance; the door to the classroom is jealously guarded. Few instructors have access to aides; few seem to want them. They accept the idea of student evaluation of their instruction and are willing to listen to colleagues' comments. Everyone else—administrators, instructors from other sectors, the public— is ignored. Some other dimensions of professionalization have not changed either. The years of schooling experienced before entering the profession have been the same for at least twenty years, and licensure requirements are static.

Some dimensions suggest a retreat. Income levels have declined relative to other occupations with equivalent responsibilities, especially to university positions. Professional association membership is down, whether measured by disciplinary association, general faculty association, or community college–specific association. For most instructors, the longer they are at the college, the weaker their affiliation with an academic discipline becomes.

Some commentators have reasoned that the community college is best served by a group of instructors with minimal allegiance to a profession. They contend that professionalism invariably leads to a form of cosmopolitanism that ill suits a community-centered institution—that once faculty members find common cause with their counterparts in other institutions, they lose their loyalty to their own colleges. This argument stems from a view of professionalism among university faculties that has proved detrimental to teaching at the senior institutions: that is, as faculty allegiance turns more to research, scholarship, and academic disciplinary concerns, interest in teaching wanes.

That argument, however, suggests that a professionalized community college faculty would necessarily take a form similar to that taken by the university faculty. It need not. It more likely would develop in a different direction entirely, tending toward neither the esoterica of the disciplines nor research and scholarship on disciplinary concerns. The disciplinary affiliation among community college faculty is too weak, the institutions' demands for scholarship are practically nonexistent, and the teaching loads are too heavy for that form of professionalism to occur.

A professionalized community college faculty organized around the discipline of instruction might well suit the community college. The faculty are already engaged in course modification, the production of reproducible teaching media, and a variety of related activities centered on translating knowledge into more understandable forms. A profession that supports its members in these activities would be ideal. Teaching has always been the hallmark of the colleges; a corps of professionalized instructors could do nothing but enhance it. This form of professionalism might also be applied to curriculum construction. Whereas instructional concerns have been left to the faculty, the propagation of curriculum has been more an administrative charge. A professionalized faculty might well direct much of its attention to designing a curriculum to fit an institution that shifts priorities rapidly.

A professional faculty in charge of the essential conditions of its work could also reconceptualize the academic disciplines themselves to fit the realities of the community colleges. As an example, many of the traditional liberal arts courses are ill suited to students in the occupational and developmental programs that constitute much of the community college effort. More apposite instructional sequences could be designed for those students. Whether a professionalized community college faculty could succeed in the necessary curriculum reformation is not certain; it is certain that a disparate set of instructors cannot do so and that university professors or community college administrators will not lead in this essential reconstruction. Such disciplinary reconceptualization takes stimulation from peers, the contribution of individuals acting as proselytizers, and the application of thought about the core principles in each discipline as they pertain to the variant teaching roles that must be adopted for the different clients. These activities require a professionalized faculty.

A few indicators of professionalization have long been apparent. National journals directed toward two-year-college instructors in mathematics, journalism, and English were established many years ago along with several state-level journals in California, Florida, Michigan, Virginia, and elsewhere. Statewide academic senate groups have expressed interest and gained power in curricular affairs. Professional associations, such as the American Mathematical Association for Two-Year Colleges and the Community College Humanities Association, have been formed. Some institutions have fostered professionalism by supporting individual instructors through internal grants for course revision and media preparation. In colleges that employ instructional aides and paraprofessionals, the faculty play a managerial role. The number of foundation and federal grants available to community college instructors has increased, thus offering those faculty members with considerable professional commitment the opportunity to magnify their influence by managing curriculum development projects. In a few colleges, the faculty have developed their own projects to modify institutional practices in testing and placing new students.

Institutional-level activities can also keep the faculty engaged in fulfilling the responsibilities of teaching that reach beyond the classroom. For example, the colleges might provide funds and release time to those who would build better instructional materials or conduct research on their programs' effects such as the classroom assessment practices popularized by Angelo and Cross (1993), a technique already being employed in several colleges (Rouseff-Baker and Holm, 2004). Instructors may well expand their role beyond that of classroom teachers to become presenters of information through colloquia, seminars, lectures, recitals, and exhibitions offered for both students and the lay public. Most faculty members in the academic areas feel there are too few such presentations at their own colleges and want to devote more time to them. The more sophisticated contracts make provision for instructors to act in such capacities and also to manage learning laboratories, prepare reproducible media, or coordinate the work of the part-time faculty.

Some instructors understand the value of presenting information in large lecture sections. Departments that can generate sizable ratios of student contact hours have often taken advantage of large classes to support their more specialized courses. Similarly, to enhance flexibility in instruction, college administrators might consider paying instructors from one department to teach short portions of courses in another, or using community service funds to augment instructional budgets. These types of funding arrangements have proved difficult to effect, but formulas that pay colleges for total programmatic emphases might make them more feasible.

Although instructors at two-year colleges may be moving toward the development of a profession, its lines are as yet indistinct. The teaching loads take their toll, but as long as instructors insist on moonlighting and on having close personal contact with students in classes—the smaller, the better—the attendant high cost of instruction makes it difficult for colleges to fund the alternatives that could be pursued. The most positive note is that the community college has become a well-known, visible workplace, not only among its own staff but also among the legislators and agency officials who make decisions affecting its directions. And as a group, faculty members no longer look to the universities for their ideas on curriculum and instruction, nor do they see the community colleges only as stations on their way to university careers. In recent years, fewer have indicated they would find a university position attractive. Community college instruction has become a career in its own right.

Issues

Many of the key issues affecting faculty center on the continuing untoward separation of the occupational and the academic, the private world of instruction, the separation of the remedial instructors, and the uncomfortably slow development of a unique professional consciousness. Some of these issues can be feasibly managed; others will persevere because of the nature of the profession and the institution.

Will adversarial relations between the faculty and boards and administrators subside? Are they related primarily to contract negotiations or based in the essence of the institution?

Can teacher dissatisfaction be mitigated through deliberate modification of the working environment? Or are moonlighting and psychological early retirement to be permanent conditions?

Will faculties engage in the necessary reconceptualization of their academic disciplines to fit the realities of their colleges? Or will the collegiate programs survive primarily as intellectual colonies of the universities?

Will instructors realize that paraprofessional aides are important for their well-being over the long term?

Will administrators continue employing part-timers for the short-term salary savings that accrue? Or will they allow the faculty to build its profession and help it by minimizing the annual influx of teachers?

What do full-timers do for the college in addition to classroom teaching, and does that justify their higher pay?

All these questions relate to the history of the colleges, the funds available, and, above all, whether college leaders perceive their institutions as labile structures responding readily to the whims of all comers or as centers of teaching and learning with an ethos of their own.

4

Organization, Governance, and Administration

Managing the Contemporary College

The terms *governance and administration* or management are not discrete. They overlap and are often used interchangeably, not clearly depicting either institutional functions or precise activities. Peterson and Mets (1987) defined them as encompassing both structure and process: governance relates to decision making, management to executing the decisions. Corson defined governance as though the college itself were a government: "the process or art with which scholars, students, teachers, administrators, and trustees associated together in a college or university establish and carry out the rules and regulations that minimize conflict, facilitate their collaboration, and preserve essential individual freedom" (1960, pp. 12–13). However, he also noted the difficulty of separating the established policies from the practices maintained on their behalf; the act of administering a policy is as much a part of that policy as is the statement of rules or laws on which it is based.

This chapter traces some of the common forms of organization, governance, and administration, including types of governing units, state-level coordination, local governing boards, and models of district and college organization. It considers also accreditation, trustee functioning, administrative patterns, the effects of collective bargaining, and efforts at efficiency. These areas change continuously as new ideas for managing these institutions become popular. The one constant is that colleges are complex entities, and a description of one never quite fits the others.

Categorizing Governance

Numerous attempts to categorize governance and management have been made, most stemming from observations of university systems. Linear, adaptive, and interpretive systems constitute one set of categories. The linear are directly linked, the adaptive are responsive, and the interpretive are more culturally based (Chaffee, 1986). Other models of governance have attempted to separate the collegial from the political, viewing both as different ways of sharing authority. A management science approach views governance as rational, focused on decision making. A different model for college operations uses the term *organized anarchy* as a way of describing an environment in which no individual or group has much influence (Cohen and March, 1986). Weick (1976) popularized the term *loosely coupled systems* to describe colleges as groups of subunits that interact with one another in unpredictable ways.

In general, it seems that most of the excessively analytical models that purport to explain the workings of universities do not aptly cover the less complex community colleges. Richardson (1975) nevertheless suggested that models must be constructed if the colleges are to be understood. He therefore offered three major models to explain why colleges appear as they do. The *bureaucratic* model presents the college as a formal structure with defined patterns of activity that relate to the functions spelled out in law and policy decisions. The positions are arranged in the shape of a pyramid, and each series of positions has specified responsibilities, competencies, and privileges. This organization is held together by authority delegated from the top down, with persons at the top receiving greater benefits than those at the bottom; the lowest levels of the triangle are occupied by faculty and students. The *political* model postulates a state of conflict among contending forces—students, faculty, administrators, and trustees—each with different interests. In a quixotic plea for the colleges to become shared learning communities, he sketched a *collegial* model: "Instead of being at the bottom of a pyramid, faculty and students are part of a community of equal partners. Authority is not delegated downward as in the bureaucratic model; rather, trustees share their authority with students and faculty as well as with administrators. Students and faculty members communicate directly with the board rather than through the president" (p. ix). The model is based on group process, the concept of community, the sharing of authority, and the making of decisions within a framework of participation and consensus. (It should be characterized as the Snowball in Hell model.)

The bureaucratic and political models seem most applicable to community colleges. The institutions are organized hierarchically, and compromises among contending forces chart their directions. Colleges are social organizations with their own rules. Despite all the rhetoric about satisfying student and community needs, the procedures maintained in community colleges tend toward protecting the staff's rights, satisfaction, and welfare. The collegial or participatory model is a delusion; the notion that students have much voice in college administration has little basis in reality.

Not overly concerned with theoretical models, community college managers conduct their affairs typically embroiled in the complexities of the moment, perhaps hearkening to a golden era when rules were few and administration was simple. In its early years, when the junior college was often an adjunct of the local secondary school, the institution was usually administered by the high school principal or a designate responsible to the principal. The local school board took up junior college affairs as part of its regular responsibilities. As the colleges separated themselves from the local school districts, the newly established boards of trustees similarly concerned themselves with budgetary matters and the selection of presidents who would keep the staff content and the college running smoothly, or at least keep the problems from becoming apparent to the public. Yet as long ago as 1931, Eells noted in his book on the junior college that the areas of governance and administration were too varied and comprehensive to be treated completely. Although boards of trustees and administrators may have been able to govern without apparent conflict, issues of financing, staff morale, and conformity with state laws have always been present.

Governing Units

Different forms of college control have been popular at one time or another. In the past two decades, the independent, nonprofit junior colleges have declined, the proprietary for-profit organizations and multiunit college groupings have increased, and nearly all colleges affiliated with local public school districts have severed that connection. The public colleges are now arrayed in single independent districts; multiunit independent districts; state university systems and branch colleges; and state systems, some with innovative patterns, such as noncampus colleges. Individual comprehensive colleges may include specialized campuses or clusters organized around curricular themes.

Independent two-year colleges, a category that includes church-related institutions and private nonprofit colleges, have varying patterns of control. The ultimate control of church-related colleges is vested in the governing board of the church itself. Boards of control for other independents may be associated with the occupations emphasized, or they may be self-perpetuating bodies composed of concerned philanthropists. Directors of development, that is, the fundraisers, are usually prominent in the college's organizational chart. Because many private colleges still maintain residence halls, there may be a director in charge of campus life.

Proprietary schools are organized quite like the business corporations that they are, with sales and marketing as central features. In fact, some function as little more than the training and credentialing arm of companies that are involved in other enterprises. They differ from the nonprofit sector in several respects: few if any full-time faculty; no faculty participation in governance; rarely a distinctive campus; no lay governing board; instructional programs that can be started or ended without consulting any outside agency. Until recently few were accredited by the regional associations, but more have applied for such status in return for access to federal financial aid for their students.

Regardless of organizational form, size seems to be the most important variable. In study after study—whether the topic of concern is students, curriculum, library holdings, or unit costs— institutional size, more than any other characteristic, differentiates publicly supported institutions from one another. In addition, the significant differences between public institutions and private junior colleges (which are almost all quite small) appear to be related as much to size as to control.

The Local District

Most public colleges in the nation are organized within single districts. A board of trustees, either elected locally or appointed by a governmental agency, establishes policy for the institution and employs a chief executive officer. Vice presidents or deans manage business affairs, student personnel, academic instruction, and technical education. In most colleges, the department chairpersons report to the dean of instruction or vice president for instruction. In larger institutions, as shown in Figure 4.1, assistant superintendents and vice presidents may be added to manage detailed operations under each of the main functions. A college with over 20,000 students may have more than fifty administrators, including a president, vice presidents, deans and associate deans, directors, and project managers, plus over forty managers of

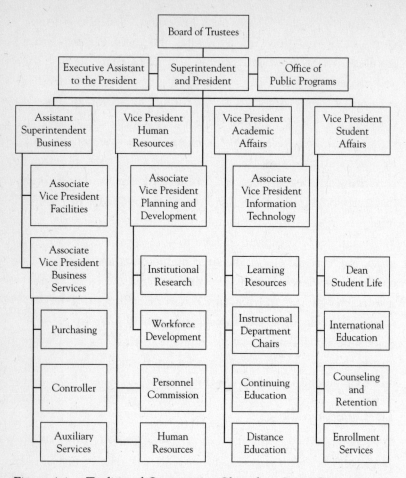

Figure 4.1.   Traditional Organization Chart for a Large Community College

campus police, facilities, custodial operations, auxiliary services, international studies, and so on. A college with fewer than 2,000 students may have considerably fewer administrators but still a president, a dean for administrative services, a dean for learning and student development, and one for community and professional education, plus over twenty managers for food services, media center, financial aid, continuing education, and so forth (Figure 4.2).

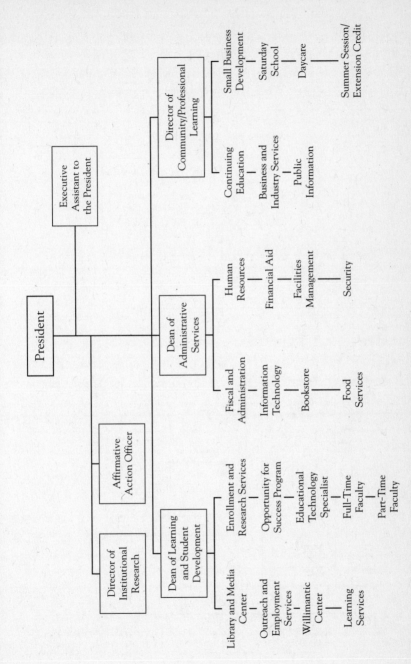

Figure 4.2. Organization Chart for a Small Community College

The multiunit independent district dates from the 1930s, with Chicago and Los Angeles as early examples. The multiunit districts usually arose when a college opened a branch campus that eventually grew to a size warranting an independent administration. As shown in Figure 4.3, these multicollege

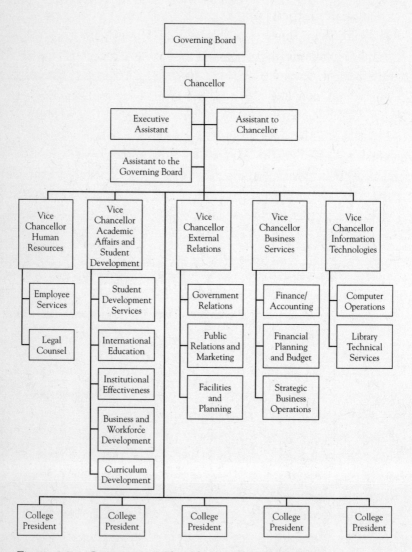

Figure 4.3.   Organization Chart for a Multicollege District

districts operate with a central district organization headed by a president or chancellor and staffed with research coordinators, personnel administrators, business managers, and numerous others responsible for overall academic, fiscal, and student services. Some multiunit districts, such as St. Louis, operate under a single-college, multicampus format.

Multiunit districts are far more complex, structured, and formalized than single-college districts. Those who advocate centralizing administration generally stress greater economy and uniformity of decisions. As long ago as 1969, Kintzer, Jensen, and Hansen concluded that although highly centralized colleges are characterized by maximum uniformity, impartiality, and efficiency, the risks are of depersonalization and low morale increased. Lander (1977) showed that when multiunit districts in Arizona were formed, another stratum of administrators was inserted between the first-line administrators at each college and the district's chief administrator. He concluded that increased size—the major factor contributing to structural differences—forced increases in complexity of function, formality in communication, delegation of responsibility, and centralization of ultimate authority.

Reducing duplication is the centralized structure's main benefit. It brings together purchasing, data processing, facilities planning, personnel research, finance, physical plant, and contracting; standardizes recruiting, fringe benefits, and payroll and affirmative action procedures; provides specialized personnel for collective bargaining purposes; fosters the equal treatment of support services, salaries, promotions, grievances, and resource allocation; minimizes rivalry and competition between campuses at the same time that it enhances recruitment campaigns, publicity, grantsmanship, community service, and coordination; facilitates educational program coordination and staff development; and permits the formation of vocational advisory committees for each vocational field rather than one area on separate campuses.

But balancing the district's needs to centralize functions with the campus staff members' desires for autonomy is a continuing challenge. Ideally, participation in decision making would be shared at all levels, from the central office to the various campus departments, but power tends to gravitate toward the central district administration. As an example, in nearly all multiunit districts, budget requests may be generated on each campus, but only within the guidelines and limitations set down by the central authority. The central district offices often also maintain separate legal-affairs offices to ensure that all decisions on personnel selection and assignments are made in accordance with the terms of the contracts and laws governing the institution.

The issue of participation is important in an era when empowerment and involvement of all campus constituents has become a guiding principle of administration. In California, shared governance was mandated in the late 1980s as a way of ensuring that the faculty and the rest of the staff could give input on all decisions. The result has been a flurry of documents that have attempted to sort out responsibilities among faculty associations, academic senates, classified staff organizations, local boards, local and district administrations, and the state board and chancellor's offices. Shared governance varies, depending on state laws and court decisions. In 2007, the faculty senate at Diablo Valley College (California) objected to an administrative decision to replace part-time faculty administrators with full-time professional deans, thus changing a forty-year tradition of academic administration. But a court of appeals moved that such reorganization is an administrative prerogative (Freedman and Freedman, 2007).

Investigating the extent to which shared governance changed administrative patterns and decision making in California's community colleges after the 1988 state mandate, Flanigan (1994) found that faculty involvement on committees had certainly increased, but that neither the quality of committee meetings and reports nor the level of trust between faculty and administration had changed. What had changed was that the decision-making process slowed because of the need to involve groups of administrators, faculty, and classified staff, each with its own special interests. Schuetz (1999) concluded that implementing shared governance may slow decision making and polarize rather than unite campus constituencies. On the other hand, shared governance may also help improve campus communication, increase the breadth of understanding related to issues, and promote buy-in to decisions by all parties. In addition, whereas other constituencies may feel able to represent their interests through alternate means, such as collective bargaining, students may feel that shared governance is a particularly valuable procedure—perhaps the only workable avenue for their input.

The State

Publicly supported colleges are under the control of a single authority in numerous states. In 1965, Blocker, Plummer, and Richardson identified twenty states where the community colleges were under the control of a board of education and six where the colleges reported to a state department or superintendent of education. Separate junior college boards or commissions existed in only six states; in thirteen others, the colleges were under a board of higher education or the board of a four-year state university. Kintzer (1980a) found fifteen states with boards responsible for community colleges only.

The state has since become even more prominent. Tollefson, Garrett, and Ingram (1999) found some form of state-level coordination in all fifty states and identified five primary models. A state board of education governed seven states' community college systems (for example, Idaho and Oregon); a state board or commission of higher education coordinated twelve (for example, New York and Texas); a statewide coordinating board ran twelve (for example, California and North Carolina); a state governing board controlled five (for example, Delaware and

Colorado [for state system colleges]); and a state board of regents coordinated ten states' community college systems (for example, Alaska and Hawaii). Some states were not typical of any of the five models or contained coordinating bodies with overlapping authority. Maine's community colleges were monitored by the Board of Trustees for Maine Vocational Technical Institute Schools; South Dakota's vocational schools were run by local school districts. Several states, including Louisiana, Wisconsin, South Carolina, and New Mexico, had dual systems of governance: vocational or community colleges, along with two-year branches of university systems that were governed by the university boards. Tollefson has concluded that with minor variations, the same five models are in place, but a few states have shifted from one category to another (e-mail communication, August 29, 2007).

In states where the public community colleges are under state board control, decisions of funding and operation have become maximally centralized. Connecticut and Delaware, for example, have what appears to be one community college with several branches, whose presidents report to the state chancellor. Statewide bargaining and budgeting are the norm, although some autonomy in curriculum planning has been reserved for the individual colleges. Figure 4.4 shows the organization pattern typical of such states. However, depending on the authority of the state board and its responsibilities, there is still much variation among the states. Hale (1994) displays the organization charts for the state offices managing community colleges in Washington, Oregon, and California. Among the differences, highly centralized Washington has an extensive planning and information services unit and numerous budget specialists, whereas the Oregon Board of Education's commissioner of community college services has a minimal staff. The California Community College Board's Chancellor's Office has five vice chancellors in charge of everything from legal affairs and governmental relations to student services and curriculum and instruction.

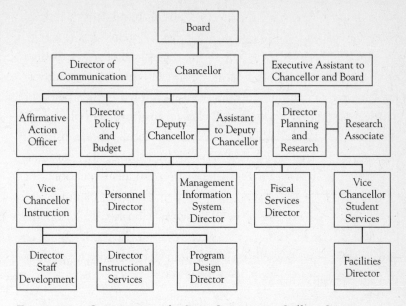

Figure 4.4. Organization of a State Community College System

A combined state university and community college system has been established in many states in order to implement state-level management. More than one hundred two-year colleges, campuses, or institutes affiliated with state universities have been established in eighteen states; such institutions are prevalent in Ohio and Wisconsin. All public community colleges in Alaska, Hawaii, Montana, and Nevada are under the state university system. The university president is the chief executive officer, and the presidents of the colleges answer to the university executives rather than to their own governing boards (see Figure 4.5). The university boards of regents establish policy. The University of Wisconsin system operates more like a statewide multicampus district, with a chancellor heading the system and each campus under the direction of a dean. The community colleges, state university branches, and technical colleges in Minnesota were combined into one system in 1995 (the University of Minnesota was excluded from the merger).

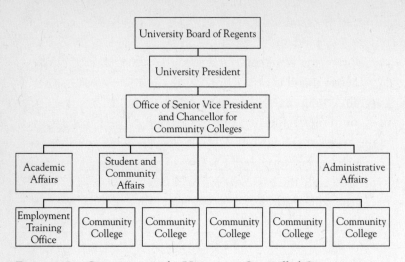

Figure 4.5.   Organization of a University-Controlled Community College System

A single state community college board that can exert influence on the legislature, compete with the university for funding, and coordinate a statewide college development system seems appealing. If the boards responsible for community colleges were also responsible for all of higher education, a thoroughly coordinated, economical, and articulated pattern of higher education for the state might result. Ideal in theory, this practice has not been universally adopted, and where it has, its benefits have not been uniformly realized. Institutional competition for support defies any organizational plan.

Increasingly, state agencies have assumed control over expenditures and program planning and have promulgated rules for nearly all aspects of college functioning, from the employment of personnel to the space a college should allocate for different functions. Numerous authors have documented complaints about duplication, contradictory regulations, and the mass of approvals that must be garnered from various regulatory agencies before college leaders can make a move. The problem is not merely one of decision-making authority between the colleges and the state board; it relates also to other agencies. Washington, for example, has a state board and thirty district boards. In addition, executive orders from the governor, directives from the Office of Financial Management, and contractual controls, legal opinions, and audits stemming from numerous state agencies "must be taken into account in the decision-making process and in the actual operation of the colleges" (Mundt, 1978, p. 51; confirmed by Sutton, personal communication, November, 2001). Information demands alone are high: "Recently the president of Highline Community College . . . found the college was reporting to twenty-nine outside, third-party agencies in one way or another" (p. 53). Elsewhere, state laws may provide for public hearings to precede any major change in college procedures, from the fees charged to program modifications.

In most states, college autonomy is continually compromised. In 2006, the thirty-nine community college districts in Illinois sued the state, asking the court to declare the colleges as local agencies so that their staff would not be classified as state employees and thus have the state ethics rules supersede those of the local districts ("Illinois Colleges," October 24, 2006). But Virginia has introduced an ambitious program designed to allow greater autonomy among its higher education institutions. As the effort develops, the public colleges within the state will be allowed to earn interest on the tuition and fees they collect, carry over unexpended balances into successive years, and seek increased operational authority "in areas including procurement, leases, personnel, and capital outlay" (Couturier, 2006). The initiative is set up so that as an institution demonstrates responsibility it may petition for autonomy in additional areas such as selling surplus property, using locally developed construction management contracts, and establishing policies for designating which staff are classified as administrators and which as faculty. Eventually, an institution may have such powers that it functions nearly as a charter school, establishing its own tuition and fees and finance and accounting mechanisms.

Many commentators believe that state-level coordination has made college leaders' jobs more difficult and the colleges less responsive to local communities. However, the advantages of greater state-level coordination have also been documented. Funding has been made more equitable than it was when community college districts depended on local tax revenues and the gap between richer and poorer districts was pronounced. Some states have developed sophisticated management information systems and student information systems whereby all colleges provide data in uniform fashion; the data then can be cross-tabulated for the benefit of planners at individual institutions and can be used to generate reports for other state and federal agencies. Articulation between community colleges and public universities in the same state has also been enhanced when statewide coordination is evident. In addition, a state board is better able to speak to the legislature with a single voice.

The line between statewide coordination and state control is fine. Many educators would prefer that the resources be provided with no strings attached, contending that state mandates regarding the programs and services to be provided unduly restrict their efforts to offer the proper services for their constituents. State-level coordination has certainly moved decision making to broader political arenas, and it has fostered the development of administrators whose chief responsibility is to interpret the codes. But it has also yielded more stable funding, more services for certain groups of students, such as the disabled, and higher standards of operation; and it has helped minimize program duplication. The question of whether it has been of general benefit or detriment cannot be answered. We can say only that it has changed the ground rules for institutional operation, the professional outlook of the staff, and the way the colleges are perceived by the public, who may see the college as no longer their local school but as a part of a remotely controlled state system.

It has given the top administrators a new role as well. Weisman and Vaughan's 2006 survey of more than five hundred public community college presidents reported that 93 percent of them visited the state legislature the last time it was in session to advocate for their institutions. Half of them said they spoke with state representatives and state senators more than ten times a year, and two-thirds reported speaking with their Congressional representative or U.S. Senator two to ten times yearly. Furthermore, associations often encourage their members to write their representatives about issues or to invite them to visit their campuses. This type of activity adds to costs: "80 community colleges spent a total of about $4.3 million in 2005, with 12 of them reporting expenditures of at least $100,000" (Lederman, 2006, p. 3). This does not include the professional associations whose governmental relations offices spend much time and resources in what is called *providing information* on pending legislation. The American Association of Community Colleges and most statewide institutional associations are deeply involved in such activities; scan any issue of their newsletters. As long as they do not advise their members specifically to "Call Congressman Miller and say you want him to vote for the bill," they avoid being tagged as lobbyists under the Federal Lobbying Disclosure Act or the Internal Revenue code. But they operate in a gray area.

Establishing a new community college has certainly become a more complex undertaking since state-level coordination became prominent. In the 1920s, a local school may have done little more to start a college than to get the state board of education's approval to offer some postsecondary classes. The 1907 California enabling act stipulated merely that the board of trustees might charge tuition for such classes. Gradually, the criteria expanded to include minimum enrollments, minimum district population, and tax support.

By 1960, the general guidelines for establishing community colleges included "(1) general legislative authorization of two-year colleges, (2) local action by petition, election, or action by local board of control, (3) approval by a state agency,

(4) a minimum assessed valuation considered adequate for sound fiscal support of the college, (5) a state or local survey to demonstrate the need for the college, (6) a minimum population of school age, (7) a minimum total population of the district, (8) a minimum potential college enrollment, (9) types of educational programs (curricula) to be offered, (10) availability and adequacy of physical facilities, (11) compliance with state operating policies, (12) proximity of other institutions" (Morrison and Martorana, 1961). By the 1970s, Evans and Neagley (1973) had authored an entire book showing the various patterns of college establishment. They discussed state regulations, local needs studies, and ways of securing local support; spelled out guidelines for appointing and organizing the board of trustees; and presented sample organizational charts and recruiting and selection procedures for staff.

The growth rate ended abruptly, and few community colleges were established during the 1980s and 1990s. One of those, Cascadia Community College (Washington), required a ten-year process involving population, participation, and feasibility studies to demonstrate need for the college; legislative processes to authorize the college and fund preplanning studies, which proceeded with the participation of the sixty-member Citizen's Advisory Committee; site acquisition studies and funding; coordination with the Higher Education Coordinating Board and the University of Washington; planning of curriculum by an established college under direction of the State Board of Community and Technical Colleges; development of a master plan; and phased construction of facilities under compliance with state and local codes. Cascadia opened for regular classes in fall 2000, with 2010 as the anticipated completion date for campus facilities.

However, the process is not always that complicated. In 2007, voters in two Idaho counties gave a two-thirds majority to a proposal to organize a community college in Boise. They were assisted by voter-registration and advertising campaign supported by local businesses, and Boise State University agreed to donate one of its campuses until funds for additional facilities could be collected (Guess, 2007).

Federal Role

The federal role in community college management has not differed much from its role in all of higher education. The community college sector has taken advantage of federal funding available for certain programs—for example, programs to train technicians, displaced workers, and various categories of underprivileged people. The colleges have eagerly sought these types of funds and built programs accordingly. Federally guaranteed student loans and other categories of financial aid have affected the community colleges less than they have the higher-cost universities, but they represent an important source of funds for the institutions—and, in the case of proprietary schools, survival.

Since the federal government has insisted that minorities, women, and the disabled gain access to higher education, the colleges have had to modify their employment practices in response to affirmative action rulings. However, each state has had a considerably greater influence than the federal government on the policies governing the colleges within its borders.

Accreditation

Accreditation, the external review of institutions and programs, began in the early twentieth century as institutions of higher education sought to establish minimum standards for student admission, faculty qualifications, and institutional resources, including finances, curriculum, and library holdings. The earliest junior colleges were accredited by nearby universities. The University of Chicago approved the courses offered by Joliet Junior College, and by 1929 the University of Missouri had accredited eighteen colleges in the state. The universities in several other states performed similar functions, and in some states, the state departments of education accredited the junior colleges.

The standards for accreditation varied greatly, and the regional accrediting associations soon attempted to adopt standards that would apply across the colleges in their area of oversight. The North Central Association and the Southern Association were early in that process. By 1930, all the regional accrediting agencies had adopted minimum standards that centered on faculty qualifications and teaching schedules, student admission and graduation requirements, curriculum, college revenue, buildings, equipment, and size of library holdings. Although the universities have abandoned the practice of accrediting community colleges, they still have an effect on college programs because of the requirements that most of them impose on the transferability of student credits.

Accreditation serves several purposes, including ensuring quality, easing transfer, and sending signals to employers and the public that programs have met certain minimal standards. Accreditation is also required for access to federal funds, since the federal government relies on accreditors to determine which institutions and, indirectly, which students are eligible to receive federal aid. Recognition by a federally approved accreditation agency thus serves in lieu of a governmental monitoring agency. In fact, it has been federal demand for accreditation that has converted what was formally a voluntary process into a mandatory procedure.

The accrediting procedure rests on several characteristics. The accrediting agency sets standards, and the institution seeking accreditation conducts a self-study that considers college performance in the light of those standards. A team selected by the accrediting agency visits the institution and, assuming it is satisfied that the applicant has reported its practices accurately, reports back to the accrediting agency, which thereupon grants accreditation status. This process is repeated periodically.

The regional accrediting association process often overlaps with similar reviews conducted by state-level governing boards. According to Ewell and Jones (1994, as cited in Laanan, 2001), four statewide indicator systems are typically used. First is one similar to that found in K–12 systems, in which inputs, processes, and outcomes are examined in order to measure value added. Second is resource use and efficiency, physical resources, faculty, and space. Third is the magnitude of state returns on investment, typically the preparation of skilled workforce and the number and quality of graduates to fill jobs. And last is customer need and return on investment; this one considers rates of persistence, degree completion, and employment.

The state agencies have emphasized these types of institutional outcomes, sometimes called effectiveness measures, which often include licensure pass rates. Although the accrediting agencies also consider such measures, they have been increasingly more concerned with direct evidence of student learning. As an example, the Southern Association in 1986 adopted an "institutional effectiveness" standard that required every institution to provide evidence of its goals for student learning (Smith and Pather, 1986). All the regional accrediting organizations had similar kinds of policy in place by the mid 1990s. Industry-based skills standards have grown as well, thereby effecting a form of accreditation manifest by business and industrial companies.

Criticisms of the accreditation process take many forms. One concern is that the regional accrediting associations vary in their standards and treatment of colleges with different emphases. They vary also in the extent to which they apply the same or different standards to associate degree-granting proprietary schools. Obstacles to outcomes-oriented standards include limited research expertise among community college staff members, the vagueness of the accreditation guidelines, and the tendency of colleges to formulate goals as statements of process rather than statements of outcomes (Palmer, 1993). Ewell has summed up some of the criticism, saying that few colleges "have progressed beyond superficial engagement with 'assessment,' though accrediting organizations have been asking them to do so for years" (2001, p. 4). A question still remains open about the extent of overlap, similarity, or differences among the standards, often written as "indicators," that accrediting associations and state governing boards, agencies, and commissions have proposed.

A particularly thorny issue in accreditation is centered on assessing distance-education programs. Among the seventeen recognized regional and national institutional accreditors that scrutinize distance learning, standards and guidelines vary widely, not least because traditional standards of faculty contact, library access, and campus facilities do not apply. Nonetheless, the recent moves toward assessing institutional effectiveness, outputs, or outcomes indicate a shift away from almost total reliance on institutional resources and processes. As with any other major paradigm shift, it is taking many years to find its way into the main currents of thought manifest by practitioners.

Nontraditional Organizations

Regardless of the form of institutional control, different organizational patterns have been tried. The "noncampus" college became popular in the 1970s. Because such institutions typically employed few full-time instructors and offered much of their program through reproducible media, often including open-circuit television, their administrative patterns differed. A president would report to a districtwide chancellor, but program directors or associate deans would take responsibility for separate geographical service areas. Furthermore, because of the emphasis on rapid change in course design, instructional planners would be more prominent than department or division chairpersons. Coastline (California), Rio Salado (Arizona), and the Community College of Vermont were notable examples of colleges without walls, functioning much like the extension divisions of universities.

At the other extreme, the continuing search for ways of bringing the decision-making process closer to faculty and students led to the development of cluster colleges, or small, semiautonomous units. The more freedom the smaller unit has to design its own academic program and to set its own rules of conduct for staff and students, the more it fits the ideal of a sub-college operating under the umbrella of a parent organization that provides budgets, legal authority, and general administration, along with access to a central library, auditorium, and sports facilities. Traditional academic departments have been conspicuously absent in most cluster college plans, and student services are usually decentralized, each cluster having its own set of counselors. Advocates of cluster colleges have put them forth as the best system for bringing students and staff into the process of making decisions about the types of programs that should be presented.

Other special organizational forms have included colleges organized for particular purposes, for instance, technical institutes built as separate colleges in multicampus districts. Some of these, such as the Los Angeles Trade and Technical College, have a long history. San Francisco's Community College Centers were formed in 1970 to coordinate all noncredit activities. Miami-Dade's Medical Center is of more recent vintage and is even more highly specialized. Santa Monica's Emeritus College (California), designed for and operated by senior citizens, is another form of a college within a college.

Early College and the Baccalaureate

Early college high schools and the community college baccalaureate are two rapidly growing innovations. Both demonstrate the colleges reaching for new service areas and clientele, one picking up students at grade 10 or 11, the other reaching toward grades 15 and 16. Together, they represent a two-way stretch.

The seamless web, schools organized so that students might progress with minimal disruption from grade one through graduate education, has long been a chimerical goal. The American system of primary, middle, and secondary schools, community colleges, bachelor's degree–granting colleges, and graduate schools, all of which may be organized apart from each other, have made transfer between institutions a capricious process. Ideally, each state's public education system would be governed uniformly and curriculum would build sequentially. But despite sporadic efforts to achieve such systems, they are as elusive as ever.

Many community colleges have attempted to minimize the barriers by reorganizing. Some have expanded in the direction of the secondary schools through Early College High School Initiatives, offering accelerated programs that lead to high school diplomas and associate's degrees. Several foundations have supported these ventures: Bill and Melinda Gates Foundation, Ford Foundation, W. K. Kellogg Foundation, and the Carnegie Corporation. State and local policies must often be adjusted to accommodate the modifications, including lifting restrictions on the number of college courses that high school students may take and for which the school district will be reimbursed, and state and union regulations that prohibit college instructors from teaching in high school and vice versa. These programs can be quite salutary, especially where they encourage financially and educationally disadvantaged ninth graders to graduate from high school and earn associate's degrees in four or five years instead of the traditional six (Kisker, 2006).

Other colleges have expanded into the realm of four-year institutions by offering bachelor's degrees; Navarro College (Texas) in 1985, Utah Valley Community College in 1997, and Westark College (Arkansas) in 1994 were pioneers in this move. In 2001, the Community College Baccalaureate Association held its first annual conference. These institutions vary considerably; some offer programs located on the community college campus with degrees awarded by a senior institution (actually a long-standing practice), whereas others present their programs on a university campus. Some formed university centers, often located close to or at the community college but with several institutions participating. Examples of the latter were Northwestern Michigan University Center, which included eleven four-year institutions; North Harris Montgomery Community College (Texas) with six public universities; and Broward Community College, with a campus at the home of Florida Atlantic University (Floyd, Skolnik, and Walker, 2005). Some of these have been identified by the Southern Regional Education Board as hybrids, associate/baccalaureate institutions that grant associate degrees primarily but also the baccalaureate; examples include Dalton State College and Macon State College (Georgia). The trend to offer the baccalaureate grew so that in 2005 the Carnegie Classification of Institutions of Higher Education created a new category: *baccalaureate associate college*, institutions offering at least 10 percent of their degrees as baccalaureate, and fifty-seven institutions were so designated (Townsend, 2005, p. 180).

Evolution has been occurring rapidly. Utah Valley Community College became Utah Valley State College in 1994 and Dixie College became Dixie State College of Utah in 2000. Westark College was designated University of Arkansas at Fort Smith in 2001. In Florida, St. Petersburg Community College, one of the state's oldest, and Miami-Dade Community College, the state's largest, along with three others, have dropped *community* from their names. All of Hawaii's community colleges have changed names to reflect their changed status, and because the Southern Association of Schools and Colleges so mandated, the institutions that the Texas Higher Education Coordinating Board has authorized to offer the B.A. have become four-year schools.

By 2007, community colleges approved to offer the B.A. were in Florida, Hawaii, Indiana, Nevada, New Mexico, New York, Texas, Vermont, Arkansas, Georgia, Louisiana, Utah, North Dakota, and Oklahoma. In Florida, the four-year programs offered at community colleges more than doubled since 2001–02, but some limitations were being implemented: the colleges were allowed to "continue offering bachelor's degrees, but only in nursing, teaching, applied sciences," and workforce-oriented degrees in high need/high demand fields" (Garmon, Feb. 2, 2007, p. 9).

Local Governing Boards

The idea of a lay governing board is an old concept in American education; public education has used elected boards to reflect the collective will and wisdom of the people since earliest times. Ideally, the local board is the bridge between college and community, translating community needs for education into college policies and protecting the college from untoward external demands. This places the board in the role of mediator, conveying information from college to community and back. The board agenda is that the college maintain a positive image, which translates into continued public support.

The demographics of community college governing boards are similar to those of university trustees. After reviewing several studies of trustee composition and attitude, both Piland (1994) and Vaughan and Weisman (1997) reported that whether elected or appointed, the board members are predominantly white male, college graduate, high-income, middle-aged people with professional or managerial occupations, who tend to hold mainstream views on college admissions policies and traditional program functions. But those are national averages; the board members in large, urban districts increasingly are more representative of minority populations.

Community college boards usually consist of from five to nine members elected from the district at large for four-year terms. They may meet once or twice a month, and sometimes weekly. Their responsibilities include selecting, evaluating, and dismissing the president; ensuring professional management of the institution; purchasing, constructing, and maintaining facilities;

defining the role and mission of the college; engaging in public relations; approving programs; determining staff salaries; and contracting for services. But these powers vary among states; the local boards in Illinois, for example, set the student fees, whereas in California they do not.

Because the boards are public corporations, they are legally responsible for all college affairs. This status involves them in legal actions regarding personnel and the purchase of materials (competitive bidding, advertising, special designs). Therefore, as Potter (1976) has shown, a board must have a working knowledge of educational law and be able to recognize potential legal problems before they develop into actual litigation. He offers examples of litigation brought on by students, faculty members, and other parties—for example, suits by students in relation to tuition or over disruptions on campus (which, they contended, interfered with their education) and suits by faculty members, who have usually engaged in litigation because of dismissal from their jobs. Cloud (2004) has traced legal issues ranging from students' rights to risk management. Maintaining student rights is essential because "courts of law have consistently found that the relationship between students and their postsecondary institutions is a contractual one" (Mawdsley, 2004, p. 5). As consumers, students have the right to services as advertised. As citizens they have the right to due process regarding dismissal or expectations about their behavior. Students are also entitled to a safe campus environment.

Due process also comes into play in considering the dismissal of faculty members. For the most part dismissal can be successfully pursued if an instructor can be shown to be incompetent, insubordinate, immoral, or neglectful of job responsibilities (Fossey and Wood, 2004). Ownership of material prepared for distance education is another point of institutional concern. College policies typically divide ownership of such material depending on how it was prepared; if created by faculty members on their own time, they would retain ownership, but if commissioned by the institution and the college has contributed faculty time and other resources, the institution would retain ownership.

Governing boards are political entities, and the selection of a trustee may be viewed as a political act in which the appointing authority or the voters weigh costs and benefits. A trustee appointment by a governor may be used to mend political fences but it may also alienate members of the public who are opposed to the appointees. The elected trustee usually has more power or political independence than the appointed one, but only at the price of the financial and emotional rigors of a political campaign. In instances where the faculty union has contributed heavily to a trustee's election campaign, its influence may be palpable—for example, when the newly elected trustee votes immediately to dismiss a chief executive officer who has fallen out of favor with the union.

State associations for community college presidents and trustees have been prominent in about two-thirds of the states. These voluntary organizations typically coordinate statewide conferences and meetings, conduct professional development workshops for various types of administrators, arrange orientation sessions for newly appointed trustees, prepare and distribute newsletters, and monitor legislation. They provide an avenue for chief administrators and trustees from the colleges within a state to meet and discuss topics of common interest. Active associations that cross state lines, such as the New England College Council, operate in similar fashion. Support for these associations most often comes from members' dues, but some have received funds from the state or a philanthropic institution.

The Association of Community College Trustees (ACCT) has also been active in apprising board members of their need to take a prominent role in college affairs. Since the ACCT was organized in 1972, its publications and conferences have been directed toward moving board members away from a rubber-stamp mentality that approves everything the college administration presents. Along with the Association of Governing Boards, it has stressed the importance of the board's monitoring the college's fiscal affairs and public relations and the necessity for open communication between the board and the college president. State offices in North Carolina (Dowdy, 1987) and Florida (Florida State Board of Community Colleges, 1990), among others, have also published manuals for trustee guidance.

The way that many board members approach their work has changed during the history of the community college. Certainly, the organizations have become more complex, and board members must respond to more initiatives from personnel organizations in the college and from monitoring and controlling agents outside the college. Furthermore, the notion of trustee liability, well documented by Kaplin (1985), has become more pronounced. Less frequently seen in the literature but nonetheless prevalent are contentions that trustees sometimes go too far in their tendencies to manage the colleges. Greater control seems inevitably to follow greater responsibility.

Administration

All colleges must have administration, although the way this function is organized and staffed differs from one college to another. In the medieval university, students were powerful, often fixing tuition charges and determining the curriculum; nevertheless, the faculty was the controlling wheel of the institution. During the nineteenth century, a system of centralized control developed in the United States, and faculty power diminished as the administration took over the university. The professors concentrated on their research, scholarship, and teaching, and professional managers controlled the affairs of administration, thus dividing the ranks between administrators and teachers. The role of the president changed as colleges grew larger. And as faculty and community advocate groups grew stronger, it became ever more circumscribed. Still, the president was the spokesperson for the college, interpreting it to the public on ceremonial occasions. The president was also the scapegoat when staff morale or funds for a favored program diminished.

Community colleges with roots in the secondary schools usually were managed by former instructors who had become first part-time and then full-time administrators. Monroe described many of them as autocrats who had freed "themselves from the control of their superiors and the general public. They assumed a paternalistic, superior attitude toward the teachers. Administrative decisions of the past have often gone unquestioned by governing boards. The members of the boards rubber stamp administrative policies and decisions so that, in practice, the college's administrators become the decision makers of the college" (1972, p. 305). But he was speaking of a time gone by. In the 1970s, the all-powerful president had disappeared from all but the smallest colleges, and the governing boards had become ever more intrusive.

The tenure of presidents is typically shorter than faculty tenure but certainly sufficiently long to suggest that the job is not particularly precarious. The 2006 average of seven years was little changed from the means reported in surveys over the previous twenty years (Weisman and Vaughan, 2007). Twenty-eight percent had moved into their current position from another community college presidency and 35 percent came from other positions in the same institution. Nineteen percent were members of minority groups. Female presidents accounted for 11 percent in 1991, 28 percent in 2001, and 29 percent in 2006.

Primarily, the president carries out general administrative duties and has periodic meetings with the board and the heads of state agencies. To a lesser extent, the president makes decisions on faculty recruitment and selection, conducts public relations activities, and coordinates the college program with programs of other institutions and community groups. Fundraising, always high on the list of responsibilities assumed by presidents of private colleges, has recently come to occupy more of the public college president's time, too. Vaughan and Weisman (1998) detail several areas of presidential focus, including mediating disputes, acting as an educational leader, and serving as an institutional symbol. Moriarty (1994) lists the president's tasks under the major headings of leadership (college mission, values, resources), management (administrative staff and functions), and direct office functions (personal, social).

In their discussion "Leadership Blues," March and Weiner assert that the problems affecting administrators are usually not major issues of educational policy but reflect campus struggles. The outcomes of these contentions usually "involve short-term political advantage and some redistribution of power and influence on college campuses." Furthermore, "loss of employee morale or trustee confidence is a likely ticket out of town for an administrator, whereas institutional ineffectiveness, stale curricula, or anemic graduation or student transfer rates can often be lost in the noise of campus politics" (2003, p. 8). The points of contention need not be very large to elicit much anger, posturing, and bad feelings and to result in lingering resentments. In summation, the style or intentions of leaders often founder on the rocks of personal relations. That is why relationship building is as important as fundraising and financial management.

Administrative Patterns

So many administrative patterns have been advocated that it is impossible to describe an ideal form. In the line-staff organization recommended by Blocker, Plummer, and Richardson (1965), the president reports to the board of control, and a business manager and a director of community relations report to the president. Under the president on the organization chart is a dean of liberal arts and sciences, a dean of technological science, a dean of students for vocational education, and a dean of continuing education. Under the deans are department or division chairs and guidance personnel, and under them the faculty. According to Blocker and his coauthors, such an organization places the major emphasis on college functions.

The college deans are usually line officers in charge of planning and supervising one or a combination of college programs concerned with instruction, student personnel services, evening division, or community services. The larger colleges may also have deans for college development and for admissions, but deans of men and women, prominent in the early colleges, have disappeared from the public colleges. Like the president, each dean becomes involved with legal issues, public relations, intra-institutional administration and personnel matters, budgeting, and liaison with state and federal agencies. Most deans serve as part of a president's council or cabinet and the position itself is frequently labeled vice president.

Designating faculty and instructional managers as vice presidents for academic affairs instead of deans of instruction suggests some broader changes in management that have occurred gradually in recent years. Formerly the deans were directly responsible for assigning and evaluating faculty, planning curriculum, and introducing and evaluating instructional processes. Now those activities have been relegated to the departmental or divisional level, much as they are in the universities where overall instructional planning and management is virtually nonexistent. In many colleges the tension between the academic senate, a faculty organization, and the administrators nominally in charge of academic affairs makes broadscale management of curriculum and instruction nearly impossible.

Departmental Structure

The academic program in community colleges has usually been provided through departments or divisions organized around a cluster of academic disciplines or related teaching fields. The primary objective in creating academic departments, inherited from the universities, was to create manageable organizational units, not necessarily to interrelate the teaching of certain subjects or to build interdisciplinary courses. The number of departments is often related to institutional size; in small colleges where not more than one or two instructors may be teaching in any subject field, the combination of teaching fields within a single unit may be quite broad. In the larger institutions, the number of departments has often increased as the number of instructors teaching a single discipline has grown.

The academic department has been a basic building block in the organizational structure in nearly all community colleges. Its influence has been quite marked. As an example, the administration may organize collegewide orientation sessions for new instructors, but true indoctrination takes place when the neophytes begin maintaining their offices in the suite assigned to the academic department of which they are members. And in-service faculty development workshops conducted on an institutionwide scale pale in comparison with the influence exerted by a senior departmental colleague's pointed comment, "That's not the way we do it around here!"

Departments often are responsible for constructing class schedules, assigning instructors, allocating funds for auxiliary employees and services—in short, for acting as miniature governmental units within the larger college structure. For this reason, many senior administrators have sought to retain control by minimizing departmental power; hence the move toward the larger organizational unit of the division. Other administrators have attempted to restrain the power of the department by having faculty members from different departments share office space or otherwise mixing the staff. But departments have survived in most institutions, probably because the affinity among instructors teaching the same courses or courses in the same academic fields remains strong. Furthermore, some department chairpersons have served the administration well by maintaining certain records, supervising staff, screening applicants for positions, and reconciling conflicts among staff members and between staff members and students that might have been blown out of proportion if they had reached higher levels of arbitration.

Until the spread of collective bargaining in community colleges, the academic department remained the most popular organizational unit. However, as bargaining units were established, the chairpersons with managerial responsibilities were often designated as administrators and thereby removed from the bargaining unit. At that point, the move toward organizing larger units or divisions accelerated, lest a college have thirty or forty administrators, each supervising only a few instructors. The distinction was not clear, though, and department chairpersons were considered faculty members in some contracts and administrators in others.

Lombardi (1974) reported studies showing lengthy lists of responsibilities for department chairpersons: sixty-nine discrete items in one statement, fifty-one in another. However, he suggested that the duty statements appearing in collective bargaining agreements seldom contained more than fifteen items. Not much has changed. The negotiated contracts of the 1970s circumscribed the chairs' ability to hire and fire instructors, and the shared governance of the 1990s further restricted their powers as it brought the faculty more toward negotiating their perquisites and working conditions directly with the chief administrators. A study of supervisors, chairpersons, and faculty at Delaware Technical and Community College (Winner, 1989) found all three groups agreeing that the chairs had major responsibility for identifying departmental personnel needs, evaluating the staff, establishing departmental curricular goals, evaluating instructional materials, and representing the department to the administration and the public. But at least forty additional tasks that chairs should perform, most of them quite generalized, were also identified.

Hammons (1984), who studied department chairs extensively, reviewed a great number of studies of chairperson responsibilities and activities and identified at least forty different functions categorized under five major headings: administration, student oriented, business and financial, faculty oriented, and curriculum and instruction. Finding a major problem to be that few of the chairs had received any preservice assistance in learning what their responsibilities were or how to fulfill them, he concluded that the role of the chair is among the most nebulous in the institution. Numerous responsibilities, most of them vaguely worded, are assigned, but few opportunities to learn how to manage them are provided. Portolan (1992) confirmed that the instructional administrators she studied seemed to be experiencing a middle-management syndrome of feeling ineffective and powerless. Faced with changing student populations, limited resources, and a range of faculty issues they had not been prepared to handle, they were developing feelings of alienation toward their work. The Academy for Leadership Training and Development has offered a year-long, skills-based program since 1992, but most chairs, and indeed most chief instructional officers, have received little preparation for their specific jobs.

Collective Bargaining

Collective bargaining swept into higher education on the coattails of legislation authorizing public employees to negotiate. As these laws were passed in various states in the 1960s and 1970s, employee groups ranging from refuse collectors to prison guards gained union representation and began negotiating contracts. Within education, elementary and secondary school teachers were first to take advantage of the legislation, possibly because they were the furthest from professional autonomy (Kemerer and Baldridge, 1975). Community college faculties were next most likely to be represented by a bargaining agent, with the National Education Association and the

American Federation of Teachers their two most prominent agents. By 1980, authorizing legislation had been passed in half the states. However, the spread of collective bargaining slowed notably; by 2001, a total of twenty-nine states had passed authorizing legislation (Kearney, 2001). In 2005, 43 percent of the full-time faculty members in public community colleges were working under contracts negotiated collectively. The 361 contracts noted in Table 4.1 covered more than 140,000 faculty, or nearly half the total teaching staff. (Overall, the union membership for government employees in America in 2006 was 36.2 percent, compared with 7.4 percent for private industry workers [U.S. Bureau of Labor Statistics, 2005].) Sixty percent of the community colleges where faculty are working under negotiated contracts are located in just five states: California, Illinois, Washington, New York, and Michigan. And, 80 percent of all part-time faculty covered by contracts are in those five states (Moriarty and Savarese, 2006).

Table 4.1.   Number of Faculty Collective Bargaining Contracts at Two-Year Colleges by Agents, 1966–2005

Year	National Education Association	American Federation of Teachers	American Association of University Professors	Independent	Other (including a combination of agents)	Total
1966	1	1	0	0	0	2
1970	6	3	1	10	7	27
1975	71	52	3	23	1	150
1980	141	72	5	16	2	236
1985	171	82	4	25	4	286
1987	172	84	4	27	8	295
1994	184	104	6	30	2	326
1998	188	110	9	29	8	344
2005	186	120	8	29	18	361

Sources: National Center for the Study of Collective Bargaining in Higher Education and the Professions, 1974–1994; Moriarty and Savarese, 2006.

The expansion of collective bargaining brought about a shift in administrative roles. In general, it marked the demise of the concept of paternalism, with the president as authority figure, and opened an era of political accommodation among contending forces. These changes were difficult for many administrators whose experience had not prepared them for their different roles, but the realities of management within the confines of a negotiated contract so confronted them that they either learned to live with the restrictions or left the practice. Lombardi (1979), who traced the effects of collective bargaining on administrators, showed that most accepted it reluctantly, recognizing that it reduced them to ministerial functionaries carrying out the decisions made during the negotiations. Other administrators welcomed collective bargaining—some because it enabled them to join forces with the union bureaucracy in controlling the faculty and some because it gave them the opportunity to avoid responsibility for their decisions. It has also increased administrators' reliance on attorneys, whose role is to interpret the contracts.

The scope of contracts suggests the magnitude of their effect. Contract coverage includes contract management procedures; rights of bargaining agents; governance items, such as personnel policies and grievance procedures; academic items, such as class size and textbook selection; economic benefits; and working conditions, such as parking facilities and office space (Ernst, 1985). Under these broad headings, practically everything concerning institutional functioning is negotiable.

Collective bargaining drew a legal line between members of the bargaining unit and those outside it—between faculty, on the one side, and administrators and trustees, on the other. It also expanded the number of detailed rules of procedure. It prevented administrators from making ad hoc decisions about class size or scheduling, faculty assignments, committee structures, budget allocations, funding of special projects, and a myriad of other matters great and small. It forced a more formalized, impersonal pattern of interaction, denying whatever vestige of collegiality the staff in community colleges might have valued. It brought the role of the legal expert to the fore and magnified the number of people who must be consulted each time a decision is considered.

The effects of collective bargaining on staff salaries and morale have been examined repeatedly. Wiley's (1993) review of several compensation studies concluded that a negotiated contract elevates salaries initially but after a few years, the difference between unionized and nonunionized campuses is minimal. Studies of staff satisfaction find only small differences but with a tilt toward greater satisfaction for the faculty on nonunionized campuses in areas such as governance, support, recognition, and workload (Finley, 1991). Still, once the faculty vote to establish a bargaining unit, they rarely decide to return to nonunion status. Overall, regardless of whether their campus has a bargaining unit, more than two-thirds of the faculty feel that collective bargaining by faculty members has a definite place in a community college (Outcalt, 2002).

Collective bargaining seems to have accelerated a move to larger institutional units. In multicampus districts where the faculty bargains as a districtwide unit, the district-level administration aggregates power, weakening the autonomy of the individual campuses. In states where the faculty bargaining unit negotiates a master contract for all the colleges, power gravitates toward the state level. At one extreme, this concentration of power may result in a federal system, in which certain powers are reserved for the individual colleges; at the other extreme, the colleges may become single statewide institutions, with branch campuses in the different localities.

Overall, under collective bargaining, the faculty gained prerogatives in establishing the conditions of the workplace, up to and including a voice in institutional governance. Administrators lost the freedom to act according to general principles and were forced to attend to the procedures specified in the contracts;

both parties were restrained from reaching private agreements. In general, an informal relationship of faculty and administration as unequal parties became a formal compact of near equals. And governance and management patterns shifted notably as union representatives, administrators, and various committees and associations composed of people from within and outside the college district made more of the decisions affecting college operations.

Leadership

When a character in Cervantes's epic novel *Don Quixote* is directed to sit at the head of the table, he responds, "Wherever I sit will be the head of the table" (2003, p. 699). This aphorism, put in the mouths of various people over the past four hundred years, has become a symbol of leadership.

Why are some colleges consistently more successful than others in effecting student learning, sustaining staff morale, presenting a positive public image, managing growth, raising funds, and answering every challenge promptly and efficiently? According to many commentators, leadership is the answer. The successful colleges are blessed with the proper leaders: people who know how to guide their colleagues, stimulating each to put forth maximum effort toward attaining the proper goals.

Studies of leaders and leadership have a long history in the literature of higher education. Some analysts have sought the common traits exhibited by people in positions of leadership, usually concluding that effective leaders are flexible, decisive, moral, courageous, goal-directed, scholarly individuals who are willing to take risks and have a concern for others; Vaughan (1994) covers these concepts for the administrators in community colleges. Others, Richardson and Wolverton (1994) and Fryer and Lovas (1991), for example, consider leadership from a contextual perspective asking how leaders behave when confronted with situations in various academic cultures. Astin and Leland (1991, p. xv) attempt to merge traits and contexts to describe leaders and leadership in terms of "vision, personal commitment, empowerment, and risk." Together with Bensimon (1994), they relate these characteristics to a feminist perspective that views the college not as a rationally managed, hierarchical organization but as a collectivity of interacting people.

Several of the broader works on leadership also articulate the necessity of viewing leadership as an interactive process. Burns's classic, *Leadership*, separates the positions of power from the influence that true leaders have over those who follow them without coercion: "Some define leadership as leaders making followers do what followers would not otherwise do, or as leaders making followers do what the leaders want them to do; I define leadership as leaders inducing followers to act for certain goals that represent the values and the motivations—the wants and needs, the aspirations and expectations—of both leaders and followers" (1978, p. 19). Wills agrees: "Where coercion exists, leadership becomes unnecessary or impossible to the extent of coercion's existence. . . . Coercion is not leadership any more than mesmerism is. . . . The leader is one who mobilizes others toward a goal shared by leader and followers" (1994, p. 70). In sum, leaders are leaders only if they have others following them, and people are willing to follow only if they feel their goals are being furthered.

Leadership is thus a transaction between people, not a quality or set of traits held by a person who is in a position of authority; a leader may not even hold a position of authority. Power is interactive. For a leader to exercise power, the other parties to the transaction must grant it. They must be convinced that it is in their interests or in the interests of the organization of which they are members that they strive toward the goals that the leader has articulated. Under the guise of democratic leadership, an administrator in a position of authority may appoint a committee to prepare a position statement or make recommendations regarding a decision that must be made. In such a case, the administrator has suspended leadership until such time as the committee's report is received, but the necessity for exercising leadership has not disappeared or even changed. The leader still must assess the committee's findings and convince the rest of the staff that they are worthy of acceptance.

In an institution where the product—human learning—is infinite and the lines of authority not clearly demarcated, one does not issue orders and expect them to be obeyed pro forma. The astute leader knows that delivering broadsides, memoranda, newsletters, and the like has little influence on the way decisions are made or people behave. Face-to-face contact, small group meetings, and one-on-one explanations are the dominant influences. Administrators who exercise leadership interact with the people involved. They personally negotiate among warring factions and talk with those who are instrumental in implementing new methods or procedures. They do not take everyone's advice or imply that they are going to, but they do ask questions, listen to the answers, and take them into account when it is time to make decisions.

Walker has characterized less effective administrators as those who need to "defend the sanctity of their office" and react with "counteraggressive behavior when under attack." They believe that they are supposed to make decisions, even unpopular ones, and to see that their orders are obeyed and the rules enforced. "They view decision making as a series of personal acts of courage, will, and purpose" (1979, pp. 2–3). The more effective administrators are those who "accept the privileges and status of their office, but wear them lightly. They separate themselves, as individuals, from their office" (p. 4). They consider administration a process, not a series of discrete events, and they tend to be good politicians. Walker concludes that the personality of the administrator seems the most important ingredient; some administrators have succeeded admirably and others have failed terribly, even while adhering to ostensibly similar administrative styles in the same type of organization.

Regardless of concepts of leadership, the context of college management is being reshaped continuously. In order to ascertain compliance with state and federal regulations, the college counsel has become central to decision making. Where a bargaining unit exists, the union must be consulted on all but the most trivial decisions. The organization chart may show a staff pattern, but lines of authority do not follow boxes and arrows. State-level associations of deans, faculty members, and various college officers often take positions on legislation affecting the colleges that may run counter to the position that a member's home institution would prefer. Although the conferees are staff members at locally governed colleges, they exert a form of state-level management. A shadow government has reduced the local districts' powers.

Issues

Several issues swirl around the concepts of governance and administration. Which elements of control should be maintained by state agencies? Which should be reserved for the local institutions? Is multicollege or multicampus the better form?

The college as learning enterprise does not operate well when it is managed as a factory with inputs, process, and outputs as the model. Can anarchical elements of collegiality coexist with contracts negotiated by distant representatives? How does the flat profile of shared governance and interactive leadership change institutional functioning?

Issues of productivity and accountability have been raised repeatedly. How can staff members be held responsible for their actions when most of the decisions that affect them are beyond their control? Does the larger bureaucracy protect the staff from external scrutiny? Will the staff ever seriously consider performance indicators or outcome measures?

A historical view sees the colleges on firm ground. They have always faced crises of one type or another. In the 1950s their identity as prebaccalaureate or postsecondary vocational institution was in question. In the 1960s they expanded so rapidly that finding adequate staff and facilities was an issue. In the 1970s collective bargaining and affirmative action were major concerns. In the 1980s administrators wondered how they would accommodate the rapid shift away from local and toward state financing. The 1990s saw funding limitations coupled with the threat of enrollment caps. Most recently, legislative demands for outcomes indicators and institutional accountability are prominent. And even though none of the crises is ever fully resolved, newer exigencies arise to shunt them aside.

As the colleges have grown larger and more complex, administrators, faculty members, and trustees all have had to adjust. The only certainty is that regardless of the form of governance and the models of administration adopted, these adjustments will have to be made with increasing frequency.

5

Finances

Sustaining and Allocating Resources

Trends in financing community colleges follow shifts in institutional purpose and modes of organization. Institutions that enroll half the people who begin higher education can no longer be considered merely alternatives for students who do not wish to leave their home town to go to a university. They have become large enterprises, some with budgets exceeding $100 million. This chapter traces the sources and allocation of funds, the implications of tuition and student aid, and the ways that community colleges have attempted to balance income and expenditures.

Sources of Funds

When the colleges were small, they made modest demands on public funds. Few people outside the institutions cared where the colleges' money came from or how they spent it. But when they and their budgets grew large and began competing for sizable funds with other public agencies, they became much more prominent. And when inflation and rapidly increasing enrollments drove costs upward at a phenomenal rate, the public colleges' support base came under ever increasing legislative scrutiny. Now that their budgets total more than $21 billion annually, they command serious attention.

The public colleges have always had to operate in a political arena. Since 1907, when the first junior college enabling legislation was passed in California, there has been continual legislative activity on their behalf. The colleges had been organized as extensions of the secondary schools, deriving their support throughout the public school budgets, but that changed as soon as independent community college districts were organized. The state helped somewhat; for example, in 1920, when a federal law ruled that money derived from mining and producing oil and gas on public lands would be turned over to the states, the California legislature decided to give these proceeds to the junior colleges—but their support continued to come predominantly from local tax funds. The usual pattern was for the local district to provide a fixed sum of money per student in attendance, with state aid minimizing the differences among districts of varying wealth. The proportion of state aid was quite small. Augenblick (1978) reported it at an average of less than 5 percent of all public college revenues in the 1920s. During most of the pre–World War II era, student tuition and fees provided more funds to the community colleges than the states did. Richardson and Leslie (1980) noted that in 1934, local districts provided 84 percent of the colleges' support, with student fees accounting for most of the remainder. But even in those early years, there was much variation among states. Eells (1931) showed that student tuition made up 77 percent of the financial support for the Texas colleges, whereas in California, taxpayers from students' home districts provided the colleges with 81 percent of their operating funds.

Over the years, community college funding has been marked by shifting proportions coming from tuition, local taxes, and state revenues. As shown in Table 5.1 and detailed later in this chapter, the trend has been toward increased dependence on tuition as a source of revenue. (State and federal grants and loans to students are included in the tuition line.) The other major trend is for the states to pick up an increasingly larger share than the local districts do. This trend was accentuated in the late 1970s when California's Proposition 13 limited property tax to 1 percent of 1975–1976 assessed valuation, with a maximum of a 2 percent

Table 5.1. Percentage of Income from Various Sources for Public Two-Year Colleges, 1918–2000

Source	1918[a]	1930[a]	1942[a]	1950[a]	1959	1965	1975	1980	1990	1997	2000
Tuition and fees	6	14	11	9	11	13	15	15	18	21	20
Federal funds	0	0	2	1	1	4	8	5	5	5	6
State funds	0	0	28	26	29	34	45	60	48	44	45
Local Funds	94	85	57	49	44	33	24	13	18	19	20
Private gifts and grants	0	0	0	0	0	1	1	1	1	1	1
Sales and services	N.A.	N.A.	N.A.	N.A.	12	6	6	3	7	6	5
Other	0	2	2	2	2	7	1	3	3	4	4

[a]Includes local junior colleges only.

Sources: Starrak and Hughes, 1954; Medsker and Tillery, 1971; NCES *Digest*, 1990–2006.

annual increase. Local community college districts found their major source of funds effectually capped and were forced suddenly to look to the state for their funds. Within two years, the state's share of community college revenues increased from 42 to nearly 80 percent. Several other states—notably Arizona, Colorado, Hawaii, Illinois, Massachusetts, Oregon, and Washington—passed legislation similar to California's Proposition 13.

Support patterns vary considerably. The colleges in many states with large systems (California, Colorado, Florida, North Carolina, Virginia, and Washington) receive 75 percent or more of their funds from the state. There, the community college share of state money going to all of higher education ranged from 18 percent in Colorado to 37 percent in Washington (Palmer and Gillilan, 2000). The colleges in several large states (Arizona, Illinois, Michigan, and Oregon) still receive a sizable percentage of their money from local districts. In 2004, the cost per student FTE in Kansas Community Colleges was $8,275, of which 48% came from local sources (Kansas Board of Regents, 2005). Although tuition charges account for one-fifth of the colleges' operating budgets nationwide, the colleges in several states derive more than one-fourth of their revenue from their students, whereas students in California pay one-tenth of the cost of their education.

Changes in support vary as well from year to year. In constant 1996 dollars, the colleges spent $5,815 per student in 1971, $5,902 in 1983, $6,583 in 1985, $6,518 in 1993, $7,180 in 1996, and $8,623 in 2001. In short, expenditures per year were flat during the 1970s, reflecting a decline in the percentage of full-time students, but turned up in the mid-1980s, remained stable for several years, and increased in the mid-1990s (NCES *Digest*, 2005). During the lean years, the colleges made up for the shortfall by increasing the percentage of the operating budget contributed by tuition and selling services or renting out land. They tended also to decrease current expenditures by deferring maintenance and equipment purchases, freezing new employment, reassigning staff, and increasing the use of part-time faculty.

Capital-outlay projects have usually been funded differently from operating budgets. Some states require the colleges to present long-term plans on the need for buildings and facilities, plans that have been difficult to defend in an era of rapidly shifting enrollments. And when appropriations become hard to obtain, capital-outlay projects are among the first to be curtailed. Some states require a bond issue to finance college buildings. Although the community colleges in many states occupy handsome quarters, their policies of reaching out to offer classes in a variety of off-campus localities have reduced their need for new buildings for traditional instruction. Special-purpose buildings, especially for newly evolving technical programs, are in high demand.

Allocation Patterns

Increased complexity in patterns of state reimbursement has accompanied the increased proportion of funds coming from the state. Wattenbarger and Starnes (1976) listed four typical models for state support: negotiated budget, unit-rate formula, minimum foundation, and cost-based program funding.

Negotiated budget funding is arranged annually with the state legislature or a state board. Used especially in states where all or nearly all the community college funds come from the state, negotiated budgets demand a high level of institutional accountability for funds expended. Budgets tend to be incremental; one year's support reflects the prior year's, with increases or reductions based on funds available, changing costs, and the introduction or suspension of various programs.

Under the unit-rate formula, the state allocates funds to colleges on the basis of a formula that specifies a certain number of dollars per unit of measure, which may be a full-time-student equivalent (FTSE), the number of students in certain programs, the credit hours generated, or some combination of measures. This pattern is in use in a majority of the states (Education Commission of the States, 2000).

The minimum foundation plan is a modification of the unit-rate formula. State allocations are made at a variable rate that depends on the amount of local tax funding available to the institution. The allocation may be expressed as either a set dollar amount minus the local funds available per student or a proportion of the approved district budget minus the amount provided by the local contributions. In either case, the intent is to provide more state funds to colleges where local support is less. Inequities in local support among community college districts are smaller than those among lower-school districts because community college districts tend to be larger and therefore are more likely to include both wealthy and poor neighborhoods. Still, considerable variation exists because community college attendance is not mandatory, and districts can differ widely in the proportion of the population they serve.

The cost-based funding formula provides support based on actual expenditures. In this model, state funds are allocated on the basis of program functions, specifically budgeted objectives, and detailed instructional categories. Local tax funds may or may not be factored in, and the appropriations vary greatly among institutions, depending on the costs of the programs they offer.

The funding formulas are often complex, and whichever is used benefits certain institutions, certain programs, and certain classes of students while penalizing others. The common practice of reimbursing colleges on the basis of FTSEs may penalize institutions having higher proportions of part-timers. Although reimbursement for occupational students may be made at a higher rate than for those enrolled in the lower-cost academic programs, as in Illinois and New Jersey, costs vary among all the programs. And because of the differences in facilities used, staff salaries, types of students enrolled, and so on, absolute parity among institutions can never be achieved.

There is no consistent pattern in state funding for special student groups or for students in particular curricula. Some states run support to the colleges according to enrollment in several different curriculum categories, each carrying a different reimbursement formula, and provide additional funds for particular groups of students. In half the states, senior citizens are given waivers of tuition or fees, and displaced homemakers or displaced workers get various types of aid. Unemployed students and prisoners sometimes also receive aid. These inconsistencies make generalizing about funding a complicated exercise. Categories of curriculum and students qualifying for various levels of aid shift continually.

Over the years, the community college funding agents have attempted to solve several complex problems. The first is for state aid to be equalized, so that colleges in districts with less of a local tax base do not suffer excessively from lower funding. Differential program payments point up another dilemma. Some programs are of most public benefit and therefore worthy of the highest support. General education, a low-cost program, falls in this category. The highest-cost programs, such as some of the technician-training curricula, demand more money per student, but their benefit may be more for the individual than for the public. Continuous adjustment of budget formulas in every state points up the impossibility of reconciling that issue.

Another major issue in funding is the linkage between funding and enrollment. An enrollment-based funding pattern calculates allocations by using student head count or FTSE to appropriate funds. Many efforts have been made to separate funding from this pattern, because costs of instruction—which are nearly all based on academic staff salaries and libraries—are constant, whereas enrollments fluctuate. If each year's appropriations are based on student enrollment, great distortions in revenues calculated against expenditures can result. However, alternative patterns of funding, such as a certain base rate calculated according to overall district population regardless of enrollment, have never succeeded. The proponents of decoupling, as that is called, have argued that expenditures for the various categories of activities need not be related to enrollments. For example, the expenditures on physical plant depend more on the age of the buildings than on the number of students occupying them. The net result, however, is that the formulas for funding become more complex. But there is one constant: every state uses some measure of enrollment as the centerpiece of its allocation process.

Tuition and Student Aid

Questions of the proper formulas for funding are no more controversial than the issues surrounding the tuition and fees paid by students. In an era of frequent tuition increases, it seems difficult to recall that when the colleges were deriving half their funds from local sources, many two-year college leaders were advocating a no-tuition or low-tuition policy for their institutions, which they felt were natural extensions of the free public schools. Their views were not shared by many outside the institution.

After studying the history of tuition charges, Lombardi (1976) concluded that the issue was not whether tuition should be charged but how much. He reported a 1941 survey of a national sample of educators, editors, and other officials that found only a small majority affirming free tuition for public junior colleges. And although the 1947 President's Commission on Higher Education stressed the importance of making public education free through grade 14, nearly all the community colleges organized in the 1950s and 1960s charged tuition. In 1970, the Carnegie Commission on Higher Education urged that students pay a larger share of instructional costs as a way of saving the private sector of higher education. The concept of no tuition was destined to abort early in its development. Perhaps Eells anticipated what was coming when he quoted a speaker at the 1928 annual meeting of the American Association of Junior Colleges, who said, "Many people, including those who are careful students of education finance, share the opinion that when the student has monetary investment, he is going to attack the problem of education more seriously than . . . when it is handed to him for the asking" (1931, p. 123).

The pressure for increasing tuition has usually come from state legislators seeking ways of holding down appropriations. Echoing Eells, their arguments have been that the people who benefit from going to college should pay and that students will take their education more seriously if their own money is at stake. The counter-arguments are that the entire population benefits when more of its members have been educated and that equity demands that low-income students not be forced to pay the same tuition as the sons and daughters of wealthy parents, because such charges represent a higher percentage of family income for the former group.

The most common type of tuition is a fixed rate for full-time students and a uniform credit-hour rate for all others. When full-time rates are charged, they act as an incentive for students to enroll in more courses per term. Where rates per credit hour are charged, they usually eventuate in the part-timers paying a higher rate per course.

Whereas tuition usually represents a portion of the costs of instruction, student fees are assessed for special services that may not be required for all students. Optional fees include use of laboratories or special equipment for certain courses, parking fees, library fines, and special fees for late registration or changes of program. Some states limit the total amount or the types of fees that colleges may charge, but in others, the colleges attempt to collect reimbursements for a wide array of services.

Tuition recently has increased rapidly. Whereas the average tuition for full-time students stayed under $100 per year from the beginnings of the community colleges throughout the 1950s, it moved to $100–199 in the 1960s and $200–299 in the 1970s.

By 1980, it was over $300; by 1987, it had more than doubled to almost $700; and by 2000, it had doubled again. In 2007, it was $2,361. The differences among states are enormous, ranging from $721 in California to $5,338 in New Hampshire. Hawaii and New Mexico are toward the low end; Vermont and Minnesota toward the upper. Although the average full-time student receives around $2,000 in grants and tax benefits, according to Horn, Nevill, and Griffith (2006), when the costs of housing, food, health care, child care, transportation, and textbooks and supplies are added in, the overall cost of attending a community college averages over $10,500 per year. For California students, Zumeta and Frankle contend that "fees represent less than 5 percent of the total attendance cost" for students not living with parents and not receiving fee waivers (2007, p. iv).

Colleges that derive much of their support locally are usually permitted to establish their own tuition within certain limits. Out-of-state and foreign students pay at a higher rate, as do certain categories of part-time, adult, and evening-division students. In some states, at least a minimum tuition must be charged; in others, the legislature establishes a maximum, as in North Carolina, where in 2006 the tuition was capped at $1,264 per year (North Carolina Community College System, 2007a, 2007b), and in Illinois, where the colleges could not charge tuition that exceeded one-third of per capita costs (Illinois Community College Board, 2005). But state policy almost invariably fixes community college tuition at a lower rate than for the public senior institutions because legislators usually want the community colleges to serve as a low-cost alternative for beginning college students. And nationally, it averages nearly 40 percent less.

In the early years, tuition and fees represented a major source of institutional income. They declined as a percentage of total revenues in the 1950s but, as indicated in Table 5.1, then began a steady rise. They have provided a conduit for federal aid that might not otherwise run to the community college. And although mechanisms for distributing state financial aid to students are imperfect because of the limitations on part-time attendance, problems of assessing the financial condition of students' families, and the difficulty in accommodating adult, independent students—all three conditions more prevalent in community colleges than in other sectors—the states have been able to enhance equity by providing funds to the lower-income groups. This method of equalizing opportunity has proved significant. South Carolina, for example, provides full-time equivalent (FTE) student aid at a ratio of 41 percent of the cost of tuition (Dougherty and Reid, 2007).

In reviewing the issues of equity and efficiency in tuition charges, many economists argue for higher tuition coupled with higher aid. It is possible for colleges to set tuition at a level that reflects the balance between private and public benefits and still maintain equity by running financial aid to low-income students. The problem of aid systems that penalize students who enroll for only one or two courses can be offset by a state's paying the tuition for anyone taking a course considered of prime use—for example, a person on welfare who takes a course in an occupational program. Increased student aid should properly be used for tuition payments, lest the incentive for students to enroll in college and receive financial aid for paying living costs lead to the system's being viewed as an adjunct to welfare.

By the mid-1980s, federal and state aid to students had become a foundation stone of college funding. In 1993, $34.5 billion was being advanced to higher education in the form of grants to special categories of students and loans to students from middle-income as well as low-income families. By 2000, this figure had doubled (a 50 percent increase in constant dollars): $35.1 billion in student loans from the federal government, $3.6 billion in state grants, and $13.3 billion in grants from the institutions. Federal Pell Grants, awards given on a sliding scale depending on family income and college costs, totaled $12.7 billion; the community

Table 5.2.   Shares of Pell Grants by Sector, 1973–2003

Year	Public Two-Year Colleges	Public Four-Year Colleges	Proprietary
1973–74	24.8%	41.4%	7.4%
1975–76	26.1	39.0	9.0
1977–78	24.3	42.8	8.9
1979–80	21.8	39.6	10.5
1981–82	18.7	40.7	13.5
1983–84	18.5	38.0	18.8
1985–86	18.8	37.0	22.1
1987–88	18.5	34.8	26.6
1989–90	21.1	35.8	23.1
1991–92	24.3	35.5	20.7
1993–94	30.0	35.9	15.3
1995–96	32.7	36.0	12.5
1997–98	32.8	36.4	12.2
1999–00	33.4	34.8	13.1
2001–02	35.0	33.0	14.2
2003–04	32.8	34.0	16.5

Sources: Gillespie and Carlson, 1983; Lewis and Merisotis, 1987; Knapp and others, 1993; Phillippe, 1994; College Board, 2000, 2005.

college share was $4.1 billion (College Board, 2006b). Table 5.2 depicts the proportions going to the public and proprietary institutions. The national community college associations were united in their support of student aid programs, even though the funds were a mixed blessing because they enabled potential students to matriculate at the higher-cost universities and proprietary vocational schools. Without the availability of aid, the latter group, the fastest-growing sector and the colleges' main competition in many areas, would close their doors.

Overall, 38 percent of all community college students enrolled for credit received financial aid. Fifty percent of the full-timers received grants, and 17 percent loans, which in 2000, averaged $3,900. The latter represents a sizable increase over 1990, when

9 percent of the full-timers borrowed an average of $2,000 (Dowd, 2003). Of these, 35 percent received federal grants; 19 percent, state grants; 14 percent, institutional support; and 10 percent received funds from other sources, usually local (Horn, Nevill, and Griffith, 2006).

Breneman's review of federally guaranteed student loans (1991) recounted the difficulty of estimating an exact federal contribution because students who receive loans are expected to repay them. The contribution appears in the form of interest that is paid while the student is enrolled and the loss incurred if the student defaults. By 1990, the interest subsidy to students in school, default payments, and special allowances to leaders reached $4 billion annually. Changing populations and different types of schools involved in the programs led to higher default rates. At traditional two-year and four-year colleges, the highest defaults (35 percent) came from the vocational students and from those with a family income of less than $10,000 (21 percent). Subsequent changes to the rules stipulated that colleges where 25 percent or more of the students were in default over a three-year period could be excluded from participation in federal loan programs. The proprietary schools were the most vulnerable sector, but in the mid-1990s, a few community colleges were on the restricted list (U.S. Department of Education, 1998).

When the loan programs began in the mid-1960s, most of the students were of traditional college age and going to traditional colleges, and more than one-third of them were in private institutions. In the mid-1970s, after attempting various programs, including state-guaranteed loans and means-tested grants and loans, the Basic Educational Opportunity Grant program (Pell Grants) was formed and the Supplemental Educational Opportunity Grant program was also retained. The Student Loan Marketing Association was supposed to provide funds stemming from private loan capital. Needs testing was introduced, and the programs became ever more complicated as older, part-time students began matriculating in ever greater numbers and as proprietary schools were included. Probably the most significant change was this latter development; by 1988, the students attending profit-making trade and technical schools were receiving one-fourth of all Pell Grants and one-third of all guaranteed student loans.

The rationale for the various grants and loans comes from the theory of human capital, which suggests that an investment in people's health and skills yields an economic return similar to investing in physical plant and infrastructure. Thus, college is an investment, and the case for borrowing to finance that investment is clear. The big problem with financing students is that they "offer no collateral, they have no credit record, they cannot make payments easily while enrolled, they have little current income, and many would simply be poor credit risks if standard measures were applied" (Breneman, 1991, p. 3). But from the perspective of higher education, the colleges have become fully dependent on the existence of credit, and from the standpoint of the students, borrowing to go to school is increasingly the norm. Changes making the federal government the direct lender in the early 1990s did not modify those basic characteristics of the program.

Problems in Funding

Increases in tuition and financial aid to students and the shifting of the major source of support from local to state tax revenues were the most dramatic, but not the only, problems affecting community college finance. Sizable salary gains were made by instructors working under negotiated contracts, but staff productivity, by any measure, did not increase. This was no surprise to students of educational structures; in fact, Coombs (1968) had outlined an impending educational crisis worldwide: because teachers' productivity does not rise along with their salaries, the costs per student must rise. Hence, each year, an educational system needs more finances simply to accomplish the same results as the previous year. As he put it, "To assume that costs per student will be held at a standstill by far-reaching, economy-producing innovations still to be introduced is to indulge in fantasy" (p. 51). No innovation can rescue educational systems from serious financial difficulty as costs accelerate in what he called one of the last handicraft industries.

Fiscal problems were accentuated by the different types of students. Many observers had applauded the institutions' attempts to reach new sorts of students, but few considered the added costs that came along with them. "New or expanded functions of the colleges such as community services, career education programs, special programs for disadvantaged and minority students, financial aid, health services, and counseling accompany the increases in enrollment. Instructional innovation generates experiments, new teaching methods, and technical devices that often cost more money and usually increase the unit cost of education" (Lombardi, 1973, p. 13). The extra costs of campus law enforcement, utilities, and theft that resulted from offering night classes for part-timers were rarely calculated. And few colleges could properly fund the small classes and personal attention necessary to teach the less-well-prepared students who have so swelled enrollments since the 1960s. Even extramurally funded programs added to costs when more people had to be employed to administer them.

Controlling expenditures has been difficult because education is labor intensive, but it is not impossible. If it were, expenditures would not differ from college to college as much as they do. The per capita cost, the most common measure, is generally derived by dividing the total cost of operation of a college by the number of FTSEs. Sometimes it is determined by cost per credit hour, that is, total cost divided by the number of credit hours taken by students. This concept of per capita costs nearly always refers to current expense of education and rarely to capital-outlay expenditures. The cost per student varies according to the mix of programs that a college offers; some courses cost more than others.

Another element of per capita costs is the price of the instructors. Instructors with long tenure and doctorates cost more than those with shorter tenure and no doctorates.

Bowen (1981) reported considerably less difference in expenditures per student among types of institutions than among different institutions of the same type. Using data from 268 institutions sampled from among those that had reported in the Higher Education General Information Survey in 1976–1977, he showed that the median expenditure per full-time freshman or sophomore student equivalent was $2,020 at public research universities, $2,025 at comprehensive universities and colleges, and $1,959 at two-year colleges. But the range for public two-year colleges was from $1,102 to $4,150. Data from each state also revealed wide disparities, although the range within states was not nearly as great. Bowen ascribed these differences among community colleges to variance in the relative emphasis on expensive occupational programs and less costly academic programs. (He was writing prior to the rise of the Tribal Colleges, which spend double the national average.)

Where does the money go? Forty-six percent is devoted to instruction, 24 percent to administration, 11 percent to student services, 10 percent to physical plant operation and maintenance, 4 percent to scholarships, and less than 2.5 percent each to libraries and public service.

Solving the Problems

In order to balance budgets, the colleges have given financial planning a more prominent role and periodically have instituted hiring freezes and made selective cuts in personnel, equipment, courses, activities, and services. Cuts in personnel are the most difficult to effect because of contracts, tenure, and seniority, to say nothing of the personal upheaval they entail. The colleges have tried to foster managerial efficiency by employing efficiency experts and training staff members in budget management. They also have responded to fiscal exigencies by making more effective use of physical facilities, including year-round use of buildings, scheduling patterns that distribute class offerings over more of the day, and the use of rented space.

For decades, numerous commentators have detailed these and other ways of controlling expenditures, including reducing the number of low-enrollment classes; restricting staff leaves and travel; employing more hourly-rate faculty members; offering courses in rented facilities off campus; encouraging early retirement of staff; reducing student support services, such as tutoring, counseling, athletics, and placement; freezing orders for supplies and equipment; and offering students credit for experience. Placing faculty members in contact with more students through larger classes or increased teaching hours has been a perennial recommendation, but that has not been an easily implemented reform because of the tradition of equating low teaching load with quality. Most recently, distance learning and technological infrastructure have been hailed as leading to potential cost reduction and great savings, but this promise has not been realized. For the present, the demographics of aging (and therefore higher-paid) faculty are inexorable in increasing college costs, and the employment of part-time (and therefore lower-paid) faculty is the preferred mode of decreasing them.

The world of politics, public relations, and illusion surrounds all public educators, who recognize the importance of maintaining an institutional image of fiscal prudence. But a public agency must spend all the money available to it; therefore, an educational system will be as inefficient in its use of resources as it is allowed to be, because efficiency leads to reduction in funding. College managers find it difficult to shift away from that concept, the bedrock of public agency maintenance. If cuts become necessary, managers try to keep all programs, services, and functions intact in order to avoid the difficult decisions to drop any of them.

If further cuts become necessary, they are made where they will be most visible. And larger units, such as multicampus districts, may give the appearance of fiscal prudence because they have fewer top-line administrators, even though the infrastructure may in fact be more expensive.

Alternative Funding Sources

Alternative funding sources, or revenue diversification, has been practiced by higher education institutions for decades. Notable examples can be observed in institutions that have sizable properties; Stanford University, for example, earns millions of dollars from its shopping center and industrial park. Brightman (1989) showed how separate corporate organizations can be set up for the ventures that earn income, such as food catering services for other organizations in the community, retail sales, and facilities leasing. He noted also that these are not activities that should be pursued by some fully engaged administrator as an add-on to regular professional responsibilities; rather, they are deserving of specially designated staff members who can ensure that the planned programs do not run afoul of state statutes or tax laws.

Numerous other nontraditional sources of funds have been reported. Some colleges aggregate supplemental funds by selling custom-designed instructional television and training special groups of professional people, often through interactive media. Teleconferencing can also be a fiscal generator. State funds outside the normal budget sometimes have been retrieved to perform a special function; Belmont Technical College (Ohio) received funds from the state department of natural resources "to reclaim land abandoned by former coal mining companies" (Lestina and Curry, 1989, p. 53). Selling or leasing of college lands is another major source of funds. Cerritos College (California) leased a parcel to a developer to construct and manage an assisted-living facility for forty years. The college not only receives a revenue stream, but it has gained an on-campus laboratory in which students in its nursing, physical therapy, cosmetology, and culinary arts programs can gain experience. (S. Helfgot, personal communication, October 4, 2001). Many colleges have arranged short-term leases with agencies wishing to stage athletic events, county fairs, swap meets, and horse shows. A college with good athletic or convention facilities is in a position to generate considerable income thereby.

One of the more effective, and rapidly expanding, ways in which colleges are offsetting increasing costs is to augment their budgets by establishing their own foundations to serve as vehicles for receiving funds from alumni, other donors, and philanthropic agencies. Most colleges have foundations, with median annual revenue of around $250,000 and market value of $2 million. These organizations are usually holding corporations, with fifteen or more board members and a full-time director. Their funds come primarily from local businesses and people not affiliated with the college and from the foundation board members, with personal solicitation the most important fundraising activity. Because the foundation is legally and organizationally independent, it is able to promote the well-being of the college without the statutory limits placed on the college's governing board and staff. Most of their funds are distributed for scholarships, student and program support, and equipment. One Florida college raised $1.6 million for teaching chairs, 60 percent from donors, and 40 percent from the state (McGee, 2003).

The colleges have also started to build endowments by soliciting funds from donors, just as four-year colleges have done for all of their history. Fundraising campaigns are often coordinated by outside professional organizations. Van der Werf (1999) noted several examples of successful large-scale fundraising efforts conducted by community colleges in Kentucky, Arizona, Washington, Florida, and elsewhere. New Mexico Military Institute, with $298 million, has by far the largest endowment. The next five highest community college endowments range from $53 million to $19 million;

California's 109 community colleges average less than 2.5 million each. These numbers pale in light of university holdings, among which the institution one-hundredth from the wealthiest boasts an endowment in excess of $500 million, but they show how far the community colleges have come in a short time.

Justifying the Costs

Periodically, after they have exhausted their efforts to reduce expenditures, colleges are forced to make policy changes. For example, the colleges' tradition of taking all who applied and keeping them as long as they wanted to stay came under attack. First, state legislatures threatened to impose enrollment ceilings if costs per student were not reduced. In addition, many colleges were required to tighten their standards for academic progress. Gradually, community college advocates realized that their proudly voiced claims of unlimited enrollment growth had become passé. As Richardson and Leslie stated, "The current practice of accepting all who apply regardless of the funding authorized conveys several messages to legislators, all of them undesirable. The first message is that quality is not an important concern of the community college. . . . A second . . . is that very little relationship exists between the amounts appropriated and the numbers of students served" (1980, p. 7). Richardson and Leslie recommended that college administrators gain prior state approval for specific curricula and services and that they introduce first-come, first-served enrollment procedures— in short, maintaining the open door only to the extent that resources permit and ensuring that quality be a hallmark.

The issue was quite straightforward. The lower schools had no choice in the number of students they admitted; every child not only had a right but by law was required to attend school. Community colleges were different; they could restrict their enrollments by cutting the variety of programs offered, by marketing less vigorously, and through numerous other stratagems, including dismissing students who were not making satisfactory progress toward completing a program. The only question was whether colleges would do so voluntarily or wait until the legislatures mandated the changes. Most college leaders waited. By the mid-1990s, most legislatures had acted to specify enrollment limits.

Issues of efficiency and equity arise in any discussion of financing. Efficiency relates to the ratio between the benefits deriving from some good or service and the costs of producing it. Equity relates to the extent to which different members of society attain similar benefits from public expenditures. In publicly supported education, the two obviously overlap: a highly efficient institution would spend its dollars only on the people who would use their training to make substantially greater incomes, thus paying back significantly more in taxes than their education cost. But such an institution would be inequitable because the members of certain social groups would not receive any of its educational benefits.

A Century Foundation analysis of funding categories and values concluded that "public policies have tilted away from low-income and working-class students to more economically advantaged students who would likely go to college with or without government aid" (Kahlenberg, 2004, p. 3). This is manifest in the increased share of aid in the form of loans and in the relative reduction in funding for federal programs created as early as the 1960s to assist low-income students: TRIO reaches "only 10 percent of those eligible" (p. 8) and GEAR-UP, designed to build mentoring partnerships between colleges and middle schools with high rates of poverty, receives less than 5 percent as much as the Pell program. The result: "74 percent of students at the nation's top 146 colleges come from the richest socioeconomic quartile and just 3 percent come from the poorest quartile" (p. 9). In the community colleges, 26 percent of the students are in the lowest quartile (Horn, Nevill, and Griffith, 2006).

How do the community colleges fit in? Economists often categorize school expenditures as investments in general human capital, specific human capital, and consumption benefits with little investment value. The classifications "academic," "occupational," and "community service" fit these respective categories rather well. Developmental programs help people become productive members of society and thus benefit the public by reducing transfer payments. However, the cost is high because of the high-risk nature of the students. Vocational programs benefit society because of the increased productivity of the labor force, the higher probability of students' going to work after graduation, and the aid to industries that will stay in an area where a trained workforce is available. Thus, although students benefit individually from occupational training, substantial public benefits are also present. Community services are most likely to be of the consumer education type, with benefits accruing primarily to the individual, not to the public. Accordingly, following the practice in university extension divisions, community colleges should charge the consumers for the full cost of providing these services. However, certain types of community service or noncredit courses, such as courses on child care, family nutrition, or energy efficiency, seem to slide over into the category of public benefits.

Many attempts have been made to demonstrate more direct effects, with studies using a bewildering array of categories, both direct and indirect. The direct effects include college-related business volume; value of local business property because of college-related business; expansion of the local bank credit base resulting from college-related deposits; college-related revenues received by local governments; cost of local government services attributed to college-related influences; number of local jobs and personal income of local citizens from college-related activities; and purchases made by the colleges and their employees, students, and visitors. The net effect is calculated by totaling all expenditures and subtracting the local district's contribution to college revenues. The studies invariably find a sizable effect on all indicators, not a surprise because institutions such as hospitals, universities, prisons, and governmental agency buildings yield similar results.

The indirect benefits are even more varied: increased income exhibited by former students, sometimes converted to additional sales and income taxes paid; employee training supported by the college; availability of college students as part-time employees for local businesses; the college's contribution to new business formation; increases in property values and real estate taxes paid resulting from staff purchases of homes; the value of college facilities that are used by community organizations; workforce productivity and involvement in civic affairs on the part of alumni; lower unemployment rates and greater lifetime earnings that translate into more taxes paid; public radio and television stations maintained by the college; and a variety of community services, such as opening college facilities to other organizations, career planning, and continuing education for professionals.

Studies using the above-named variables have been reported for several decades. After reviewing the flow of state funds that the college brought into the local area, Littlefield, a Long Beach City College (California) instructor, referred to the impacts that "cannot be readily quantified . . . Suppose there are 1000 male high school graduates. Five and a half percent, or 55, would have been unemployed . . . If these 55 enroll in a community college, we would expect their unemployment rate to drop to 4.2 percent after graduation. The number unemployed would thus drop from 55 to 3, a 95 percent reduction . . ." (1982, p. 45). A comparable calculation found a 95 percent reduction in the number of families receiving public assistance (p. 50). Furthermore, since people who have been to college earn considerably more than people who have not been to college, and since 16,000 people attend the college, multiplying the earnings differential by the total student body yields a "Total Annual Income Increase" of $45,600,000 (p. 37). And, because 94 percent of the prison population had not been to college, the community was saving an additional $18,000 per student per year, the difference between keeping a person in college or in jail. Bottom line: the college saved the community $263 million per year. (After twenty-five years, the screams of the tortured statistics still have not subsided.)

The most prolific set of reports dates from 1999 when the Association of Community College Trustees contracted with a group to develop a generic tool for documenting college benefits. The resultant template was based on four types of benefits: college expenditures on salaries; the higher earnings accruing to former students; social benefits such as reduced expenditures for prisons, welfare, and medical care resulting from the more healthful life style exhibited by alumni; and overall return to the public relative to their support of the colleges. Over 500 studies resulted, some relating to all community colleges in a state, others to individual institutions. One example of the former reported that the 14 community college districts in Oklahoma paid $200 million in direct salaries and spent an additional $2.6 billion in salaries off campus. Over time, taxpayers will see a return of 14.9% on their annual investments in the colleges, students will enjoy a 23% annual return on their investment, and the state will save more than $38 million per year through "improved health and reduced welfare, unemployment, and crime" (Christophersen and Robison, 2003b, p. 3). Furthermore, because 95% of the students remain in the state, they will contribute further to the economy. According to their analyses, the fifty-eight colleges in North Carolina "account for $1.4 billion" in the state's economy, "$13.3 billion" in alumni earnings, and "$184.1 million per year" in social benefits, while the state's taxpayers "see a real money 'book' return of 16.8%" on their annual investments in the colleges (2004a, p. 1). Comparable figures for Connecticut's twelve colleges show $24 million per year in social benefits and a return to taxpayers of 14.6 percent (Christophersen and Robison, 2004b). And the thirty Washington colleges save the state $168 million in improved health and lower incarceration rates, while the taxpayers receive a 19.6 percent return (Christophersen and Robison, 2003a). The same group has used that formula to report data on numerous individual colleges. Their review of Grand Rapids Community College (Michigan), published in 2006, indicated contributions of close to $1 billion in higher earnings; reduced medical costs (employer savings from reduced absenteeism, and reduced smoking and alcohol abuse among alumni); and reduced incarceration rates among students. Similar accounts report contributions of Ivy Tech Community College (Indiana) as more than $700 million; Housatonic Community College (Connecticut), $60 million; and so on (Dembicki, 2006).

The economic impact studies stand apart from studies of college effects on student access, learning, and progress through the higher education system. The studies on learning and progress through the system are rarely conducted routinely unless mandated by state or accreditation agencies, a recent phenomenon, whereas those on student access have long been used as marketing and public relations tools. Schuyler (1997) summarized methodology, models employed, and findings of nineteen economic impact studies conducted by colleges over a twenty-year period and concluded that most were "geared toward policy makers, incorporating factors that exemplify the worthiness and value of the community college, and written so as to highlight the positive outcomes" (p. 76). In sum, studies of student learning as related to cost are rarely seen, possibly because of the difficulty in combining these variables; concepts of efficiency and learning may be ultimately incompatible.

Issues

College leaders will be forced to face several issues regarding finance in coming years.

How can costs be managed in a labor-intensive enterprise? Bargaining units will restrict the savings that managers formerly gained by employing part-time faculty members and increasing class size. Reproducible media demand sizable start-up costs and have yet to yield far-reaching financial benefits.

How can accounting procedures document the additional costs to the institution engendered by categorical aid and demands for special programs stemming from external agencies? More broadly, on what grounds can an institution that has prided itself on offering something for everyone refuse to begin a new service that costs more than the revenues it generates?

Does low tuition make sense in the light of substantial student aid? At what point does tuition without offsetting financial aid reduce equity? What are the actual, as opposed to the conceptual, relations between levels of tuition and institutional efficiency? In brief, can benefits be run to one group without offsetting losses to another?

Developmental studies and high school completion courses seem destined to occupy a major portion of the community college effort. A plausible case can be made for reorganizing many colleges along the lines of the 6–4–4 plan that was in effect in some districts in the early years. How can they obtain funds to teach the basic education that was supposed to have been completed in the lower schools?

Those portions of vocational education that benefit certain industries are difficult to justify on the grounds of efficiency. How can the colleges expand the targeted portions of their occupational education and defray the costs by entering into greater numbers of contracts without damaging the integrity of a publicly supported institution?

What measures of institutional productivity can be introduced so that increased costs can be justified? Answers to that question depend on the results the institution is trying to achieve. Can education be defended in its own right, or must the criterion always be the financial return to the students and the community?

These are all difficult questions. College administrators who would be educational leaders will see them as challenges and take them up with vigor.

6

Instruction

Methods, Media, and Effects

Instruction is the foundation of all schools, colleges, and universities, and several perennial issues surround this basic activity: Who does it? How? With what effect? Undergraduate teaching in the universities particularly has commanded attention recently. Books and articles exhort professors to spend more time with their students even if that means they do less research. Anyone with a historical perspective finds it mildly amusing to see the number of comments deploring the status of undergraduate instruction in the universities; the same contentions have been raised for the past one hundred years.

Because community college instructors have never devoted much time to research or academic discipline–based scholarship, they have been free to address nearly their full attention to instructional processes. The colleges have emphasized the importance of good teaching since their earliest days, and their observers have reported unanimously that teaching was their raison d'être. Eells called the junior college "a teaching institution par excellence" (1931, p. 389). Thornton proclaimed instruction the primary function, saying that it had to be better in the two-year college than in the university because the students covered a broader range of abilities and their prior academic records tended to be undistinguished: "It is fair to say that most community college students are able to learn but are relatively unpracticed. Under good instruction they can succeed admirably, whereas pedestrian teaching is more likely to discourage and defeat them than it would the more highly motivated freshmen and sopho- mores in the universities." He concluded that either the college "teaches excellently, or it fails completely" (1972, p. 42).

Other writers followed these exhortations regarding good teaching with the observation that it was indeed to be found in the two-year colleges. Although rarely heard since the colleges grew large, the pronouncement that instruction was better because of the small classes was often voiced in an earlier time. In addition, junior college instructors were considered to be better than those in the universities because their pedagogical preparation was more evident and they were bona-fide instruc- tors, not teaching assistants. Koos reported that "classroom procedure in junior colleges is assuredly on at least as high a plane as is instruction of freshmen and sophomores in colleges and universities" (1924, p. 219). He pointed to the "superiority of teaching skill" found among instructors at two-year colleges because, unlike their counterparts at the universities, most of them came from the ranks of high school teachers and had train- ing in pedagogy (p. 201).

Even the way the colleges are organized suggests a commitment to teaching. An administrator, formerly a dean, now more typically a vice president for instruction, oversees the formal educational program and usually chairs a curriculum and instruction commit- tee responsible for all major changes in those areas. The com- mittee comprises program heads, department chairpersons, and representatives of the library and counseling services. This alloca- tion of instructional leadership to the administrators has enabled them to coordinate the work of the faculty members and offer incentives through instructional development grants, sabbaticals, and release time to develop new techniques. The evolution of the library into a learning resource center and the widespread use of tutors and reproducible media also attest to an orientation to teaching.

This chapter discusses instructional technology and considers varied techniques as television, computers, online instruction, writing across the curriculum, and supplemental instruction. Also included are comments on mastery learning, learning resource centers, and competency-based instruction. A discussion of the assessment of instructional effects—its pros and its cons—completes the chapter.

Before recounting the use and effects of some of the many instructional forms in place, it should be noted that traditional classroom instruction, that is, one teacher interacting with a number of students, still dominates. Most students still learn by sitting in classrooms, listening to lectures, watching demonstrations, participating in discussions, reading books, and writing examinations. Class size has varied little over the years. Dickmeyer (1994) reported that one-third of the classes overall had between ten and nineteen students, and one-third enrolled between twenty and twenty-nine. The other third was about divided equally between classes with fewer than ten or more than twenty-nine students. The 1998 survey conducted by the Center for the Study of Community Colleges found that class size averages had barely changed in the past twenty years. Fine and performing arts had the smallest classes, averaging between twelve and sixteen students per class; applied and advanced mathematics, foreign languages, social and ethnic studies, English, engineering, physics, chemistry, and interdisciplinary sciences also tended to be smaller than the norm. Arts and music history and appreciation classes, earth and space sciences, and introductory classes in psychology, sociology, and history were typically larger, averaging twenty-seven or more (Schuyler, 1999a). More recently, a national survey found composition teachers with a mean of ninety-four students per semester (Jaschik, March 27, 2007). And in Illinois, excluding adult basic education, English as a Second Language, and independent study courses, the average class size was eighteen (Illinois Community College Board, 2005).

The Technology and Discipline of Instruction

One of the most persistent ideas in education is that individual-ization must be the goal in every instructional program. Numerous articles have begun with the statement, "Let's assume that the best ratio of teachers to learners is one to one," and then gone on to explain how one or another instructional strategy might be tailored to fit each student. The most extreme version of individualiza-tion was realized when colleges began granting credit for experi-ence gained anywhere. Core courses taught in singular fashion and required of everyone were at an opposite extreme. Each had its proponents, and both were evident, often in the same institutions.

A technology of instruction in which goals are specified and a variety of learning paths designed so that most students may reach those goals has made some inroads, but progress has been slow. The definitions of *instruction* that are in use offer a clue. *Instruction* may be defined simply as "an activity that implements the curriculum." This definition assumes a set of courses that must be brought to the students. Another definition is "a sequence of events organized deliberately so that learning occurs." This defi-nition does not depend on a curriculum, but it does include the word learning, and it implies a process leading to an outcome. But most instructors seem still to define *instruction* not as a pro-cess but as a set of activities (lecturing, conducting discussions, cajoling, and so on) in which teachers typically engage. Such a definition ignores both the courses and the learners.

Regardless of the medium employed, the basic model of instructional technology includes clearly specified learning out-comes or objectives, content deployed in relatively small portions, learning tasks arrayed in sequence, a variety of modes of present-ing information, frequent feedback on student performance, and criterion tests at the ends of instructional units. The instructors are part of the technology of instruction when they define the objectives, write the tests, select and present the media, and in general connect students to the learning tasks.

The technology of instruction has been important for two-year colleges, typically commuter institutions in which the environment of a learning community is not available to exercise its subtle yet powerful influence on the students. The tools basic to an instructional technology have been available ever since words were first put on paper. The expansion in variety and use of other forms of reproducible media have made additional sets of tools available. However, except for institutions that have adopted competency-based education and its companion form, mastery learning, the concepts of instructional technology have not been widely adopted. It is as though new types of hammers, saws, and trowels had been taken up by artisans unaware of the shape of the houses they were attempting to construct.

Instructors of developmental courses have been among the leaders in adopting concepts of instructional technology. During the 1970s and 1980s, this group moved steadily from the periphery of the educational establishment toward the mainstream. They became not only teachers of remedial classes but also managers of student flow, and their learning centers became more nearly integral parts of the instructional programs. They expanded their provision of academic support services to instructors in the academic and occupational areas, and they became more deeply involved in measuring instructional outcomes. As a group, developmental instructors became more professionally aware, and this awareness was reflected in their participation in vigorously functioning professional associations—the National Association for Developmental Education and the College Reading and Learning Association. Conceptually, they coalesced around instruction as a discipline. Many of them had begun as teachers of reading, English, mathematics, or psychology, but as they became deeply involved in the learning resource centers and the remedial programs, their connections with their academic disciplines weakened. They became much more concerned with the technology of instruction.

As would be expected in this era of technological upswing, developmental instructors rely heavily on computers and computer-assisted instruction for math, reading, and writing courses. This use can take on numerous forms: incorporation of established software programs; student use of personal computers to revise writing; electronic bulletin boards and chatrooms; review of classroom learning; self-paced courses; online courses; and use of study skill Web sites. In addition to computers, other instructional methods and academic support strategies such as learning assistance centers, supplemental instruction and adjunct course offerings, collaborative learning, linked courses, tutoring labs, structured study sessions, and mastery learning are also embraced by developmental instructors.

Eventually, remedial instructors began teaching large numbers of freshmen not only at their own colleges but at neighboring universities. In 1993, 35 percent of the entering freshmen at the University of California at Davis were taught remedial English by instructors from Sacramento City College. In fall 2001, the university offered seventy-nine developmental education courses in English, math, and chemistry, serving over twenty-one hundred students in the process; by 2006, this involvement had grown to eighty-one sections of math, English, and chemistry plus courses in less commonly taught foreign languages. All of these courses were taught by instructors from Sacramento City College (J. E. Ruden, e-mail correspondence, August 28, 2001; H. Paik, e-mail correspondence, April 10, 2007). Similar arrangements were in place between the University of California at San Diego and the San Diego Community College District. Symbiotically, the university faculty who have never wanted to teach remedial studies contracted with a group who have become experts in the task.

Television

Television, one of the most generally adopted teaching tools, is presented on closed circuit for students in the classrooms and through open circuit for the benefit of the public. Many of the open-circuit televised courses can be taken for college credit, and some institutions have generated a sizable proportion of their course enrollments through the use of that medium. Enrollments in the Dallas County Community College District's TeleCollege rose from their beginnings in 1972 to over ten thousand per academic year in eighteen courses in 1978 and fifteen thousand in 2002 (Dallas County Community College District, 1979, 2002). The City Colleges of Chicago organized TV College in the 1950s, and several other community colleges also received licenses for the cultural enrichment and entertainment of the public, as well as for credit-course instruction.

Interest in television led many colleges to develop their own materials. Video production facilities were constructed in most of the larger institutions; by 1980, two-thirds of the instructors nationwide had access to them. A few college districts—most notably, Miami-Dade (Florida), Coast (California), Chicago, and Dallas—became widely recognized for the sophistication of their programming. (Interestingly, whereas a university's prestige often rests on its faculty's scholarship and research discoveries, the export of high-quality television programs provides one of the few ways that a community college can gain a reputation beyond its own district's boundaries.) Interdistrict cooperation in production and distribution of televised courses became common, and several consortia were developed to share programs and production costs.

The use of televised instruction grew steadily throughout the 1980s, with open-circuit courses offered for college credit one of the more popular options. Surveys consistently found that tele-course students were more likely to be women and older than their counterparts taking courses on campus. Students were taking the classes because they did not have time for regular attendance on campus or because it was more convenient for them, although their purposes for taking the course were similar to those of people who took regular classes. Most of them learned about the courses through mailings or newspaper advertisements. Televised instruction had become well established.

Television as a method of instructional delivery has remained popular. In fact, among all the institutional types (public two year, public four year, and private four year), public two-year institutions were the most likely to use one-way prerecorded video, including prerecorded television broadcasts and cable transmissions. Compared to other modes of delivery, television instruction (one way, prerecorded), which was used by 60 percent of the two-year institutions, was the most common distance-education method until the late 1990s when it was overtaken by online instruction.

Computers

The advent of the computer gave the colleges another opportunity for instructional innovation. A Washington State report on the use of computers in instruction divided patterns of usage into (1) computer-based instruction, the use of specialized computer programs, such as models and simulators, in the teaching of economics, business, and engineering; (2) computer-managed instruction, which supports teaching by maintaining student records, administering tests, generating progress reports, and prescribing the most suitable types of instruction; and (3) computer-assisted instruction, the presentation of linear and branching instructional programs (Howard and others, 1978).

In the 1980s, the personalized computer gave considerable impetus to this form of education, and the community colleges were not remiss in taking advantage of it. In 2001, they led in the percentage of courses reporting classroom computer technology usage. But with respect to the number of institution-owned desktop or notebook computers and workstations, public universities boasted one computer and workstation for every 4.3 students, whereas public two-year schools had 5.6 students per workstation (Green, 2001). In 2006, community colleges were still leading in classroom computer use but lagging in instruction-owned desktops and work stations. Institution-owned work stations averaged 1 per 6.7 students in community colleges versus 1 per 2.9 students in all institutions. Community colleges reported one workstation per 10.8 students whereas the average for all institutions was one per 9.8 students. User support persons varied dramatically; community colleges had one user support person per 912 students relative to one per 277 students in all institutions. Wireless networks reached 60 percent of all college classrooms but less than 45 percent of classrooms in community colleges. The total central computing budget averaged $2.2 million in community colleges, $5.6 million in all institutions. Yet information technology budgets totaled 8.2 percent of overall campus expenses in community colleges relative to 6.5 percent of expenses in all institutions collectively (Green, 2006).

Financial issues affect the community colleges' capacity to provide instructional resources for students and faculty. As of fall 2006, more than one-third of the courses in community colleges had a website (up from 25 percent in 2002) but well below the more than 50 percent in public universities and four-year colleges. Similarly, the faculty in less than one-third of community college courses were using learning management software, compared to 54 percent in public universities. And less than one-third of community colleges provided online course reserves, compared to 84 percent for public universities. Despite a long history of underinvestment in information technology to support instruction and administrative operations, community colleges clearly have done much with considerably less.

Since the 1970s, computer technology has had a role in managing student records, supplementing course material, administering tests, and assessing student progress. In addition to computer-managed applications, which have become the norm in most colleges, computer-assisted and computer-based instruction in the classroom have undergone innovative developments over the past few years. Often these developments enhance teaching practices. At Johnson County Community College (Kansas), organic chemistry courses incorporated an interactive software package that allowed visual material to be presented electronically (Byers, 1997; J. Gadberry, e-mail correspondence, April 12, 2007). Elsewhere, computer-based classroom communication in college physics classes (Dufresne and others, 1996) and architecture design classes (Perryman, 1998) improved active participation. Distance education students in an American government course at Kirkwood Community College (Iowa) used a statistical analysis and data retrieval program as a part of their computer-based exercises (Rosberg, 1997). At Dekalb College (Georgia), computer-assisted techniques, including Internet access to the library catalogue during class, an online version of the course syllabus, online course supplements, and newsgroups and e-mail, were used in literature classes (Nunes, 1996).

Computer-based instruction has been especially important to students in language education. Electronic chat sessions, made possible through collaborative writing software, helped English as a Second Language (ESL) students build vocabulary, reading, and writing skills at the same time that they became more proficient with computers. At Pierce College (California), students with disabilities benefited from the Individualized Vocabulary Instruction program, which provided instruction, offered opportunities for practice and repetition, administered tests, and monitored progress (Crozer, 1996).

Numerous studies have analyzed the effectiveness of computer-based and computer-assisted instruction. For adults, computer-based instruction was found to produce greater gains than did traditional instruction in algebra (Oxford, Proctor, and Slate, 1998). Reed (1996) described computer-based writing classes as "inclusionary" and "more democratic" because such environments encourage student collaboration in evaluating their writing, and Hansman and Wilson (1998) contended that computer use is a necessary component of teaching adult students to write well. According to Klemm (1998), computer conferencing enables creativity, student engagement, and collaboration in the classroom to a greater extent than does lecturing; incorporating this technique increased teaching efficiency and improved the quality of students' work. Despite these positive claims, Pankuch (1998) reported that students welcomed computerized illustrations, simulations, and graphics in chemistry courses but that the effects of computer-based instruction lessen once the novelty wears off. And very few significant differences in retention rates and success emerge between students in traditional classes and those in computer-based math classes.

Writing Across the Curriculum

Writing Across the Curriculum (WAC) is an instructional methodology in which students develop writing assignments in classes in addition to English composition. In some applications, the papers are submitted to a writing instructor, who assists in evaluating them; in others, the students in composition classes work on papers that are related to the content of subject-specific classes. During the mid-1970s, WAC programs gained popularity. Responding to a perceived deficiency in students' writing and thinking abilities, advocates of this approach urged the incorporation of writing into all classes and all disciplines.

WAC programs continue to be implemented. Tidewater Community College (Virginia) had a WAC program that existed informally for twenty years. Faculty from diverse fields met regularly to discuss student writing and the implementation of writing activities into curricula (Reiss, 1996). Monroe Community College's (New York) WAC program provided students with centers that assisted individuals with their writing in all disciplines (Dillon, 1998). A 1991 issue of *New Directions for Community Colleges* (Stanley and Ambron, 1991) described rather fully the history of WAC and presented various approaches to its implementation. In general, WAC programs have been popular for decades but require dedication and enthusiasm to maintain them. The Tidewater program described above ceased functioning when a key faculty member retired (M. Summers, e-mail correspondence, April 10, 2007).

Critical Thinking

Critical thinking as a pedagogical reform has been promoted for several decades. It has many definitions, including tying it to the kinds of thinking that professionals in a discipline use, enhancing a student's ability to be open minded and restrain impulsivity, or "thinking that explicitly aims at well-founded judgment" (Elder and Paul, 2007, p. 43). Elder and Paul link critical thinking with creative thought. They define *talent, gifted, aptitude,* and *genius* as innate endowments, whereas *intelligent, brilliant, accomplished, proficient,* and *virtuoso* are qualities that can be taught and learned.

Critical thinking should be familiar to all instructors who have studied academic disciplines in their own college careers because each academic discipline "is a system of interrelated meanings with definite logic that presupposes and uses critical thinking concepts and tools" (Paul, 2005, p. 29). Furthermore, the massive efforts to teach literacy are often centered on improving writing by analyzing and assessing draft papers, a critical thinking activity. Critical thinking has been linked with Writing Across the Curriculum and with efforts to elevate community college instruction to a level of what has been termed *higher learning,* or at least *collegiate.* Sullivan (2003) has suggested redefining the term *college level writer* to "college level reader, writer, and thinker." Hennessy and Evans (2005) trace Writing Across the Curriculum, noting that it has not lived up to its promises because it has not been coupled with systemic reform both in English composition and in all academic courses in the college. And critical thinking itself has been examined from numerous viewpoints by Barnes (1992, 2005) and McMahon (2005), whose volumes of *New Directions for Community Colleges* review not only the concept but also numerous ways of introducing it and sustaining it in community colleges. One of the more positive developments for the concept is the way that promoters of the learning college concept have tied it to institutional reform. Elder (2005) calls critical thinking "the key to the learning college" (p. 39), showing how it provides the key set of concepts for faculty development, outcomes assessment, and evolution of the college culture. Many educators have commented on the difficulty of assessing critical thinking, but Bers (2005) lists a dozen standardized instruments, some of which have been around for decades.

Supplemental Instruction

Supplemental instruction (SI) uses course content as the basis for skills instruction after identifying high-risk courses (basic or introductory classes with unconscionably high dropout or failure rates) rather than high-risk students. Pioneered at the University of Missouri at Kansas City, it is designed to teach students to read the texts and interpret the tests used in the academic classes they are taking. In these programs, students work outside class with tutors, who attend all lectures for the targeted course. A reader coordinates the work of the tutors with that of the instructors who have agreed to participate by encouraging their students to take advantage of the tutoring. Supplemental instruction is associated with extracurricular peer studying, and it has been used in comprehensive programs designed for ESL students. Where SI has been institutionalized, the key people are a supervisor who identifies the target courses and trains the SI leaders, the instructors of those courses who agree to participate, and the students or learning center staff members who "attend course lectures, take notes, read all assigned materials, and conduct three to five out-of-class sessions a week" (Arendale, 2005). At Santa Monica College (California), supplemental instruction is arranged by linking two or more classes and having students who have previously taken them assist the new groups (Santa Monica College, 2007). It has been shown to have a positive effect on first-year persistence because it provides students with what they most need: additional time spent on learning skills they must have if they are to succeed in required, basic classes.

Mastery Learning

Mastery learning, a technology of instruction, has been described and advocated by several educators, especially by Bloom (1973) of the University of Chicago. The intent of mastery learning is to lead all students to specified competencies (as opposed to programs that have the effect of sorting students along a continuum of individual ability). In a mastery learning plan, competencies are specified in the form of learning objectives. Practice tests, corrective feedback, additional learning time for those who need it, and a variety of instructional techniques are provided to ensure that all, or at least most, of the students attain mastery of the concepts or skills at the prescribed standard.

Proponents of mastery learning have pointed to sizable student gains on test scores and in personal development when this strategy is used. The gains have been attributed to more focused teaching, cooperation instead of competition among students, the definition of specific learning objectives, the amount of class time actually spent in learning, practice and feedback before the graded examinations, and teachers' expectations that most students will attain mastery.

Mastery learning procedures have been adopted in some community college courses and programs, even becoming prominent for a while at City Colleges of Chicago, but for many reasons the concept has not swept the field. Faculty members and administrators who have shied away from mastery learning say it costs too much to develop and operate programs with a sufficient variety of instructional forms; it takes too much of teachers' and tutors' time; outcomes for most courses cannot be defined or specified in advance; allowing students time to complete course objectives interferes with school calendars; students may not be motivated if they are not in competition with their fellows for grades; employers and the public expect the college to sort students, not pass them all through at prescribed levels of competency; and accrediting agencies and other overseers demand differential grades.

McIntyre (1991) reported that a combination of teacher overload and a lack of administrative support interferes with the implementation of mastery learning, while Kulik and others (1990) and Slavin (1990) discussed effects of mastery learning, based on 108 controlled evaluations. Aviles (2001) found that students preferred mastery instruction over nonmastery instruction, even though achievement levels were the same for both types. A synthesis of findings from forty-six studies of group-based applications of mastery learning strategies was reported by Guskey and Pigott (1988). In general, the findings were that mastery learning techniques are rarely installed in pure form but that when they are, the effects on student learning are salutary.

Competency-Based Instruction

Also making inroads in community colleges, competency-based education is an approach that depends on the specification of desired competencies to be exhibited by the students but does not include all the specific instructional strategies of mastery learning. The Competency-Based Undergraduate Education Project, sponsored in the 1970s by the Fund for the Improvement of Postsecondary Education, wrestled with defining the outcomes of liberal education. Ewens found a paradox in attempting to convert liberal education to competencies. It was the seemingly insoluble dilemma of converting higher education from an ideal-referenced standard to criterion-referenced or norm-referenced standards. "Ideal-referenced judgments presuppose some notion of the good, the excellent, the higher, the best" (Ewens, 1977, p. 19), but most education now deals with minimal competencies, functioning in an environment, and meeting acceptable standards of behavior. There is no room for the ideal when we ask, "What is a competent person?" The dilemma appears with force in the tendency of all education to teach job-related skills. One's job is what one does; one's work is what one is. If education teaches for jobs, ignoring what the person is, it runs the risk of creating a corps of dissatisfied graduates when they find that a job is not enough for a satisfactory life—not to mention the issue of whether they find jobs at a level for which they were trained.

For many years, state oversight and regional accrediting agencies have requested that the colleges specify and assess the competencies to be learned in all programs, but especially those leading to employment. Numerous colleges have done so, using Developing a Curriculum, a program for aligning curriculum with specific job requirements, defining competencies, and developing course syllabi. The Carl D. Perkins Vocational and Applied Technology Act of 1990 brought the federal government into the picture by stating that the programs should include competency-based applied learning in academics, problem solving, work attitudes, and occupationally specific areas.

However, specifying tangible, desired outcomes has never been easy, even in the occupational areas. The span from broadly stated college goals to tasks to be performed by students at the end of a portion of a course is long, and the connections may be difficult to make. The links among "making people better," "helping them cope with society," "training them for jobs," "preparing them for clerical positions," and "students will type seventy words per minute on a word processor" may be too tenuous. A technology of instruction puts responsibility for learning jointly in the hands of instructors and students; both must participate. Perhaps educators despair of being called to account if they fail. Teaching is not like building a wall; the chances are good that a brick will remain in place, whereas the influences on students, the myriad impressions they receive in addition to their instruction, and the predispositions they bring to the task can change program results.

Still, the most successful adoptions of competency-based education have been in vocational studies and in adult basic education. Numerous colleges have established a Comprehensive Adult Student Assessment System, which incorporates competency-based approaches to instruction. Supported by a combination of state, federal, and local funds, CASAS provides programs with the resources to establish indicators of performance in adult basic education that integrates literacy and occupational skills instruction, primarily for the unemployed. The system emphasizes documenting outcomes (Council for the Advancement of Adult Literacy, 2003). Competency-based instruction has been implemented in Indiana to enhance workforce training in numerous fields. Certificates of technical achievement are awarded when students meet the given standards for their vocational and technical programs (Indiana Department of Workforce Development, 1996). At Lane Community College (Oregon), a collaboration between the college and local businesses resulted in a workforce training project that used competency-based curricula. All involved parties (including the learners) expressed satisfaction with outcomes, and 82 percent of the students completed the program with the required competencies (Lane Community College, 1998).

Competency-based instruction has also been used as a basis for articulating secondary school occupational programs with their community college counterparts, and it has been employed in high school completion programs. But it has not been widely adopted in general education or liberal arts programs. When it has been applied for this purpose, it has been most successful where working face-to-face is feasible for a critical number of the entire staff, that is, at small colleges such as Kirkwood Community College (Iowa), where competency-based education has become the foundation of the liberal arts program.

Learning Communities

The term *learning community* is often used for instructional innovations that build on concepts of mutual support. Defined as "clusters of courses that are taught as an integrated instructional unit or through linking one course with one another" (Van Middlesworth, 2004, p. 36), they promote social integration by affording students multiple courses within a specified time, the same cluster of students enrolled in all courses, faculty collaboration, and students engaging in collaborative learning through classroom projects. Some colleges pair basic skills courses, such as writing, with courses in academic content areas. The concept of supplemental instruction, noted earlier, is often augmented with linked courses taken by the same groups of students acting cooperatively instead of competitively. These classes may be supplemented with field trips and related support activities. A number of institutions have begun designating themselves *Learning Colleges* in a hubristic attempt to call attention to their having adopted many of the instructional innovations noted in this chapter. They emphasize that although learning is presumptively the central feature of all colleges, the paradigmatic underpinnings of an institution determine the extent to which learning outcomes are emphasized. And, they subscribe to Barr and Tagg's contention that higher education is moving away from the "instruction paradigm" toward the "learning paradigm." The instruction paradigm, historically the dominant of the two alternatives, "mistakes a means for an end" (1995, p. 13), looking to teaching instead of to the outcomes produced by teaching. This acknowledges that within higher education, the definition of instruction as "an activity in which teachers engage," rather than "a process that causes learning," has been dominant.

In numerous publications, O'Banion (1996, 1997, 1999) has documented the characteristics common to learning colleges. Generally, traditional institutions are constrained by time, location, bureaucracy, and the customary roles of faculty and students (the teacher as the bearer of knowledge and the student as a passive receptacle). These limitations have the potential to hinder learning, according to O'Banion, making it essential for learning colleges to work to overcome such obstacles. He expects that learning colleges will

- Allow students to engage in the learning process as full partners who share in the responsibility for their own learning
- Offer a wide variety of options for learning, including numerous alternatives in terms of time, place, structure, and delivery methods
- Incorporate opportunities for students to collaborate with others in learning communities
- Document the learning that takes place

The literature on learning colleges has consistently evoked O'Banion's principles, if not verbatim then in theme. Overall, learning colleges are realms (not tied by place and time) where diverse students find opportunities to grow academically and personally. The faculty become facilitators of the learning process, open to new methods and technologies now available. These learning colleges are responsive to workforce needs, lifelong learners, and nearly everything else that learners demand. They document assessment, maintain accountability, and attempt to please all stakeholders.

Does the learning college represent reality or is it yet another example of good intentions that fail to materialize? Certainly, the movement has been popular, especially among college administrators. And if it but serves only to shift the working definition of instruction from an *activity* to a *process* leading to predictable goals, it will have made a major contribution. It will bring about lasting change only if its proponents recognize and successfully promote the conceptual link between learning and instruction. However, although the term has become popular and numerous institutions have so characterized themselves, as Roueche, Kemper, and Roueche point out, "None of the colleges about which we read, nor the documents they have produced can prove that they have become actual learning colleges in their entirety . . . Progress overall has been painfully slow" (2006–2007, pp. 30–31). So far, the term seems as tautological as "eating restaurant."

Student Engagement

Student involvement in college has been long recognized as an important contributor to overall success and achievement. Studies conducted over several decades and using various valid instruments have verified the relationship between student effort and the effects of college that Pace (1979) postulated and that A. W. Astin and V. Tinto popularized subsequently. In a nutshell, the model holds that all learning requires investment of the students' time and effort, and student development in every dimension depends on the scope and quality of that effort. Although Borglum and Kubala (2000) reported that they found no correlation between academic/social/integration and withdrawal rates, Marashio (1999) emphasized the importance of student engagement through learning communities, and others have identified student effort (defined as participation in library, class, fine art, writing, and science activities and as interactions with faculty and peers) to be a key predictor of perceived gains in general education, as well as in personal and social development. In general, though, community college students are less engaged in college than are students at four-year institutions, a phenomenon certainly related to the nonresidential nature of most community colleges and the external constraints that occupy students' time.

Recent efforts to assess the extent of student involvement have been undertaken by the developers of a community college version of the National Survey of Student Engagement. Educational practices such as academic challenge, active and collaborative learning, enriching college experiences, and a supportive environment are all considered proxies for student learning. Learning outcomes are not measured directly; instead, student perceptions are used to evaluate how well colleges are performing. Survey questions ask about students' time management; self-perceived gains; student interactions with peers, faculty, and staff; types of activities that students are encouraged to undertake; and the degree of support that students feel they are receiving from the college. The Community College Survey of Student Engagement focuses especially on student involvement, their working on projects with other students, the time they spend in preparing class assignments, and their communications with instructors in and out of class. Staff members may compare their students' engagement in collaborative learning, student-faculty interaction, and so forth, with national benchmarks.

Learning Resource Centers

Community college libraries are curriculum driven, containing materials that directly support coursework, with only an occasional nod to faculty research. Many share facilities and collections with university or public libraries in order to maximize resources. Relative to the number of students they serve, the libraries have modest budgets and holdings, averaging $433,000 and 44,311 volumes, compared with $1,574,390 and 269,000 volumes in the average academic library in all of higher education. Less than two-thirds have reference services available through e-mail or the Internet (Holton, Vaden, O'Shea, and Williams, 2006).

Most community college libraries underwent a major transformation in the 1970s and 1980s when they became learning resource centers (LRCs). In some colleges, the library remained intact, with facilities added for individual study through the use of self-instructional programs. But in many, totally new LRCs were built to encompass a library; a learning assistance center; audio and video learning laboratories; a center for the distribution of audiovisual materials; and centers for tutorial services, graphic and photographic reproduction, and video production. About one-third of the LRCs also had career information centers and computer-assisted-instruction terminals.

The evolution has continued, with some LRCs now operating learning enrichment, tutorial, or survival-skills centers or labs. Some learning centers have taken on a status apart from library functions, operating chiefly as coordinating agencies for tutoring, remedial instruction, student orientation, and independent study. In other applications, LRC staff have provided material for grant writing, faculty development, and curriculum design. The LRCs often house production libraries for faculty to develop media. They have expanded to include such electronic formats as on-line services, CD-ROM, and multimedia products. Automation within LRCs includes the conversion of traditional card catalogues to digital databases that are often accessible to faculty and students through college local area networks, making the LRCs gateways to the Internet, other library catalogues, on-line indexes, databases, and texts.

Interactive Media

Interactive media is a broad term for several functions and technologies, including video and audio live broadcasts or tapes, CD-ROMs, and other computer-based forms. The common element is that the user must be able to control the pace and direction of the presentation. These media combine several features. They are like telephones in that it is possible to speak readily to people anywhere in the world and with more than one person at a time; like answering machines with infinite storage capacity; and like teaching machines that allow students to create their own learning paths. They enable searching of dictionaries, encyclopedias, and all the databases, abstracting services, and related information sets. They enable people to revise form, combining books and artwork, blurring the line between creator and critic. Using these media requires no special skills. Children play games on interactive machines, and e-mail is as easy to use as the telephone. Selecting index terms and surfing across databases are relatively straightforward.

With the growth of user-controlled media, the school becomes more important than ever before because education, critical thinking, and functional literacy are essential for sorting out the messages. Just as reading a book has always required the intelligence to decode print as well as to differentiate arguments, interactive media require the ability to vet the information, determining which signals are important, which are true, and which are relevant.

The more sanguine proponents of interactive media, Lanham (1993), for example, project the form's effect on freedom, responsibility, and individuality. Heretofore, teachers, editors, critics, and publishers have screened the various products, thereby controlling access to ideas. But by placing the individual in a position of searching all databases, interacting with everyone on the Internet, interpreting and idiosyncratically reforming all types of emanations past and present, the experts will be circumvented. All to the good, proponents say, because no one should have to suffer the biases of someone else's selection.

Many years ago, arguments in favor of universal literacy centered on the notion that all people should be able to read the Bible for themselves without the interpretation of religious leaders. Applied to education, similar thinking suggests that people should be empowered to learn independent of school. The ultimate in interactive media allows the learners to form their own questions, find their own answers, construct their own texts, and develop their own knowledge.

Within the schools, interactive media must contend with several traditions that militate against their immediately displacing extant instructional forms. At the heart is the core of instruction itself. Devotees of interactive media and all sorts of reproducible instructional situations have been constantly stymied by the difficulty of duplicating a live learning situation. Whether one-on-one tutorial or small class or large lecture hall, the live learning situation involves more than information transmission on the part of the instructor or responses to student questions. The live instructional situation has nuances of body movement, voice intonation, expression, and cues from the instructors and other students that come through the communally breathed air. What tone is being employed? How important is the message that is being transmitted, as indicated by the speech pattern or body language of the person transmitting it? What needs to be repeated because the respondents indicate by their faces a failure to understand sufficiently?

If these verbal and nonverbal cues were not as critical as they are, the various reproducible instructional programs available for half a century would have made more inroads than they have. True, some people learn through using programmed instructional materials, and these materials have become an important part of education in America, just as the mass media have become important. But the predominant form of school-based instruction is still centered on live people talking with live people and picking up all the nuances of behavior that human beings have learned to associate with messages since the beginnings of speech. Reproducible media hold a continuing allure, a promise of low-cost information transmission, but they do not contain the subtle cues to meaning that emanate from the face-to-face contact of a classroom. A nod, a frown, a smile, the shifting of bodies in chairs, the winks and blinks and twitches all have meaning that cannot be duplicated readily through a medium outside the individual.

It is reasonable to assume that in an institution dedicated to "good teaching" since its inception, new instructional forms will be tried. However, despite the spread of reproducible media, traditional methods of instruction still flourish. Visitors to a campus might be shown the mathematics laboratories, the media production facilities, and the computer-assisted instructional programs. But on the way to those installations, they will pass dozens of classrooms with instructors lecturing and conducting discussions just as they and their predecessors have been doing for decades. Media are being used widely, but usually in association with or adjunctive to live instruction. Many faculty members continue to believe that close personal contact with students is the most valuable and flexible instructional form that can be developed.

The Power of Inertia

Media-based techniques are not the only instructional forms that meet resistance. Why don't the faculty require more writing? Many reasons can be advanced, but the one that the faculty often give is that they have too many students in their classes, that if they require their students to write more, then they (the teachers) are required to read more. In most classes, too few papers are assigned because the instructors cannot accept alternatives to their reading them. Either outside readers are not available to them, or they do not trust anyone but themselves to read their students' written work—and probably some combination of both. Nor have the faculty ever accepted the notion that student writing can be sampled, with only every second or third paper read or each paper read only for certain restricted characteristics. They still act as though every practice session must be critiqued, whether the student is practicing the piano, hitting baseballs, or writing compositions.

Anything that lessens direct contact with students or demands more of the instructors' time stands a good chance of meeting resistance. The ad hoc lecture requires the least preparation time. And innovators must prove the positive effects of their techniques, while traditionalists can usually go their way without

208 THE AMERICAN COMMUNITY COLLEGE

question. Teaching as a profession has not developed to the point at which proper conduct in the instructional process can be defined and enforced in the face of individual deviation. Whereas lower teaching loads would allow more time for instructional reform, they would not be sufficient to revise instruction; merely giving people more time to do what they are bent to do does not change the perception of their role, which is a major reason that PowerPoint presentations have become popular; the instructor is still in charge of the pacing and the presentations and never out of sight of the students. Still, nearly all public two-year colleges provide support for instructors who develop reproducible instructional software and courseware.

The rapidity with which new media appear and the stability of the academic culture are at odds. Five hundred years after the introduction of moveable type, the book and the lecture still share the territory of instruction. The inexpensive, readily available book did not displace the lecture in transmitting information; it became an additional form. Each has valuable features that the other cannot duplicate. In this respect, the academic culture resembles its societal context. Cinema did not replace live theater, nor did television replace radio. For that matter, the ascendancy of science over the past three hundred years has not fully displaced belief in the supernatural, and the vision of authority based on superior training must continually contend with a stubborn reliance on folk wisdom.

Distance Learning and Online Instruction

Distance learning expanded notably when online instruction became available. The number of course enrollments in distance education in postsecondary institutions nearly doubled between 1998 and 2001, with community colleges leading the way. By 2004, Internet-based instruction had outpaced telecourses as the primary distance education delivery mode by more than two to one.

Nearly 3.2 million postsecondary students were taking at least one online course in fall 2005, an increase of over 800,000 since the previous year; more than half of those were in community colleges. Eight percent of the students in Washington community college were enrolled in online learning; in Bellevue Community College, online enrollment represented 12 percent of the total college enrollment (Washington State Board, 2006). In California community colleges, the credit students enrolled in distance education totaled 8.6 percent of total enrollments, and in North Carolina online enrollments accounted for 12 percent of the total. A national survey found that online enrollment increased by 15 percent on average over the previous year, with 70 percent of the responding institutions saying there was more demand than they could meet. Most students were taking online courses in addition to classes taught in the traditional mode while they were on campus (Jaschik, April 16, 2007).

Retention and completion rates in online instruction have increased, ranging usually between 50 and 75 percent but always less than in traditional classes. In California, they equal 57 percent compared to a completion rate of 64 percent for students taking face-to-face classes. At Bellevue Community College, they are closer to the 75 percent mark, 10 percent lower than for on-campus courses; and when F grades and dropouts are eliminated, both types of courses have essentially the same grade point averages. Around one in seven California colleges offers full degree and certificate programs via distance, but this is lower than the national average of 31 percent of the colleges having such programs. The larger the institution, the more likely it is to provide opportunity for students to get all of their coursework online.

When students are asked why they choose an online course they usually respond that they like the flexibility of the format and that their schedule does not allow them to attend classes on campus. Those who don't complete the courses frequently give the same reasons for dropping out as those found in surveys of students in traditional classes: too difficult to combine coursework plus employment or family responsibilities; and personal problems. One college's survey of dropouts found many withdrawing in order to take the same class in a traditional classroom setting. Most academic leaders indicate that the learning outcomes in online instruction are the same as or superior to those in face-to-face courses, but a majority also feel that students need more self-discipline in order to complete an online program.

Although a majority of institutions offer online courses, a minority of instructional faculty have taught such courses: 18 percent of full-time faculty compared with 6 percent of the part-timers (NCES *Digest*, 2004). However, some colleges have made online instruction a centerpiece of their offerings. Rio Salado College (Arizona) is one that has combined the savings presented by employing adjunct professors with a corps of instructional designers. Nearly half of its students access courses online and 80 percent of those complete the courses they start. They can sign up for any of the institution's more than four hundred courses every two weeks. The college serves more than 46,000 students and employs thirty-one full-time faculty members who earn between $70,000 and $80,000 annually, and nine hundred part-timers paid an average of $2,100 per course. The full-timers develop the courses and around half the part-timers teach them online. The per credit hour tuition charged for the online course is the same as for the students who take classes at one of the Maricopa District's on-site colleges. And with half of its total enrollment taking classes offered electronically, Rio Salado operates at a cost that is 34 percent below the average of its nine sister colleges.

Distance learning has been handicapped by policies that treat it differently from traditional on-site classes. Students who need state or federal aid may find different policies controlling the amount they can receive if they want to take all of their classes online. Furthermore, many states and individual colleges treat funding for distance learning as a special budget item rather than incorporating it into the regular annual budgetary process. And distance learners residing out of state may be charged out-of-state tuition.

Successful installations of distance education depend on the advocates' ability to overcome obstacles such as lack of support from most people within the institution, necessary changes in student support services, and changes in institutional culture. Oliver (2004) offers several maxims crucial to creating successful online instruction: institutional commitment; investment in instructional development and staff training; development of a technical infrastructure and support network; and recognition that electronic learning changes rapidly and leads to further costs. As Cox concluded, "the enthusiastic rhetoric of possibility continues to outpace the empirical evidence" (in Bailey and Morest, 2006). Bailey found a disjuncture between administrators and faculty, with the former saying they had to introduce online instruction in order to remain competitive with other sectors, whereas the latter were more concerned that online courses lacked quality and increased their workload. Constructing high-quality distance education programs often demands more resources and a greater commitment than most college administrators are willing to expend.

Assessing Instructional Effects

No type of instructional technology has been sufficiently powerful to overcome the traditional educational forms against which it has been pitted. With rare exceptions, an institutionwide commitment to demonstrable learning outcomes has foundered on the rocks of inertia and on an inability to demonstrate that it is worth the effort entailed. Assessing student learning is, however, as important a component of instruction as any other aspect of the process.

Is the community college the home of "good teaching"? Information on the effects of instruction is always hard to obtain because of the number of variables that must be controlled in any study: the entering abilities of the students, the criterion tests and instructional procedures used, and the level of the course or learning unit, to name only a few. Comparative studies are especially difficult because of the infeasibility of matching student groups and instructional presentations (are any two lecture sessions really the same?). Rather than try to compare learning attained, many studies have used student and instructor preferences as the dependent variable. Researchers have measured the value of online instruction by asking students whether they preferred it to live lectures. The reports usually indicate that many students prefer the interpersonal contact with instructors, but many others do quite well with the instructional programs presented through the computer. But pre- and postinstructional assessments of student learning rarely yield significant differences between treatments.

An intractable problem with research on instruction is that no method can be shown to be consistently superior to another. Dubin and Taveggia reanalyzed the data from ninety-one studies conducted between 1924 and 1965 and concluded "that there is no measurable difference among truly distinctive methods of college instruction when evaluated by student performance on final examinations" (1968, p. 35). The conditions of instruction are so fluid, the instructors so variant, the students so different that true experimental conditions cannot be applied. McKeachie (1963) reached similar conclusions.

In the 1980s, new efforts were made to assess effects broadly, by measuring student learning through statewide, interinstitutional, and institutionwide studies, for example. Although such studies are common in most other countries, they are alien to American higher education, where responsibility for measuring cognitive change in students has been relegated to classroom instructors. Therefore, efforts to institute such studies have been greeted with little enthusiasm. Leaders in many institutions have given lip-service to the importance of student outcomes measurement, but beyond a flurry of study groups and the usual skittishness displayed by educators who are faced with a potential change in their routine, little was effected.

Many states, New Jersey, Tennessee, Florida, and Texas, among others, have emphasized testing in basic skills for all entering freshmen. The colleges are then encouraged to link these data with graduation and retention rates. Most such programs have progressed slowly, stung by questions of enforcement, rewards for compliance, and penalties for noncompliance. But where they really run into difficulty is when they include recommendations for content testing, learning measures to be administered as students progress through their undergraduate years.

Still, the press for assessment has continued. Alarmed at the rapid increase in cost per student, especially since the public pays most of it, and prodded by constituents who deplore the low success rates for minority students, the legislatures and appointed officials in many states have insisted on more direct measures of college outcomes. What proportion of the matriculants obtain degrees? How many pass licensure examinations? How many are employed in areas for which they were trained? And—most disturbing of all for a professional group that has taken pride in its vaguely defined goals and processes—how much did the students learn? For the faculty especially, this last query cannot be set aside as beyond their purview. Influential outsiders are demanding to know just what is happening as a result of their ministrations.

Collecting student retention and follow-up data is one thing, but a test of student knowledge administered at the conclusion of the sophomore year is quite another. Complaints about outside control of the curriculum and the demise of academic freedom and similar lamentations have become common. Examinations that reveal student learning to people outside the confines of the single classroom are anathema in academe. Few within the colleges have any notion of how to construct them. Except in rare instances, the staff makes no effort to collect and use such information until the state legislatures tie the process to college funding or student access.

Assessment changed form again in the 1990s as legislatures in some states mandated that the colleges validate their student placement procedures. Because placement testing in community colleges has provoked heated debate in many states, legal actions have led to regulations requiring institutions to provide predictive validity evidence for their placement tests and course prerequisites. Also, other measures of student aptitude must be considered for placement purposes. After evaluating placement test validity, Armstrong (2000a) reports that although correlation coefficients show a statistically significant relationship between placement test scores and resulting grades, these coefficients are not practically significant. Similarly, weaker correlation coefficients are found at the lower curriculum levels (developmental course work), suggesting little connection between placement test scores and course grades in remedial instruction. Conversely, student demographics and situational, and especially dispositional, variables are strongly related to course grades and retention. In fact, student disposition is a much more powerful predictor of success than test scores. Armstrong (2000b) demonstrated his point further when he found that for an English placement test, there was virtually no relationship between the test and student performance in class.

The Pros and Cons of Assessment

The way colleges are organized leads most staff members to resist measurement of learning outcomes. Students are supposed to learn history, music, and mathematics in separate courses and departments. Some students learn more efficiently than others, and classroom tests have always been used to determine which students are better than their fellows. The national testing organizations that offer subject tests from biology to sociology, used to determine which students deserve entry to further school programs, play into this form of normative measurement. They work well when the purpose is to spread individuals along a continuum because they emphasize variation in student ability. This variation is so strong that the difference in scores made by students in a single course will often be as great as the difference between the class average and the scores made by another group of students who have never taken the course.

This normative model, useful for assigning places in a program or grades to students within it, is different from the criterion-referenced measures usually employed when a program or an institution is being assessed. Criterion-referenced measurement refers to the learning obtained by individuals as measured against a standard. If all students answer all questions correctly, then the entire group has learned everything that the test asked, and if the test was designed as a sample of all knowledge to be gained in a course, program, or institution, then the instructional unit has been a total success. However, applying criterion-referenced analysis in an institution with a history of normative-referenced testing requires a complete shift in the way the staff view their work. Easy to conceptualize, that form of outcomes assessment bogs down in practice. Rare is the institutional leader with sufficient patience or skill to turn the group away from its traditional way of looking at student-learning measures. Rare is the leader who can explain the value and purposes of population sampling and test development that demands items that are not course specific.

Regardless of the impetus for assessment or the model that is pursued, certain principles should apply:

- The results of an examination should not be tied to a single course or instructor; causal inferences should not be sought, nor should the findings be used to judge an instructor, a department, or a discipline.

- The items used must not be course specific but should cover concepts that might have been learned anywhere.

- Scores on the examination should not be made a condition of graduation for the students.

- The student population should be sampled; universal assessment systems are too cumbersome for most colleges to manage.

- Alternate forms of the numerous entrance examinations should be used as measures of student knowledge at the completion of certain numbers of units.

- The faculty must be involved as much as possible in test selection, design, item construction, and test scoring. Installation of the process should not be delayed until all are in accord.

- Specialists in testing who are sensitive to the staff should be employed, with the understanding that although assessment is a group effort, staff members will not be forced to participate.

- No one set of measures should be used to provide data for different purposes. Different measures should be used to evaluate student progress, college processes, and the college's contribution to its community, for example.

- The temptation to subdivide scores according to student characteristics should be resisted because such tabulations direct attention away from college contributions to overall student learning.

- A belief in the value of individualization need not extend to variant curricular objectives for everyone; if shared understandings and values contribute to social cohesion, then some consistency in college goals and measures of college outcomes should be maintained.

Issues

The major issues in instruction center on the extent to which a technology of instruction will progress. Will more instructors adopt instruction as a process instead of an activity? What types of instructional leadership can best effect this change?

Assessing instructional outcomes is an integral part of instructional technology. Will persistent calls for mandatory assessment spread from such measures as graduation and licensure-pass rates to systematic measurement of learning attained?

Will the learning college ideal and the contemporary external pressure for funding on the basis of outcomes act synergistically to make assessment of student learning a routine activity?

The consequences of a turn away from print as the primary mode of information transmission have not yet been fully realized. What impact on instruction will be made by students who have gained much of their prior knowledge through nonprint sources? Does an instructional program centered on teachers in classrooms best accommodate them?

Mastery and competency-based instruction have made inroads in developmental and vocational education. Can they spread to the collegiate function?

Although each new instructional medium, from radio to the computer, has forced educators to examine their teaching practices, none alone has revolutionized teaching. A general acceptance of instruction as a process that must, by definition, lead to learning might do more in actualizing the prime function of the community colleges.

7

Student Services

Supporting Educational Objectives

The instructional process is complemented by a range of ancillary activities known as student services. The rationale for these services stemmed originally from the institution's need to regulate its clients' activities and was founded in the academic side of the college in the appointment of faculty members to positions of student advising and deans of students. As stated by O'Banion (1971): "One of the historical models for the student personnel worker is that of regulator or repressor. The student personnel profession came into being largely because the president needed help in regulating student behavior" (p. 8). In other words, students need to be managed for the sake of institutional order, a rationale underlying not only the guidance of students into the proper programs but also admissions and registration, student activities, student government, and record-keeping functions. As a result of larger institutional size and the imposition of extramural directives, student services now include recruitment and retention; counseling; orientation; student activities; judicial affairs; student health; financial aid; academic supports; supplemental services such as transportation, child care, and book supply vouchers; and services tailored for specific populations of students.

The rationale evolved also so that student services were presumed to be positively supportive of student development. Reporting findings of the Committee on Appraisal and Development of Junior College Student Personnel Programs,

Collins (1967) wrote, "The student personnel program should be the pivot, the hub, the core around which the whole enterprise moves. It provides the structure and creates the pervasive atmosphere which prompts the junior college to label itself as student-centered" (p. 13). Eventually, student services combined both regulatory and developmental elements.

A basic difference between community colleges and four-year institutions is the availability of student residence. Although over two hundred public community colleges have on-campus housing, nearly all of them are in small, rural institutions with an average of just over two hundred beds. Most community colleges lack the pervasive sense of community that is more common in four-year residential situations. Therefore, a prime challenge for student services professionals in community colleges is to engage students through counseling, student activities, ongoing orientation, and so forth, to keep them connected to the campus long enough to achieve their academic goals. The students may have myriad other influences that guide their life plans more than the attainment of a degree or certificate.

The most prominent of those distractions results from students' living off-campus. Astin notes that the more involvement, or physical and psychological energy, invested in the college experience, the more successful a student's learning and development will be: "It is obvious that students who live in residence halls have more time and opportunity to get involved in all aspects of campus life" (1999, p. 523). "One of the challenges confronting student personnel workers these days is to find a 'hook' that will stimulate students to get more involved in the college experience: taking a different array of courses . . . joining student organizations, participating in various kinds of extracurricular activities, or finding new peer groups" (p. 526–527). The Opening Doors Project found that many younger students (twenty and under) reported they attended college largely to please their parents and did not feel a strong personal motivation to attend, whereas many students between the ages of twenty-one and twenty-five said they enrolled in college to escape low-wage work and provide a higher standard of living for their families; parenting responsibilities of students with children often interfered with their ability to succeed in college; and making friends in college was only marginally important to them (Gardenhire-Crooks et. al, 2006).

This chapter describes the scope and various emphases of student services. Of particular note are efforts in recruitment and retention, counseling and the areas of specialization within the counseling process, orientation, student activities such as student organizations and study abroad, financial aid, services for specific populations of students, and other supplementary services.

Scope

Consensus has never been reached on the precise role of student services. How much emphasis should be placed on helping students develop? To what extent should the services specialize in assisting students in navigating the bureaucracy, centering on registration and financial aid? Dassance (1994) outlines these issues, pointing out how such role ambiguity has not been resolved. He concludes that above all, student services must link all college functions and work with the faculty in order to be maximally effective.

Several listings of the categories of services have been published. In 1989 the League for Innovation in the Community College issued a set of concepts regarding student development that included thirty-one directives organized under seven major headings (Doucette and Dayton, 1989). The Board of Governors of the California Community Colleges in 1990 listed the responsibilities of student services that should be incorporated in matriculation activities: admissions, orientation, academic assessment, counseling and advising, follow-up on academic progress, research and evaluation, and coordination and training of staff. The list was extended in 1998 to include other support services: financial aid, health services, campus employment placement, Educational Opportunity Programs and Services, campus child care, tutorials, disabled student programs and services, and specialized curriculum offerings such as precollegiate basic skills and English as a Second Language. The board also included reference to populations of students who may need special accommodations, such as ethnic or language minority students and students with disabilities (California State Board of Education and California Community Colleges, 1998; A. Ely, personal communication, March 9, 2007). The Opening Doors project added more developmental aspects: transfer and career counseling, which encompasses aptitude assessment and career planning; personal guidance and counseling, including crisis intervention, mental heath and life-skills counseling; and supplemental services, such as child care subsidies, transportation passes, and book and supply vouchers (Purnell and Blank, 2004, p. 7).

Organizing Student Affairs

Once considered the supplemental administrative services needed to assist students as they made their way through college, student services now play an important role in the total student experience. Student affairs professionals have a complex job, with an understanding of various student cultures their most recent challenge. Lee and Ramsey state: "Multicultural counseling takes into consideration the cultural backgrounds and individual experiences of diverse clients and how their psychosocial needs might be identified and met through counseling" (2006, p. 3). An additional challenge is in addressing the mental health needs of students, as many are arriving on campus with serious medical, psychological, and social problems, and these may not even include the high levels of stress and anxiety experienced by a great many normally functioning people. Student services leaders must be "efficient administrators, effective problem solvers, and sensitive handlers of crisis" (Sandeen, 2004, p. 31).

The student services function is typically organized as a separate administrative division headed by a vice-president or a chief student development officer. Subdivisions may include a dean of students supervising counselors, athletic directors, and coordinators of disability services and student activities. Under their aegis would be student publications and events, along with placement testing, advising, and student rights and responsibilities. A dean of enrollment services would supervise registration, admissions, financial aid, recruitment, high school relations, student records, work-study arrangements, and grants and scholarships.

Recruitment, Orientation, and Retention

Ideally, recruitment, orientation, and retention strategies are an ongoing, unified process. The efforts to engage students in the educational process and in the campus environment often touch prospective students before they arrive on campus. Because the colleges try to serve as many people as feasible, the staff have engaged in extensive recruitment activities. These activities, which accelerated as the population of eighteen-year-olds declined after peaking in the late 1970s, were especially vigorous in communities where the percentage of high school students beginning college decreased. More recently, as the number of high school graduates has grown, the recruitment function has become less pronounced. However, colleges are still actively seeking students, especially those from underrepresented groups.

Most community colleges have links with their surrounding high schools as participation in a recruitment program increases students' likelihood to attend college. These efforts include visiting high school campuses to provide information about college; administering tests in academic subjects and then helping students and their parents interpret the results; providing college facilities for activities attracting high school students; presenting videotaped, online, and personal recruitment promotions; offering advanced placement classes to qualified students; disseminating radio, television, mailed, and online information to potential students informing them about campus events; and even assisting students in the matriculation process by walking them through the admissions, registration, and orientation on site. The idea is that by frontloading students with information about services and activities available to them early on, they will be less likely to drop out since such resources are the keys to retention.

Butte Community College (California) provides an example of such a liaison between the college and local school districts. The forerunner of Butte's liaison programming was an orientation program for high school seniors that offered college-level courses on high school campuses, provided college catalogues and other information, and facilitated assessment tests to high school students (Butte Community College, 1990). Since 1995, Butte's programming has evolved into the Reg to Go program, which provides information to high school students and offers them the opportunity to complete the college matriculation process (B. Zuniga, personal communication, March 28, 2007).

At Sacramento City College (California), a peer-to-peer recruitment program called RISE (Respect, Integrity, Self-Determination, and Education) involves community college students serving as mentors to high school students. RISE students also participate as in-class tutors, assist students struggling with course material, and contact students if they stop attending class (K. Muraki, personal communication, April 26, 2007). Sacramento also has a recruitment program called City Vets specifically targeted at veterans.

Transitional bridge programs are pre-enrollment activities that begin during the summer prior to the students' entering college and may last through the first year. The aim is to help students develop academic skills and make the transition into college through establishing social networks among their peers, as well as to connect students with the college early on. Such programs are in place in a sizeable number of colleges. Examples include Gateway Community College (Arizona), which has a five-week program allowing high school seniors to earn six college credits; Montgomery College (Texas), with a three-week program for students who did not pass the Texas Assessment of Knowledge and Skills; Kapiolani Community College (Hawaii), a four-week orientation, study skills, and math review; Pima Community College's (Arizona) Upward Bound Pre-College Program for low-income students; and a "Native Science and Engineering Program" functioning since 1998 as a cooperative endeavor among institutions in Alaska, Hawaii, and Washington.

For several years, the National Science Foundation has supported a Science, Technology, Engineering, and Mathematics Talent Expansion Program (STEM) that seeks to increase the number of students majoring in and receiving degrees in those fields. The community college–based programs begin with summer bridge activities and continue with first year experience coordination plus curriculum modification in succeeding years. Pasadena City College (California) emphasizes student recruitment, tutoring, and mentoring, as well as faculty development. Kirkwood Community College (Iowa) supports students in making the transition from high school through the two-year curriculum and on to four-year degree programs. Turtle Mountain Community College (North Dakota) awards stipends to tribal students preparing for college-level courses in the STEM areas.

Generalized orientation programs are designed to provide students with a map of educational requirements and services available to them and to connect them with the college. Several formats are popular, including orientation offered during the summer preceding the term, in one- or two-day sessions at the beginning of the term, classes meeting throughout the first term, and seminars for special groups of students. Orientations may provide workshops; various types of interest inventories; registration procedures; discussion of college programs, student services, and resources; advising regarding student strengths and weaknesses; participation in small groups that are led by college leaders; and campus tours.

One college offered a three-day retreat for the first 150 freshmen to sign up with the faculty members who helped in leading the activities. Another maintained a series of weekly lectures on issues of concern to students throughout the term. Bronx Community College (New York), Chaffey Community College (California), and Portland Community College (Oregon) offer semester-long courses to help students develop educational plans, set career goals, implement time management and study skills, take part in tutoring, and understand how to navigate the campus and use resources such as the library (Purnell and Blank, 2004, p. 17). Valencia Community College (Florida) offers an elective, three-credit course called "Student Success." Students who completed this course averaged 6.5 percent higher reenrollment rates between the 2005–06 and 2006–07 academic years (J. Cornett, personal communication, May 11, 2007). Santa Monica College's (California) Student Success Project involves an ongoing orientation, developmental and intrusive advisement, co-curricular experiences, peer support, and tutoring; all of which are co-hosted by instructional and counseling faculty members (Tovar and Simon, 2003). Brevard Community College (Florida) created the First-Year Experience program that includes mandatory advising, educational planning, and career guidance; advising workshops with small groups, as well as individual sessions; and a clear goal of identifying a major. All first-time college students registered for one or more developmental courses at Brevard are assigned a student services mentor who provides additional guidance and helps the student connect with tutoring and other services (Community College Survey of Student Engagement, 2006, p. 19).

Online orientation is an innovation that has grown out of the programmed advising booklets that were popular decades ago. Mount San Antonio College (California) displays an interactive orientation where students browse page by page through relevant campus information examining components of matriculation and take short assessment tests at the end of each of four modules. Information about and direct experience with online counseling with one of the college's full-time advisors are included. In this way, students experience counseling as a requirement of the orientation and are thereby familiar with the service for future use (R. Rodriquez, personal communication, March 28, 2007). If organized correctly and made a requirement for matriculation, students can be required to engage in online counseling, whereas other forced counseling experiences can be negatively perceived. Furthermore, they can be quizzed to fulfill the orientation requirement and ensure understanding and completion of the process. Overall, though, online or in person, orientation programs are most effective when they are well-planned and semester-long or involve ongoing programming, or both.

Efforts to retain underrepresented student populations have given rise to special services such as the Extended Opportunities Programs and Services (EOP&S) program (California), the TRIO Student Support Services (SSS) program (national) for disabled students and those with low socioeconomic status, the CalWORKS Community College program (California) for first-generation, low income, educationally disadvantaged students, the Access to Better Jobs program (Ohio) for nontraditional students, the Puente Project (California) for Latino students, and others. These programs encourage students to become involved with the campus, registration assistance, mandatory multiple counseling sessions, progress monitoring, basic skills and special instruction, needs assessment, tutoring, child care, peer advising, education mentoring, and single-parent support groups.

Counseling and Advising

Counseling and advising have been at the core of student services since the earliest years. Counseling centers were initially developed to assist students "find and effectively use the information, skills, insight, and understanding they need in order to be successful, first and primarily in the college and secondarily, later in life" (Helfgot, 1995, p. 49). The contention has been that students need help moving into the college and out again into careers and other schools, and that individualized instruction through various kinds of counseling and other nonclassroom-based activities, such as academic support in the form of study skills classes, tutoring, and mentoring, is essential. Counseling may exist in a variety of forms, including academic and educational planning; personal counseling for life skills, mental health and other personal concerns that may impede students' academic progress; transfer counseling; career counseling; mentoring, group counseling, and peer advising; direct academic support in the forms of study skills courses, seminars and workshops, tutoring; and online services—and all this with an average full-time student-equivalent ratio of 1 to 434, nationwide (Douglas and Harmening, 1999). On a head-count basis, the ratio is considerably lower. For example, Lorain County Community College (Ohio) had nine full-time academic advisors and six full-time counselors on staff to serve approximately 9,600 students, or about 1,067 students per advisor and 1,600 students per counselor (Scrivener, Wavelet, and Sagness, 2003).

As a key element in student development, counseling must be integrated with other campus activities, focusing on educational, personal, social, and vocational development, and should take into account students' interests, aptitudes, needs, values, and potential. Comprehensive counseling should include goal setting, personality and skills assessments, development of change strategies, strategy implementation, evaluation, and recycling of the whole process for each student, all the while keeping the students' personal goals and interests in view.

This therapeutic view affirms the belief that the best way to educate people is to integrate all their objectives and all their ways of functioning: cognitive, affective, and psychomotor. It holds that students are active and responsible participants in their educational growth and process, and that with help and support they will make decisions that affect their lives and deal with the consequences of their decisions. Assessments of student services' effects are sometimes based on this holistic development model. Measures based on psychological constructs have been applied, and the level of satisfaction that students feel has been a favorite measure. Follow-up studies showing that most students value their college experiences for their contribution to self-understanding, further schooling, social interaction, and job skill training are not uncommon. However, personality development concepts are more applicable in institutions that control most aspects of the person's life. Apparent change in the developing personality is more likely to be revealed in a four-year residential college than in a commuter institution where most students attend part-time. The character-formation, moral-development thread that appeals to many student services professionals seems rather irrelevant in a college where half the entrants drop out before completing one term's worth of credit.

Brick questioned whether psychological counseling is "an educational function which should be implemented by an educational institution, or … a public health function which should be implemented by a public health agency" (1972, p. 677). Students may bring personal problems to counselors such as stress and anxiety, depression, suicide, domestic violence, substance abuse, eating disorders, racism, prejudice, and other concerns of societal marginalization. Those with serious mental health problems may be referred to services off campus. At Cabrillo College (California), counselors engage in a referral process called the Fast-Track-to-Work program whereby students are recommended to visit professionals elsewhere in the community. A few licensed psychologists are staffed at Palomar College (California) counseling center, but they may still make referrals to off-site specialized services (J. Fernandez, personal communication, February 9, 2007).

Academic guidance has always been intended to match applicants to the programs best suited to their own goals and abilities and to help students recognize their academic abilities and limitations in an organized and caring manner. Some colleges take active steps to conduct follow-up on academic progress with students with whom they remain in contact, as is the case at Hazard Community and Technical College (Kentucky). Hazard uses an "early-alert system," in which students may be contacted by phone or mail by the appropriate staff, administrator, or faculty member if they are identified as struggling academically or otherwise (Purnell and Blank, 2004). On the other hand, the counselors engaged in the Opening Doors Project at Kingsborough Community College (New York) acted as the academic early warning system themselves (Gardenhire-Crooks and others, 2006).

Regardless of the concepts undergirding their efforts, academic counselors face unremitting conflict between guiding students into the programs most consonant with their abilities and allowing them to reach for their own preferred goals. Many students want to go in one direction but seem better qualified to go in another, a long-familiar group most recently characterized as "drifting dreamers" or students with "misaligned ambitions" (Schneider and Stevenson, 1999, p. 7).

Transfer counseling assists students by ensuring that they meet associate degree requirements, as well as those of four-year institutions. Transfer counselors may hold information sessions, arrange site visits to four-year college campuses, and offer orientation programs to help students transfer from the environment and culture of the community college to the four-year institution. Most counselors are well versed in the transfer requirements for the major universities and colleges, and many colleges have established distinct transfer centers.

Career counseling links with students' academic goals by assisting students to choose a degree that matches their desired career. Many students' goals in attending school are for career enhancement only, whether that means acquiring work skills or earning a degree or certificate to gain them entry into a given field. In either case, occupational outcome is a high priority for students. However, Cowles (2002) found that counselors spend the greatest percentage of their time on academic and transfer counseling, followed by personal counseling, with career counseling third in emphasis.

Alternative methods for specialized counseling methods include group counseling, mentoring, peer advising, and tutoring. Group counseling is used in some instances to serve specialized needs and problems of students such as eating disorders, abusive relationships, parenting, and alcoholism. Mentoring can involve counselors, administrators, faculty, coaches, community leaders, and alumni who work with students to guide them in personal and career concerns on a more informal basis. Mentors are often matched with students based on their similar interests or backgrounds and take into account students' personal experiences in order to best guide them through the educational and developmental processes. Peer advising usually involves student-to-student guidance for personal, academic, and career concerns; all of which serve a recruitment or retention function. In most cases the peer advisor is trained by student services professionals in a specific area of expertise, whether for social, academic, or mental health support.

Online services are an innovation that may buffer the shortage of student services professionals. They provide an array of benefits both to the counselor and student such as the convenience of access, speed, and comfort. Geisel (2006) states that innovative applications are available for a range of services, including online freshman and course orientations, financial aid, library access, career planning, student news, and testing. At Lorain County Community College (Ohio), online advising is provided under the pseudonym of "Auntie Carol" to answer student queries via e-mail. This option allows the advisor to direct students to one of the college's websites. If the student's concern is too complicated, sensitive in nature, or raises concerns of ethics and confidentiality, the advisor can suggest that the student come in for an appointment.

Counseling and guidance services are less likely to be questioned now because of their presumed usefulness in maintaining student flow into the programs for which they are best suited and on through to successful program completion. Faculty advisors used to sustain the responsibilities now carried out by counselors to assist in educational planning and follow-up but cannot now reasonably be expected to carry the entire burden; in fact, one study found that 21 percent of the students whom the faculty had advised to take certain courses had not met the prerequisites for those courses (Heard, 1987). However, student development theory may be less applicable to the counseling situation because of the wide range of student age. It is difficult to apply concepts of adolescent development when half the students are age twenty-three or older and when students' consistency in attendance is sporadic. In addition, many of the students are responsible not only for their own behavior but also for that of their dependents, and a high proportion of students are employed, often on a full-time basis.

Group-Specific Services

Some colleges maintain centers with counseling and other services available specifically for international students; students with disabilities; lesbian, gay, bisexual, transgender students; and a variety of other student interest groups. All counselors at Santa Monica College (California) are versed in academic and transfer counseling, but its counseling division includes nineteen other distinct services for specific student needs, including those for students with disabilities, student government members and honors students, international students, new students, student athletes, veterans, Black students, Latino students, students from underserved communities, services for specific state-funded assistance programs such as TRIO/Student Support Services and EOP&S, career services, psychological and health counseling, and financial aid counseling (B. J. Benson, personal communication, April 26, 2007). But these extra centers are extremely uneven, ranging from collections of brochures to centers staffed by part-time counselors to those "with trained career counselors providing a range of assessments, inventories, workshops, job placement, and ties to community networks" (Grubb, 2001, p. 8). Minority students are more likely to stay enrolled and progress toward program completion at colleges with "minority inclusive campus environments" and "specialized retention services" that are aligned with mainstream student services, not "small-scale, boutique" programs (Jenkins, 2006, p. 4).

Provisions for students with disabilities are common, especially as state and federal laws mandate that colleges be accessible to that population. All colleges provide access for students with mobility-impairment, which is the most common type of disability at about 26 percent (Ash, 2005). Similarly, most colleges provide assistance for visually or hearing-impaired students and students who experience depression, mental illnesses, or learning disabilities. The range of services for students with disabilities includes adaptive equipment, readers, classroom note takers, interpreters, tutors, alternative exam formats, assistance with registration, and course substitution. According to the National Postsecondary Student Aid Study of 2000, 12 percent of all community college students with disabilities used an alternative exam format, which was the most utilized service, closely followed by the use of tutors. A more recent innovation is online courses especially designed for this population of students. At St. Petersburg College (Florida), this service focuses on simplifying the presentation of online courses by decreasing the number of windows, using straightforward language, limiting excessive movement on Web pages, and synching videos in real time with text (Boulard, 2007).

Twelve percent of the degrees and certificates awarded by the Michigan Community College system in 2002–03 went to students with disabilities.

Student Activities

Community college student activities programs are difficult to popularize because most students have outside jobs, few reside on campus, and many high school student leaders elect to attend universities. Although it is not easy to involve students in activities outside their regularly scheduled classes, various types of extracurricular activities have been in place since the earliest institutions organized student clubs and athletic events. Eells (1931) listed numerous student activities in the junior colleges of the 1920s, mentioning in particular Pasadena Junior College (California), with seventy active clubs. The most popular were athletic clubs, with literary groups, musical activities, and religious and moral organizations following. Today, Pasadena City College students are still involved in over seventy clubs but the types have shifted somewhat toward identity groups such as Chicano students, and gay, lesbian, bisexual, and transgender students. Other activities include community service; environmental issues; student government and publications; and various campus-sponsored events such as speakers, musicians, plays and musicals, dancers and other performers. Elsewhere, cultural and political events, film showings, gaming and arcade areas, leadership programming, and legal advice services are in place, often financed in part by student activity fees.

Low rates of student involvement in extracurricular activities are reflected in the level of student activism on community college campuses. Culturally or ethnically oriented student groups often demonstrate on behalf of hiring more minority instructors or giving more attention to minority concerns in the curriculum. But in most cases, the activism has not reached the level of disruption that it has taken at the universities. Community college activism has generally involved student attempts to be free of restrictive rules on their conduct. Student newspapers have often caused difficulty, especially when an editor or staff writer decides to test the boundaries by printing a provocative article, story, or poem. The college's right to guide student conduct thereupon comes into conflict with First Amendment rules governing freedom of the press, and these cases are sometimes taken up by the students at large as evidence of how the school administration tends to treat them as children.

Student government has many purposes. It may provide student leadership training programs, with workshops on group dynamics and communications skills; involve students as full voting members of faculty committees; assign responsibilities to student government committees; assign faculty members to student organizations as consultants rather than as advisors; allocate funding to student services departments for programming; and instruct student government representatives in procedures for polling student opinion on pertinent issues. It also spills over into coordinating student involvement in community service and student club activities.

As a way of involving more students, some commentators have called for student activities and organizations centering on academic departments. At Harper College (Illinois), administrators of student activities conduct focus groups with students to survey interest in campus activities, but their primary method for organizing events is not based on student interest as much as the need to increase student attendance. This is done by coordinating activities with faculty who can offer extra credit to students who attend events. Faculty may also be willing to feature campus speakers or performers in their classrooms. Though students plan some of their own events at Harper College, attendance is typically higher when an event involves faculty sponsorship (M. Nejman, personal communication, April 17, 2007).

Athletic activities vary widely. Some colleges field intercollegiate teams but nearly all offer intramural sports for interested students and even courses centered on sports activities. Clubs and ad hoc groups organized to engage in hiking, cycling, scuba diving, backpacking, and jogging have become widespread. Exercise classes open to staff members as well as students have also sprung up as the concern for physical fitness has grown among people of all ages. Aerobic dancing, swimming, and weightlifting have gained in popularity. In general, though, small percentages of students participate.

More community colleges are providing leadership programming for students, a trend that is growing at four-year colleges as well. Sandeen states: "Among the most promising student affairs/academic affairs collaborations in recent years have been student leadership-development seminars, inter-group relations retreats, values-development workshops, and programs to improve academic integrity and honor codes" (2004, p. 32). Student leadership participants cite increased confidence in their abilities, leadership skills, and willingness to serve in leadership roles (Cress et al., 2001). Harper College's (Illinois) Excel Leadership program is one such example. It is based on the Social Change Model of Leadership (Astin and Astin, 1995) and includes monthly workshops on topics such as team-building, diversity, and conflict management, along with a service-oriented learning project (M. Nejman, personal communication, April 17, 2007). Harper boasts of high attendance at the workshops and participation in the program but defers partial credit to the fact that many student organizations attend the workshops en masse, which supports the assertion that student activities are most successful if they foster support networks among academics, service, and vocational activities.

Study abroad is another extracurricular activity, often overlooked because of the paucity of students who can afford it. However, many colleges offer programs that are shorter, less expensive, and more flexible than the traditional semester or yearlong programs offered at most four-year institutions. Brookdale

Community College (New Jersey) offers shorter programs, such as five weeks abroad in Ecuador for the study of Spanish and Ecuadorean history (Brookdale website, April 29, 2007). Vocational programs, such as nursing, are sometimes offered as study abroad opportunities, which provide an incentive of utility. Howard Community College (Maryland) has grant money available from endowments made by staff members and other donors for study abroad. Borough of Manhattan Community College (New York) has student activity fees available to offset students' study abroad costs (Blum, 2006). Like their peers at four-year colleges, community college students may seek funds from the federal government as well.

In 2003–04, about 5,800 community college students studied abroad: a number roughly equal to 3 percent of the college students who study abroad each year. Though study abroad programs are promoted at many community colleges, it is not unusual for them to be cancelled outright for lack of student attendance, whether as a result of lack of interest, lack of information, or inability to attend due to financing, child care reasons, and so forth. The College of DuPage (Illinois) aims to curtail misinformation that students and their parents may have about study abroad by hosting informational events, as well as making the opportunity to study abroad more feasible for students by offering brief two- to three-week programs. It also has a faculty committee that raises funds on behalf of students interested in studying abroad (Zinta Konrad, personal communication, April 26, 2007).

Financial Aid

Federal financial aid to students began with the Servicemen's Readjustment Act (GI Bill) in 1944 and was expanded with the National Defense Education Act in 1958, but the community colleges were slow to seek these funds. Not until passage of the Basic Educational Opportunity Grant (now called Pell Grants) program in 1972 did the majority of community colleges organize financial aid offices. One reason for the slow start was the misperception that because of the comparatively low cost of community college education, students did not need financial assistance. However, students still had to spend money to live, still commuted to classes, and, by attending school, were forgoing income that they could otherwise have earned. Furthermore, since community college students were typically from lower-income groups, their needs were greater even though the cost of college going was less. By the 1980s, the financial aid offices in most community colleges had gained the ability to direct grants and loans to students who needed them. In the 1990s, student aid increased dramatically as the availability of state grants grew more rapidly than the federal funds.

Financial aid for students is now an outstanding feature throughout higher education and affects student decisions both in enrolling initially and in maintaining continuing attendance. Federal and state funds administered through Pell Grants, Supplemental Educational Opportunity Grants, Guaranteed Student Loans, College Work-Study Aid, and State Student Incentive Grants, to name only some of the programs, have grown so that any shift in their availability has an immediately discernible impact on enrollments. Aid is so much a part of the college system that when the California legislature mandated a $100 per year fee to be paid by community college students, it made $52.5 million available as student aid in the same bill (California State Postsecondary Education Commission, 1984).

Still, because of the relatively low tuition costs and because of various aid program restrictions, such as discrimination against part-time or non-degree-credit attendees, community college students have not received their proportionate share of financial aid. From the mid-1970s through the mid-1980s, the federal scholarship and fellowship funds received by community college students remained at around 16 percent of the total awards, if the proprietary schools were not included, even though the colleges enrolled over 25 percent of all full-time students and an even higher percentage of the part-timers. In 2003–04, 49 percent of full-time community college students received federal aid compared to 62 percent of all full-time students enrolled in higher education. This proportion varied greatly between states, depending on the percentage of a state's students enrolled in community colleges and the relative level of tuition charged. Students in community colleges in Arizona, Florida, Mississippi, and Oregon received more than 25 percent of the scholarship funds going to college students in those states, whereas those in Maine, New Hampshire, and Louisiana, with relatively low community college enrollments, received less than 5 percent of the grant monies (NCES *Digest*, 1986, 2005). Students in Maryland community colleges were receiving 21 percent of the total aid awarded to undergraduates in the state; Illinois students received 17 percent of the aid distributed in that state; Texas students received 13 percent. However, when compared to the percentage of the students enrolled in community colleges in those three states, the figures are low.

The total number of students receiving aid also varies among states. In 2003–04, 42 percent of public two-year college students in California received some kind of aid, compared with 51 percent of those in Alabama. The national average was 47 percent. Among full-time students, 62 percent received aid: 49 percent of them received federal aid; 18 percent, state; 14 percent, institutional; and 15 percent, other. Among part-timers, 44 percent received aid: 28 percent, federal; 9 percent, state; 6 percent, institutional; 14 percent, other (NCES *Digest*, 2005). As of 2005, three states were allowing undocumented students access to financial aid and nine were granting in-state tuition privileges.

Many states have sought to increase funds and make procedures more navigable. Connecticut streamlined its student aid system, thereby doubling the percentage of students receiving financial aid from 20 to 42 percent between 2001 and 2007. Since centralizing financial aid services for the entire Connecticut

Community College System, administrators have seen a 64 percent increase in aid applications, a 63 percent increase in Pell Grant recipients, a total of $46 million in financial aid awarded to 19,200 students in 2005–06, and a 21 percent increase in minority enrollment since 2001 (Prince, 2006). New Jersey also saw increases in its financial assistance programs. The New Jersey student tuition assistance rewards scholarship program showed an increase of more than 50 percent between 2005 and 2006 in students receiving assistance through the program: a total of 3,100 students. High school seniors graduating in the top 20 percent of their class are eligible for the state scholarship. The program also allows students who meet all transfer requirements to enter as juniors in the state's public four-year institutions and have their tuition and fees covered for the last two years toward a bachelor's degree (Chappell, Jan. 19, 2007).

The U.S. Department of Education regulates federally funded guaranteed loans, which have a maximum of less than $18,000 and an interest rate capped at 6.8 percent, but not private loans, which carry variable rates (like credit cards) up to 20 percent. Students may borrow as much as a bank will advance them. Since 2005, federal law has precluded students from declaring bankruptcy as a way of discharging their student loan debt (Lederman, June 7, 2007).

Funding and Effectiveness

Student services for adult students (defined as those working at least twenty-five hours per week or responsible for one or more dependents) have expanded. Child care services have become widespread, and offices have been opened to assist students with various types of disabilities. Job placement services, always a feature in community colleges, have grown as the proportion of students seeking immediate job entry has increased. Student services also have been extended to accommodate an increase in the prevalence of entrance testing.

For the first time in the history of the community college, the 1980s saw a trend toward funding student services on soft money—that is, extracurricular funds targeted to assist certain types of students. In some cases, special state funds have been made available. In others, Vocational Education Act funds, Title III monies, EOP&S funds, and various state and federal programs supporting disabled students and those in other special categories have been used. Although the student affairs division might be organized on a line-and-staff basis, the subordinate offices might expand or contract with the availability of funds to support them.

The effectiveness of student services has been a perennial issue. Student access and success are assessed regularly, and these variables may be taken into consideration by state policymakers and local college officials in policy decisions and budget allocations. But with student services, evaluation largely depends on reports from students about how well they perceive the usefulness of one or another aspect. Students at Howard Community College (Maryland) gave high marks to all services; however, when those ratings were combined with students' level of involvement with or use of the services, only academic advising received a high rank, at a 97 percent satisfaction rate, whereas all other student services fell below 50 percent. Nationally, 43 percent of the students said that faculty were their best source for academic advising, and 26 percent indicated "friends, family, and other students." Students in developmental programs were more likely than others to find the services "very important" (Community College Survey of Student Engagement [CCSSE], 2006, pp. 17–18).

Evaluation of student services is typically not well conceived. The evaluators often try to assess everything in the student services purview: orientation, counseling, financial aid, student activities, testing—all different forms of service, all different purposes and conceptual bases. Asking the students, "How well did each of these services meet your expectations?" is not useful.

Most students were never touched by most of the services; for example, studies often find that half the dropouts never saw a counselor.

More sophisticated evaluations have been tried recently, particularly attempts to determine how student retention and achievement are affected. The evaluations are made in terms of each service or cluster of services separately. One study found that in order to promote student success, student services such as orientation, advising, early warning systems, and academic support services need to be coordinated with other divisions and programs throughout the campus (Jenkins, 2006). Most studies of orientation and advising have found a positive relationship between completing orientation and retention and graduation, as well as between advisor-student contact and increased retention and graduation. After instituting the full-time Advisors in Residence program in seven departments at St. Philip's College (Texas), in two and a half years the number of associate degrees and certificates awarded increased by 68 percent. At Sinclair Community College (Ohio), the Individual Learning Plan (ILP) was implemented by counselors to assist new students with career selection and plans to pay for educational expenses. Between 2003 and 2005, ILP students were found to have consistently higher retention rates than non-ILP students and all first-time degree-seeking students, and furthermore, the students reported that ILP helped them overcome obstacles (CCSSE, 2006, p. 19). In general, the more that students used services, the more successful they were, a finding confirming the adage that research is often a way of lending credence to what we already know.

Issues

As a whole, the colleges' services to students have grown faster than the instructional activities, but the various services have shown different patterns. Counseling and guidance declined early in the 1970s in response to students' demands to be admitted to courses of their choice and to the increase in part-time students, but these services increased in the 1980s as tight budgets forced the colleges into streamlining their procedures for guiding students through the system. Recruitment and retention also became prominent concerns of the student affairs personnel, who gradually adopted concepts other than those set down by theorists whose model was the full-time resident student. Student activities supporters especially have had difficulty in converting their programs to fit students who are on campus for only an hour or two at a time.

One issue affecting not only student services but other programs as well is the way they are conceptualized. As an example, student recruitment, retention, orientation, graduation, and transfer or job placement should be organized not as discrete activities but as part of a whole process. And each should be viewed as it contributes to the overall process of meeting the students as individuals and sending them on to further pursuits. This type of overall coordination has been growing, but haltingly.

The challenge for college leaders has been to maintain a balance among all services and coordinate them with the formal instructional program. But issues of educational philosophy swirl around the questions of student services work. How much responsibility does the college have for the lives of its students? How personalized can an institution dedicated to mass education afford to get?

Although between-sector comparisons are precarious because of differences in institutional mission, the question of whether community college students receive as much financial aid as their university counterparts has not been resolved, nor has the question of whether undocumented students should be eligible.

Answers to these questions will determine the future course of student services in the community colleges. As with all other questions about the types of services colleges provide, the answers rest on the energy and political skills of the advocates of one or another activity. And that, above all, is why the services vary as much as they do in colleges across the country.

Much of the funding for student services is obtained through grants directed toward assisting special student groups. This soft-money base makes it difficult to build sustaining assistance, yet student services are still rarely perceived as deserving the type of permanent funding on which the instructional programs are based. Can that support be built?

8

Vocational Education

Occupational Entry, Change, and Development

A group of prominent citizens called together in 1964 by the American Association of Junior Colleges (AAJC) to serve as a National Advisory Committee on the Junior College concluded that "the two-year college offers unparalleled promise for expanding educational opportunity through the provision of comprehensive programs embracing job training as well as traditional liberal arts and general education" (American Association of Junior Colleges, 1964, p. 14). The committee recommended that "immediate steps be taken to reinforce occupational education efforts" (p. 1), a statement similar to those emanating from many other commissions and advisory groups, including the AAJC's own Commission on Terminal Education a quarter-century earlier. Its words were notable only because they came at a time when the floodgates had just opened and a tide of vocational education programs was beginning to inundate the two-year colleges.

The year 1963 marked the passage of the federal Vocational Education Act, which broadened the criteria for federal aid to the schools. Along with the new criteria, Congress appropriated funds generously—$43 million in 1968, $707 million in 1972, and $981 million in 1974—and these funds were augmented with additional monies for vocational programs for the disadvantaged and for students with disabilities. On this surge of funding, occupational education swept into the colleges in a fashion dreamed of and pleaded for but never previously realized by its advocates.

In this chapter, we consider various aspects of vocational education, including the growth, successes, and limitations of courses and programs designed to lead to initial job entry with no further schooling or to modify the skills of people who have already been employed. Also covered are the broader implications of vocational education: Is it a deterrent to baccalaureate seekers? How can its social benefits and individual benefits be disaggregated? How successful are students in obtaining employment in the fields for which they have been prepared?

Early Development

One of the criteria for professionalization is the number of years of schooling that a group requires before allowing neophytes to enter their rank. A major impetus to the expansion of higher education early in the century was the drive toward professional status made by numerous occupational groups. And as these professions developed, a set of auxiliary or support occupations, sometimes called semiprofessional, developed around them. Professional training moved into the university, but the training of the auxiliaries remained outside. The community colleges grew in part because some of their earlier proponents recognized the coming need for semiprofessionals and despaired of the universities' adjusting rapidly enough to provide this less-than-baccalaureate education.

Calls for vocational education in the two-year colleges had been made from their earliest days. In 1900, William Rainey Harper, president of the University of Chicago, suggested that "many students who might not have the courage to enter upon a course of four years' study would be willing to do the two years of work before entering business or the professional school" (cited by Brick, 1965, p. 18). The founders of the junior colleges in California postulated that one purpose of their institutions was to provide terminal programs in agriculture, technical studies, manual training, and the domestic arts. Alexis Lange (1927) indicated that the junior colleges would train the technicians occupying the middle ground between manual laborers and professional people, and Koos (1924) described and applauded the occupational curricula in the junior colleges of the early 1920s.

Arguments on behalf of vocational education were raised at the earliest gatherings of the AAJC. At its organizational meeting in 1920 and at nearly every meeting throughout the 1920s and 1930s, occupational education was on the agenda. Brick traced these discussions and noted that "the AAJC was aware that it had to take a leadership role in directing the movement for terminal education" (1965, p. 120). He quoted C. C. Colvert, president of the association, who, in a 1941 address, had admonished junior college educators for not encouraging the national government to fund occupational education for people of junior college age: "Had not we of the junior college been so busy trying to offer courses which would get our graduates into the senior colleges instead of working and offering appropriate and practical courses—terminal courses—for the vast majority of junior college students, we might have thought to ask for, and as a result of having asked, received the privilege of training these young people" (cited by Brick, 1965, p. 121).

The thesis of Brint and Karabel's book *The Diverted Dream* (1989) is that the AAJC was the prime force in effecting a change in community college emphasis from prebaccalaureate to terminal-occupational education. The extent to which local school boards and college leaders were attentive to the national association is debatable, but there is no doubt that AAJC had been diligent. In 1939, it created the Commission on Junior College Terminal Education, which proceeded to study terminal (primarily vocational) education, hold workshops and conferences on its behalf, and issue three books summarizing junior college efforts in its area of interest. Much had been done, but as the commission noted, more remained to do: "At the present time probably about one-third of all the curricular offerings in the junior colleges of the country are in the nonacademic or terminal fields. Doubtless this situation is far short of the ideal, but it shows a steady and healthy growth in the right direction" (Eells, 1941a, pp. 22–23).

In 1940, terminal programs were offered in about 70 percent of the colleges. The most popular were business and secretarial studies, music, teaching, general courses, and home economics. Over one-third of the terminal students were in business studies; enrollments in agriculture and home economics were quite low. Tables 8.1 and 8.2 present data on the numbers of colleges and programs.

Definitions

The terminology of vocational education has never been exact: the words *terminal, vocational, technical, semiprofessional, occupational,* and *career* have all been used interchangeably or in combination, as in vocational-technical. To the commission and the colleges of 1940, *terminal* meant all studies not applicable to the baccalaureate, but programs designed to lead to employment dominated the category. Earlier, *vocational* had generally been used for curricula preparing people for work in agriculture, the trades, and sales. *Semiprofessional* typically referred to engineering technicians, general assistants, laboratory technicians, and other people in manufacturing, business, and service occupations. *Technical* implied preparation for work in scientific and industrial fields. *Occupational* seemed to encompass the greatest number of programs and was used most often for all curricula leading to employment. *Career* education was coined in the 1950s to connote lower-school efforts at orienting young people toward the workplace. The title was applied to several programs sponsored by the U.S. Office of Education after Sidney Marland became commissioner in 1970. Currently, terminal is no longer in use, but all the other terms are. *Vocational* adorns most governmental acts concerned with this area of the curriculum.

Table 8.1.   Percentage of Total Curricular Offerings Classified as Terminal or Vocational in Junior Colleges, 1917–1937

Investigator	All Junior Colleges		Public Junior Colleges		Private Junior Colleges	
	Number of Colleges	Percentage of Offerings Terminal	Number of Colleges	Percentage of Offerings Terminal	Number of Colleges	Percentage of Offerings Terminal
McDowell (1917)	47	14	9	18	28	9
Koos (1921)	58	29	23	31	35	25
Hollingsworth-Eells (1930)	279	32	129	33	150	29
Colvert (1937)	—	—	195	35	—	—

Source: Eells, 1941a, p. 22.

Table 8.2. Number of Students Enrolled in Each Terminal Field, 1938–39

Number Enrolled in Group	Number Enrolled in All Terminal Curricula	General Cultural	Agriculture	Business	Engineering	Fine Arts	Health Services	Home Economics	Journalism	Public Service	Misc.
All institutions	41,507	6,205	1,673	14,511	4,449	3,406	1,603	1,387	808	6,500	965
Public	30,261	4,724	1,631	11,278	3,915	2,341	1,029	876	673	3,033	761
Private	11,246	1,481	42	3,233	534	1,065	574	511	135	3,467	204

Source: Eells, 1941a, p. 239.

Although the college-parallel (collegiate) function was dominant in community colleges until the late 1960s, the structure for vocational education had been present from the start. The community college authorization acts in most states had tended to recognize both. The California District Law of 1921 allowed junior colleges to provide college preparatory instruction; training for agricultural, industrial, commercial, homemaking, and other vocations; and civic and liberal education. The comparable 1937 Colorado act defined a junior college as an institution providing studies beyond the twelfth grade along with vocational education. Mississippi required that the junior college curriculum include agriculture, home economics, commerce, and mechanical arts. By 1940, nearly half of the states' junior college laws specifically set forth the terminal functions along with the college-parallel studies. The national and regional accrediting associations of the time also wrote that provision into their rules.

Enrollments in vocational programs did not reach parity with those in collegiate studies, however; well into the 1950s, they accounted for only one-fourth or less of the whole. In 1929, 20 percent of the students in California and 23 percent in Texas were in terminal programs (Eells, 1941a, p. 24), and not all of those were in occupational studies; the figures include high school postgraduate courses for "civic responsibility." Eells reported 35 percent in terminal curricula in 1938, but when nonvocational terminal curricula were excluded, the percentage dropped to less than 25, a figure that held constant until 1960. Although 75 percent of students entering junior college as freshmen did not continue beyond the sophomore year and hence were terminal students by definition, only about one-third of them were enrolled in terminal curricula. "The difference of these two figures shows that more than 40 per cent of all junior college students are enrolled in curricula which are not planned primarily to best meet their needs" (p. 59).

Limitations on Expansion

Why did the vocational programs fail to flourish before the 1960s? First, their terminal nature was emphasized, and that tended to turn potential students away; few wanted to foreclose their option for further studies. For most students, going to college meant striving for the baccalaureate, the "legitimate" degree. That concept of collegiate education had been firmly established.

Another handicap to the growth of vocational programs was the small size of the colleges. Average enrollment remained below one thousand until 1946. Colleges with low enrollments could not offer many occupational courses; the costs were too high. Eells reported a direct relation between size and occupational enrollments. Small colleges (up to 99 students) had 10 percent in terminal curricula; medium colleges (100–499 students), 32 percent; large colleges (500–999), 34 percent; and very large colleges (1,000 and over), 38 percent (Eells, 1941a).

A third reason for limited terminal offerings was the association of many early junior colleges with high schools. In these colleges, administrators favored collegiate courses because they were more attractive to high school students than vocational courses, they entailed no new facilities or equipment, they could be combined with fourth-year high school courses in order to bolster enrollments, and they would not require the hiring of new teachers.

The prestige factor was important. Most of the new junior colleges were opened in cities and towns where no college had existed before. Citizens and educators alike wanted theirs to be a "real college." If it could not itself offer the bachelor's degree, it could at least provide the first two years of study leading toward one. In the eyes of the public, a college was not a manual-training shop. Costs were an important factor. Many vocational programs used expensive, special facilities: clinics, machine tools, automotive repair shops, welding equipment. By comparison, collegiate studies were cheap. The transfer courses had always been taught in interchangeable classrooms. The same chairs and chalkboards, and often the same teachers, can be used for English, history, or mathematics.

And last, the secondary schools of the 1920s and 1930s provided education in shop trades, agriculture, secretarial skills, bookkeeping, and salesmanship. Vocational education in community colleges could not grow until employers in these fields began demanding some postsecondary experience and until the health, engineering, and electronic technologies gained prominence.

For all these reasons, and despite the efforts of Eells and his commission and subsequent AAJC activities, college leaders did not rally around the calls for terminal occupational studies. In some states—Mississippi, for example, where occupational education was a requisite, and California, where the institutions were large enough to mount comprehensive programs in both occupational and collegiate studies—occupational education did well. But in the smaller institutions in states where the popularizing function, that of promoting higher education, was dominant, sizable vocational programs were not developed until much later.

Growth

Vocational education enrollments began growing at a rate greater than liberal arts enrollments in the 1960s and continued to do so for twenty years. This rise is attributable to many causes: the legacy left by early leaders of the junior college movement and the importunities, goading, and sometimes barbs of later leaders; the Vocational Education Act of 1963 and later amendments; the increase in the size of public two-year colleges; the increase in part-time, women, disadvantaged, disabled, and older students; the community colleges' absorption of adult education programs and postsecondary occupational programs formerly operated by the secondary schools; and the changing shape of the labor market.

The Vocational Education Act was not the first to run federal funds to two-year colleges. The 1939 Commission on Junior College Terminal Education had noted that at least sixty-two junior colleges in fourteen states were receiving federal funds that had been appropriated under the 1917 Smith-Hughes Act and the 1937 George-Deen Act. The federal monies were earmarked for institutions where education was less than college grade: "It does not mean that the institution must be of less than college grade—only that the particular work offered, for which federal aid is received, must be of less than college grade" (Eells, 1941a, p. 29). The U.S. Office of Education called programs of trade and industrial education less than college grade if college entrance requirements were not prerequisites for admission, the objective was to prepare for employment in industry, the program did not lead to a degree, and the program was not required to conform to conditions governing a regular college course. According to Dougherty (1988), as early as 1937, the AAJC was lobbying for the repeal of the provision restricting support to programs of less than college grade.

The 1963 Vocational Education Act and the amendments of 1968 and 1972 vastly augmented the federal funds available to community colleges. Other federal programs provided additional funds that the community colleges shared: the Comprehensive Training and Employment Administration (1973), Job Training Partnership Act (1982), and Carl D. Perkins Vocational Education Act (1984). Subsequent years saw Job Opportunities and Basic Skills, Omnibus Trade and Competitiveness, Worksite Literacy, and Cooperative Education—programs that were superseded, modified, or extended when the School-to-Work Opportunities Act of 1994 and the Workforce Investment Act of 1998 were added to the set. In 1994, the Advanced Technical Education program was passed and the National Science Foundation subsequently funded more than 200 programs, along with laboratory improvements. In summation, several specific acts were marked clearly for workforce preparation and occupational studies, whereas most federal funds dedicated to other types of education were run through Pell grants and loan programs directed toward individual students. The federal government's direction was evident.

The states were active as well. In Illinois, where many of the new districts were formed on the promise to the electorate of having more than 50 percent of the programs in career education, 1,871 curricula, or 66 percent of all curricula, were occupational (Illinois Community College Board, 1976). In Florida, associate degree and certificate occupational programs exceeded two hundred. The small Hawaii system offered eighty different programs. As detailed in McCabe's 1997 review, "The states . . . are better positioned than the federal government to reform workforce development. Although workforce reform has traditionally centered on federally funded programs, state expenditures for these efforts far exceed federal monies" (p. 9).

Although many individual colleges offered one hundred or more different occupational programs, those that led to the greatest variety of career options were the most popular. Programs in business drew the most students because of the breadth of opportunity they presented. The health professions and the engineering technologies drew large numbers of students because of the expanding base of the professions in those areas and the ever-growing need for support staff. Computer science became popular in the 1980s because of the rapidly expanding applications of computers in all career fields. Other programs ebbed and flowed depending on job markets.

The growth in students with disabilities and part-time, women, disadvantaged, and older students also reflected the rise in occupational enrollments. Disadvantaged and disabled students were encouraged to enroll in occupational programs through special grants funded by a succession of federal acts. A national study conducted in response to Perkins legislation reported that 43 percent of the total community college student population and more than half of the disadvantaged and disabled students were enrolled in vocational education programs. Ninety-three percent of the colleges were providing such programs and of those, 80 percent were receiving funds appropriated under the Perkins Act. The colleges were averaging twenty-seven vocational programs each, with federal funds accounting for 18 percent of the cost. Other support was coming from the states (47 percent), tuition (19 percent), and local funds (15 percent) (*Vocational Education*, 1993).

Some of the enrollment increases resulted from the upgrading of institutions and the transfer to the community colleges of functions formerly performed by other segments of education: secondary and adult schools, technical institutes, and area vocational schools or centers. This trend was most marked in Florida, where fourteen of the twenty-eight community colleges had a department designated as an area vocational education school, and others had cooperative agreements with school boards that operate area vocational-technical centers; in Iowa, where all the public community colleges were merged with area schools; in Nebraska, where the state was divided into technical community college areas; in North Carolina, where the technical institutes were part of the community college system; and in Chicago where the adult and vocational education programs were transferred from the city schools to the community college system (Lombardi, 1975).

The combination of these forces counteracted to a considerable degree those forces that caused students and their parents to value the baccalaureate over the occupational programs. In its statewide master plan for 1978 to 1987, the Maryland State Board for Community Colleges reported that the "increasing emphasis on occupational programs reflected changing values and attitudes among students and their families as to the level of education required to qualify for desirable employment opportunities. This shift was reflected in national projections predicting that throughout the next decade, 80 percent of available jobs would require less than the bachelor's degree" (1977, p. 34). U.S. Department of

Labor data listed as the main areas of job openings in the 1980s retail salesclerks, cashiers, stock handlers, and similar jobs for which a bachelor's degree is not required; "Managers and Administrators" was the only job category in the top fifteen to suggest baccalaureate training (Kuttner, 1983).

Stability

The growth in occupational enrollments that began in the second half of the 1960s is revealed in the enrollment figures shown in Table 8.3. Obviously, this percentage increase could not continue indefinitely, and it began leveling off in the 1980s. The 1991 Center for the Study of Community Colleges (CSCC) survey found that 44 percent of the class sections offered nationwide were in occupational curricula; the 1998 survey found 45 percent. Enrollment in career programs in Illinois stabilized at 34 percent of the head count in 1983 and has remained there. Florida's 33 percent has also been consistent. Washington's and Michigan's held steady at around 40 percent from the early to the

Table 8.3. Enrollments in Terminal-Occupational Programs in Two-Year Colleges as a Percentage of Total Enrollments, 1963–1975

Year	Total Enrollments	Terminal-Occupational Program Enrollments	Percentage of Total
1963	847,572	219,766	26
1965	1,176,852	331,608	28
1969	1,981,150	448,229	23
1970	2,227,214	593,226	27
1971	2,491,420	760,590	31
1972	2,670,934	873,933	33
1973	3,033,761	1,020,183	34
1974	3,428,642	1,134,896	33
1975	4,001,970	1,389,516	35

Source: National Center for Education Statistics, 1963–1975.

late 1990s, but both increased subsequently. By 1992, the ratio of occupational-curricula degrees to all degrees awarded had fallen back to the 1979 figure of just over 60 percent, where it remained throughout the 1990s and then declined, primarily because of the increase in bachelor's degree-seeking students (see Table 8.4).

Because of frequent changes in ways of classifying programs and enrollments, it is perilous to compare data between states or even within the same state in successive years. As an example, Indiana's Ivy Tech Community College, which formerly awarded diplomas in vocational fields exclusively, has begun college transfer programs and in 2005–06 awarded nearly 7,000 degrees and certificates, half of them associate in science degrees (Ivy Tech, 2007). For that reason, the national data shown in Table 8.3 cannot reasonably be updated beyond 1975. The wide variation among states results partly because of varying community college missions and partly because enrollment data are not reported uniformly between states: the unit of measurement—head count, or full-time-student equivalent—varies, and some reports indicate opening fall enrollments, whereas others report fiscal year enrollments. The data have been unstable also because the higher funding patterns for vocational education encouraged colleges to designate as vocational many programs that had been classified previously as general education or liberal arts. In order to show high enrollment in career programs, educators also may have classified as occupational students those who took one occupational course, even though they were actually majoring in a liberal arts transfer program.

Although only a minority of community college matriculants complete programs, the figures on associate degrees awarded provide a measure of the popularity of vocational education. Tables 8.4 and 8.5 show the percentage of career-related degrees and the fields in which awards were made. Associate degrees conferred showed liberal and visual arts increasing from 34 percent of total awards in 1996–97 to 38 percent in 2003–04. Business,

Table 8.4.   Associate Degrees Conferred by Institutions of Higher Education by Type of Curriculum, 1970–71 to 2003–04

Year	All Curricula	Arts and Sciences or General Programs	Percentage of Total	Occupational Curricula	Percentage of Total
1970–71	253,635	145,473	57	10,862	43
1973–74	347,173	165,520	48	181,653	52
1976–77	409,942	172,631	42	237,311	58
1979–80	405,378	152,169	38	253,209	63
1982–83	456,441	133,917	29	322,524	71
1984–85	454,712	127,387	28	327,325	72
1987–88	435,085	148,466	34	286,619	66
1991–92	504,321	195,238	39	309,083	61
1995–96	555,216	211,822	38	343,394	62
1999–00	564,933	249,975	44	314,958	56
2003–04	665,301	308,064	46	357,237	54

Source: NCES Digest, 2005.

management, and marketing degrees dropped from 19 percent to 14 percent, while degrees in computer and information sciences increased from 2 percent to 6 percent. Overall, occupationally oriented degrees accounted for 54 percent of the awards.

Much of the shifting in awards has been related to the process of certification. A student wishing to enter a career as a health service worker or a laboratory technician often must present the degree, whereas for the student wishing to transfer credits to the university, the associate in arts degree is usually superfluous; the student need only show a transcript of courses completed.

In summation, linking data from state reports with national data on degrees awarded and on program and course enrollments yields a figure of 40 to 45 percent for the community colleges' overall degree-credit effort in areas designed for direct employment.

Table 8.5.   Main Fields in Which Associate Degrees Were Conferred, 2003–04

Main Fields	Associate Degrees	Percentage of Total
Liberal arts, general studies, and humanities	227,650	34
Health professions and related sciences	106,208	16
Business, management, and marketing	92,065	14
Computer and information science	41,845	6
Engineering and engineering-related technologies	39,652	6
Visual and performing arts	23,949	4
Security and protective services	20,573	3
Mechanics and repairers	12,553	2

Source: NCES *Digest,* 2005.

This ratio has been steady since the mid-1970s, declining slightly as more vocational education moves into noncredit offerings and into prebaccalaureate programs in health, high tech, and law enforcement, increasing slightly when additional funds, such as those provided through federal programs for special purposes or special populations, become available.

Program Success

Career programs are established with the intention of preparing students for employment and serving industries by supplying them with trained workers. The college staff presumably initiate programs by perusing employment trends in the local area and surveying employers. Program coordinators are appointed and advisory committees composed of trade and employer representatives are established. Funds are often secured through priorities established by state and federal agencies. The entire process suggests rational program planning. Nonetheless, questions have been raised about the appropriateness of certain programs and whether the matriculants are well served, and much research on program effects has been mandated by state and federal funding agencies.

Most students in vocational programs seem satisfied with the training they receive. Follow-up studies routinely find 80 to 90 percent of the program graduates saying that they were helped and that they would recommend the program to others. Among the students who do not complete the program, a sizable number usually indicate that they dropped out because they received all the training they needed in the courses they took, not because they were dissatisfied with the program. Employers seem satisfied as well. Respondents to surveys of businesses and industries usually give high marks to community college–based training programs. A national study found 90 percent or so of the employers saying that the colleges' "quality of training provided," "responsiveness to employer needs," and "cost of training" were "Good" or "Excellent" (Quinley and Cantrell, 1998). Surveys of major employers of recent graduates in Tennessee received "overwhelming positive results, ranging from satisfied to very satisfied" (Tennessee Higher Education Commission, 2003, p. 3), but the employers appear to be less satisfied with communication skills . . . than with other skills" (p. 3). In 2005–06, 97 percent of responding employers of community college graduates in North Carolina said they were satisfied with their job preparation (North Carolina Community College System, 2007b).

Several statewide data sets showing the number of students who obtain employment are available. Among Wisconsin Technical College graduates, one year later, 76 percent of those employed were in jobs related to their training (Wisconsin Technical College System, 2006). The numbers of employed graduates elsewhere were 81 percent in Illinois and Washington; 78 percent in Connecticut; 70 percent in Wyoming; 85 percent in Florida; and 99.58 percent(!) in North Carolina (Illinois Community College Board, 2000; Washington State Board for Community and Technical Colleges, 2006; Connecticut

Department of Higher Education, 2006; Wyoming Community College Commission, 2004; Florida Department of Education, 2007; North Carolina Community College System, 2006). But the reliability of these types of data is dubious. The employer satisfaction reports invariably rest on response rates from a minority of those surveyed. The employment studies may or may not include students continuing their education; those working in fields unrelated to the programs in which they were enrolled; their initial intentions; whether they received a degree or certificate; students in prison; those for whom data are missing; and those working out of state.

Furthermore, the data on program success must be interpreted in the light of the programs' features and the students enrolled. The number of students who are already employed and enter vocational programs only to get additional skills must be factored in. Students who leave before completing the programs and enter employment in the field for which they are prepared should be considered program successes; these "job outs" account for as many as 75 percent of the students in some programs (E. Powers, personal communication, Sept. 26, 2006). Students who graduate but do not obtain employment because they have entered related baccalaureate programs should not be counted among the unemployed. And it is misleading to categorize vocational programs as a unitary group, because there are high- and low-status programs. Also, there are programs preparing people for areas of high demand, such as health care and law enforcement, and programs in areas for which the market is not as distinct, such as real estate or retail trade. Much depends also on the time that has elapsed since the students were enrolled; the ordinary drift of careers suggests that fewer students will be employed in jobs related to their program several years after they have left college.

Some critics of vocational education are concerned that the programs do little in equalizing status and salaries among types of jobs. They view with alarm the high dropout rates without realizing that program completion is an institutional artifact. The degree is not as important as the skills that the applicant manifests. To the student who seeks a job in the field, completing the program becomes irrelevant as soon as a job is available. The categories "graduate" and "dropout" lose much of their force when viewed in this light. This phenomenon is not peculiar to community colleges: generations of young women participated in teacher-training programs in universities even though few of them expected to teach more than a few years and fewer than half entered teaching at all. If one merely surveys the vocational program graduates who are working in that area or places graduates in one category and dropouts or job outs in another, the true services rendered by those programs may be lost.

Few critics of vocational education acknowledge that questions about its value are much more complex than simplistic data on job entry and first salary earned can answer. What is the value of a vocational program when an enrollee hears about an available job, obtains it, and leaves after two weeks? In that case, the program has served as an employment agency of sorts. What is the value of a program in which a person who already has a job spends a few weeks learning some new skills and then receives a better job in the same company? There the program has served as a step on a career ladder. What of the person who enrolls to sharpen skills and gain confidence to apply for a job and ends up doing essentially the same work but for a different company? And what of the students who enter occupational programs but then transfer to other programs in the same or a different college?

A curriculum is a conduit through which people move in order to prepare themselves to do or be something other than what they were. Yet for some people, the curriculum has served an essential purpose if it but allows them to matriculate and be put in touch with those who know where jobs may be obtained; and, indeed, half or more of the students who obtain jobs learn of them through their program contacts, in many cases where, as Rosenfeld notes, "close ties between faculty and employers and informal labor market information networks make traditional college placement services superfluous" (1998, p. 18). At the other extreme are the students who go all the way through the curriculum and learn the skills but either fail to obtain jobs in the field for which they were trained or, having attained them, find them unsatisfying. For them, the institution has been a failure. The critics cannot seem to accommodate the fact that for many dropouts, the program has succeeded, while for many of its graduates, it has failed.

Success may be measured in many ways. Bailey, Alfonso, Scott, and Leinbach analyzed data from three national longitudinal studies and found the completion or transfer rates for occupational entrants to be between 7 and 11 percent lower than for students in academic programs, even after controlling for their background characteristics and enrollment patterns "that are identified with local levels of completion in college. One reason could be that many of them are seeking specific skills rather than degrees" (2004, p. 4). Other studies of both graduates and nongraduates of vocational programs have shown that although most enrolled to obtain job entry skills, many sought advancement in jobs they already held.

Around 60 percent of the respondents to a survey of career program completers in a Kansas community college gave "prepare to enter job market" or "to change careers" as their reason for enrolling, whereas 13 percent had sought to improve their skills in jobs they already held (Conklin, 2000); comparable figures at a Wisconsin Technical College were 63 percent and 12 percent (Waukesha County, 1999). The figures on job skill upgrading are notably steady; 11 percent of the students in vocational programs in California in 1979 had enrolled to improve skills for their current job (Hunter and Sheldon, 1980), and in 1999, 13 percent of Wisconsin Technical College graduates so indicated (Wisconsin Technical College System Board, 1999). Such data often fall between the planks when program follow-up studies or comparative wage studies are made.

Another important finding in studies of graduates and current enrollees in vocational programs is the sizable number who plan to transfer to four-year colleges and do eventually transfer. In a California statewide study, 25 percent of students enrolled in vocational curricula said that they intended to transfer (Hunter and Sheldon, 1980), and national data compiled by the CSCC in 1986 yielded a similar figure (Palmer, 1987a). Regardless of their intentions when they enrolled, from 5 to 30 percent of the vocational program graduates transfer immediately to baccalaureate institutions, as indicated in several statewide studies. The figures show 5 percent of the vocational program graduates transferring in Illinois (Illinois Community College Board, 2000, p. 5), 12 percent in Florida (Windham, 1996), 16 percent in South Carolina (South Carolina Technical College System, 1997), and 27 percent in Maryland (Maryland State Board for Community Colleges, 1983). Thirty percent of the students transferring to the University of North Carolina system in 1993 came from that state's community college technical programs (Fredrickson, 1998). Yet a transfer percentage double that of the national norm is seen in programs that are directly linked to the baccalaureate, as in teacher education and several health fields. Although the term *vocational program* includes several types of activities, from noncredit certificate and associate in applied science to associate in science, the relationship between these programs and further education is well established.

Can students from occupational programs receive course credit when they transfer to baccalaureate-granting institutions? A national study by the CSCC accounted for the percentage of courses in the non–liberal arts that transferred to both research universities and comprehensive colleges and universities. Considerable variation was shown in both the types of courses that transfer and among types of universities, with the flagship institutions accepting fewer courses than the four-year colleges that had high numbers of career-related programs of their own;

as an example, Illinois State University and the California State University system would give credit for more than 60 percent of the occupational courses, whereas the University of Illinois and the University of California accepted only around 20 percent of them. But the overall transferability of the non–liberal arts suggested that "except for trade and industry courses, the concept of 'terminal education' should be laid to rest" (Cohen and Ignash, 1994, p. 29).

Because vocational education has several purposes, the measures of success that can be applied to it vary. It prepares people for specific jobs. How much do business and industry gain when their workers are trained at public expense? It assists the disadvantaged and people with disabilities to become self-sufficient. How much is that worth to society? It aids economic development. How much does a locality or region gain thereby? It enhances individual income generation and career mobility. What value has been added, person by person? Indicators of success and, indirectly, legislation and funding depend on which purpose is being reviewed.

Benefits to the Individual

Analysts of vocational education often consider the economic benefits to the enrollees. Because of the difficulty in disaggregating vocational and liberal arts curriculum and the motives and subsequent earnings of the students who complete the programs or leave without a degree or certificate, the analyses usually relate cost of attendance and incremental earnings for matriculants overall as well as for vocational program graduates. After reviewing several studies Kane and Rouse (1999) reported, "the average community college entrant . . . who enrolls but does not complete a degree, earns 9 to 13 percent more than the average high school student." Put another way, "each year of credit at a community college is associated with a 5 to 8 percent increase in annual earnings—which happens to be the same as the estimated value of a year's worth of credit at a four-year college" (p. 73). Larger returns are enjoyed by students in health and technical fields, while courses in sales, basic education, and the liberal arts show relatively negligible earnings increments.

Completing a program makes a difference. Sanchez and Laanan (1998) calculated that students under age twenty-five who were working during their last year in college earned twice as much three years after receiving a degree or certificate. Those aged twenty-five or older showed lesser percentage gains, primarily because their earnings while they were in college were substantially higher. Grubb (1999) reported a 54 percent increase for associate degree holders, 29 percent for those gaining a certificate, and 8 percent for those who leave with less than twelve credits. Students who left job preparatory programs in Washington short of completion in 2005–05 were nine months later earning 8 percent less than completers. But students in basic skills and vocational training concurrently did better (Patton, 2007). Nationally, by 1998, of the students who entered in 1995–96, 63 percent reported salary gains if they had attained a degree or certificate, compared with 29 percent of the noncompleters (Hoachlander, Sikora, and Horn, 2003).

Many of the economic benefits studies consider cost of attendance as well as earnings increments. Because community college tuition is low, most of the cost to the students is in the form of forgone earnings, what the students could be making on a job if they were not spending the time in school. This is difficult to estimate precisely because most students work while attending. The sheepskin effect, the fact that possession of a degree is essential before one can obtain a job in certain fields (as in nursing), comes into play as well. For this reason, associate degree and certificate holders display considerably greater rates of return. Other variables include the different rates of employment and wages in different fields and the earnings displayed soon after leaving college as compared with those enjoyed one or several years later. Nearly all analysts conclude that community college attendance yields a net benefit. They differ only on the amount of gain.

The Broader Implications

Vocational education has other implications: To what degree should the schools be in the business of providing trained workers for the nation's industries? None, say the academic purists; totally, say many community college leaders. A lengthy list of commentators and educational philosophers would argue that the preparation of people specifically to work in certain industries is not the school's purpose because it should have broader social aims and because the industries can do the particular job training much more efficiently. And those who take this approach are not necessarily those who plead for a return to an era when the purpose of higher education was to provide gentlemen with a distinctive set of manners.

The pattern of workforce training in other industrialized nations offers a few insights. Some countries depend on postsecondary institutions to carry the main burden, some on schools in the compulsory sector, and others on adult education that is provided by other than formal educational institutions (see Table 1.2). For example, vocational education in Canada is centered in the community colleges; in France, it is in the high schools and apprentice training centers; Germany has a dual system, with students pursuing vocational education through the upper secondary schools and in on-the-job training; Italy depends on technical schools and non-school-based vocational programs; Japan has special training schools at the postcompulsory level; and the United Kingdom provides vocational training through institutions of further education and apprenticeships. The greatest proportions of students in vocational programs in formal postsecondary structures are in Japan, Germany, France, and Italy (NCES, 1994d).

Is vocational education primarily an individual or a social benefit? Individuals gain skills that make them more employable and at higher rates of pay; society gains skilled workers for the nation's businesses and technologies. Solmon (1976) argues that community colleges can and should work closely with employers to facilitate students' passage through to the labor market. To the extent that they do, everyone benefits: students, their families, the colleges, business, and the general public. And he contends that the costs must be maintained by all. Although employers must provide expensive apprenticeships, they can benefit by using cooperative programs to identify students whom they would like to retain. The colleges lose some control over their students when business firms decide whom to involve in cooperative programs and when those programs become more susceptible to external evaluation. However, they gain by doing a better, more direct job for students and by keeping them enrolled longer.

Nevertheless, other writers in education, and certainly the majority of those who comment on the role of the community colleges, suggest that education is an essential expenditure for economic growth, a common good, and is not merely a nonproductive sector of the economy, a form of consumption. To the extent that the schools are viewed as investments of this type, educators can make a more effective claim on national budgets. To justify this claim, the schools must be brought in line with the goals of society; if they are to foster economic growth, they must provide trained workers, and the more they provide trained workers, the more they will be looked on to fit those trainees to available jobs. Hence, they can be criticized to the extent that their graduates do not obtain jobs or are not able to function effectively in the jobs they get. And the term *overeducated* can be used to describe those who are prepared for nonexistent jobs or have jobs to which they do not apply the type of education they received.

Should the colleges get paid on some pro rata basis only when the trainees have been employed? The notion is seductive but fraught with problems. First, the institutions' managers might be tempted to select at entry only those people who are likely to be employable, leaving behind the difficult ones. Second, depending on the institution to provide data about who is employed and for how long before funds are released begs creative data reporting. Third, employers prefer a larger pool of potential employees rather than the smaller pool that this type of contracting for performance would effect. Still, the specter of institutional accountability looms over the occupational programs.

Eells deplored the fact that 66 percent of the students were enrolled in programs designed primarily to prepare them for what 25 percent would do: transfer to the upper division. At the time he was writing, there was no great difference between the public and the private junior colleges: "The problem is essentially the same for both types of institutions" (1941a, p. 63). However, Eells also noted that "of all groups, only the private junior colleges of the New England states and the public junior colleges for Negroes report an enrollment in terminal curricula which even approximates the proportion of terminal students" (p. 59). Now, there were colleges that knew what they were doing! The private junior colleges of New England could fit the young women for homemaking, sales, and secretarial work, and the public junior colleges for blacks in the South could prepare their students for the manual trades.

The idea of vocational education reflects a belief that separate curricular tracks are the best way to accommodate the varying educational objectives and characteristics of the students. However, Palmer (1987a) suggests that the organization of career education as a separate curricular track stems from several viewpoints other than student intentions. The first is a political agenda held by state legislators and college planners. According to this agenda, occupational programs are supposed to serve students whose primary educational objective is to gain skills allowing them to enter the workforce. Second is the terminal education agenda, which sees vocational studies as a way of serving academically less able students, who are not likely to obtain the baccalaureate. Third is the economic agenda, which holds that occupational studies improve the economy through labor-force development and thus serve society. These three agendas, embedded in the history of the community college, have been put forth by national leaders from Eells (1941a, 1941b) to Parnell (1985). A fourth, the hidden agenda, has been postulated by other commentators who charge that vocational programs channel low-income and minority students away from academic studies and the upward social mobility attendant thereon.

Palmer's study demonstrates that the career programs in community colleges may have been furthered by leaders who subscribe to those beliefs but that the agendas do not accurately reflect what the curricula do. Occupational studies actually serve a much broader diversity of students, with a wide range of abilities and goals. The programs are not exclusively related to the workforce or the economy; they also serve individuals wishing to obtain skills for their personal interest, students who take vocational classes "for their intrinsic value and not necessarily for their vocational import" (1987a, p. 291). Palmer based his assertions on the 1986 CSCC survey of students enrolled in all types of classes in community colleges nationwide. In that survey, 16 percent of the students in occupational classes indicated that they were not enrolled in an occupational program, and 26 percent of the students who were in occupational classes or programs said that they intended to transfer. He rejects the charge that community college students are counseled into career programs on the basis of their academic ability and hence their socioeconomic status. His analysis shows that the enrollment patterns in high-status and low-status occupational classes deviate considerably from what would be expected if curricular tracking were efficiently carried out. Low-income students enroll in high-status and low-status program areas in almost equal numbers, and highly self-confident students equally tend to enroll in low-status program areas, just as students with below-average self-ratings of ability are as likely to enroll in high-status programs. "Many students clearly go their own way, regardless of whether counselors try to track students by ability" (p. 305).

Thus, an oversimplified view of vocational education as a track leading away from the baccalaureate gives ground to several errors. It neglects the extent to which occupational classes serve avocational or community service functions. It contributes to the confusion of curricular content with student intentions. It suggests that vocational education serves an ever-changing middle-level portion of the job market, which supposedly requires some college study but not the baccalaureate, thus ignoring the high transfer rates exhibited by career program graduates. And it perpetuates the myth that vocational studies are the exclusive domain of low-ability or low-income students.

Whether or not vocational education is useful or proper, it has certainly captured the community colleges. The 1960s to 1980s enrollment surge and financial support from business, industry, and government have given occupational educators a buoyancy that shows up in new courses, programs, and teaching strategies. They have a large reservoir of funds, mostly public but some private and foundation, to undertake studies on every aspect of occupational education: preparing model courses and programs, conducting follow-up studies of graduates, assessing employment trends, establishing guidelines for choosing new courses and curricula, and developing criteria for weeding out the obsolescent and weak courses and programs or for upgrading others to conform to new job specifications. The U.S. Department of Labor has been involved through its Secretary's Commission on Acquiring Necessary Skills, which has defined competencies needed in the workplace. And the Developing a Curriculum occupational analysis methodology, a low-cost way of determining tasks that persons need for certain occupational areas, has formed the basis of hundreds of studies since the 1970s (O'Brien, 1989). Nothing remotely comparable has taken place in the liberal arts.

Despite the widespread support for vocational programs, many college leaders view with concern the growth of the proprietary or for-profit schools. This group, the fastest-growing sector of postsecondary education since the 1980s, includes cosmetology and barber colleges, schools for computer and health fields, and business and secretarial institutes, along with several other less populous categories. In 1988, 92 colleges and business schools belonging to the association offered associate in arts or science degrees, up from 62 only a year earlier. And 144 additional institutions offered specialized associate degrees in occupational studies, applied sciences, and business, up from 119 in 1987. Ten years later, the NCES reported 173,089 students enrolled in 453 accredited proprietary schools (NCES *Digest*, 2001). A decade further on, NCES (NCES *Digest*, 2006) found that the number of schools and enrollees had doubled. Supported in the main by students who were receiving federal and state aid with which to pay their tuition, this group was proving a most effective set of competitors in the market to provide vocational training. Their students were more likely to attend full time and to attain certificates and degrees in less time. The for-profit institutions accounted for only 4 percent of the students in the two-year sector but awarded 13 percent of the degrees and certificates (Bailey, Gumport, and Badway, 2003). Depending on the types of credentials they offered, tuition in the for-profit institutions ranged from $5,196 to $11,183. Together with fees for room and board, they charged $20,418, double the cost of public community colleges (Goan and Cunningham, 2007). Their students were more likely to collect federal financial aid—in 2006, 72 percent received Pell grants and 91 percent, Stafford loans.

Merging Academic and Vocational Studies

The separation between the career and collegiate functions is more organizationally than conceptually inspired. Consider the following statement: "Students will learn to plan more efficient use of time, analyze written communications, understand interpersonal relations, respond appropriately to verbal directives, evolve alternative solutions, maintain involvement with tasks until resolution, communicate effectively verbally." Are those goals related to vocational or to baccalaureate studies? They are likely to appear in course syllabi from either area.

For decades, pleas have been made for reducing the separation between vocational and liberal studies. Solmon (1977) surveyed graduates of all types of programs several years out of college and found them wishing they had had more preparation in English, psychology, and ways of understanding interpersonal relations. Employers, too, frequently expect higher levels of competency, especially in writing, mathematics, thinking, computer literacy, leadership abilities, and interpersonal or team relationships (Hickman and Quinley, 1997). Salzman, Moss, and Tilly reviewed changes in the workplace and found "increased demands for soft skills and basic literacy for the lowest-level jobs" (1998, p. 3), along with entry- to middle-level jobs that are "increasingly based on formal education and training that is not possible to obtain through internal training and learning on the job" (p. 18). Thus, hiring criteria are no longer based on "a person's ability to perform a particular function . . . but rather on an assessment of his or her ability to master a host of skills and responsibilities" (p. 18). They concluded, "Ironically, one of the reasons community colleges seem like an ideal candidate for deepening and broadening the skill base of the workforce is their broader focus on skill which in turn is due to their dual educational mission modeled at least in part on four-year colleges" (p. 28).

Harris and Grede (1977) predicted a breakdown in the rigid dichotomy between liberal arts and vocational curricula or between transfer and nontransfer curricula in community colleges. This prediction has not come to pass, not least because of the rigidity of the separate funding channels through which support flows into the vocational and the collegiate courses. The crossovers that do exist tend to be at the microlevel. A few courses in some colleges have been designed so that they incorporate elements of both the liberal arts and career studies; Grubb and Kraskouskas (1992) and Bailey (2000) mention several examples. But in the main, the proponents of the liberal arts have depended on accreditation and state requirements to sustain their offerings in programs leading to associate degrees in career fields.

Of itself, occupational training involves a higher risk for the student than does liberal arts education. The costs in tuition and forgone earnings may be the same for both, but occupational training is almost entirely wasted if there is no job at the end. The liberal arts at least hold the person's options open, a perception certainly accounting for some of the continuing popularity of liberal arts among students. Since it seems impossible to predict with much accuracy the types of jobs that will be available by the time an entering student leaves school, the problem can be accommodated in two ways. First, the educational system can be made open enough that people may return successively for retraining throughout life. Second, the initial training can be made sufficiently broad that the skills learned are applicable to a variety of situations. The argument can be made that all contemporary education is vocational, since it is designed for people who will one day work. Furthermore, the concept of work is sufficiently broad to accommodate people who are less interested in doing or making things than they are in maintaining jobs for their status, social connection, and the human interaction they provide. Many people define themselves by their role but not by their work; it is easier for them to say that they are the assistant manager of something than it is for them to recount exactly what it is they do.

In the long run, vocational education usually fails if it is focused narrowly on job skills. Knowing how to produce something is quite different from all of the other requirements for sustaining employment. Functional literacy is basic, along with interpersonal relations and knowledge of how to find a job in the first place. Furthermore, the concept of matching a trained worker to an available job is not as prominent now in the overall picture of employment as it was previously, predominantly because more production is occurring in structures that have less distinct boundaries, in other words, networks, or virtual corporations. Entrepreneurship, too, is the place where many new jobs are created. It involves not only skills but knowing how to find capital, knowing about the marketplace, knowing all that it takes to organize a business. A growing proportion of occupational training has been directed toward helping people create their own jobs through small-business development.

A major change in recent years has been that vocational programs in community colleges increasingly became feeders to senior institutions, which were undergoing their own form of vocationalization. Students were finding that many of the credits they earned in their two-year occupational programs were acceptable for transfer. Thus, the categories "vocational" and "transfer" became inadequate to describe the realities of the community colleges, and "terminal" certainly became obsolete. Sizable percentages of the transfer students sought leisure-time pursuits; sizable percentages of the vocational students desired certification for transfer. A view of the community colleges as terminal institutions and of the universities as institutions for students interested in the liberal arts is woefully inaccurate.

In his book *The Two Cultures*, the English writer C. P. Snow (1959) posed a distinction between the humanities and the sciences. The scientific culture attempts to describe laws of the natural world and is optimistic that problems can be solved. The other culture, the literary world, is pessimistic about the likelihood of solving major problems and regards members of the scientific culture as barbarians. According to Snow, the literary intellectuals or artists lack foresight, are unconcerned about their fellow humans, and do not understand what science can do. The scientists regard the artists as lacking precision in thought and action, as speaking in phrases capable of a myriad of interpretations.

There are other ways, however, to contemplate a gap between two cultures. Perhaps on one side are those who have a vision of the future; who work with discipline, pride, and rigor; who articulate their ideas through language that has consistent meaning; who value the intellect. On the other side are those who demand quick gratification; who refuse to be told what to do or what to study; who are antiliterate, rejecting language; who deal with feeling, not thinking, with emotions, not intellect. If these are the two cultures, the split is not between the liberal arts on the one hand and occupational education on the other. That argument is passé, although community colleges are still organized as though the real distinction were between people who were going to work and those who were not. Work in the sense of vocation demands commitment, planning, delay of gratification, application of intelligence, acceptance of responsibility, a sense of present and future time. As such, it differs less from the concepts surrounding the liberal arts than it does from the antiliterate, language-rejecting, stultified group, who cannot understand themselves or their environment in terms that have common reference.

As though it anticipated later developments, the AAJC's 1964 National Advisory Committee concluded, "Time must be provided, even in a two-year curriculum, for at least basic courses in languages, arts, and social sciences. The technicians of the future must be inoculated against the malady of overspecialization. . . . They must not be forced to concentrate so narrowly on technology that they cannot be useful citizens or cannot accommodate changes in their own specialties" (American Association of Junior Colleges, 1964, p. 14). Nearly a quarter-century later, an AACJC-sponsored group reiterated a concern for combining career and general education: "Many students come to the community college with narrow backgrounds, and, for them, career education may mean only gaining skills for a specific job. . . . Through lack of attention to general education, community colleges often exacerbate this tendency toward narrowness. . . . We recommend that the core curriculum be integrated into technical and career programs" (American Association of Community and Junior Colleges, 1988a, pp. 17–19).

Some things don't change very much.

Issues

The phenomenal growth of vocational education in the 1960s and 1970s stabilized in the 1980s at 40 to 50 percent of total enrollment. Will this figure remain stable? How much will competition from the proprietary schools affect it?

Can vocational education be effectively merged with the collegiate function? Few prior attempts to integrate aesthetic appreciation, rationality, ethics, and other elements of higher learning with programs training people for particular jobs have met with success. Can the staff itself do it? Does the community college leadership want it?

The lines between vocational and collegiate education have become blurred since as many students began transferring to universities from community college career programs as from the so-called transfer programs. Questions of the conceptual differences between occupational and liberal studies have often been raised, but the answers have yielded little to influence program design in the community colleges. What type of staff training, program reorganization, or external incentives might be provided to encourage faculties and administrators to reexamine both programs in the light of the practicalities of their own institutions?

Programs designed to prepare students to work in particular industries should be supported, at least in part, by those industries; many examples of this type of support have been set in place. But how can industry be assigned its proportionate share of all training costs? What channels can be opened to merge public and private funds so that an equitable share is borne by each?

The full effects of vocational education as a primary function have yet to be discerned. The public's view of community colleges as agents of upward mobility for individuals seems to be shifting toward a view of the institutions as occupational training centers. This narrowing of the colleges' comprehensiveness could lead to a shift in the pattern of support.

9

Developmental Education
Enhancing Literacy and Basic Skills

Nothing is easier to decry than the ineffectiveness of the schools. One observer of American education noted:

> Paradoxical as it may seem, the diffusion of education and intelligence is at present acting against the free development of the highest education and intelligence. Many have hoped and still hope that by giving a partial teaching to great numbers of persons, a stimulus would be applied to the best minds among them, and a thirst for knowledge awakened that would lead to high results; but thus far these results have not equaled the expectation. There has been a vast expenditure . . . for educational purposes . . . but the system of competitive cramming in our schools has not borne fruits on which we have much cause to congratulate ourselves [Parkman, 1869, p. 560].

The sentiments in this passage, written in 1869 by the American historian Francis Parkman, have been echoed countless times since. One hundred years after Parkman's comment, the American poet and critic John Ciardi complained that "the American school system has dedicated itself to universal subliteracy" (1971, p. 48). The novelist Walker Percy has offered this devastating critique: "Our civilization has achieved a distinction of sorts. It will be remembered not for its technology nor even its wars but for its novel ethos. Ours is the only civilization in history which has enshrined mediocrity as its national ideal" (1980, p. 177).

A steady outpouring of books has continued the critique. Hirsch begins his best-seller with the words, "The standard of literacy required by modern society has been rising throughout the developed world, but American literacy rates have not risen to meet this standard" (1987, p. 1). Harman's examination of illiteracy describes how "more and more working members of mainstream America are found to be either totally illiterate or unable to read at the level presumably required by their job or their position in society" (1987, p. 1).

The conventional belief is that literacy has declined. But how much? And by what measurement? Certainly the colleges are deeply involved with developmental studies, but at what cost to their image? And to what effect? In this chapter, several dilemmas surrounding the tracking of students into less-than-college-level courses are explored, especially the difficulty in assigning standards and definitions and assessing program outcomes. Some examples of the practices in which the colleges are engaged are also noted.

Decline in Literacy

Broad-scale denunciations are one thing, accurate data quite another. Information on the literacy of the American population over the decades is difficult to compile, even though data on the number of people completing so many years of schooling have been collected by the Bureau of the Census for well over one hundred years. Intergenerational comparisons are imprecise because different percentages of the population have gone to school at different periods in the nation's history and because the United States has never had a uniform system of educational evaluation. Still, an understanding of the importance of literacy, concern about its decline, and the need to do something about it have become widespread.

Eight National Education Goals were set into law on March 31, 1994, when President Clinton signed the Goals 2000, Educate America Act. One of the eight goals was that every adult would be literate, possessing the knowledge and skills to compete in the workplace and exercising the responsibilities of citizenship. Although the act itself has been superseded, its emphasis on standards, norms, and instrumentation so that measures of literacy in all age groups could be reported according to common referents has survived, incorporated into the contemporary emphasis on accountability. Subsequent federal legislation has emphasized testing students periodically, with the intention of encouraging schools where students score below the norm to improve (as though the staff in those schools were not already aware of their students' level of literacy).

Concerns about literacy came as no surprise to educators who have reviewed the scores made on nationally normed tests taken by people planning on entering college. The available evidence suggests that the academic achievement of students in schools and colleges registered a gradual improvement between 1900 and the mid-1950s, an accelerated improvement between the mid-1950s and the mid-1960s, and a precipitous, widespread decline between then and the late 1970s, before stabilizing in the early 1980s. The Scholastic Aptitude Tests (SATs) taken by college-bound high school seniors show mathematical ability at 494 in 1952 and 502 in 1963; it dropped as low as 466 in 1979 but by 2004 had reached 520. Verbal ability went from 476 in 1952 to 543 in 1966, then dropped in 1975 to 509, where it stabilized; it was 508 thirty years later (College Board, 1994; NCES *Digest*, 2001). Renamed the Scholastic Assessment Test, with the scores recalibrated, math scores showed a gain although verbal scores remained flat.

The scores made by students who participated in the American College Testing (ACT) Program between 1995 and 2004 reveal a similar pattern (Table 9.1). In that decade, reading and science scores were stable, English showed a slight increase, and math a

Table 9.1. ACT Test Scores for High School Seniors

	1995	2004
Composite	20.8	20.9
English	20.2	20.4
Math	20.2	20.7
Reading	21.3	21.3
Science	21.	20.9

Table 9.2. SAT Scores for College-Bound Seniors

	1966–67	1975–76	2004–05
Verbal	543	509	508
Math	516	497	520

greater increase. The overall composite went from 20.8 to 20.9 (NCES *Digest,* 2001). Declines in academic achievement during the 1970s and subsequent stabilization were confirmed by the National Assessment of Educational Progress (NAEP) studies of seventeen-year-old students (see Figure 9.1). After bottoming out in the early 1980s, students' performance in math rose, so that their average score in 2004 was higher than in 1973. Over the same period, their scores in reading showed a gain in the 1980s but dropped back to the twenty-five-year-earlier level thereafter.

No one can say with assurance which social or educational condition was primarily responsible for the decline in student abilities that apparently began in the mid-1960s and accelerated throughout the 1970s before leveling off. Suffice it to say that numerous events came together: the coming of age of the first generation reared on television, a breakdown in respect for authority and the professions, a pervasive attitude that the written word is not as important as it once was, the imposition of various other-than-academic expectations on the public schools, the increasing

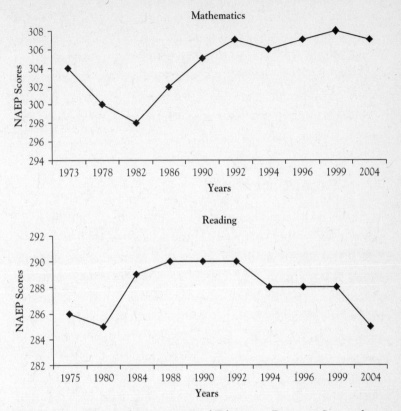

Figure 9.1.   National Assessment of Education Progress Scores for
Seventeen Year Olds, 1973–2004
(*Source:* National Center for Education Statistics, *Digest of Education Statistics,*
2006)

numbers of students whose native language is other than English,
and a decline in academic requirements and expectations at all
levels of schooling. The time that the current generation has spent
in destroying the Xyklorbs from Galaxy Zorx hasn't helped either.
The effect of schooling and the availability of other educational
opportunities is suggested by the relationships between family
income and SAT scores. According to the College Board (2007),
scores made by the more than one million college bound seniors
who took the SAT showed a straight-line, positive correlation

with family income. Those with income greater than $100,000 averaged 544 in reading, 556 in math, and 537 in writing, while those with income less than $10,000 scored 427 in reading, 451 in math, and 423 in writing. Since students from low-income families are considerably more likely to attend community colleges than universities, these figures do much to explain patterns in the colleges' student body.

School Requirements

Of all the listed conditions, academic requirements are the only ones that are within the power of the schools to change directly. Several premises underlie schooling—for example, that students tend to learn what is taught, that the more time they spend on a task the more they learn, and that they will take the courses required for completion of their programs. Hence, when expectations, time in school, and number of academic requirements are reduced, student achievement, however measured, seems certain to drop as well. In its 1978 report, *The Concern for Writing*, the Educational Testing Service noted, "The nub of the matter is that writing is a complex skill mastered only through lengthy, arduous effort. It is a participatory endeavor, not a spectator sport. And most high school students do not get enough practice to become competent writers" (p. 4). In the 1960s and 1970s, the schools put less emphasis on composition, and even in composition courses, "creative expression" was treated at a higher level than were grammar and the other tools of the writer's trade.

Copperman (1978) recounted the depressing statistics regarding deterioration of the secondary school curriculum. Specifically, the percentage of ninth- through twelfth-grade students enrolled in academic courses dropped between 1960 and 1972, from 95 to 71 percent in English courses and proportionately in social studies, science, and mathematics. In other words, the average high school graduate had taken four years of English in 1960 and only three years in 1972. And the curriculum in English shifted from sequential courses to electives chosen from courses in creative writing, journalism, public speaking, classical literature, science fiction, advanced folklore, composition, mass media, poetry, and a host of other options. Not only were students taking less science, math, English, and history, but in the academic classes they did take, the amount of work assigned and the standard to which it was held deteriorated as well.

During the 1980s, school reform shifted toward educational excellence and outcomes assessment. At the same time, increased requirements for high school graduation and state-centered student testing programs became prominent. By 1990, most states had changed their curriculum requirements for graduation, with the majority of changes directed toward increases in the number of math and science studies. Between 1982 and 2004, the average number of Carnegie credits taken by high school students increased from 21.7 to 25.8 (Guess, 2007); twelfth grade GPAs rose from an average of 2.68 in 1992 to 2.98 in 2005 (Landsberg, 2007). Student testing had increased as well, with more than one-third of the states requiring a minimum competency test for high school graduation. But as the SAT, ACT, and NAEP results show, overall gains in literacy have come slowly, if at all.

A recent report from Educational Testing Service reveals that, despite all types of school reforms in the past generation, little has changed. High school completion rates (exclusive of GEDs), 77 percent in 1969, fell to 70 percent in 1995 and have remained close to that level, which has resulted in the United States dropping behind all but five of twenty-one countries listed by OECD (Kirsch, Braun, Yamamoto, and Sum, 2007). Noteworthy here is that during that same period, total spending per pupil in public K–12 schools doubled in constant 2004–05 dollars, the student-teacher ratio (class size) dropped by half, and the percentage of teachers with at least a master's degree doubled. One in four ACT-tested high school graduates of 2005 who took the core curriculum—four years of English and three each of math, science, and social studies—met the ACT College Readiness Benchmarks in all four subjects; one in five failed to reach any of the benchmarks (E. Redden, May 16, 2007). Just over half the graduates met the standard for reading, a decline from the peak of 55 percent reached in 1999. ACT found that, "more eighth and tenth graders are on track to being ready for college-level reading than are actually ready when they graduate . . ." and suggests that, "state standards in high school reading are insufficient—or nonexistent." More than half of the 49 states with reading standards fully define them "only through the eighth grade" (American College Testing, 2006, p. 3). ACT's "college readiness benchmarks" for biology, algebra, and English composition showed a 22 percent rate in 2004 (Kirst, 2007).

College Admissions

Because each college set its own standards and because the founding of colleges preceded the development of a widespread secondary school system, the early colleges displayed a wide variety of admission requirements. By the late nineteenth century, most were operating their own remedial education programs. In 1895, 40 percent of entering students were drawn from preparatory programs operated by the colleges and universities themselves (Rudolph, 1977, p. 158).

Numerous attempts to stabilize college admissions have been made. In 1892, the National Education Association organized the Committee on Secondary School Studies, known as the Committee of Ten, which was to recommend and approve the secondary school curriculum for college matriculation. In 1900, the College Entrance Examination Board began offering a common examination for college admission. Nonetheless, the wide variety in types and quality of colleges in America made it impossible to devise uniform admission standards. There has never been a standard of admission to all colleges in the United States. The Educational Testing Service and the ACT Program offer uniform examinations across the country, but each college is free to admit students regardless of where they place on those examinations.

Of all postsecondary educational structures in America, the public community colleges bore the brunt of the poor preparation of students in the twentieth century. When sizable cohorts of well-prepared students were clamoring for higher education, as in the 1950s and early 1960s, the community colleges received a large share of them. But when the college-age group declined and the universities became more competitive for students, the proportion of academically well-prepared students going to community colleges shrank. Thus, the colleges were dealt a multiple blow: relaxed admission requirements and the availability of financial aid at the more prestigious universities, a severe decline in the scholastic abilities of high school graduates, and a greater percentage of applicants who had taken fewer academic courses. And although the recent upturn in the eighteen-year-old population has lowered the median student age in community colleges, it has done little to elevate the students' abilities.

The community colleges responded by accommodating the different types of students without turning anyone away. They have always tended to let everyone in but have then guided students to programs that fit their aspirations and in which they have some chance to succeed. Students who qualified for transfer programs were never a serious problem; they were given courses similar to those they would find in the lower division of the four-year colleges and universities. Technical and occupational aspirants were not a problem either; vocational programs were organized for them. Internal selectivity was the norm; failing certain prerequisites, applicants were barred from the health professions and technology programs. The students who wanted a course or two for their own personal interest found them both in the departments of continuing education and the transfer programs.

The residue, the poorly prepared group of high school pass-throughs, has been the concern. What should the colleges do with marginally literate people who want to be in college but do not know why? How should they deal with someone who aspires to be an attorney but is reading at the fifth-grade level? Shunting these students to the trades programs was a favored ploy, giving rise to Clark's cooling-out thesis (1960). Another ploy was to offer a smattering of remedial courses where students would be prepared, more or less successfully, to enter the transfer courses— or entertained until they drifted away. But the decline in achievement exhibited by secondary school graduates and dropouts in the 1970s hit the colleges with full force. The problem of the marginal student became central to instructional planning.

The Magnitude of Remediation

In practice, definitions of basic skills and remedial studies vary little. A team from the Research and Planning Group of California Community Colleges offered, "Basic skills are those foundation skills . . . which are necessary for students to succeed in college-level work" (RP Group, 2007). Grubb and associates (1999) define remediation as activities for "students who initially do not have the skills, experience, or orientation necessary to perform at a level that the institutions or instructors recognize as 'regular' for those students" (p. 174). Thus, the institutions make the determination but that is only the beginning, because the students who are referred to remedial coursework are a diverse lot, including those who have done poorly in all subjects and those who are deficient in just one, older students who did well in their high school studies but whose skills have fallen into disuse, those with poor study habits who have learning problems, and recent immigrants, to name only a few subsets.

Data on entering students who need remedial help suggest the magnitude of the problem. Since New Jersey began giving its

College Basic Skills Placement Test in the early 1980s, more than half of the students entering the county (community) colleges have needed remediation in verbal skill, computation, and algebra (New Jersey State Department of Higher Education, 1994). Forty-six percent of the recent high school completers (92 percent of the GED graduates) entering Kentucky's public institutions in 2004 were underprepared for college (Kentucky Developmental Education Task Force, 2007). In 1989, 39 percent of the students in Georgia's two-year colleges were enrolled in one or more remedial courses (Hamilton, 1992). In California, half the entering students were directed to basic skills courses (although more than one-third of them did not enroll in these courses) (Academic Senate for California Community Colleges, 2004). In Washington, nearly half the students entering community colleges took at least one developmental course (Washington State Board for Community and Technical Colleges, 2006). Nationwide, 44 percent of first-time community college students enroll in between one and three developmental courses, 14 percent in more than three, and 42 percent take no remediation (Attewell, Lavin, Domina, Levey, 2006).

Many studies of single colleges have found similar percentages. More than 40 percent of the entering students at Rockland Community College (New York) were directed to the developmental studies department (Brown and others, 1989), and 88 percent of the first-time students entering Shelby State Community College (Tennessee) were placed in remedial and developmental studies courses (Hobbs, 1988). In Prince George's Community College (Maryland) 70 percent of the entrants were identified as needing remedial work (Prince George's Community College, 1999). Clearly, curriculum revisions, higher standards, and graduation examinations in high schools had yet to yield substantive change in entering college students' abilities.

Remedial and *developmental* and, less often, *compensatory* and *basic skills* have been used more or less interchangeably for courses designed to teach literacy—the essentials of reading, writing, and arithmetic—plus broader skills for living—time management, how to study, coping with family crises. Students have been advised to enroll in those courses on the basis of entrance tests or prior school achievement. The courses are not often accepted for credit toward an academic degree, but their funding comes through the regular academic instructional budget, sometimes augmented by special state or federal program appropriations to assist disadvantaged students.

Although the decline in student ability stabilized in the 1980s, developmental education grew until it leveled off in the 1990s. The rise in remedial course enrollment occurred because student ability had sunk so low that college staff members, legislators, and the staff of the universities to which the students transfer had had enough. The dropout and failure rates were unconscionably high. When the population was expanding and an ever-increasing number of new students showed up each year, the problem was not as acute, and few colleges did anything about coordinating developmental education. In the late 1970s, however, the attitude shifted as the college staff realized that it was more feasible, not to say socially and educationally defensible, to keep the students enrolled than to let them drop out as a result of academic failure.

All public two-year colleges offer remedial courses. The Center for the Study of Community Colleges (CSCC) tallied the sections offered in a national sample of colleges in 1977–78 and found that about three in eight English classes were presented at below-college level; in nearly one in three mathematics classes, arithmetic was taught at a level lower than college algebra; and remedial classes accounted for 13 percent of the enrollments in chemistry. In 1998, CSCC again tracked credit courses and found developmental studies continuing their prominence; 29 percent of the scheduled class sections in English and 32 percent in math were so designated (Schuyler, 1999b). These data were corroborated in state studies: 14 percent of the credit-course enrollment in Illinois, 17 percent in North Carolina, and 23 percent each in Florida and Washington community colleges were in remedial courses (Illinois Community College Board, 2005; North Carolina Community College System, 2007a, 2007b; Florida Department of Education, 2007; Washington State Board for Community and Technical Colleges, 2006).

Revised Practices

Developmental courses and programs can be built within the colleges, but several questions remain: Is developmental education effective? How does it affect the college staff? How can it be conducted in the context of an open-admissions institution without jeopardizing the college's standards and its legitimacy in higher education? How can segregated developmental education programs respond to charges of racism and class-based tracking? How many times should the public pay the schools to try to teach the same competencies to the same people?

Placement testing and integrated developmental education services have dominated recent efforts in remedial studies. Beginning in the late 1970s, the nation's community colleges moved toward a system of placement testing, restricted admissions to many courses and programs, integrated developmental programs complete with counseling and tutorial services, and assessment of the efficacy of these procedures. In the 1980s, state-mandated placement testing was installed, first in Florida and Georgia, subsequently in Texas, California, and New Jersey, and by 2000, in twenty more states. These requirements affected all the publicly supported institutions.

More than half the states have regulations governing remedial instruction. Some have mandated that it not be offered in the public universities; Florida, Missouri, South Carolina, and Arizona are notable examples (Roueche and Roueche, 1999; Massachusetts Community College, 1998). Others have placed limits on the number of developmental courses a university may offer and directed the universities to arrange remedial instruction for their students with the community colleges, thus inflating their numbers of developmental students. Since half the freshmen entering the twenty-two campuses of the California State University in 1994 needed remedial work, the system's governing board proposed shifting nearly all remedial studies to the community colleges. Illinois law stipulates that "the primary emphasis on postsecondary remedial programs [is] at Public Community Colleges" (Ignash, 1997, p. 7), an example of persuasiveness seen also in several other states.

Some of the states that have mandated assessment and placement have specified tests and cutoff scores. Most of the Massachusetts colleges use the College Board Computerized Placement Test, and its cutoffs for reading and math fall within a narrow range (Massachusetts Community College Developmental Education Committee, 1998). The Texas Academic Skills Program (now called the Texas Success Initiative) has established a "college-readiness standard" on the Texas Assessment of Knowledge and Skills, required of all exiting high school students who plan on entering college (Texas Higher Education Coordinating Board, 2004, p. 5). California allows its 108 colleges to choose their own measures and 128 different instruments were in use (Academic Senate for California Community Colleges, 2004). Other states have taken the process a step further by requiring the colleges to place students in courses that demonstrably match the students' abilities. Berger's succinct analysis of the process points out that "if students are required to have certain skills or bodies of knowledge before they take a particular class, that class should, in fact, operate in such a manner that those skills or knowledge are actually needed for success." In brief, across-the-board entrance requirements have not been challenged as being biased against certain ethnic groups, but have pointed toward a "course-by-course scrutiny of outlines, textbooks, examinations, syllabi, and the like, ending in a clear listing of entry and exit skills for each course" (Berger, 1997, p. 37).

Programs

Proceeding in tandem with the state mandates have been a number of integrated programs combining instruction in the three Rs with counseling, tutoring, study skills seminars, and a variety of special interventions. Special counseling procedures are established, and each student's attendance and progress are monitored. The courses may include remedial reading and writing, and adjunct classes centering on certain content areas also may be provided. The students may be tutored individually by professionals or peers. The programs frequently include reproducible instructional sequences presented through learning laboratories. Nearly half use computers as an interactive instructional tool for on-campus reading, writing, and mathematics, and one-fourth offer developmental courses through distance instruction. In some of the more sophisticated developmental programs, remedial classes are offered through the English and mathematics departments, adjunct courses or study programs are offered through the learning resource center, study skills activities are presented by members of the counseling staff, and tutorials are coordinated by any of these divisions.

Numerous descriptions of such programs may be found. Some are organized as bridge programs designed to assist recent high school graduates in making the transition to college. These programs include counseling and efforts to direct the students toward career goals, as well as emphasizing basic academic skills. The Freshman Year Initiative Program in Bronx Community College (New York) was organized as a comprehensive academic and counseling program for first-semester students who required at least three remedial courses (Baron, 1997). The twelve-week Transition Class, nongraded and offered to prospective students free of charge at Parkland College (Illinois), emphasized academic skills, social skills, career exploration, and goal setting, along with the usual reading, writing, and mathematics instruction (Koehler and Burke, 1998). Santa Monica College (California) offers a Summer Bridge and Learning Communities Program through its First Year Institute.

Many other permutations can be cited. Some programs allow students to enter the academic courses but insist that they take advantage of tutorial assistance available to help them with their course work. This is an old approach, matching learning laboratories with the specific course areas. Some of these labs are dedicated to math, others to reading or writing. Also prevalent are open-entry, open-exit courses, where students can drop in at any time and work with an instructor on specific problems. However, where these are volitional, they may be playing into the students' tendency not to place extra effort on their college work.

Overall, numerous patterns are in play: self-standing developmental courses; learning assistance keyed to students in regular college classes; supplemental instruction for students in high-risk courses; precollege bridge programs; learning communities; and combinations of all of these. The point is that the colleges have now abandoned the practice of allowing students to drop in and drop out at will and have moved distinctly into a mode of mandatory assessment and placement in sequences designed to keep students in school and to help them improve their basic skills so that they can complete an academic or vocational program satisfactorily.

Program Effects

Hundreds of studies reported in the published literature and in the ERIC files suggest that student placement procedures are valid and that students learn to read and write in the remedial classes. The integrated developmental programs, designed to effect retention as well as learning, similarly show positive results. These effects are not surprising; when staff members are involved in a comprehensive program, they pay close attention to students, integrate teaching with counseling, provide a greater variety of learning materials than ordinary students receive, and motivate their enrollees to devote more time to their studies. In short, when special treatment is applied; when students are given supplemental counseling, tutoring, and learning aids; and when they are singled out for additional work, they tend to remain in school. Special treatment of any sort yields special results.

How do college faculty members who face students daily feel about massive developmental education efforts and the poorly prepared students in their classes? Students' abilities exert the single most powerful influence on the level, quality, type, and standard of curriculum and instruction offered in every program in every school. Other influences—instructors' tendencies, externally administered examinations and licensure requirements, the entry levels imposed by succeeding courses in the same and other institutions—are of lesser importance. Nothing that is too distant from the students' comprehension can be taught successfully. All questions of academic standards, college-level and remedial courses, textbook readability and coverage, and course pacing and sequence come to that.

Students are part of the instructors' working conditions. Except for faculty members recruited especially to staff developmental programs, most feel that their environment would be improved if their students were more able. In the CSCC's 1977 national survey of science instructors at two-year colleges, respondents were asked, "What would it take to make yours a better course?" Over half noted, "Students better prepared to handle course requirements," a choice that far outranked all others in a list of sixteen (Brawer and Friedlander, 1979, p. 32). More than twenty years later, Outcalt (2002) found almost the exact response among the academic faculty he surveyed.

If students cannot be more able, at least they might be more alike, so that instruction can be better focused. Teaching groups of students whose reading or computational abilities range from the third to the thirteenth grade is demoralizing; everything is more difficult, from writing examinations to showing group progress—hence, the unremitting pressure for ability grouping, remedial courses, and learning laboratories that serve to remove the poorer students from the classrooms.

As integrated developmental programs grew in the 1980s, separate divisions combining faculty members, counselors, and support staff were formed to accommodate them. As noted in Chapter Six, this separation of the developmental education staff from the academic discipline–centered faculty has led to an increased level of professional consciousness among members of the former group. They publish their own journals, which carry articles on peer tutoring, the pros and cons of mandatory testing, ways of organizing reading and writing laboratories, and the various treatments they apply to students who come within their purview. In some colleges the academic instructors still treat them as pariahs, but they have their own colleagues and support groups. A continuing problem, however, is that an overwhelming number of remedial instructors—57 percent in California—are part-timers (Academic Senate for California Community Colleges, 2000).

Although only a minority of developmental programs in community colleges are evaluated in a regular and systematic fashion, many reports indicate varying effects. The measures usually employed are student retention, grade point average, remedial course completion, successful transitions to the college-level programs, and graduation rates. Levin and Calcagno cite studies showing that "about seventy percent of students pass the reading and writing remedial courses they enroll in, but only thirty percent pass all their remedial math courses" (2007, p. 4). A study of 36,123 first-time students entering Florida community colleges in 1999 showed that after five years, those who had completed a Student Life Skills course were considerably more likely to have earned an award or still be enrolled (Florida Department of Education,

November, 2006). Pascarella and Terenzini's meta-analysis found academic interventions such as remedial programs "at least modestly effective in helping students overcome deficiencies in their pre-collegiate academic preparation and associated disadvantages" (2005, p. 398).

Even though some single-college studies, such as one reported by Hammons and Mathews (1999), have found enrollment in developmental courses to have no effect on subsequent achievement, the inconsistency seems to relate both to the way programs are organized and to the variations among types of students. The integrated program, combining remedial instruction with counseling, tutorials, and assistance specifically tailored to the other courses that the students are taking, seems to have a more salutary effect when compared with the free-standing or separate remedial classes, which have lower retention rates and lower long-term success rates. Levin and Calcagno (2007) summarize the effects, saying that isolated courses are considerably less effective than linked programs that rest on any of three categories: restructuring curriculum, developing new institutional structures, and employing specific instructional strategies. They point out that many models exist for this type of redesign, including linking basic skills courses with credit-bearing courses, implementing supplemental instruction, and establishing learning communities. They point to successes attained through learning assistance centers that include career counseling, tutoring, and other enhancements. They also contend that instruction in critical thinking, complex problem solving, and abstract reasoning can be salutary for remedial students. Their designs for evaluating developmental education are summarized in Chapter Twelve.

The differences among students classified as needing remediation is also an influential issue. Gallegos describes one type, the non-native English speaker, with several risk factors: "There is overwhelming evidence that developmental students and traditional students are, on the average, fundamentally different in many ways that will not be affected by successful remediation" (2006, p. 35). Developmental students often have high high-school grade point averages, suggesting grade inflation. They are more likely to be bilingual, often from the first generation in their family to attend college, from low SES backgrounds, have dependents, and attend part time. Evaluating "the effectiveness of developmental programs by comparing the academic success of students exiting these programs to that of students placed initially in the corresponding college-level course" (p. 57) is often undertaken but in many cases, students will continue to speak Spanish to anyone they spoke Spanish with before, disabilities and financial disadvantages will persist, their numbers of children will remain the same, and the educational level of their parents will not change.

Student age is another difference. In a study of 30,000 first-time traditional students and 5,700 older students, the Community College Research Center at Teachers College found older students more likely to need remediation as a refresher: "It is likely that older students, having been out of school longer, were more likely to need some remediation (but not a lot) because their basic skills were merely 'rusty' rather than grossly deficient" (Calcagno, Crosta, Bailey, and Jenkins, 2006).

Even among older students, further subcategories yield different findings. Prince and Jenkins used data from the Washington State Community and Technical College System to track the progress of low-skill students 25 or older with no more than high school diplomas who entered the system in 1996 or 1997. They were subdivided into low wage-earner, precollege, welfare recipient, and resident of low-income zip code area. Only 13 percent of the ESL students went on to earn some college credits; clearly the colleges provided a special service for that group. Around 30 percent of the ABE/GED students entered college-level courses, with 5 percent earning 45 units or a certificate or degree within five years. As for the programs' value to students' earnings: "Attending college for at least one year and earning a credential provides a substantial boost in earnings . . . Short-term training such as that often provided to welfare recipients may help individuals get into the labor market, but it usually does not help them advance beyond low-paying jobs." Gains of 8 percent in employment probability and over $1,100 per quarter were seen in those who went through occupational degree programs. But adult basic skills programs did not have a positive impact on wages. The authors concluded that the "colleges ought to make taking at least one year of college-level courses and earning a credential a minimum goal for the many low-skill adults they serve" (2005, p. 23).

Legitimacy

The question of legitimacy is one of image in the eyes of the public, the potential students, the funding agents, and the other sectors of education. Like any other public agency, an educational institution must maintain its legitimacy. The community colleges have strived to maintain their claim to a position in the postsecondary sector through numerous stratagems. In the 1950s and 1960s, for example, they sought people with doctoral degrees to serve as staff members and rewarded current staff members when they obtained the higher degree, even though possession of a doctorate bore little or no relation to a faculty member's professional activities. The doctorate was a way of saying, "We are as good as the senior institutions." Similarly, they segregated their developmental programs in an attempt to regain the legitimacy lost when the colleges accepted adult basic studies and job-training programs that could in no measure be considered college level.

Actually, a school's legitimacy rests on its academic standards and the definition of its guiding principles. Academic standards certify that a student holding a certificate or degree has met the requirement for employment or for further study at another college; they are the basis for the reputation of institutions and the people who work in them. Although community colleges typically maintain open-admissions policies, they must still attend to these concerns. Their students must be certified; their instructional programs, testing and counseling services, course content, and course requirements must all relate to a shared vision of desired competencies and outcomes. Their certificates or degrees must evidence some set of proficiencies achieved at some minimum level.

What are the standards in developmental education? Here the special programs exhibit several problems in common with the traditional. One of the main problems is the difficulty in setting fixed exit criteria (grading standards) for courses and programs that have no set entry requirements. If anyone may enroll regardless of ability, a wide range of students will be attracted. Accordingly, either the exit criteria must be fluid, with a different standard for each student, or the time and type of instruction must be greatly varied, or the instructors must maintain exceedingly modest expectations. All three options are at play in practically all programs.

Standardized expectations of accomplishment, or exit criteria, suggest social norms as contrasted with standards for individuals. Social norms imply that people who would function adequately in particular social settings (the workplace, school) must act to a certain standard. The alternative, relating accomplishment to the desires or entering abilities of individuals, suggests that any accomplishment is satisfactory and that the institution has succeeded if any gain in individual ability can be shown. This conflict between social and individual standards is an issue of the absolute versus the relative, and it strikes at the heart of developmental education.

Different groups take different positions on the issue. Community college instructors tend to argue in favor of absolute standards. The Academic Senate for California Community Colleges (ASCCC) has studied the problem extensively, surveying its members and sponsoring state conferences on the issue. The ASCCC deplored some of the pressures to lower standards: students entering the college with inadequate basic skills but with the expectation of passing the courses, as they have done throughout their prior school careers; ill-prepared students insisting on enrolling in transfer courses rather than remedial courses; the virtual elimination of D and F grades and concomitant wider use of passing grades; reduction in the number of required subjects; and the cult of growth afflicting community colleges, as evidenced by aggressive student recruiting drives. In 1977, the ASCCC Academic Standards Committee recommended that standards should be maintained through the use of diagnostic and placement testing, directive counseling, academic prerequisites for courses, and proficiency testing before awarding academic degrees. These recommendations were in no small measure responsible for California's adopting matriculation standards in the 1980s.

Support for the remedial function comes from many other areas, not least the American Association of Community Colleges. As its Commission on the Future of Community Colleges pointed out, "Literacy is essential both for the individual and society . . . community colleges must make a commitment, without apology, to help students overcome academic deficiencies" (AACJC, 1988a, pp. 16–17). The association carried its point a step further when it sponsored a national study seeking to determine the long-term success of students who had participated in remedial programs. The study found that most students who had gone through the remedial programs did well in their college-level studies, entered occupational programs or direct employment, and in general joined the mainstream of American life, much like a general cohort of the students entering community colleges (McCabe, 2000).

Advocates of the concept of lifelong learning often provide an opposing view. To them, any seeker of knowledge should find the institution a resource to be used for an infinite variety of purposes. Cross, for example, has argued that substantial changes in school forms are needed, so that anyone may learn anything at any time: "My concern is that in our exuberance for recruiting adults and certifying that their learning projects meet our standards, we will corrupt independent, self-directed learners into learners dependent on someone else to determine where, when, and how people should learn. Visions of a learning society with people of all ages enthusiastically pursuing learning that interests them could so easily turn into a joyless learning society with people grimly fulfilling requirements and seeking legitimacy for every conceivable variety of learning" (1978, pp. 19–20). These opposed positions suggest differing views about current and potential students. Some see them as lethargic illiterates; others, as humanistic knowledge seekers.

The Dilemma of Tracking

Segregating the less well-prepared students has much appeal. Classes can be made more homogeneous; the bright students are not forced to wait for the less able to catch up; and, most important, the instructors whose classes have been relieved of the poorer students can retain the attitude that they are teaching in a true college. However, the practice of shunting students to developmental classes is based on tenuous assumptions, especially the assumption that student performance standards are immutable, when nearly all school programs are based on shifting norms. The concept of functional literacy provides an example.

Definitions of Functional Literacy

One definition of functional literacy is *the level of reading, writing, and calculating ability that people need to succeed in the public realm in which they choose to operate.* Under this definition, the level of literacy required to function as a citizen, taxpayer, or homemaker, or in any other instructional milieu, serves as a criterion. A second definition is *the level of reading, writing, and ability to send and receive messages that it takes to obtain and maintain a job.* Obviously, different levels of literacy are required for performance in various jobs. A third definition of functional literacy is *the level required to perform successfully in a college program.* Here again, alternative programs require different levels of competency. Harman cited a 1956 omnibus definition: "A person is functionally literate when he has acquired the knowledge and skills in reading and writing which enable him to engage effectively in all those activities in which literacy is normally assumed in his cultural group" (1987, p. 4). All of these definitions, then, can be subsumed under the statement, *Functional literacy is the ability to communicate in the symbolic language of reading, writing, and speaking that is adequate for people to maintain themselves in the context of particular situations*, or, as the NAEP defines it, "using printed and written information to function in society, to achieve one's goals, and to develop one's knowledge and potential" (Kirsch and Jungeblut, 1986, p. 3).

So defined, functional literacy is related to the milieu in which people find themselves. It is relative; there are no absolute minimum standards of competence. A functionally literate person in some school settings may be functionally illiterate in certain jobs. And a person who is quite able to communicate within the confines of certain jobs may be functionally illiterate for purposes of a college program.

The dilemma here is that institutional legitimacy and faculty predilections rest on standards, defined outcomes, and certifiable results, but the definitions guiding staff efforts and the precepts of continuing education or lifelong learning are relative. Each person brings idiosyncratic backgrounds and aspirations to the institution; each finds a separate set of experiences. How can the two be reconciled in an open-admissions institution? The question is not limited to developmental education, but the influx of students with low academic ability brought it to the fore. In addition to providing a more useful learning experience for poorly prepared students, many of the developmental education programs have segregated them into separate enclaves, thus protecting, at least temporarily, the legitimacy of the other portions of the college. As state regulations and funding have joined the battle, the war has turned in favor of normed tests and mandatory assessment.

Imprecise Criteria

Selective admission to any program is as discriminatory as it is justifiable. Regardless of the yardstick applied, the people who are shut out of the programs in which they wanted to enroll have been discriminated against. Yet with accrediting agencies, state licensing boards, and senior institutions looking on, program directors feel justified in admitting only a select few, particularly if the field of endeavor for which the program prepares people can take only so many graduates or if college facilities allow for only so many matriculants.

Should the colleges restrict admissions to certain programs? If some applicants cannot gain admission to a program because their level of literacy is lower than a cutting score, the issue is resolved for them. But if applicants are admitted to the program, then its operators are responsible for teaching the skills required for them to succeed in it. The pattern of allowing all to enter and using the program itself to screen out the unworthy should be discounted, first because one cannot simultaneously teach and judge, and second because it is too expensive, in terms of both public funds and concern for people, to allow sizable numbers to enroll with the expectation that many of them will not complete the course of study.

The pressures for selective admission to various programs have grown in recent years. In the 1950s, most colleges screened students into remedial programs if their prior high school grades or their scores on entrance tests suggested that they might not be able to succeed in the transfer programs. In the 1960s, the pressure to allow anyone to enter a transfer program grew, the reason being that remedial programs were seen as catchalls for the less worthy, as holding tanks for students who must be "cooled out" of higher education. In the 1970s, the pendulum swung back, with many institutions building developmental programs, screening students into them, moving away from the attitude of letting students try everything and fail if they must. That trend accelerated in the 1980s as state mandates spread.

However, it is quite possible to teach functional literacy in the transfer program. Some notable efforts at mainstreaming—that is, allowing lower-ability students to take the regular college classes even while they are being assisted supplementally—have been made. Many of these efforts are decades old. Some use learning laboratories. As examples, in the Developmental Studies Program at Penn Valley Community College (Missouri), the Learning Skills Laboratory (LSL) was used as an extension of the math and English classroom. Students could complete LSL instructional activities, as prescribed by faculty members, before progressing to the course or concurrently with it. Established in 1980, the Learning Center at South Plains College (Texas) integrated remedial courses with collegiate instruction in reading and human development tutorials and a variety of other study opportunities. Sacramento City College (California) initiated the Higher Education Learning Package to promote the success and retention of students with basic skill deficiencies while mainstreaming them into regular courses. Students who were reading at a sixth-grade level worked with instructors and tutors in small groups and on a one-to-one basis. A series of one-hour study skills courses coordinated with the regular academic courses in Dutchess Community College (New York) led to better grades and retention not only in the related courses but also in other classes (Weeks, 1987). Thus, remediation does not have to come in the form of segregated remedial courses.

It is likely that most students can succeed in the collegiate and occupational programs if they are required to supplement their courses with tutorials, learning labs, special counseling, peer-group assistance, and a variety of other aids. Students who were required to take the remedial reading course concurrently with various math classes in Gainesville College (Georgia) were less likely to withdraw from their class than those who completed the reading course first (Hamilton, 1998). Students who registered concurrently in basic skills classes in English and mathematics along with other within-discipline classes at City College of San Francisco had higher pass rates than those who were in separate programs (Spurling, 1998).

Denying students admission to programs of their choice is difficult to justify. The open-door philosophy of the community college implies that these students should not be denied. The fact that some can succeed also suggests that they should not be denied. And the fact that students who are denied access to collegiate programs are typically denied exposure to the humanistic and scientific thought on which these areas are based mandates that they must not be denied. Community colleges have succeeded in opening access to all; if that access is limited to a developmental program that offers primarily the same type of basic education that failed the students in the lower schools, then students have been cruelly denied access to higher learning. The colleges cannot afford to operate separate programs for the less qualified unless those programs are verifiably supportive of the collegiate and vocational programs.

Those who would impose standards for programs at any level face difficulties stemming from lack of consensus on institutional purpose, antagonism to the idea of group norms, and, in secondary schools and community colleges, the inability to impose entrance requirements. Selective screening into the collegiate programs could not be maintained in an earlier era because students demanded and got the right to fail, and that contributed to the unconscionable attrition figures of the 1970s. Selective admission into the collegiate programs has been tried again because it is easier to screen students out en bloc than to establish criteria for functional literacy course by course, as the colleges in San Diego have done. Yet unless those criteria are defined, selective admissions will again be unsuccessful. Although it is impossible to bring all students to the point at which they can succeed in the courses and programs of their choice, the community colleges must continue trying.

Reconciling the Dilemma

Three options are available to colleges that would reconcile the conflict between maintaining standards and allowing all students to enter the programs of their choice. First, they can define the specific competencies required to enter and succeed in each course. "College level," "program proficiency," and "academic standards" are not sufficiently precise. There is too much variation among courses in the same program—indeed, among sections of the same course—for these criteria to hold. Standards are too often relative instead of absolute. Screening tests can be used at the point of entry to each class. And precise exit criteria—also known as specific, measurable objectives—can be set.

The second option is to allow all students to enroll in any course but to limit the number of courses that poorly prepared students can take in any term and require that they take advantage of the available support services. Thus, students might take only one course at a time and participate in tutorial and learning-laboratory sessions on the basis of two or three hours for each credit hour attempted.

A third is to build free-standing developmental programs and insist that all students designated as reading, writing, or computing at a level precluding their passing college-level courses enroll in them. These programs would emphasize study skills, directing attention to the problems that kept the students from achieving in their earlier schooling.

All three options are now employed to some extent. The colleges that rely on precisely specified measures of student progress have built their programs on absolute standards even though assessing student performance may still be based in part on faculty judgment. Those that monitor student progress and insist that students participate in auxiliary instructional exercises or remedial courses taught within the academic departments have moved well toward building the kind of collegewide instructional effort that teaching poorly prepared students demands. But those that have erected separate programs that concentrate exclusively on remedial studies have become the most widespread, involving especially trained instructors and judging success by the number of students who pass through to the academic and vocational programs. They are effective only when they are comprehensive efforts complete with support services and connections with the colleges' other programs, such as the learning communities cited earlier.

At least two options are not acceptable: allowing sizable percentages of students to fail and reducing academic standards so that those who do get through have not been sufficiently well prepared to succeed in the workplace or in further education. High failure rates have led to numerous charges that the community colleges are a dead end for many of their matriculants, especially minority students. By reducing standards, as detailed by Richardson, Fisk, and Okun (1983), the colleges were merely pushing the problem off to the students' employers or the academic institutions in which they subsequently enrolled. Since the 1980s, the numerous state mandates designed to improve student progress reflect a decided unwillingness to allow either of those options to continue.

As community colleges become involved more heavily in developmental education, they have to reconcile their relations with the secondary schools from which they broke away. Education at any level depends on prior preparation of the students. The decline in the secondary schools during the 1970s was one of the most notable events of the decade in education, and some of the blame can be placed at the colleges' doors. The dearth of communication between college and secondary school staff members, the lack of articulation in curriculum, the failure to share teaching materials except on the basis of random encounters: all must be mentioned. Concerns for social equity replaced a prior concern for admission standards. In their haste to expand access, the colleges neglected to assist the secondary schools in preparing the people who would be coming to them and even, in many cases, to recommend the secondary school courses that the students should take. Reconciling the dilemma will force them to rectify this omission. Contemporary efforts at school–college collaboration, such as those described by Palmer (2000) and those noted in Chapter Four, suggest moves in that direction.

Issues

Whether the community colleges pick up the seventeen-year-olds who have left high school early and whether they serve as a bridge between schooling and work for their older students, developmental education fits within their mission of connecting people with opportunities. They will be involved in remedial studies in one form or another.

College staff need more information about the effects of the developmental education in which they are so heavily engaged. Do segregated remedial programs lead to higher standards in other courses? Do the faculty members outside the programs add content to the courses from which the lesser-ability students have been removed? Do they pass students through the courses more rapidly when they are relieved from having to wait for the slower students? If so, all these results should be tabulated as benefits of the separate programs. If not, the better students have not gained from the absence of the poorer ones. So far, studies of these effects have been almost nonexistent.

Several attempts to engage instructors in defining the outcomes of their courses in specific, measurable terms have failed. What forms of staff development would be successful? What incentives could be used?

Would allowing instructors to test the students who sought entry to their classes and bar those who did not pass the test suffice to encourage them to take responsibility for passing a specified percentage? Regardless of the faculty's involvement in entrance assessment, they typically refuse, individually and collectively, to be held accountable for results.

Required support services increase instructional costs. Can the colleges find sufficient funds for the necessary tutors, counselors, learning laboratory technicians, and paraprofessional instructional aides? Can the faculty be encouraged to work with these aides, so that classroom and auxiliary instruction lead to parallel objectives?

What patterns of learning are demanded of students in the courses currently in place? Finding answers to that question demands analyses of classroom tests and teaching techniques, a form of research rarely seen in the contemporary college. Will incessant pressure from legislators and governing boards eventually see it occur?

The overriding issue is whether community colleges can maintain their credibility as institutions of higher education even while they enroll increasingly less well-prepared students. If they can, they will fulfill the promises of their earliest proponents. Regardless, the United States is not going to abandon its functional illiterates, and the community colleges are going to be involved in educating them.

10

Community Education

Extending College Services and Training

Community education, the broadest of all functions, embraces adult and continuing education, contract services, and numerous other activities not part of traditional college programs. It may take the form of classes for credit or not for credit, varying in duration from one hour to a weekend, several days, or an entire school term. Community education may be sponsored by the college, by some other agency using college facilities, or jointly by the college and some outside group. It may be provided on campus, off campus, or through television, the newspapers, or radio. It may center on education or recreation, on programs for personal interest or for the benefit of specific businesses or the entire community.

The various forms of community education usually are fully supported by participant fees, grants, or contracts with external organizations. Participants tend to have short-term goals rather than degree or certificate objectives. They are usually older than the traditional eighteen- to twenty-one-year-old students, and their range of prior school achievement is more varied: many of them already hold baccalaureate or graduate degrees; many more have never completed high school. They usually attend the course or activities intermittently and part time. They have their own reasons for attending, and program managers design activities accordingly.

Found in the earliest community colleges, these activities were carried along for decades on the periphery of the vocational and collegiate functions. They expanded greatly in the 1970s, slowed in the 1980s as college services came under closer scrutiny from external budget allocators, and grew again in the 1990s as college leaders continually sought new avenues for funding services to particular community groups.

This chapter reviews the rationale for and scope of community education, emphasizing the most popular activities: continuing education, community services, and contract training. It considers also the perennial problems of funding, assessing effects, and validating these services that fall outside the traditional collegiate offerings.

Rationale

Beginning with Jesse Bogue, who popularized the term *community college* in the 1950s, and continuing with the Commission on the Future of Community Colleges' report, *Building Communities* (American Association of Community and Junior Colleges, 1988a), the leaders of the American Association of Community and Junior Colleges (AACJC) have been vigorous in their support for community education. Edmund J. Gleazer, Jr., president of the association from 1958 until 1981, wrote extensively in favor of education for direct community development, the expansion of the colleges beyond their role in postsecondary education, and continuing education as the main purpose. He emphasized the "community," rather than the "college," in the institution's title. To him, it was a resource to be used by individuals throughout their lifetime and by the general public as an agency assisting with community issues.

One of Gleazer's primary contentions was that "the community college is uniquely qualified to become the nexus of a community learning system, relating organizations with educational functions into a complex sufficient to respond to the population's learning needs" (1980, p. 10). He thought the institution capable of serving as a connector by virtue of its students and staff members, who frequently work at other jobs in the community. The college would be a link among all community organizations that provide learning activities. "Among these are radio and television stations, newspapers, libraries, museums, schools, colleges, theaters, parks, orchestras, dance groups, unions, and clubs" (p. 10). As for the money to pay for all this, Gleazer made repeated calls for fiscal formulas that would recognize the diverse programs presented by community colleges. However, he recognized that "a kind of riptide exists between the interest in lifelong education and the apparently limited financial resources available for conventional education for traditional students" (1976, p. 6).

Numerous other commentators have favored community education as a dominant function. Myran traced the community education concept through university extension services and the adult and continuing education offered by the public schools for the past century. These institutions were able to provide educational services to individuals and groups without being wed to traditional academic forms, such as credits, semesters, and grades. In Myran's view, the community-based college was eminently equipped to provide such services because of its ability "to coordinate planning with other community agencies, its interest in participatory learning experiences as well as cognitive ones, the wide range of ages and life goals represented in its student body, and the alternative instructional approaches it arranges to make learning accessible to various community groups" (1969, p. 5). Martorana and Piland (1984) similarly promoted the concept; Cross has furthered it in many of her writings, such as *Adults as Learners* (1981); and it is thematic in the quarterly, *Catalyst*, published since 1970.

Its intentions are noble. Harlacher and Gollattscheck recommended a college that would be a "vital participant in the total renewal process of the community . . . dedicated to the continual growth and development of its citizens and its social institutions" (1978, p. 7). Such a college would offer the kinds of education community members want, not the kind that pedagogues think is good for them, and at locations where the learners are, not where the college says they should be. Harlacher and Gollattscheck urged community colleges to cooperate with social, governmental, professional, educational, and neighborhood agencies in mutually supportive advisory relationships and in joint ventures.

More recently, the AACJC-sponsored Commission on the Future of Community Colleges urged the colleges to coalesce around the community education concept:

> The community college, at its best, can be a center for problem-solving in adult illiteracy or the education of the disabled. It can be a center for leadership training, too. It can also be the place where education and business leaders meet to talk about the problems of displaced workers. It can bring together agencies to strengthen services for minorities, working women, single parent heads of households, and unwed teenage parents. It can coordinate efforts to provide day care, transportation, and financial aid. The community college can take the lead in long-range planning for community development. And it can serve as the focal point for improving the quality of life in the inner city [American Association of Community and Junior Colleges, 1988a, p. 35].

This seems a large order, but the commission was dedicated to fostering the colleges as centers of community life. Its report began with the premise that "the term *community* should be defined not only as a region to be served, but also as a climate to be created" (p. 3), and many of its seventy-seven recommendations followed from that theme. Elsner and Beauchamp extended the idea: "Community building involves creating relationships that let people and organizations share values, find common interests, and mobilize resources toward solutions" (2002, p. 1).

What has stimulated these calls for completely revised structures? What has made these advocates so concerned with community building and noncampus forms? One clue is provided by the nature of the colleges' political and fiscal support. They draw minuscule funds from private donors and have few federal or foundation-supported research contracts. Instead, they depend almost entirely on public monies awarded in a political arena. And here they have difficulty competing with the more prestigious universities for support in legislatures dominated by university alumni. They seem to be turning to their local constituents, seeking links with taxpayers at the grassroots—seeking support from the business community, for example, by providing customized job-training services for local employers.

Community education proponents foster activities different from the traditional courses taught by regular faculty members, saying that these are archaic, restrictive, discriminatory, and narrowly focused. They seem to feel that doing away with the traditional forms in which education has been conducted will necessarily lead to a higher quality of service. In their desire to eschew elitism, they articulate populist, egalitarian goals. The more diverse the population served and the less traditionally based the program, the better.

The overarching concept of community education is certainly justifiable; few would quibble with the intent of an institution to upgrade its entire community rather than merely provide a limited array of courses for people just out of high school. However, the total seems less than the sum of its parts. The components of community education must be addressed separately in order to understand its scope and effect. Are all segments of equal value? Who decides what shall be presented, and who shall pay for it?

Categories

Because community education covers many areas, few of which are encompassed within traditional collegiate activities or funding lines, attempts have been made to categorize its manifold aspects.

The Carnegie Foundation for the Advancement of Teaching (2006) proposed a four-part classification system:

- Community engagement (collaborative efforts)
- Curricular engagement (community-identified needs for education and scholarship)
- Outreach and partnerships (providing institutional resources for community use)
- Curricular engagement, outreach, and partnerships, combined

In this chapter, we subdivide community education as follows:

- *Continuing education*: The learning effort undertaken by people whose principal occupation is no longer student—those who regard learning as a means of developing their potential or resolving their problems.

  Adult education: Instruction designed for people who have either completed or interrupted their formal education.

  Adult basic education: Basic skills instruction for adults who function at less than a high school level. Instruction may include English as a Second Language (ESL), General Education Development (GED), and literacy programming.

  Continuing occupational/workforce education: Any type of noncredit instruction or training designed to upgrade job skills or prepare one to enter an occupation. Courses may be tailored for a specific job or industry, or they may have broader applicability.

  Lifelong learning: Intermittent education, undertaken in school and other settings. Courses may be of a community service nature other than recreation and leisure.

Entrepreneurship training.

- *Community services*: The broadest term—whatever services an institution provides that are acceptable to the people in its service area.

Cooperative arrangements with other community agencies.

Community-based education: Programs designed by the people served and developed for the good of the community.

Recreation and leisure: Courses designed for recreational and leisure purposes often offered on a short-term basis.

- *Contract training*: Collaborations between the community colleges and business, industry, and other agencies.

Correctional education.

Training provided for, and at least partially funded by, particular industries.

Conceptually, community education includes elements of vocational, developmental, and collegiate education. Vocational education is organized around programs that prepare people for the job market, whereas community education includes short courses offered for occupational upgrading or relicensure. Collegiate education is directed toward preparing people for academic degrees, whereas community education may include regular college courses taken by adults, the awarding of college credit for experience, and noncredit courses taught at the college level—for example, conversational foreign languages. Developmental education is designed to remedy the defects in student learning occasioned by prior school failure, whereas community education may include adult basic studies that focus on literacy, high school completion, and general education development. Some elements of community education—programs for the disabled and for prison inmates, for example—may cut across all three of the other functions. However, different elements in community education relate also to providing noneducative services to the community. In this category would fall the opening of college facilities for public functions and a variety of recreational services—the community service notion. As an example, residents in rural areas may find the only readily accessible arts and cultural activities to be those presented through their local colleges.

Practically, the source of funds tends to divide community education from the other functions. Community education activities are more likely to be self-supporting, fully funded through tuition or with money provided by an outside agency on the basis of a contract for services rendered. State and federal funds earmarked for special groups are often used in community education programs. In some cases local tax monies and categorical grants are used for community education, whereas vocational and collegiate education are funded by the states through various formulas, usually based on student enrollment or credit hours generated.

Enrollments

The variations in definition and categories make it difficult to estimate the magnitude of community education. Enrollment figures, especially, are unreliable; they are usually understated except when being pronounced by advocates intent on showing that the colleges serve nearly everyone in their district. Because degree-credit courses are funded at higher, more consistent levels than most of community education, the tendency was to classify as much as possible as degree credit, thus inflating those numbers at the expense of community education enrollment figures. However, as the states placed limits on the number of credit hours for which they would reimburse the colleges, that practice was curtailed. Actually, the total community education enrollment would far exceed the combined enrollment in the career-certificate and collegiate-degree programs if people who enrolled in college-credit classes but without degree aspirations were classified instead as adult education students. But enrollees in noncredit courses and participants in community service activities are those typically counted.

The enrollment figures that are available are worth recounting. Community education enrollments (in service, recreational, and life enrichment programs that are not part of for-credit academic programs) were reported in the American Association of Community and Junior Colleges *Directory* between 1974–75, when they were 3,259,972, and 1984–85, when they totaled 3,651,225. For the decade, they ranged between 3 and 4 million per year. However, the introduction to the 1980 *Directory* states that "because these programs vary in length, with no clearly defined registration periods, it is difficult to get a clear picture. . . . Some institutions do not routinely collect enrollment figures from community education students" (p. 3). Extrapolating from the 877 institutions that did report student head count in noncredit activities in 1984–85, the compilers of the *Directory* estimated that 4,848,065 participated nationwide, with 99 percent in public colleges. The AACC has since stopped reporting these data because of the imprecision of the figures.

Data difficulties make it impossible to compare community education enrollments between states as well. Some state reports include adult basic education or participation in recreational activities (or both), and others do not. Furthermore, head-count enrollments in community education usually include duplicate enrollments occasioned when the same person participates in more than one noncredit course or activity during the year. Nonetheless, state enrollments are useful as an estimate of the magnitude and types of functions included in the community education definition.

For example, the AACJC *Directory* reported 153,086 participants in community education in 1979 in California, compared with a total enrollment of 1,101,648 students in degree-credit programs. This relatively low ratio reflects the predominance of the California secondary schools in adult education. In the three community college districts that had jurisdiction over adult education, more than half the students were classified as adults. Community education enrollments in California plummeted after the passage of Proposition 13 in 1978 cut off the local funding base for community services, but rose again when the courses were reinstated on a student-fee basis.

The total varies also in other states. In Florida, the community colleges have major responsibility for offering courses to individuals aged sixteen and older who had legally left the lower schools. In 2005–06, 57,493 were enrolled in adult education, 4,928 in lifelong learning, and 76,835 in recreation and leisure (Florida State Department of Education, 2007). In 2004–05, Mississippi had 209,795 students enrolled in noncredit courses, including adult basic education, continuing education, Graduate Education Development (GED) programs, literacy programs, high school vocational education programs, and workforce education (Mississippi State Board for Community and Junior Colleges, 2004–2005). In California, over 647,272 adults participated in noncredit courses offered by 94 of the state's 106 community colleges (California State Board of Education, and California Community Colleges, 1998).

There is no question that the demand for non-degree-related courses is high across all segments of the population. A 1991 National Household Education Survey found that one-third of all employed adults had enrolled in some type of job-related, part-time educational activity in the prior year. (NCES *Digest,* 1994). The NCES estimated that 90 million adults were participating in adult education in 1999, a substantial increase from 58 million in 1991. Work-related and personal development courses attracted the highest percentage of adults (23 percent for each activity) (NCES *Digest,* 2001).

Scope

The scope of community education is reflected in documents from colleges around the country. Continuing education alone covers a broad area. The concept describes an area of service that knows no limits on client age, prior educational attainment, interest, or intent, and the scope of offerings is limited only by staff energies and imagination and by the funds available.

Continuing Education

A Ford Foundation Study reported by Gittell (1985) found many low-income adults involved in community education and concluded that community-based colleges provide an important option for many people who are not served elsewhere. Whatever the financial circumstances, many groups of people are involved because community education addresses a wide variety of concerns, including child care, substance abuse, senior citizen services, student achievement and school effectiveness, community pride and support for schools, unemployment and underemployment, literacy and diploma and degree completion, and community economic development. When sufficient funding can be obtained, programs for special groups are provided: women, displaced workers, gerontology programs for both the general public and providers of direct services to older adults, retired persons, single parents, and displaced homemakers.

More than 500 community colleges participate in the Servicemembers Opportunity Colleges (SOC), which allows members of the armed forces and their families to enroll in college-level programs at community and state colleges and universities (Servicemembers Opportunity Colleges, Web site). It advocates flexible access to higher education for members of the armed forces and strengthens the liaison and communication between the military and higher education. In general, adult and noncredit education serve an especially versatile population: parents, older adults, disabled adults, homeless adults, out-of-school youth and dropouts, special needs adults, unemployed and underemployed adults, adults receiving public assistance and welfare recipients, persons involved with the penal system, and new immigrants.

Adult Basic Education

Continuing-education programs also serve other special groups. Adult basic education, centering on basic skills development for functionally illiterate adults, is a major component. The Florida community colleges enrolled 57,493 students in adult and secondary programs (Florida Department of Education, 2007). In the Illinois colleges, 10,892 students were in ABE and 5,857 participated in adult secondary education programs (Illinois Community College Board, 2005). Over 135,000 students, 17 percent of the total served by the North Carolina Community Colleges, were in ABE (2007b). Milwaukee Area Technical College (Wisconsin) is one of many that helps migrant and seasonal farmworkers and their dependents obtain GED (General Educational Development) degrees and either gain employment or continue their education in postsecondary institutions outside the agricultural setting (Lopez, personal communication, June 14, 2007). The need for and popularity of such programs is evident.

Entrepreneurship Training

Establishing a small business has always been a natural sequence for some graduates of community college career programs. In 1980, a congressional act created Small Business Development Centers (SBDCs), a venture funded jointly by the federal government, the U.S. Small Business Administration, and state and local public and private agencies. These centers, in many cases housed in community colleges, were designed to help individuals interested in starting a business and those who already had businesses but required management assistance.

Carmichael (1991) discusses the steps in establishing SBDCs and describes Lane Community College (Oregon), which had the first community college–based network in the nation, and Bergen County Community College (New Jersey), which had one of the first pilot programs funded by the Small Business Administration. Other exemplary programs include Montgomery Community College (Maryland) and several other colleges in the Washington, D.C., metropolitan area.

The difference between entrepreneurship training and small-business development, on the one hand, and workforce training, on the other, lies in program centers and in people for whom the programs are intended. The content of entrepreneurship training, designed to assist people starting their own businesses, ranges from developing a business plan to obtaining licenses and loans to employing other people to operate a successful business. A small number of community colleges are involved in business incubation: the practice of assisting emerging small businesses by creating an environment where business owners are provided with opportunities to develop entrepreneurial skills. However, in many cases, the colleges provide entrepreneurs with little more than space and clerical support.

The Center for the Study of Community Colleges examined the scope and magnitude of entrepreneurship training in the nation's community colleges and found that most large-city colleges had some such involvement, usually provided through their continuing-education division or through a center for economic development or small-business development institute. The programs were organized on an ad hoc basis when state, federal, foundation, or local-agency funds could be acquired. Typically, the people toward whom the training was directed could afford to pay little or no tuition (Center for the Study of Community Colleges, 1994).

In Virginia, a majority of community colleges offer at least one course treating topics of entrepreneurship and small-business management education. Two of the eleven colleges responding to a 1999 survey award associate of applied science degrees with a focus on entrepreneurship education (Drury and Mallory, 2000). REAL Enterprises (Rural Entrepreneurship Through Action Learning) operates in sixty-nine colleges, with programs focusing on the development of small businesses through experiential learning, self-assessment, community analysis, and business plan writing. Students may receive start-up support for setting up their own enterprise (Larson, King, McGee, and Shea, 1997). Several other reports describe statewide and local efforts to promote entrepreneurial competence in California (Carvell, 1988), Kansas (Gainous and others, 1987), and Clackamas Community College in Oregon (Borquist, 1986).

Special Services

Several types of cooperative endeavors between community colleges and other community agencies may be found. The AACJC's Policies for Lifelong Education project surveyed cooperative relationships between colleges and community groups and reported that arrangements between the colleges and local and state clubs and organizations as well as other educational institutions were most prevalent. Cooperative arrangements were also found with county and municipal government agencies and private enterprises, including industrial concerns. These joint ventures ranged from sharing facilities to offering mutually sponsored courses. The majority of funds came from tuition and fees charged participants, but many of the programs were supported by college community service funds, often generated by local taxes (Gilder and Rocha, 1980).

One study, conducted by the Workforce Strategy Center staff, cited community-based organizations (CBOs) as essential to the goal of community colleges to extend their education and training opportunities to wider local communities. CBOs offer services such as counseling, case management, social support, rehabilitation services, and education and training to adults in local communities who lack ties to educational institutions. Partnerships between community colleges and CBOs link these resources with accessibility for underserved adults. The study sought examples of programs focusing on economically and educationally disadvantaged adults, offering credit-bearing instruction and integrating social support and counseling. West Side Technical Institute at Daley Community College (Illinois) collaborated with Insituto del Progreso Latino to provide metalworking, machinist, adult basic education, vocational ESL, and GED programs designed to prepare economically and educationally disadvantaged adults for jobs in manufacturing. Austin Community College (Texas) partnered with Capital IDEA to provide over 600 low-income adults with postsecondary training in health care, high technology, accounting, adult education, ESL, GED, and customized training for employer demand. The study group concluded, "Making community colleges the key institution in career pathway models allows local workforce agencies, community-based organizations (CBOs), social service agencies, and employers to work together to build an effective workforce development system that enables disadvantaged individuals to achieve economic self-sufficiency" (Gruber, 2004, p. 3).

In community-based programming, promoted by the Academy for Community College Leadership Advancement, Innovation, and Modeling, community colleges act as leaders and catalysts facilitating collaboration among the community they serve and its leaders, community agencies, and organizations with the primary purpose of improving the life of the community (Boone and Associates, 1997). Community-based programming was used in Guilford Technical Community College (North Carolina) as a means to improve workforce preparedness; in James Sprunt Community College (North Carolina) with a focus on literacy and economic development; in Florence-Darlington Technical College (South Carolina) to address issues of local water quality; in Technical College of the Lowcountry (South Carolina) to spur economic development; and in Paul D. Camp Community College (Virginia) emphasizing issues related to substance abuse (Boone, Pettitt, and Weisman, 1998). Some colleges have developed community-based forums in which the participants discuss subjects reported in the local newspaper, a procedure that has been used to bring the humanities to participants through lectures, panels, debates, dramatizations, films, and radio broadcasts.

Although not included in the community education figures, the many programs that fine arts and humanities departments sponsor in cooperation with local agencies, such as arts councils and museums, are properly a part of the concept. Such activities have been promoted for decades: Fields (1962) described how Tyler Junior College (Texas) shared cultural events in its community; Goldman (1969) found rural colleges in California offering several types of cultural programs; and Terry, Hardy, and Katsinas (2007) found nearly all the rural community colleges in Alabama providing theatrical productions and musical and literary events open to the public and funded by small grants, some from the National Endowment for the Arts.

A review of other activities conducted under the heading of continuing education's special services reveals little change in scope over recent decades. Many colleges offer job fairs to help connect people who need jobs with businesses that need people, recreational activities in senior citizens' centers, parenting classes, child care training programs, and drug and alcohol abuse workshops.

Contracted Services

Contract training refers to instruction that is provided for specific occupational purposes, usually outside the college-credit program. It falls into three categories: training designed specifically for the employees of certain companies, training for public agency employees, and training for specific groups such as unemployed people or people on welfare. Funds may come from the companies or public agencies that benefit or from state or federal funds.

Contract training has become a significant portion of the community college's overall educational effort. Surveys conducted by the League for Innovation in the Community College (Doucette, 1993) and the National Center for Research in Vocational Education (Lynch and others, 1991) suggest its magnitude. Practically all community colleges in the nation are involved. The programs designed for specific companies include job-specific and computer-related training, management preparation, and workplace literacy. And in some colleges, it was big indeed; in 1991, sixteen selected community colleges reported that they had generated over $42 million through contract training during the previous year (Updike, 1991). Roueche, Taber, and Roueche (1995) describe many other types of collaborations with community agencies.

Community colleges have long taken advantage of various federal programs designed to retrain technologically displaced workers and other unemployed people, using funds provided by the Manpower Development Training Act of 1962, the Comprehensive Employment and Training Act of 1973, and the JTPA of 1983. These programs assisted the colleges in designing activities in accordance with local job needs and in cooperation with employers in their region. In 1985, the Sears-Roebuck Foundation gave a sizable award to encourage collaboration between community colleges and local employers. Through this award, the AACJC and the Association of Community College Trustees established the Keeping America Working project (American Association of Community and Junior Colleges, 1986).

Labor union leaders also have supported community education programs—for example, by negotiating tuition aid packages with employers, serving on advisory committees for the colleges' occupational programs, and helping to establish cooperative apprenticeship training programs and programs to assist union members in studying for leadership roles. Some union-sponsored activities assist members in studying the liberal arts; others are designed to help working people deal with personal problems or problems with employers.

Dougherty and Bakia (1999) examined contract training as represented in five industries—auto manufacturing, apparel making, construction, banking, and auto repair—in twenty community colleges. Programs for skilled workers were found to dominate contract training in the auto manufacturing, auto repair, and construction industries, whereas training for entry-level and semiskilled workers was scarce. Training programs are typically governed by employers and unions but community colleges have some degree of influence in curricular, selection, and evaluation-related decision making. The colleges emerged as the training partner of choice for many employers because of their low cost, reliability, and responsiveness to employers' needs and are preferred over vocational schools because of the higher value attached to the credentials they offer.

How are the colleges affected? As an important benefit, contract training boosts enrollment figures, and many students, originally taking vocationally oriented contract classes, later return to enroll in classes in general education as well. Contract training also often provides a substantial source of additional revenue for the colleges. Nonmonetary revenue from contract training includes new facilities, equipment, training aids, and training for faculty. The greater visibility and political support that contract training brings, emphasizing the colleges' role in lowering the rate of unemployment, are also among the advantages.

Contract training is associated with several negative consequences as well. Community colleges may be criticized for presenting unfair competition to private training companies by offering publicly subsidized training. Furthermore, contract training brings expanded business involvement into the colleges' internal decision-making processes and may create unease among faculty in vocational and contract training programs, since the two programs often compete for the same student population. Although the employers who benefit provide a significant portion of the cost of these programs, college funds are often used as a supplement. Because the programs are only tangentially connected with the college-credit curriculum, some faculty groups have complained that they are employing instructors who are not reviewed by the regular faculty and that they are bypassing the traditional channels of curriculum development, thus weakening the overall college program.

Correctional Education

Community education often involves providing special services to other publicly funded institutions, as in, for example, nearly every prison system in the nation. Erisman and Contardo's comprehensive study found that, "As of 2003–04 more than 85,000 prisoners—just under 5 percent of the total prison population—were taking college courses" (2005, p. 47). The largest numbers were in federal prisons (17 percent) and in Texas and North Carolina (11 percent each). Since 1967, Arizona community colleges have offered basic skills and vocational training to inmates within their prison system and in 1990 awarded more than one hundred associate degrees. In 2006, 45 North Carolina community colleges enrolled 65,000 duplicated headcount, which represents 30 percent of the inmates in 78 prisons (North Carolina Community College System, 2007a). Montcalm Community College (Michigan) enrolled 245 inmates, equal to 23 percent of the college's total student population (Michigan State Board for Public Community Colleges, 1999). Lakeshore Technical College's (Wisconsin) prison program includes ABE and secondary education, ESL, and GED testing. Coastline Community College and Palo Verde College, both in California, enroll high numbers of inmates through their distance learning programs. Chaffey College (California) and Quinebaug Valley Community College (Connecticut) have programs especially for female inmates.

These programs for prisoners seem to be effective. The Workplace and Community Transition Training for Incarcerated Youth Offenders Program in Virginia operates through seven community colleges at 17 correctional facilities and two detention/ diversion centers and offered credit and noncredit courses to 1,200 inmates between 2000 and 2004. Students in this program recidivated at a significantly lower rate than other ex-offenders (Lichtenberger and Onyewu, 2005; Cunningham, 2007). Texas prisoners who earned associate's degrees while incarcerated returned to prison at a rate of 27 percent, compared to a 43 percent recidivism rate for the state prison system as a whole. J. F. Ingram State Technical College (Alabama) inmate education program claimed a 2 percent recidivism rate for its graduates, as compared with 35 percent in the rest of the Alabama prison system (Cvancara, 1994). Legislation in 1994 eliminating Pell Grants for prisoners depressed these involvements, but ten years later, enrollments were higher than the previous level. State corrections funds and charitable donations make up for the loss of federal grants (Erisman and Contardo, 2005).

Effectiveness

Are community education programs effective? Assessing the outcomes is difficult; because the entire community is the client, effects are diffuse and subject to contamination from innumerable sources. One way of measuring the effects of continuing-education courses has been to ask the participants how they liked them. The 4,631 students enrolled in community service courses in ten Florida community colleges were asked why they enrolled and the extent to which their expectations were met. Among the twenty-two choices, the major reasons for enrolling were "to improve my chances of employment" (42 percent), "to further my cultural or social development" (39 percent), and "to learn a certain hobby" (34 percent). The only areas in which expectations were not met by at least 60 percent of the respondents were "to help with an alcohol-or-drug related problem" and "to learn about family planning" (Nickens, 1977, p. 269).

Other evaluations typically are process related. The Maryland State Board for Community Colleges has specified that in order to be eligible for state funding, continuing-education courses "must illustrate the skill or knowledge to be developed and the student outcomes expected" (1988, p. 13). McGuire (1988) has provided a set of criteria by which entire community-based programs might be measured. But these again are process criteria: the extent to which community members were involved in program planning, the linkages that were built between the college and other community agencies, the feedback received from community leaders and clients, and similar subjective measures that are dependent on an observer's interpretation. All of community education seems to be assessed as though it were continuing education for individuals raised to the level of the broader group. If the clients define the goals and the processes, success is measured by their saying that they achieved those goals. Independent ratings based on measurable change seem as scarce as advance determination of the change to be effected.

Organization and Funding

The organization of Coastline Community College (California) in 1976 as a noncampus institution devoted primarily to community education, and similar institutions in Arizona and Washington, stimulated the development of a new form of professional educator. The managers of these institutions must be not only curriculum and instructional designers, the role played by practitioners in all colleges, but also must interact with community advisory committees, find agencies to bear the cost of their programs, advertise for students, employ part-time staff members, produce varieties of new instructional media, and resolve jurisdictional disputes with other agencies; in sum, must act as entrepreneurs. Although such roles are not as well defined in the more conventional community colleges, those with sizable community education efforts of necessity have a number of people acting in those capacities.

Separate administrative entities have also been organized in several individual colleges. Valencia Community College (Florida) began the Open Campus in 1974 to coordinate all continuing education, community services, and functions that the college was providing away from the campus. Headed by a provost reporting directly to the president, the Open Campus was organized as a unit equal in autonomy to the other branch campuses of the college. The off-campus learning center operated by Lansing Community College (Michigan) included a director of continuing education, a formal contract between the college and the local school districts, a broad selection of courses, and the same basic support services that were provided at the central campus. The Extended Learning Institute at John Tyler Community College (Virginia) used television, radio, and newspapers as media for the instruction of a wide variety of students in its district. These types of organizations—which coordinate the noncredit courses, distance learning, and related community education activities—have been built in many colleges. They typically have their own staff, budget lines, and funding sources.

The ways that community education has been funded reflect its growth and variety. Some community education activities receive no direct aid; all expenses are borne by the participants themselves or by an agency with which the institution has a contract. Others are funded by enrollment formulas that tend to yield less money than the formulas used for the vocational and collegiate courses. Funding for the recreational and avocational activities within the community education definition is the most difficult to obtain because those activities seem least justifiable for support at taxpayer expense.

Some states have funded adult basic education at the same rate as vocational and collegiate programs. Others have funded them well but under different formulas. In Florida, developmental and community instructional services received nearly as much state money per full-time-student equivalent (FTSE) as the vocational and collegiate functions. However, continuing-education courses in Iowa were not eligible for state aid. Oregon reimbursed colleges for remedial and continuing-education courses at approximately the same level as for collegiate and vocational programs. Maryland funded continuing-education courses that met certain criteria, especially if they focused on occupational, developmental, and consumer education; recreational courses were not eligible for reimbursement. Noncredit and adult education programs in California, limited to classes provided free of charge to students, were funded primarily by the State School Fund, general apportionment, with additional support from the National Literacy Act of 1991; the Carl D. Perkins Vocational and Applied Technology Education Act; the JTPA; School-to-Career Partnerships; the California Work Opportunities and Responsibility to Kids Program and Greater Avenues for Independence; and Apprenticeship programs (California State Board of Education, and California Community Colleges, 1998). Once again, it is important to note that between-state comparisons cannot accurately be made because the definitions of the courses and programs included in the different categories vary widely.

There is no best plan for financing community colleges in every state, and disputes over financing often disguise disagreements over the community college mission. Haynes and Polk (1991) contended that continuing-education units designed to keep an institution viable during periods of decline were self-serving and less likely to succeed than those that identified and served a community's educational needs. State officials certainly accord lower priority to financial support of these programs, compared with the traditional academic and occupational functions. Historically, community services have been funded by local sources and as community college finance shifts toward the state level, funding becomes more precarious. In Virginia, a survey was taken of the forty members of the state senate and the presidents of the state's twenty-three community colleges to see how well these two groups agreed on which programs could be appropriately funded by state taxes. Although the senate and presidents agreed on the majority of goals, these two groups ranked "providing general interest courses and activities for senior citizens and other community members" twelfth out of fourteen categories (Ashworth and Vogler, 1991).

The precarious base of funding for community education was revealed between 1978 and 1981 when tax-limitation legislation was passed in several states and a national administration pledged to reduce taxes was elected. Soon after the 1978 passage of Proposition 13 in California, the average community services budget was cut by at least 50 percent. These cuts resulted in a 76 percent increase in courses for which fees were charged and a 24 percent decrease in courses funded through college budgets. Kintzer detailed the cuts, showing that 20 percent of the forty-six hundred noncredit courses were eliminated and 10 percent were placed on a fee basis. Recreational noncredit classes were reduced by 60 percent, and senior citizen programs were halved statewide as twenty-one colleges deleted their community service budgets. Overall, since Proposition 13 "eliminated the five-cent permissive property tax that had protected community services activities, including programs, personnel, and some capital construction, for nearly fifteen years, the fiscal basis for this function was destroyed" (1980b, p. 7).

However, the programs not only survived but expanded. In 69 percent of the colleges surveyed subsequently by Harlacher and Ireland, community services directors said that "the status of their community services and continuing education programs had increased during the past five years. Another 21 percent said that the status had been maintained" (1988, p. 3). The prime programmatic emphasis was on workforce training and retraining, with leisure-time education and economic development the secondary areas of emphasis. Despite the strength of these programs, the growing mandate for self-support by community services and continuing-education programs posed a major threat to their continued expansion. The regulations most commonly cited by their respondents were state rules regarding self-support for noncredit offerings, community instructional service, and leisure-time courses.

Other notable threats to expansion were lack of instructional support and integration, and competition from the private sector and community-based organizations.

Much of community education transfers the costs of certain programs from one public agency to another. The training programs conducted by community colleges on behalf of police and fire departments that are too small to operate their own academies offer an example. Where the departments pay the college to do the training, little changes except that the college coordinates the training. But in some instances, law enforcement programs are converted to degree- or certificate-credit programs, thus qualifying them for support through the state's educational funds. The cost of these programs is therefore transferred from the local to the state government budget. Similarly, some industries contract with community colleges to train their workers, paying for the services. But in numerous instances, targeted training programs are given for credit, thus shifting the cost from the industrial concern to the state.

College managers tread carefully when developing training programs for the employees of local industries. The programs are often presented at the plant site, using the company's equipment. There is no problem if the company pays all expenses, including the instructors' salaries, on a flat rate or cost per head. But if the programs are offered for college credit and the usual state reimbursement procedures are in effect, they must be open to all applicants, thus potentially compromising the company's work rules. In many cases, existing courses offered at the college have been modified to fit a major employer's requirements, thereby maintaining intact the faculty contracts and preexisting course accreditation. The company may provide new equipment, paying in kind for the special service. Program development costs may also be charged to the company, but the accounting procedures occasioned by the charge-back can be difficult to effect.

Contracts to train military personnel are particularly intricate. They specify the site, the curriculum, and the tuition that may be charged. They are overseen not only by the college accrediting agency but also by the military officials, the Veterans Administration, and other federal agencies. Difficulties arise when, for example, the college faculty is covered by a union contract but the military does not recognize union membership for its employees. Such involvements also add greatly to the college's administrative costs because of the complexities of arranging the contracts and maintaining elaborate files for the auditors.

In sum, the variety of activities within the scope of community education provides an opportunity not only for serving new clients but also for manipulating the funding to the institution's advantage. If a course can be designated as a degree-credit course and thus become eligible for state aid, it may be moved to that category. If a program can be offered on a contractual basis, with a different government agency or a private industrial concern paying for it, it may be so arranged and thus not drain the college's operating funds. Although administrative costs may be high, community education offers opportunities for creativity in program planning and staff deployment to college managers who find their efforts in the traditional programs hamstrung by external licensing bureaus and negotiated contracts with the faculty.

Program Validity

Advocates answer questions of validity by saying that they can serve the entire populace through community education. To them, community education is a natural extension of the open-door policy and the egalitarian impulses that gave rise to community colleges in the first place. The idea of community uplift has also been presented as a purpose. To those subscribing to that idea, the development of a sense of community is the goal. The college serves as the focal point for community pride. The events that it sponsors enhance a sense of community in the district; the act of planning, teaching, and participating in recreational programs and personal-help workshops fosters community spirit. By this line of reasoning, any activity that brings people together—a health fair, a senior citizens' day, a hobby course offered in a convalescent home, or a college-sponsored trip to a foreign country—will suffice.

Less noble, but nonetheless prevalent, is the intent to aggrandize the institutions, or at least to maintain their current size. Decline is painful. College leaders who peruse the demography charts, consider the competing institutions in their area, and study the potential market for their own programs may wonder about sources of students. Enrollment of older students enabled the colleges to avoid severe declines when the population of eighteen-year-olds dropped in the 1980s. Much of community education acts as a marketing device, not only for the activities offered within it but also for the traditional college programs. The awarding of credit for experience offers a prime example. As many as 80 percent of the people who receive such credit go on to take additional courses at the college. The term *changing markets* is frequently used by those who exhort the institutions to move into new service areas lest they suffer the fate of once-prosperous industries that failed to adapt to changing conditions.

Community education seems also a way of blunting charges of failure in other areas. In the 1950s and 1960s, there were widespread contentions that community colleges would enable the disadvantaged to move up the socioeconomic ladder and would teach skills of citizenship and literacy to people whom the lower schools had failed. College spokespersons also promised to provide an avenue to the baccalaureate for students of lesser ability and lower income. All of these goals prove more elusive than their proponents expected. It is easier to propose new roles for the colleges than to explain away their inability to fulfill old ones.

The issue of institutional credibility must also be addressed. Is the community college a true college? Most community education advocates and most of those who make fervent calls for a new mission make light of that question, but it has been posed by both members of the public and professional educators. Faculty members trying to maintain collegiate standards in their courses certainly take a dim view of most community education activities. Correspondingly, most community education proponents find little place for the regular faculty members in their programs, preferring instead to staff them with part-timers working ad hoc with little or no commitment to the institution itself. Community education has thus fostered internal dissension. Administrators may perceive the traditional faculty members as anchors dragging at an institution that would propel itself into a new era; the faculty tend to cast a jaundiced eye on the recreational activities and the contract programs that use instructors as interchangeable parts to be dismissed when the particular programs for which they were employed have ended.

To those whose memories of college center on courses in the liberal arts taught on a campus, community education threatens to debase the institution. Their perception of college is as a place of mobility for individuals who, through exposure to higher learning, take their place as productive members of society. To them, community uplift is an alien dimension; its aspects seem to be frills or peripheral functions at best, anti-intellectual at worst. They question the standards in the noncredit, open-circuit, and continuing-education programs; and they wonder about quality control in an institution lacking a corps of full-time professional scholars. They reject contentions that an institution serving up a pastiche of uncoordinated functions bears any relation to an institution of higher learning. Community education advocates may try to dismiss these critics as anachronisms nostalgic for the ivy-covered college serving an elite group, but the ranks of the critics include sizable percentages of the public, who want their community college to serve as an avenue of mobility for their children, not as a purveyor of circuses and illusions.

Future Development

The future for community education rests on its funding base and the way it is organized within the colleges. The people served through community education do not fit typical student categories. They seldom enroll in programs leading to degrees; they may not even be enrolled in formally structured courses but instead may be participating in events especially tailored to their interests. Therefore, any attempt to fund community education on the basis of average daily attendance, FTSE, or some other category that suggests students' attending courses leading to degrees or certificates on a campus is at variance with the intent of the program and the pattern of student participation.

It seems that the areas of community education most promising for further development are those that have taken the community colleges away from their higher education affiliation. But this redefinition in the direction of vocational and literacy training differs markedly from the idea of the community college as an agency of direct community uplift. It is the community college as latter-day secondary school, not as social welfare bureau. It is the community college as educational structure rather than as purveyor of recreational activities and quasi-educative services.

The prognosis for other forms of continuing education is less clear. It is certain to vary in different institutions, depending mainly on the directors' vigor in attracting funds and publicizing offerings. The large market frequently noted by proponents of life-long learning is composed, in the main, of people teaching themselves to play tennis, make furniture, cope with their families, understand their own physiology, and deal with cyclical changes in their lives. Those who need the discipline afforded by structured, institutionally sanctioned activities may be enticed away from their self-help books and informal study groups. But it is doubtful that they will greet eagerly the intervention of an agency that would coordinate all their learning efforts.

The issue of social versus individual benefits looms large in connection with community education. Most economic theorists would contend that funds collected from the taxpayers at large should be used to benefit society; hence, if a program is more beneficial to the individual than to the broader community, the person receiving that benefit should bear the cost. This is the basis for the legislative antagonism toward supporting courses in self-help and ceramics. And, indeed, many community education advocates were caught with their premises down when those human *needs* for activities that were provided by the college during the period of liberal funding dried up as the recreational programs were put on a pay-as-you-go basis, and enrollments declined to the extent that tuition advanced.

However, much of community education cannot be neatly categorized into services that benefit individuals rather than the broader society. When people complete a program in nursing at public expense and go on to work as trained nurses in the community, society gains trained nurses, and the individuals gain access to a profession in which they can earn many more dollars than they could without the training. Who benefits more: society or the individuals? At the further extreme are those forms of community education that assist society most clearly. One example is provided by community forums that explore patterns of energy use, quality of life, the effects of zoning, and the environment in the local community. Citizens are provided with information important to their making decisions within the social unit.

Those who would expand community education might do well to articulate and adhere to certain principles underlying its structure. The programs most defensibly supported by public funds are, first, those that tend toward the socially useful, such as sustainability, as opposed to the individually beneficial, end of the continuum—for example, forums instead of self-help programs. Second, they are the verifiably educative programs, as opposed to those that are predominantly recreational, which provide credentials offering the illusion of learning, or which are thinly disguised contributors to transfer payments. Third, they are programs that provide services that are not readily available elsewhere for the people they serve. Thus, the better-integrated businesses would manage their own employee-training programs while the colleges concentrated on assisting workers in less-well-organized industries, such as restaurant workers in their area, who might benefit from periodic refresher courses in health care and sanitation. Heretofore, members of these groups have been the least likely to participate in education of their own volition, but the true community service institution would bend all effort to serve them. Unfortunately for the concept of social utility, programs in which the colleges effect training relationships with Fortune 500 companies are much more common than those that support farmworkers or the homeless.

The advocates might also reduce their claims that community education has the potential for solving community problems. As Talbott observed, the college is confusing its ability to take on the whole community as its province with its ability to take on and solve all of the community's problems: "To take on the role of an omniscient social welfare agency strains the credibility as well as the resources of the college. It is not set up to revamp the courts, to change the traffic pattern, to purify the water, to clean the air of smog" (1976, p. 89).

Gottschalk (1978) also noted the dissimilarities between serving individuals and society by differentiating between problems and issues. Problems are individual; issues are broad enough to affect the community. Individuals who are unemployed have problems that the community college can mitigate by training them sufficiently so that each may obtain paid employment. But massive unemployment is a community issue over which the college has little control. Attempting to solve community issues requires political action, which the colleges cannot afford to undertake because the risk of offending important public support groups is too great. The colleges sometimes get involved in low-risk community issues, offering forums on safe topics such as energy conservation. But a forum on the history of a local labor dispute would be risky. The local arts council may often meet in a college building that is never made available as a dormitory for the homeless. Most college leaders opt for the safe course.

Issues

Community education has not reached parity with degree- and certificate-credit programs in either funding or internal and external perceptions of the college's main mission. For the foreseeable future, the community college as nexus for all the area's educational forms is an even less likely eventuality. How can an institution funded predominantly by the state respond appropriately to local needs?

Cultural and recreational activities conducted as part of community service programs have declined in the face of limited budgets and concomitant conversion of these functions to a self-sustaining basis. Should colleges try to maintain their recreational functions? Can cultural presentations be offered as part of the regular humanities programs and thus be absorbed into their funding packages?

How can quality be controlled in community education programs that do not come under the scrutiny of any outside agency or under internal curriculum review?

Any public agency ultimately can be supported only as long as the public perceives its value. The educative aspects of community education—its short courses, courses for institutionalized populations, and courses offered on job sites—are the colleges' strengths. Each noneducative function may have a debilitating long-term effect because it diffuses the college mission. Each time the colleges act as social welfare agencies or modern Chautauquas, each time they claim to enhance the global community, they run the risk of reducing the support they must have if they are to pursue their main purpose.

Collegiate Function
Transfer and the Liberal Arts

The collegiate function encompasses two concepts: student flow and the liberal arts curriculum. Student flow refers to providing education at the thirteenth- and fourteenth-grade levels for students who are moving through the American educational system, which reaches from kindergarten through graduate school. The liberal arts curriculum includes education founded on the humanities, sciences, and social sciences, the basic studies for most college students, often codified as general education.

In this chapter, we marry the two. The discussion of the liberal arts is followed by the way that these studies affect student transfer to senior institutions. Curriculum details are included. The reasons for the decline in collegiate studies in the 1970s, and their subsequent stabilization, are examined, along with the faculty as a liberal arts support group. Also included are discussions of the academic disciplines, transfer rates, ways of assessing student learning in the liberal arts, and the possibilities for merging the various curricular strands into a new conceptualization of general education.

Liberal Arts

Originally, the liberal arts embodied the collegiate function. They were the main and, in some cases, the only curriculum in the early American colleges. Codified in the medieval European universities, they were brought into the colleges as reflecting the best in human thought. From grammar, rhetoric, logic, music, astronomy, geometry, and arithmetic, all considered essential for the learned person, the humanities gradually came to include classical languages, philosophy, and natural sciences. By the end of the nineteenth century, the physical and social sciences had also shouldered their way into this curriculum.

In the late nineteenth century, the universities gained dominance over the liberal arts colleges and with them assumed responsibility for defining the educated person. Before that time, people studying the liberal arts were as likely to do so in their own home, in a society of amateurs, in a church or monastic setting, or in an independent laboratory as within a school. But the universities institutionalized the teaching of science and those aspects of the humanities that had not been part of the curriculum—modern foreign languages, literary criticism, art, and history—and made the study of them tantamount to being educated.

This institutionally based definition of education was fostered by an intramural revolution: the ascendancy of scholarship. The universities were grounded on the assumption that they would sustain the work of contemplative scholars advancing the frontiers of knowledge. For their part, the scholars felt they could best pursue their work by organizing themselves into academic disciplines. Thus, along with all other areas of intellectual endeavor considered worthy of inclusion in higher learning, the liberal arts took disciplinary form. One who would be ennobled by them studied them from the viewpoint of the disciplines as defined by the scholars. The organization of the curriculum became ineluctably associated with the form of the discipline.

This conversion of the liberal arts predated the advent of the community colleges. By the time these new institutions came on the scene, the collegiate function had already been so codified in terms of the academic disciplines that no college, no legislature, no educator's call for a "student-centered curriculum," no student's cry for "relevance" could shake it. All attempts to tailor the students' studies to their own interests produced little more than rearranging the number or sequence of courses required for graduation, wide varieties of course distribution requirements, or laissez-faire elective systems. The liberal arts were captives of the disciplines; the disciplines dictated the structure of the courses; the courses encompassed the collegiate function.

Ideally, the liberal arts provide contexts for understanding rather than the knowledge that some bit of esoterica is true or false. If the definition of education depended on knowledge of certain data, facts, or the modes of discourse in any academic discipline, then no one prior to the nineteenth century was liberally educated, because the concept of the academic discipline did not exist. The liberal arts can be useful only as they help people evaluate their society and gain a sense of what is right and what is important. This sense is not inborn; it is nourished through studies in which the relations among forms and ideas are explicated—the general education ideal. The conversion of the liberal arts from these precepts to academic disciplines reflected a major shift away from the individual to the organization as the arbiter of learning.

Transfer Courses

Thus structured, the collegiate function was adopted in toto by the community colleges. In their drive for acceptance as full partners in higher learning, with their faculty trained in university departments, they arranged their curricula in the university image. The terms *college parallel*, *college transfer*, and *college equivalent* were (and are) used to describe their academic programs. Their collegiate function, their part in the acculturation of the young, was embodied in the transfer courses. The more closely those courses resembled university courses, the higher their status.

The most pervasive and long-lived issue in community colleges is the extent to which their courses are accepted by the universities. Articulation agreements (sometimes written into state education codes), interinstitutional standing committees, and policy statements that date from the earliest years of the community colleges to the most recent all attest to the importance of transferability. For all the rhetoric emanating from community colleges about their autonomous curriculum for special students and purposes, the universities have dominated the collegiate function by specifying what they accept for transfer credit, what they require for the baccalaureate degree. Major or sudden changes in community college courses can often be traced to a nearby university's changing its graduation requirements or its specifications for the courses that must be on the transcripts of incoming transfer students.

The community colleges were less rigorous in articulating their curriculum with that of the secondary schools, which tended to neglect many of the liberal arts disciplines. U.S. history, U.S. government, literature, biology, and modern foreign languages were included in the secondary school curriculum but philosophy, anthropology, art history, Western civilization, religious studies, and interdisciplinary sciences and humanities were rarely seen. Community college practitioners of those disciplines, as well as all the other disciplines in the liberal arts, have looked to the universities for guidance in forming their courses. There has been minimal flow-through from the lower schools and a paucity of give-and-take of ideas, course patterning, or texts.

In the earliest community colleges, most of the offerings were transfer courses in the liberal arts. Koos (1924) studied the curriculum in fifty-eight public and private junior colleges during 1921 and 1922 and found the liberal arts totaling three-fourths of the offerings. Ancient and modern languages alone accounted for one-fourth of the curriculum. English composition was taught, but literature courses accounted for more than half the courses in English. Agriculture, commerce, education, engineering, and home economics, along with all other vocational studies taken together, came to less than one-fourth of the whole (see Table 11.1).

This emphasis on the liberal arts continued well into the 1960s. All observers of the community colleges were aware of it.

Table 11.1.   Average Number of Semester Hours and Percentage of Total Curricular Offerings in Junior Colleges by Subject, 1921–22

Subject or Subject Group	Number of Semester Hours	Percentage of Total Offering
English	17.1	7.9
Public speaking	2.9	1.4
Ancient languages	16.9	7.9
Modern foreign languages	40.0	18.6
Mathematics	15.9	7.4
Science	29.9	13.9
Social subjects	22.3	10.4
Bible and religion	2.3	1.1
Philosophy	2.1	1.0
Psychology	3.0	1.4
Music	6.2	2.9
Art	4.2	2.0
Physical education	2.5	1.2
Agriculture	3.0	1.4
Commerce	10.9	5.1
Education	7.9	3.7
Engineering and industrial	13.1	6.1
Home economics	12.5	5.8
Other occupational	1.9	0.9

Source: Koos, 1924.

In 1960, Medsker discussed the prestige value of "regular college work." In 1966, Thornton wrote that transfer "is still the function on which the junior colleges expend most effort and in which most of their students express interest" (p. 234). Even after the flowering of vocational education, Cosand reported that "community colleges were, are, and will be evaluated to a major degree upon the success of their transfer students to the four-year colleges and universities" (1979, p. 6).

The 1970s saw an extreme narrowing of the collegiate curriculum. Political science, history, literature, and foreign languages (especially English as a Second Language) remained strong, but cultural geography, religious studies, and ethnic studies were found in fewer than one-fourth of the colleges. Cultural anthropology, art history and appreciation, interdisciplinary humanities, theater history, and philosophy were offered in one-third to two-thirds of them. The greatest number of humanities courses was seen in the older institutions, a legacy of the days when the colleges fed from one-fourth to one-third of their students to senior colleges. The trend was decidedly toward introductory courses for the transfer students and specialized courses for adults taking them for their own interest, not for degree credit.

By the 1990s, emphasis in areas of the liberal arts had shifted once again, with several subjects showing significant increases. The number of colleges offering social and ethnic studies courses went from 15 to 42 percent between 1991 and 1998. Similar growth characterized religious studies (from 22 to 42 percent) and music history and appreciation (from 71 to 90 percent).

Tables 11.2 and 11.3 display data on the magnitude of community college offerings and the percentages of students enrolled. (Laboratory sections in the sciences are not included.) The information has been compiled from several studies conducted by the Center for the Study of Community Colleges between 1975 and 1998. Detailed descriptions of the survey procedures, along with additional information on instructional practices, may be found in *The Collegiate Function of Community Colleges* (Cohen and Brawer, 1987), "Art Education in American Community Colleges" (Center for the Study of Community Colleges, 1988), Cohen and Ignash (1992), and Schuyler (1999b).

More recently, a study of curriculum in Florida community colleges tallied the percentage of liberal arts and non-liberal arts course sections in 2007, comparing them with a similar study conducted in 2000. Overall, the later year study showed 68 percent of the class section offerings in the liberal arts versus 66 percent seven years earlier. Within the non-liberal arts the greatest changes were in the health classes, which increased from less than 14 percent

Table 11.2.   Percentage of Total Credit Curriculum by Major
Discipline Areas in 164 Community Colleges: 1991 and 1998

Discipline	Percentage of Total Curriculum	
	1991	1998
Humanities	13.42	12.82
English	12.75	12.15
Math and computer science	10.69	11.28
Business and office[a]	10.67	8.02
Personal skills, avocational[b]	8.27	6.94
Trade and industry	8.05	6.78
Technical education	7.87	8.55
Sciences	7.68	6.86
Social sciences	6.66	6.51
Fine and performing arts	5.42	5.35
Health[a]	4.44	5.78
Marketing[a]	1.46	0.95
Education[a]	1.10	1.72
Engineering technologies[a]	0.85	1.26
Agriculture (non-liberal arts)[a]	0.51	0.58
Home economics[a]	0.10	N.A.
Other	0.07	0.30
Criminal justice	N.A.	1.01
Internships, practica	N.A.	3.13

[a]Indicates vocational courses.
[b]Includes courses in freshman orientation, career and life planning, and physical education.
Source: Brawer, 1999.

in 2000 to more than 17 percent in 2007. Decreases in business, office, and avocational personal skills averaged over 10 percent each (Griffin, 2007).

Curricular Variety

Beneath the stultifying sameness of a curriculum comprising primarily introductory courses, a notable variety can be perceived. Specialized courses flourished where instructors with a bent toward

Table 11.3.   Percentage of Total Student Enrollment for All Liberal Arts Areas

Discipline	1991	1998
Humanities	26.76%	25.06%
Art history, appreciation	1.33	1.45
Cultural anthropology	0.49	0.49
Foreign languages	7.24	5.82
History	6.23	6.46
Interdisciplinary humanities	1.48	0.83
Literature	1.90	2.21
Fine and performing arts	0.47	0.54
Music history, appreciation	1.03	1.38
Philosophy and logic	2.25	2.07
Political science	3.91	3.26
Religious studies	0.22	0.34
Social and ethnic studies	0.21	0.21
English	20.70	20.26
Fine and performing arts	4.63	4.91
Dance	0.43	0.37
Music	1.51	1.66
Theater	0.31	0.57
Visual arts	2.38	2.31
Social sciences	15.13	15.36
Physical anthropology	0.44	0.25
Economics	2.73	2.75
Physical geography	0.31	0.40
Interdisciplinary social sciences	0.47	0.48
Psychology	7.15	7.30
Sociology	4.03	4.18
Sciences	13.75	12.49
Biology	6.43	7.03
Chemistry	2.05	2.00
Earth and space sciences	1.34	1.35
Engineering sciences	1.61	0.48
Geology	0.38	0.46

Interdisciplinary sciences	0.68	0.33
Physics	1.26	0.84
Math and computer science	19.03	21.94
Introductory and intermediate math	12.04	12.79
Advanced math	1.38	1.27
Applied and technological math	0.65	0.62
Math for other majors	1.57	1.55
Computer science	2.31	4.14
Statistics	1.08	1.57

Source: Schuyler, 1999a, p. 10.

designing and marketing those courses were found. Nearly every college in the Center for the Study of Community Colleges (CSCC) samples had one or a few instructors concerned with presenting something of particular interest, determined to do something different for the different students with whom they were confronted. The oft-heard contention that the curriculum cannot be centered on the collegiate function because the pragmatic students would not attend the courses did not hold. Exciting, active, lively engagements with ideas, tastes, and values did attract audiences, just as in the broader society, the cinema and the stage have survived commercial television. Faculty members who have determined to break away from their lecture and textbook course offerings have been able to do imaginative college-level work with their students.

The breadth of curriculum is moderated by institutional size. Although practically all colleges offer the basic classes, specialized courses are found in few institutions with small enrollments. Table 11.4 displays some of these relationships. The Florida study similarly found higher percentages of liberal arts curriculum in the large colleges (68 percent) as compared with the small colleges (62 percent).

A true picture of the collegiate function is obscured if it is perceived only through the filter of the transfer-credit courses. Some of the ways that the liberal arts have been modified can be

Table 11.4.   Percentage of Colleges Offering Certain Liberal Arts Classes

	Colleges with More Than 6,000 Students	Colleges with Fewer Than 1,500 Students
Art history	91%	57%
Cultural anthropology	83	15
Cultural geography	40	6
Interdisciplinary humanities	71	26
Dance	40	6
Earth, space science	81	19
Statistics	98	50

Source: Cohen and Ignash, 1994, p. 19.

discerned. Community colleges offer relatively few courses in the history of any world region other than the United States, comparative or specialized political science, literature of a single author, languages other than Spanish and English as a Second Language (ESL), and cultural geography. However, courses in social history, film appreciation, and the history of art in certain cultures have increased. Most of these changes have attracted students to areas in which enrollments were diminishing. A decline in introductory classes in music appreciation has been offset by increased enrollments in courses on jazz and other specialized forms.

These changes may be traced through most of the disciplines. Art history instructors capitalized on student affinity for certain cultures by presenting the art of Mexico or Asia to students who might have been less interested in the art of Europe. New courses in folklore, magic, and mythology attracted some students who would not have enrolled in anthropology courses dealing with kinship systems. Students who would not take classes in climatology signed up for "The Living Desert" or "Preserving the Prairies." Specialized courses in problems of the city replaced introductory

sociology, just as courses in family life took students from introductory psychology. An interest in ecology drew students who
were not interested in or qualified for courses in physics or chemistry to "The Oceanic Environment." Although precise figures cannot be obtained, taking all categories of students together, these
specialized, current-interest courses accounted for around 20 to 25
percent of enrollments in the liberal arts during the 1990s.

Student interest in careers took enrollments away from the traditional transfer programs, but the collegiate function was maintained
in a different form. Courses in political science and jurisprudence
were found in every program for law enforcement officers. Students
in social welfare programs took specially modified courses in sociology. The allied health programs in numerous institutions included
medical ethics and Spanish. And the faculty in some institutions
built such courses as "The Humanities in a Technological Society"
for vocational education students, so that they might meet general
education requirements without taking the traditional history and
literature courses.

The general education requirement of vocational programs is
reflected in the discrepancy between the percentage of liberal arts
courses in the total credit curriculum (54 percent in 1998) and
the number of associate degrees conferred in liberal arts fields. In
1997–98, of 555,538 associate degrees awarded, 42 percent were
in the liberal arts and 58 percent in occupational areas. Seven
years later, of 696,660 degrees awarded, 49 percent were in the liberal arts and 51 percent in occupational areas (NCES *Digest* 2001,
2005). The difference reflects not only the continuation of general education requirements in occupational programs but also the
increased enrollment of younger, baccalaureate-bound students.

The most rapid change in the collegiate curriculum in recent
years has been in ESL; it expanded from 30 percent of the foreign language enrollment in 1983 to 43 percent in 1986 and
51 percent in 1991 when, together with Spanish, it accounted
for 75 percent of all the foreign language credit-course sections.

Approximately 250,000 students were taking ESL for credit, and nearly as many were in noncredit courses. The decisions behind offering or not offering credit, investigated in six large ESL programs in six states, were found to be based on issues of state funding and financial aid policies, where the programs were placed (adult or continuing education), and whether ESL was classified as less-than-college-level work. If the greater proportion of a college's curriculum was devoted to credit, then ESL also tended to be offered for credit (Ignash, 1994). In 1998, more than half the colleges were offering ESL.

The collegiate function also thrived in noncredit and noncourse formats. In approximately three of every eight colleges, numerous concerts, recitals, and musical events were presented each year, and around one-fourth of the colleges mounted art exhibits. The colleges were also deeply involved in theatrical productions, film series, and lectures and seminars open to the public. These events were usually funded by the participants or by the colleges themselves, although a few colleges were successful in obtaining funding from external sources. In many cases, the colleges participated with community drama or musical groups, local art councils or museums, and secondary schools in presenting these events.

Articulation and Dual Credit

Articulation refers to the movement of students—or, more precisely, the students' academic credits—from one point to another. Articulation is not a linear sequencing or progression. It covers students going from high school to college; from two-year colleges to universities and vice versa; double-reverse transfer students, who go from the two-year college to the university and then back again; and people seeking credit for experiential learning as a basis for college or university credit. The concept includes admission, exclusion, readmission, advising, counseling, planning, and course and credit evaluation.

Articulation is certainly a state policy issue, first, because the colleges enroll masses of students who cannot qualify for admission to state universities at the freshman level. And because that group includes high proportions of students of color and those from low-income families, it is politically expedient to keep the transfer option open. Second, the community colleges cost less. In 2001–02 the average expenditure nationally was less than one-half the amount spent per FTE by the public four-year colleges, and one-third of that spent by public universities. Hence, "the transfer process meets the societal demand for access in a cost-effective manner" (California Postsecondary Education Commission, 2002, p. 1).

Until recently, articulation with the universities was largely a one-way situation, a series of policies and procedures dictated by senior institutions. But Kintzer and Wattenbarger, who individually and together studied issues in articulation, found that various senior institution policies discriminate against students who transfer even though transfer students usually perform in a manner similar to their past patterns of accomplishment. They noted that little progress had been made in smoothing transfer relations in the years prior to 1985 and concluded, "at least half of the 50 states continue transfer negotiations interinstitutionally, most on a case-by-case basis" (Kintzer and Wattenbarger, 1985, p. 40). Problems were typically related to the types of courses for which transfer credit should be given, students' finding openings in the academic major field of their choice, and the fact that in most cases, the university staff insisted that the evaluation of community college credit should be made by the baccalaureate-granting institution. Cohen, Brawer, and Eaton's 1995 study of policies and programs affecting transfer in eight states reported similar findings.

Where formalized articulation agreements are in place, they are usually brought about through the invention of state boards of higher education. Agreements on a common core of general education courses are negotiated between the community colleges and universities in several states, and in some, California and Illinois, for example, students who complete the specified course work are deemed to have completed the requirements for transfer to a public university. However, periodic negotiation is necessary to keep them current. And despite many efforts to involve faculty members from community colleges and universities in curriculum articulation, the student personnel staff typically contribute the lion's share of the effort—with counselors, admissions and records officers, transcript analysts, and articulation officers doing nearly all the work. It is one thing to make high-level pronouncements on the importance of articulation, but quite another to negotiate the details. Still, although nearly 60,000 students transfer annually to the University of California and the California State University System, the California Postsecondary Education Commission concluded that transfer did "not appear to be impacted by the advent of the many new state-funded transfer initiatives and policies that have been created. . . . " CPEC further speculated that the figures may be showing "some natural, operational ceiling," although "one that is lower than policymakers envision" (2002, pp. 11–12). Anderson, Alfonso, and Sun (2006) also found no relationship between transfer rates and the presence or absence of articulation agreements. Nonetheless, the efforts continue; New Jersey recently mandated that its public universities accept all credits transferred by associate's degree recipients (E. Redden, September 14, 2007). But no system has yet solved the overarching problem: how to ensure that a student's credits qualify as prerequisites for all majors.

In a pioneering move to stabilize community college entrance and smooth the way for ultimate transfer, Miami Dade Community College developed a comprehensive program to screen students into certain courses at entry and monitor their progress throughout their tenure at the college (Harper and others, 1981). Previous institutional practices had allowed students to take any courses and to stay at the institution indefinitely, whether or not they were proceeding toward program completion. In the new plan, students were advised of the requirements for both graduation from the college and transfer to various programs in Florida's universities. The system was mandatory; everyone who matriculated, except those who already had degrees and were taking courses for personal interest, was included in it. This system spread throughout the state, and its effect was seen in the colleges' graduation rates: in 1998, seven of the top ten associate degree–producing colleges in the nation were in Florida (Borden, 2000, p. 7).

The Florida experience was repeated in other states where various efforts were founded to identify and assist potential transfer students. Many community colleges built transfer centers to coordinate information about transfer policies and smooth course articulation, especially for minority and other underrepresented students. These efforts to enhance transfer rates were stimulated not only by state support but also by various philanthropic foundations— notably the Ford Foundation, which funded the Urban Community College Transfer Opportunities Program.

Many state systems of higher education have standing articulation committees with detailed procedures for gaining course approvals. Course equivalency guides are maintained and common course numbering systems pursued. Articulation agreements often specify the courses that the two-year colleges may not offer rather than those they must provide; junior- and senior-level courses offered by the senior institutions, particularly, are out of bounds. In some states, articulation boards review noncredit offerings as well as credit courses and act, for example, to discourage conversational language offerings in two-year colleges' community education programs because those courses are considered the province of the senior institutions.

Articulation and transfer are enhanced considerably when programs are closely coupled. The community colleges have long had an association with teacher education; in fact, in the early years of the twentieth century, when two years of college was considered sufficient for a teacher in the K–12 system, the community colleges were prominent in preparing teachers. Subsequently, as the bachelor's degree became the expected education level for school teachers around the 1930s, state colleges became the primary providers. But the role of the community colleges in teacher preparation was never abandoned, and teacher training sequences constructed in a 2 + 2 fashion (that is, two years at the community college and two at a neighboring university) have become widespread (Townsend and Ignash, 2003). Other closely articulated patterns have been developed in theater, agriculture and farm management, nursing and other health fields, and engineering technologies. Oakland Community College and Eastern Michigan University formed a 3 + 1 curriculum in construction, with students taking all but their senior year at the community college. The bachelor's degrees that graduates of the University of Southern California's program in film and media production receive do not display a notation that the awardees may have saved $45,000 in tuition by taking their first two years at Santa Monica College.

Attempts to build a system from kindergarten through grade fourteen take place within the goals of structural efficiency (reducing duplication), social equity (maximizing access for all students), and economic returns for individuals and society. Orr and Bragg (2001) cite research on K–14 collaborations that identified organizational barriers; community colleges usually serve more than one school district; workforce preparation is often a priority for community colleges whereas in the lower schools the curriculum centers on literacy and acculturation; and a common planning and governance structure for the partnership is difficult to effect.

By comparison dual credit programs are easier to create, but they suffer from similar problems: multiple school districts feeding into a fewer number of community colleges and the need for formal agreements. Girardi and Stein (2001) note that in Florida legislative mandate requires a dual credit system. Whereas Florida's system dates from the 1980s, several other states have since fostered comprehensive dual credit programs; colleges in 80 percent of the states have such programs.

Although collaboration between secondary schools and community colleges is still less prevalent than university articulation, initiatives to establish partnerships between the two educational segments continue, with dual and concurrent enrollment introduced to facilitate student flow. Adelman emphasized the importance of dual enrollment, pointing out that degree completion is greatly advanced for students who have twenty credits or more by the end of their first calendar year of enrollment, an event enhanced if they "enter higher education with a *minimum* of 6 additive credits" (2006a, p. xx).

A review of state policies governing dual enrollment (Karp, Bailey, Hughes, and Fermin, 2005) revealed the complexity and variability in such efforts: In half the authorizing states, the schools were obliged to offer it. Five opened it to all high school students whereas nine restricted it to juniors and seniors. In ten states, students paid tuition; in fifteen, the institution or the state bore the cost.

Faculty and Academic Disciplines

The collegiate function survives not least because of the faculty, who have been its staunchest supporters. When the liberal arts were brought from the universities into the community colleges, the ethos of academic scholarship did not accompany them. The colleges were not supportive of scholarship, and the university training that instructors received was not adequate to foster teachers who would attend to the reflections and meanings of their disciplines. Furthermore, too few instructors have banded together to build interdisciplinary courses in the sciences, social sciences, and humanities. The argument that the universities would not accept new types of courses for transfer credit is spurious; practitioners in two-year colleges have not pursued them with sufficient diligence.

The idea that the faculty, as independently functioning practitioners, should have the power to define the curriculum stems from the turn-of-the-century university model. The concept of academic freedom, of instructors teaching what they want within the confines of their own classrooms, was not accepted by the secondary schools. But the community colleges adopted it even though few of their instructors developed courses that fit the institutions' broader social purposes. Within the liberal arts especially (but not exclusively), the departmentally designed and administered examination is often resisted. Common textbooks for courses taught in multiple sections by different instructors are more the exception than the rule. Although community college instructors ostensibly work from common syllabi, on file in the dean's office for display to visiting accreditation teams, those documents typically serve only as general outlines for course construction.

If the liberal arts exist within an anarchy, if scientists and humanists work within different frameworks of ideas, the curricula that they articulate will be diverse. In universities, however, the expectation is that instructors will be affiliated with the academic disciplines and that the curriculum will reflect the tenets of those disciplines. In community colleges, where disciplinary affiliation is much weaker, the unseen hand of the academic discipline is much less strong as an influence on the form of courses or on instructors' activities. Accordingly, the innovation and flexibility so prized by community college spokespersons derive less from educational philosophy than from the fact that the curriculum is without a rudder. One instructor's whim will change the pattern, emphasis, and direction of a course, and hence a curriculum. Whereas the university organizes the intellectual world in a division of intellectual labor and necessarily accommodates a plurality of diverse intellectual stances, the community college organizes its world in a division of faculty labor and necessarily accommodates a plurality of diverse instructor stances. Amorphous, sporadic monitoring of instructors by department chairpersons, deans of instruction, accreditation teams, and peers is of little consequence. Instructors' work is influenced by the writers of textbooks they use, the speakers at conferences they attend, the new information they learn in in-service programs or on their own. But the enterprise is chaotic, directionless.

An example is provided by contrasting the modes of teaching the liberal arts and the occupational courses. Traditionally, the liberal arts have been taught by a teacher in a room equipped with chairs and a lectern. Instructors have acted as though contact between the students and themselves is the key element, as though all that is necessary for a person to learn is to engage in dialogue and to read and reflect in a solitary fashion. Vocational educators, in contrast, have taken the position that they need laboratories, shops, equipment, and links with the business and industry community in order to teach people a trade. They say their students must practice the craft, not merely talk about it.

What if the faculty in the liberal arts took similar views? Instructors teaching art appreciation would say that students cannot learn unless they are provided with funds to travel to museums. Anthropology instructors might insist that students be paid to work at archaeological digs. Political science instructors would have students serving as apprentices to politicians and bureaucrats in all types of government agencies. And certainly the best way to learn a language is to live in a country where that language is spoken, with the colleges sponsoring such trips. But liberal arts faculty members rarely advocate such views, whereas nursing educators and their accrediting associations insist that they must have laboratories, equipment, and clinical training. It would not occur to them to try to teach nursing in a room equipped with nothing more than chairs and a whiteboard. They get the clinics and the funds they need to maintain their small student-teacher ratios. The liberal arts instructors get eye strain from reading student papers.

These variant attitudes stem from the different ways that the vocational and collegiate functions were taught before they came into the colleges. Vocational preparation evolved from a history of apprenticeships in work settings, the traditional mode of learning a trade. The liberal arts were the province of a group inclined toward contemplation. Thus, it costs more to teach the occupations because the workplaces are duplicated or at least simulated on site. Liberal arts educators in community colleges do not even have the benefit of sizable library collections, and they do not act in concert to modify the conditions.

The collegiate function in community colleges has been characterized by a reduction in emphasis on the academic disciplines. Community college instructors tend not to conduct scholarly inquiry, not to belong to disciplinary associations, not to be excessively concerned with disciplinary purity—all to the good for faculty members who are instructed to teach in areas of current student interest and must often cross disciplinary fields. The instructor whose workload comprises one course in anthropology, another in sociology, and two in American history does not have the luxury of maintaining currency in all fields. This turn away from disciplinarianism has had some untoward effects. Many courses appeal to immediate relevance and focus excessively on what learners want, to the detriment of making intellectual demands. Under the guise of presenting a student-centered curriculum, courses that reflect the popular literature of self-help books on coping, gaining singular advantage, and other personal concerns are often built within the liberal arts framework.

Ultimately, all curricula must be based on knowledge. No matter what the intent of a student-centered course, that course cannot maintain its collegiate character unless something is being taught. That something is the subject; that subject stems from the discipline. Without the anchor of the humanistic and scientific disciplines themselves, the basis of the academic tradition, the collegiate function would be adrift. Even if the liberal arts were not a curriculum in themselves, they would still have to be maintained as the foundation of the liberal education that is provided through all the other curricula.

The decline of the academic disciplines as the organizing principle of collegiate courses has both reflected and served to limit faculty members' awareness of recent trends in their academic fields. Such an awareness is important even for such a seemingly simple task as evaluating the new textbooks that appear. But it is important for more than that: the academic disciplines need reconceptualizing to fit remedial and vocational education, the institution's dominant functions in addition to transfer. This reconceptualization cannot be made outside the colleges themselves. For the sake of the collegiate function, community college instructors must reify their own disciplines. It is difficult for a group that has severed connection with its disciplinary roots to accomplish that.

Student Ability and the Curriculum

No curriculum exists in a vacuum. The decline in the collegiate function in the 1970s and its subsequent stabilization are revealed in the liberal arts courses detailed in this chapter and in the student transfer rates documented in Chapter Two. It relates also to the changes in the academic ability of the entering students and the curriculum in the high schools from which they come.

The figures in Chapter Nine illustrate the decline and subsequent improvement in National Assessment of Educational Progress, Scholastic Assessment Test (SAT), and American College Testing performances by high school students during the 1970s and through the 1990s. In 1975, when average SAT scores had been declining for over a decade, Willard Wirtz, former secretary of labor, chaired a commission that sought to explain and resolve the lowering of educational standards. The commission found that students were taking fewer courses in general English and math and were enrolling in more vocational courses such as driver education and home economics. School days had become shorter and course textbooks weakened in quality (Ravitch, 1985). Data collected by NCES further illustrate high school students' reluctance to enroll in math, science, and English classes. In 1982, students completed an average of 3.93 courses in English, 3.16 courses in history and social studies, and 2.63 courses in math. Not surprisingly, as more students stopped enrolling in English and math courses, their performances on verbal and math ability tests dropped.

Attempts to rebuild the high school curriculum were widespread. In 1983, the National Commission on Excellence in Education published *A Nation at Risk* (Gardner and others, 1983), in which it highlighted the importance of education for the civic well-being of our nation. This report suggested that states adopt a curriculum, known as "the New Basics," to include four years of English; three years of mathematics, science, and social studies; one-half year of computer science; and two years of foreign language for students who wish to go to college. Ravitch notes that "by late 1983, a national survey found that forty-six states had either raised their graduation requirements recently or were debating proposals to do so" (1985, p. 67).

A notable shift in high school course enrollments occurred. Table 11.5 displays the changes between 1982 and 1998. All academic areas showed an increase, with mathematics, sciences, and foreign languages showing the most notable gains. In 1998, 60.4 percent of students took chemistry, as compared with 32 percent in 1982; 75.1 percent took geometry in 1998, versus 47.1 percent in 1982; 25.4 percent took biology, chemistry, and physics, compared with 11.2 percent in 1982. Overall, the high school curriculum was rebuilt to the levels of the 1950s. The effect of the strengthened requirements was a reduced number of vocational education classes (bookkeeping, typing, shop) and an increase in the totality of courses taken by graduates.

Table 11.5.   Average Number of Carnegie Units Earned by Public High School Graduates in Various Subject Areas: 1982, 1994, 1998

	1982	1994	1998
Total Carnegie Units	21.58	24.17	25.14
English	3.93	4.29	4.25
Social studies	3.16	3.55	3.74
Total math	2.63	3.33	3.40
Total science	2.20	3.04	3.12
Foreign language	0.99	1.71	1.85

Source: National Center for Education Statistics, *Digest of Education Statistics,* 2001.

In sum, students coming to the colleges in the 1990s had taken more academic courses, and their academic abilities had begun to climb. In the broadest fashion, the foundations of educational practice had been verified: students will take the classes that they are required to take, and those who take classes in a particular area of study are likely to learn something about that area. The latter is both obvious and experimentally verifiable. In 1983–84, the CSCC administered the *General Academic Assessment,* a survey and content test that would reveal student knowledge in general education and in the liberal arts. The test, with non-course-specific items in English usage, the humanities, mathematics, sciences, and social studies, was given in five forms to over eight thousand students in twenty-three colleges in Chicago, Los Angeles, Miami, and St. Louis.

Tables 11.6 and 11.7 present some of the findings, which suggest three major outcomes: (1) students who complete more college courses tend to know more, (2) students who complete courses in certain areas score higher on content tests in those areas, and (3) students know what they know: the best predictor of the students' scores on the subtests was to ask them, "Compared with other students at this college, how would you rate your ability to [various discipline-related questions]?" Findings similar to

Table 11.6.   Means on Scales by Number of Completed College Units

Total Units	Math	Literacy	Social Science	Humanities	Science	Total Liberal Arts
0–14	4.45	4.73	4.64	3.02	4.89	21.73
15–29	4.84	4.84	4.80	3.13	5.05	22.65
30–44	4.88	4.90	4.88	3.31	5.25	23.23
45–59	5.18	4.96	5.13	3.54	5.27	24.07
60 or more	5.51	5.55	5.58	4.24	5.84	26.71
Total sample	4.85	4.92	4.92	3.35	5.17	23.21

Source: Riley, 1984.

Table 11.7.   Means on Scales by Self-Rating on Scale-Related Skill

Self-Rating	Math	Literacy	Social Science	Humanities	Science
Poor	3.82	4.16	4.22	2.66	4.44
Fair	4.49	4.58	4.0	2.99	4.81
Good	5.16	5.08	5.17	3.48	5.25
Excellent	6.17	6.28	5.82	4.22	6.34
Total sample	4.85	4.92	4.92	3.35	5.17

Source: Riley, 1984.

those yielded by the General Academic Assessment were reported in a subsequent survey, the *General Academic Learning Exercise*, administered to more than 2,500 students in ten Southern California colleges in 2002 (Cohen, Schuetz, Chang, and Plecha, 2003). Older students, including those enrolled for *personal interest*, tended to score higher in English and social science, subjects often learned outside school, but lower on mathematics. A positive relationship was seen between the number of units students had completed in the subject area and the scores on the corresponding section of the test, a relationship especially strong in science but less significant for humanities. Students' self-assessments of their abilities in liberal arts subjects were remarkably accurate.

Other studies have employed ACT's *Collegiate Assessment of Academic Proficiency* (CAAP) on samples of graduating students.

The College of Dupage (Illinois) administered it to sections of introductory courses in the fall and to advanced courses in the spring. After controlling for dropouts and transfers they were able to compare a pool of entering freshmen with a set of sophomores and to use the results to modify courses where students showed weakness (Geesaman, Klassen, and Watson, 2000). Ivy Tech Community College of Indiana system has adopted CAAP for assessing student outcomes on its 23 campuses ("Ivy Tech CC System Assesses General Education Outcomes with CAAP," *Activity*, 2007). Educational Testing Service has been promoting a Measure of Academic Promise and Proficiency (MAPP), which assesses "critical thinking, reading, writing, and mathematics with one integrated test" (ETS, 2007).

The Transfer Function

One of the community college's primary purposes has been to accept students from secondary school, provide them with general education and introductory collegiate studies, and send them on to senior institutions for the baccalaureate. An associate degree usually qualifies the recipient to enter the university as a junior. In many states, the degree guarantees junior status. However, certain courses may not be acceptable, some university departments may require alternate courses, and transfer may not guarantee entry to the particular program a student desires. Since most students attend two or more institutions on the road to the baccalaureate, the issue of course-credit transferability is at least as important as student demographics and abilities in understanding student progress.

One of the thorniest problems is that of determining which community college courses are acceptable for graduation credit in which university. Practically all the liberal arts classes qualify, but courses in the trades and technologies are variable. As an example, the University of California accepts only 27 percent of the non–liberal arts classes offered in that state's community colleges, but the California State University awards credit for 73 percent of them (Striplin, 2000). Course transferability rates are even more variant at the University of Illinois, Urbana, and Illinois State University, with the former taking 16 percent and the latter 80 percent of the non–liberal arts, even though Illinois has had statewide agreements on general education core curriculum for decades. The University of Texas, Stephen F. Austin State, and Southwest Texas State are much more uniform: 35 percent of the non–liberal arts classes are acceptable at the junior level at the University of Texas at Austin and 42 percent at the state university branches. In all three examples, the differences relate most to the correspondence of programs in particular fields. The University of California and the University of Illinois have no undergraduate majors in marketing, trade and industry, or engineering technology, and few in health or technical education, whereas those fields can be found in the California and Illinois State University systems. Majors are more evenly distributed across the university types in Texas (Cohen and Ignash, 1994).

The collegiate function is intact. The decline in liberal arts studies and student transfer rates that was manifest in the 1970s and 1980s has been stemmed. Although the transfer rate had been stable up to the mid-1990s, it began to increase by the end of the decade. Collegiate and vocational studies stood together as the college's primary functions. Even so, the proponents of one or the other function have not slackened their efforts. The notion that vocational studies should be primary has been advanced repeatedly by those who view the community college's main role as helping people prepare for the workplace. They usually neglect to acknowledge that cultural and basic literacy, the ability to communicate in context, understand societal conditions, and similar goals of a liberal arts education are essential for practically every job. Those who advocate the liberal arts often ignore the realities of their students' lives; all of them are or will be in the workforce, and most will require some form of specialized training.

The waves of fashion, trends in funding, interests of students, and imaginativeness of the faculty all affect the prognosis for collegiate studies in community colleges. Several trends favor expansion. Aspects of finance favor them because they are less expensive than vocational programs. Tradition is on their side; they have been present since the first days of the institutions, and tradition (or inertia) plays an important role in education. Those who would abandon collegiate studies must answer to charges that they are thereby denying opportunity to the great numbers of students who still see the community college as a stepping-stone to higher learning.

For the collegiate function to reach its full potential and involve all students, it must not be sequestered away from the vocational programs. Instead of depending exclusively on graduation requirements to attract vocational education students to their classes, the faculty might integrate the liberal arts with career education through a merger of principles stemming from both the humanities and the sciences. Technology is ubiquitous; students would have little difficulty understanding generally how the history of politics, ethics, sociology, and philosophy of science and technology affect their world. Those who would be more than job holders would attend to the fundamental assumptions undergirding what scientists and technologists do. In general, literature and art in the community colleges have not dealt sufficiently with technology, but a fully integrated course could be required in all vocational programs. Similarly, portions of the liberal arts could be designed especially for key courses in the vocational programs. In fact, the 1990 amendments to the Perkins Act emphasized such integration.

If the collegiate function weakens, it may be a result of continuing high levels of funding for vocational programs without sufficient intramural concern for general literacy and social awareness. Furthermore, students reared on a diet of instant information presented through electronic media may find the reflectiveness and self-discipline basic to the collegiate function difficult to master. Although some imaginative efforts at integrative courses presented through television have been made, the long-term effects of a turn away from print have not yet been fully appreciated. Communication through nonprint images is pervasive. The spoken word is carried across distance not by a courier with a packet of letters but through wires and waves. The ubiquitous hand-held calculator has done for arithmetic what the invention of movable type did for storytelling. Supermarket checkers rely on bar codes; restaurant cashiers, on pictures of the product superimposed on a register key that records the cost of an item and the amount of change to be tendered. Why, then, should educators be concerned about teaching the liberal arts? Advocates of the collegiate function would argue that the failure to do so only perpetuates social class divisions and increases the benighted individual's reliance on authority. Any educator with less than a totally cynical view of society would agree.

General Education

The liberal arts are defended by those who subscribe to the concept of general education: the process of developing a framework on which to place knowledge stemming from various sources, of learning to think critically, develop values, understand traditions, respect diverse cultures and opinions, and, most important, put that knowledge to use. It is holistic, not specialized; integrative, not separatist.

Statements on behalf of general education have been advanced not only by educators as far back as the earliest writers on community colleges—Lange, Koos, and Eells—but also by groups outside the academy. In 1947, the President's Commission on Higher Education noted the importance of semiprofessional training but contended that it should be "acquired in an environment that also cultivates general education, thus offering the student

'a combination of social understanding and technical competence'"
(Park, 1977, p. 57). Ten years later, President Eisenhower's Committee on Education Beyond High School also articulated that
combination, viewing it as the particular responsibility of the
community colleges. Subsequently, an American Council on
Education task force recommended that any institution offering
an associate degree should attest that its students have become
familiar with general areas of knowledge and have gained "competency in analytical, communication, quantitative, and synthe-
sizing skills" ("Flexibility Sought in Award of Educational Credit,"
1978). The degree should state not only that the students gained
their training in a college but also that the training included a
general education component.

General education received widespread publicity in 1977
when the Carnegie Foundation for the Advancement of Teaching
published *Missions of the College Curriculum*. This report was followed by several others on the same theme emanating from other
agencies: *Involvement in Learning*, a report by the Study Group
on the Conditions of Excellence in American Higher Education
(1984), formed under National Institute of Education auspices; a
National Endowment for the Humanities report, *To Reclaim a Legacy* (Bennett, 1984); *Integrity in the College Curriculum*, sponsored by
the Association of American Colleges (1985); and a subsequent
Carnegie Foundation report, *College: The Undergraduate Experience
in America* (Boyer, 1987).

General education has a venerable history, dating from the
moral philosophy courses found in American colleges during their
first two hundred years. These integrative experiences often were
taught by the college president and presented to all students.
However, that type of general education broke apart in most colleges in the second half of the nineteenth century, to be replaced
by the free-elective system. The old classical curriculum died out,
taking with it the idea of the curriculum as a unified whole to be
presented to all students.

The initial reaction against the free-elective system gave rise to distribution requirements, groups of courses specified in the process of political accommodation among academic departments. But the success of distribution requirements as an organizing principle for curriculum did not stop those who advocated curriculum integration. Their early attempts to return order were founded in survey courses; Columbia University's "Contemporary Civilization" course, first offered in 1919, is usually seen as a prototype.

In his history of the undergraduate curriculum, Rudolph traced the concept to the 1970s and concluded, "Where highly publicized general education requirements reshaped the course of study in the 1940s and 1950s, less publicized erosion of those requirements took place in the 1960s and 1970s" (1977, p. 253). Then, according to Rudolph, general education fell victim to faculty power, lack of student interest, increased demands on faculty time, difficulties in integrating the disciplines, and, most of all, its own lack of demonstrated value and the superficiality of the presentations. General education has remained a noble idea but a practical backwater in most of American higher education.

General education is often defined in terms of the competencies to be gained by those whom it touches. A group studying general education in California community colleges in the early 1950s offered a list of twelve competencies to be exercised by a person who is generally educated:

- Exercising the privileges and responsibilities of democratic citizenship
- Developing a set of sound moral and spiritual values by which he guides his life
- Expressing his thoughts clearly in speaking and writing and in reading and listening with understanding
- Using the basic mathematical and mechanical skills necessary in everyday life

- Using methods of critical thinking for the solution of problems and for the discrimination among values
- Understanding his cultural heritage so that he may gain a perspective of his time and place in the world
- Understanding his interaction with his biological and physical environment so that he may adjust better to and improve that environment
- Maintaining good mental and physical health for himself, his family, and his community
- Developing a balanced personal and social adjustment
- Sharing in the development of a satisfactory home and family life
- Achieving a satisfactory vocational adjustment
- Taking part in some form of satisfying creative activity and in appreciating the creative activities of others [Johnson, 1952, pp. 21–22]

This list, or portions of it, was duplicated verbatim in many community college catalogues because it gave the appearance of being competency based even though it was sufficiently broad to justify any course or program.

In 2001, fifty years after Johnson's list appeared, the Accrediting Commission for Community and Junior Colleges in California drafted a set of "comprehensive objectives" for general education that included most of the same competencies:

- An introduction to the content and methodology of the major areas of knowledge: the humanities and fine arts, the natural sciences, and the social sciences.
- Capability to become productive workers and lifelong learners: skills include oral and written communication, scientific and quantitative reasoning, critical analysis/logical thinking, acquisition of knowledge, computer literacy, and ability to work with others.

- Ability to become ethical human beings and effective citizens: qualities include respect for others, interpersonal skills, civility; appreciation for aesthetics, cultural diversity, ethical principles, creativity, and historical perspective; and willingness to assume civic, political, and social responsibilities [2001, p. 5]

Despite its superficial appeal, defining general education as "that which everyone should know" has never been easy to codify, and recently two additional forces have afflicted it. One set of contentions holds that no knowledge is basic to everyone because everyone has a different background that gives rise to a unique outlook; a man cannot understand a woman's perspective, a person whose forebears came from Africa cannot understand the viewpoints held by one whose ancestors were European, and books written by members of one group are irrelevant to others. The second antagonistic force is that language, values, and understandings evolve so rapidly that no reference is more relevant than another, none has permanence, none survives a new season's television shows. Add to those the fact that most universities still define general education as a set of discipline-based courses.

The rationale for general education in the community college is the freedom enjoyed by the informed citizen. Only when people are able to weigh the arguments of the experts are they truly free. These experts may be discussing issues of the environment, whether to put power plants or oil docks in or near cities. They may be advising on governmental questions. Or they may be deciding who may be born, who has a right to live, what it means to be healthy, and how, where, and when one should die. People need to understand how these things work: social systems and persuaders, artists and computers. General education is for the creation of a free citizenry, the Greek ideal of the citizen participating in the polity. Because we are embedded in families, tribes, and communities, we must learn to be free-thinking citizens, learning the literacy necessary for life in a civil society, the competence to participate in the broader community, the ability to think critically. A general education that leads to the ways of knowing and the common beliefs and language that bind society together is offered in every culture through rituals, schools, and apprenticeships. The community colleges are responsible for furthering it in the United States. But it cannot effect its mission as long as it is defined as a set of distribution requirements, as it is in most universities, where the academic discipline-bound faculty control the curriculum.

Sustainable Development and Service-Learning

The essential parts of a reformed program are in the community colleges now in the form of service-learning, or civic engagement, and the nascent sustainable development curriculum, which can be brought together as a rigorous, modern program to teach what the proponents of general education have sought for generations.

The efforts to integrate service-learning into the community college curriculum in the 1990s echoed the general education ideal. Service-learning emerged as an attempt to reduce the growing disparity between the liberal arts as portrayed in the disciplines and its original purpose of placing learning in its larger societal context. As an instructional methodology, service-learning "combines community service with classroom instruction, focusing on critical, reflective thinking as well as personal and civic responsibility" (Robinson, 1999, p. 1). Service thus forms a direct part of students' learning experience, with a clear connection between academic courses and real-world problems, allowing students to experience the extent of the impact they can have on their community and surroundings. In 1995, 31 percent of the community colleges incorporated service-learning in their courses, and by 2003 this number had doubled (Prentice, Robinson, and McPhee, 2003). The two major forums for service-learning in community colleges were the Service-Learning Clearinghouse hosted by the American Association of Community Colleges and the Campus

Compact National Center for Community Colleges at Mesa Community College (Arizona).

Campus Compact surveyed its member colleges in 2006 and found that nearly one-third of the students participated in volunteer and service-learning work, contributing an average of 5.6 hours per week. The most common engagements were in providing tutoring and mentoring to pupils in local schools, but students were also involved with social and health services and senior centers. The faculty in the social sciences and English were most likely to sponsor service-learning, along with partners from community-based organizations. Participating students were more likely to stay enrolled; Brevard Community College (Florida) found its service-learning students had higher graduation rates than its non-participants over a six-year period ending in 2005 (Robinson, 2007, p. 3).

Sustainability and civic engagement round off a curriculum emphasizing service-learning. Sustainable development refers to several types of activities: biological, economic, and social. It rests on environmental sustainability, improved standards of living, renewable resource use, ecological economics, and "progress as if survival matters" (Hawken, 2007, p. 288). Environmental education aims to make people "aware of, and concerned about, the environment and human impacts on the environment" (p. 233). *Green schools* teach ecological awareness and encourage students to take environmentally responsible action. Overall, sustainable development seeks to enhance the quality of life for everyone and to teach stewardship of sustainable resources. Hawken's book *Blessed Unrest* has a 110-page appendix listing so many nongovernmental organizations dedicated to sustainability education, and similar concepts dedicated to a healthy earth, that he has labeled it a movement without leaders or ideology. College staff would have no difficulty in identifying organizations with which to arrange partnerships. Students connected with these agencies would gain experience with forms of civic engagement.

Various projects have been funded in an effort to infuse this type of reform in community colleges, although, as Barnes (2005) reports, many of these initiatives vanish when their funding ceases. All curriculum and instructional reforms require one or more on-site champions; they do not sustain themselves. The successful programs would be integrated with traditional course offerings in order to satisfy the four-year college and university expectations that transferring students are prepared for upper-division work and to satisfy those legislators whose focus is on narrowly construed vocational education. The foundation for an integrated sustainability curriculum is in place in a large number of colleges and universities. Campus Compact National Network was created in 1984 to promote public service opportunities in all of higher education. The National Society for Experiential Education and the Corporation for National Service date from the 1990s. The Association for Sustainability in Higher Education has hundreds of institutional members. And the grassroots organizations that Hawken identified number in the thousands worldwide; nearly 12,000 in environmental education alone, plus thousands more in natural resource education, sustainability education, energy efficiency and conservation, renewable energy, and so on (2007, pp. 233–236). Butte College (California) is a leader among colleges that have begun linking service-learning with sustainable resources by modifying courses in life and social sciences (Meier, 2008). Kirtland Community College (Michigan) has demonstrated how rural colleges can involve high percentages of their students in civic engagement (Holton, 2003). General education is poised to thrive, both for the hundreds of thousands of transferring students and for those who leave formal education after their community college experience. But it will take modified form.

Issues

The overriding issue is whether the community colleges should maintain their position in higher education. If they should not, no deliberate steps are necessary. Continued deterioration in course requirements will suffice. But if they should, what can they do?

Can the collegiate function be expanded beyond the college-parallel courses? Can it be made part of the vocational programs? What can the liberal arts say to students who want nothing more than job upgrading or new skills?

Must the collegiate function decline along with the decline in students' tendency to read and write? Can the liberal arts be offered in a manner that fits less-well-prepared students' ways of knowing?

Advisory committees comprising concerned citizens, labor leaders, and employers have been influential in connecting the occupational programs to the world of work. Can lay advisory committees for the liberal arts similarly help connect those programs to the broader society?

Will the college leaders who recognize the value of general education, reformed around principles of service-learning and civic engagement centering on sustainable resources, be able to build and maintain it?

The collegiate function has many advocates within and outside the colleges. The future of the community college as a comprehensive institution depends on how they articulate its concerns.

12

Scholarship and Assessment

Research in and About the Colleges

The amount spent for research in social service institutions is low in comparison with that in the commercial sector. Research in education commands a minuscule proportion of education expenditures and has even decreased as a proportion of overall budgets since the early 1970s. A major reason for this meager support is that, until recently, few legislators, members of the lay public, or education practitioners have thought that research about education was useful, or that it had anything to contribute to productivity or efficiency. The words *community college*, *junior college*, and *two-year college* do not appear in the index to Feldman and Newcomb's two-volume compendium of research, *The Impact of College on Students* (1969), and only a few dozen studies that include community college student data are among the more than three thousand reports cited by Pascarella and Terenzini in their successor volumes, *How College Affects Students* (1991; 2005). Thus, according to those who study the effects of postsecondary schooling, nearly 40 percent of America's college students, the proportion enrolled in the community colleges, have not even been important enough to tabulate.

However, this lack has become less pronounced in recent years as more studies of community college functioning are being undertaken. As abbreviated as this research effort is in comparison with the magnitude of the enterprise, it is worthy of note. The research is conducted by professors and graduate students; national organizations, sponsored primarily by foundations and membership fees; federal and state agencies concerned with postsecondary education; and researchers within the colleges. It takes several forms: historical and sociological analysis; state and national data compilation; data that set norms for interinstitutional comparisons; and information such as program review, student satisfaction and behavior, community relationships, and student placement validation that may be used for intramural planning. Much of it is driven by external mandates, especially the calls for institutional accountability, and it has yielded a substantive increase in assessment and outcomes studies. More research on community colleges has appeared in the past fifteen years than in the previous fifty.

This chapter reviews the groups that conduct these studies, the types of research they report, and some of their findings and persistent problems. Much in the chapter highlights inconsistencies in assessment, which perhaps gives it a negative tone. But the contemporary research on community colleges is inchoate. The institutions are assailed with demands for data showing their effectiveness. College leaders know that they live in a world of images and applaud reports displaying any type of institutional success, while ignoring or attacking those showing negative outcomes. State officials demand to know how policy and funding relate to accountability. The researchers themselves waver between attempts to present scientifically verifiable evidence and that which a lay audience can understand, even while relying on mushy definitions and data. All this is to be expected because the studies do not stem from a tradition of valid research designed for knowledgeable audiences. They are still dominated by the need for positive public relations, an imperative guiding many of the studies reported in this chapter.

Sources of Research

Except for the college-based institutional research officers, nearly all the researchers who study community colleges are affiliated with universities or federal or state agencies. An occasional report written by a private, nonprofit corporation or an ad hoc commission may appear, but the extramural studies are usually conducted by university professors and students in the social sciences, most of them in schools of education. Just over one hundred university professors are exclusively concerned with teaching and writing about community colleges. Perhaps one hundred more have some interest in the institutions and occasionally conduct a study or prepare a commentary. However, these researchers are responsible for the lion's share of the analyses that appear as published documents. Graduate students working under their direction collect original data or write theses based on existing data sets; many of the reports written by community college practitioners about their own institutions are prepared while they are concurrently enrolled in graduate programs. A limitation to these studies is that, in order to legitimize education as a profession and education departments as worthy of status in graduate schools, the professors must obey the university imperative to emulate scientific methods. Accordingly, their studies and those of their students typically display a strained connection to theory and often employ high-powered statistical analyses of soft data.

Much of the expansion in research on community colleges has resulted from two sources. The major impetus has been from state legislatures demanding justification for their appropriations. A lesser, but important, thrust has come from organizations concerned with student access and attainment, especially those from low-income families. Lumina Foundation has been a leader in this effort; its Web site lists dozens of grants and resultant publications.

The magnitude of state-agency efforts varies, depending on state-governance structures. Some states (for example, Florida, Illinois, and Washington) have sophisticated research offices as arms of their governing or coordinating boards. Where the community colleges are part of the state university system (as in Hawaii and New York, for example), reliable data collection and analysis may result. In other states, such as Colorado, Oklahoma, and North Carolina, the university and the community college systems cooperate closely in compiling and reporting data about both sectors. But across the nation, the state-agency effort has grown. Ewell and Boeke describe the Unit Record systems tracking student progress in public institutions in forty states, which have grown more sophisticated and reliable. They conclude, however, that "little progress has been made in sharing across state lines" (2007, p. 7) and see that as the next frontier.

Much research on the national level centers in the U.S. Department of Education. Its National Center for Education Statistics sponsors the Integrated Postsecondary Education Data System (IPEDS), the most comprehensive compilation; the Center reports annually on the number of community colleges, institutional services provided, revenues, costs, expenditures, enrollment, degrees conferred, and staff composition and salaries. In recent years, it has expanded its efforts far beyond IPEDS to assess school dropout, academic progress, literacy development, national goals, and a host of interrelated issues; it publishes separate reports of those data.

Other agencies, especially the American Association of Community Colleges, extract the community college-related data from the NCES reports and publish their own compendia. The Education Department also funded the ERIC Clearinghouse for Community Colleges, not a research agency but a collector, indexer, abstractor, and disseminator of research reports that, between 1966 and 2003, added over twenty thousand documents to the ERIC database, providing an easily accessible archive and resource for everyone studying the institutions.

Some useful work has been done by a few groups studying higher education overall, including the National Center for Postsecondary Improvement and the National Center for Public Policy and Higher Education. Organizations dedicated especially to studying community colleges from a national perspective include the Center for Community College Policy at the Education Commission of the States; the Community College Research Center at Teachers College, Columbia; the Center for the Study of Community Colleges at the University of California, Los Angeles; the Community College Leadership Program at the University of Texas, Austin; and the Institute for Community College Development, Cornell University.

Various national professional and institutional membership associations conduct a few specialized studies: the National Association of College and University Business Officers collects financial data, and the American Association of University Professors collects salary data. The League for Innovation in the Community College, a membership organization, has sponsored research on several aspects of institutional functioning. Many of the other professional and institutional associations serve the research enterprise by encouraging philanthropic foundations and governmental agencies to sponsor studies of community colleges as unique entities, and to use paradigms that fit the colleges' mission and role. Some collect information of a type that supports their lobbying efforts.

Institutional Research Offices

Institutional research (IR) in the colleges manifests a pattern ranging from the sophisticated to the rudimentary. Except in a few colleges, it has never been well supported. A 1968 study reported by Roueche and Boggs found full-time research coordinators in only about one in five community colleges, usually the larger institutions. In two of five colleges, responsibility for institutional research was assigned to an administrator who also had other duties, and in two of five, no regular staff member was responsible for coordinating institutional studies. Knapp (1979) found IR offices typically staffed with only one or two persons. In 1987 the community colleges of southern California averaged only

0.67 full-time-equivalent (FTE) institutional researchers each, hardly enough to fill out the data request forms that flowed in from governmental agencies (Wilcox, 1987), and fewer than half the colleges in the South employed as much as a half-time institutional researcher (Rowh, 1990). Little has changed. A recent survey found that about half the colleges employed "just one or fewer IR staff persons on an FTE basis" (Morest and Jenkins, 2007, p. 6). The larger and the older colleges had more staff.

State after state has generated demands for outcomes assessment, but the IR offices have not grown nearly so much as the requests for additional information would warrant. A centralized research effort depends on someone at the community college level to provide the basic information. Thus, the IR function is heavily involved with compliance reporting or performance accountability, in which rates of student retention, transfer, graduation, job placement success, performance on licensing exams, and student satisfaction are the targets. After compliance reporting and enrollment reports, the third major function is preparation for accreditation visits. Such information systems are not designed with research in mind; they are rather for record-keeping purposes and financial administration, facility use, and class scheduling. In a few colleges, highly qualified IR personnel use sophisticated methodologies, but these are not really necessary for the job. "Indeed, the more sophisticated IR work may be done for the purpose of journal submissions and conference presentations rather than for college management" (Morest and Jenkins, 2007, p. 3). Their study found "a cultural resistance to complex research." College presidents, vice presidents, and IR staff themselves said that complex studies were not useful, there were simply too many variables to account for when analyzing education outcomes, and that there was "simply no audience for complicated analysis" (p. 11).

Calls for assessment assail the colleges relentlessly: state-level mandates, federal reporting regulations, accrediting agency requests. First come the requests for data, then the suggestions for how the data should be arrayed, and finally the requirements to do it, or else. These requests and demands seek a variety of types of information: program accountability, outcomes assessment, transfer rates, employment placement validation, graduation rates, evaluation criteria, satisfaction measures, job performance—there is no end to the types of information sought. The research office must have ready access to all the information banks in every college office: personnel, admissions, student records, and the like. The task is easier now because of the greater data processing capability that has become economical and readily available in recent years. But the community colleges with research offices averaging one or two FTE staff members per campus can barely keep up with the demand.

Understaffed as they are, the IR offices produce a sizable number of reports useful not only to their own colleges but also to analysts seeking data about program effects. Relating student progress to placement and testing procedures is popular. The IR offices also occasionally design community surveys, asking, "How many of our district's high school graduates attend our college?" They conduct studies of student aspirations, attempting to link them to program design and student success: "Why did the students enroll? Did they get what they were looking for?" They do program review, often under the impetus of an external agency's request: "Is this program properly staffed? Does it attract students? Is it cost effective?" They include comparative studies: "How do other colleges in our state organize their orientation programs?" They conduct academic validation studies: "Which tests best predict course grades?" They study student learning, using standardized instruments to test student gains in writing, mathematics, reading, and critical thinking. And they do attainment studies: "How many of our graduates obtained jobs or went on to further education?"

The audience for these reports varies. The state agencies that have requested the data receive copies, as do the college's senior officials and board members. The institutional researchers' state and national associations publish selected data compilations. Some institutional researchers condense their reports into short memoranda that they distribute to everyone on the campus. The general availability of desktop publishing equipment has made the production of these types of quick releases feasible. They usually include a bar graph or pie chart or some eye-catching artwork and an amount of information sufficiently abbreviated so that the casual reader might still find something of use. The computer has simplified this aspect of the institutional researcher's work, but office support and staffing still lag.

Although most IR reports circulate only within the college, some are distributed to a broader audience. Several state and national faculty associations organized along disciplinary lines publish journals and sponsor conferences in which their members report on studies of their own; the Community College Humanities Association and the American Mathematical Association of Two-Year Colleges are prominent. The journals *Community College Enterprise*, *Community College Review*, *Community College Journal of Research and Practice*, *Journal of Applied Research in Community Colleges*, and *New Directions for Community Colleges* carry articles by both practitioners and researchers. Various state groups, including two-year college trustee, administrator, institutional research, and faculty associations, report their members' studies in their own publications; examples are *Inquiry*, the journal of the Virginia Community Colleges, and *Visions*, the journal of applied research for the Florida community colleges. Several national forums welcome presentations of research. Among the more prominent are the Association for Institutional Research, Society of College and University Planners, Association for the Study of Higher Education, National Council for Research and Planning, American Association of Community Colleges, Division J of the American Educational Research Association, and the Council for the Study of Community Colleges.

Forms of Research

Historical and Sociological Studies

Several treatments of the formation and development of junior (later community) colleges have been written from the viewpoint of history or sociology. Those with a historical bent look for documentation and details of the founding of individual institutions, such as Bishop's *The Community's College* (2002), hoping that when such examples are strung together, a picture of nationwide institutional formation will emerge. The sociologists usually work from the top down, seeking to connect institutional formation with broad social forces and theories of institutional formation. Interesting also are the biographies of early leaders, attempting to place the great person at the center of institutional development.

Much of the sociological and political science–based research linking college development to broad social forces is reviewed in the following chapter. A few of the historical treatments include books by Eaton (1994), Vaughan (1980), Dougherty (1994), Frye (1992), and Witt and others (1994), and a dissertation by Pedersen (2000). Articles have been prepared by Gallagher (1994), Murray (1988–89), Plucker (1987), and Wagoner (1985). Some trace college genesis to the influence of local officials, such as school superintendents and university presidents, or of business and community leaders. By showing how these actors brought about the community colleges in their areas, the authors rebut the arguments that the colleges were products of a national agenda. If university leaders wanted to give a boost to undergraduate education (Gallagher, 1994), if business leaders wanted a precollegiate structure as an ornament of civic pride (Frye, 1992), and if school officials built the colleges despite reluctance on the part of state legislators (Dougherty, 1994; Pedersen, 2000), then the thesis of response to directives from a national association breaks down. Whether these local leaders were acting from noble or base motives seems irrelevant.

The contemporary dominant historical view is that prior to the 1950s, the colleges were formed as local institutions in which recent high school graduates could get a start at a collegiate career. Most of the colleges were organized in small towns, far from universities; if the intent had been to form colleges for terminal students, the presence of a university would not have been a limiting factor. Furthermore, if vocational education were the guiding reason for establishing the colleges, they would have been organized first in the big industrial states, not in Iowa, Missouri, Texas, and California. After the 1960s, when sizable funds for occupational education were made available and large numbers of poorly prepared students sought college entry, the vocational and remedial functions became prominent along with collegiate studies.

These analyses have served to fill a gap in the research on the community colleges. Several of them have contributed to the ongoing debate over the motives of the early promoters and leaders of the institutions. Were the institutions formed because of the pleadings of national organizations, or did they develop in response to local enthusiasts? Did they arise in response to broad social forces, or to the determination of individual opportunists? Do they evidence a capitalistic society's conspiracy to keep the lower classes in their place? Are they a major democratic force, assisting people in moving toward the American dream of higher-status' jobs and social position? Depending on the author's biases, the colleges are either the greatest invention of the twentieth century or the social tragedy of the era. Still, it has been refreshing to see the institution analyzed, even if the analysts range from neo-Marxists to Chamber of Commerce–type hagiographers.

Large-Scale Efforts

Although large-scale compilations obscure information about single colleges, they provide useful overviews. The NCES collects data on all sectors and publishes numerous reports; nearly two dozen are cited in this book. Beyond its routine census-style reports of enrollments, its data reflect congressional concerns. Because of the various forms of federal aid awarded to postsecondary students, NCES summarizes data on college revenues, expenditures, and tuition. Federal affirmative action rulings require the colleges to report data on the gender and ethnicity of college staff, students, and graduates, and NCES compiles them. Federal regulations regarding discrimination against, or special funds available for, students with disabilities have led to various data on special services provided.

Recent legislation has added to the types of information compiled. In an effort to reduce loan default and abuse of financial aid, regulations such as Student Right-to-Know have brought forth calls for data on student success in the various programs. The Student-Right-to-Know graduation rate is based on assessing all first-time-in-college, full-time, degree-seeking students who enroll on a certain date. The rate is calculated at 150% of the time normally required to complete the degree (which is two years for an associate's). But the data are inexact because "for purposes of calculating the rate, once students are included in the cohort they remain in it, even if they switch to part-time enrollment or are no longer enrolled" (Bailey, Crosta, and Jenkins, 2007, p. 1). Also, students who transfer are counted as noncompleters, even if they obtain a degree at a different institution. This yields some weird data because close to half of all first-time community college students eventually attend more than one institution. Furthermore, three years is too short to measure community student outcomes. The National Postsecondary Aid Study did a cross-sectional survey of all students enrolled during an academic year and found that "only 22% of all students enrolled in credit-bearing courses in a community college during 1999–2000 enrolled full-time and for the full academic year" (Bailey, Crosta, and Jenkins, 2007, p. 2). The authors conclude that using the Beginning Postsecondary Student Survey, the graduation rate would double if six years were allowed and if students were tracked after they left their initial institution.

The Carl D. Perkins Vocational and Applied Technology Education Act, passed in 1990 and reauthorized several times since, instructed the colleges to provide data on student job attainment and maintenance. Two other federal initiatives of the 1990s impinged on data collection. Goals 2000 was designed to stimulate attempts to develop national curriculum standards, along with information on student literacy and other capacities. State Postsecondary Review Entities (SPRE) directed colleges to provide data on graduation rates, student withdrawal, licensure exam pass rates, and several other categories. Although both initiatives have been rescinded, they reveal how the federal government is involved in setting a research agenda for the colleges.

National data are an essential beginning point for any community college studies, but various types of information useful for a more complete picture of college contributions are not being compiled routinely. The American Association of Community Colleges (1994) pointed to some of these gaps by citing several core indicators of effectiveness, including student persistence, satisfaction, and goal attainment; transfer and job placement numbers and success ratios; literacy and citizenship skill development; and college relationships with the community. Alfred, Ewell, Hudgins, and McClenney (1999) have further described fourteen of these indicators, and the association subsequently published a third edition of core indicators, this time with sixteen measures listed (Alfred, Shults, and Seybert, 2007). The League for Innovation in the Community College detailed sixty-nine measures of institutional effectiveness that could be reported (Doucette and Hughes, 1990). Participants in a conference sponsored by the Spencer Foundation listed one hundred questions, most so broad that they could be used to justify any types of research (Ashley, Barr, and Lattuca, 1999). Other suggested assessment frameworks include combinations of multiple forms: exams, hands-on learning activities, Web-based designs, opinion polls, and diagnostic tests. All these plans suffer from complexity in design and attempts to account for too many arcane variables. As Gleick stressed, "The choice is always the same. You can make your model more complex and more faithful to reality, or you can make it simpler and easier to handle" (1987, p. 278).

The U.S. Education Department has continued the efforts it made in the early 1990s toward drafting specifications for a national collegiate assessment system. In various ways it has attempted to pressure all of higher education to set standards that the states and the accrediting agencies would enforce; the Secretary of Education's Commission on the Future of Higher Education (Spelling Commission) held hearings in 2006–2007 on those and related topics. The purpose of its recommendations was to develop procedures for continuous monitoring of access and outcomes, the rate at which students entering colleges complete their programs, and various indicators of student learning. Primarily, the group was looking for uniform reporting formats and some set of indicators beyond accreditation standards that could be readily understood and generally accepted. Along with SPRE and the National Education Goals of the 1990s, this activity marked a notable departure from the American tradition of leaving goal setting to state and local authorities. But such changes were not to be easily effected. Despite some acceptance of the idea by a public concerned about its schools, many politicians and college officials opposed what they characterized as a usurpation of authority by the federal government and an invasion of student privacy.

The types of data that state agencies compile differ greatly because of the variant place of community colleges in state higher education systems and because each state legislature and governing board enacts different regulations. State agencies typically receive data from the colleges and publish statewide aggregates regarding college expenditures, graduation rates, staff salaries, student ethnicity and age, and other areas. Some of these *fact books*, such as those published annually in Florida, Illinois, North Carolina, and Washington, are useful in making interinstitutional comparisons. Some are quite comprehensive; a California report tallied college effectiveness on more than fifty performance measures ranging from adult population participation rates to the college's fiscal condition (Walters and Shymoniak, 1996).

More often, the state agencies act as NCES does in responding to legislative mandates. The law directs the colleges to initiate a program—student matriculation, for example—and directs the state agency to collect data on program effects, whereupon the agency draws guidelines for the colleges to use in assessing students at entry. The colleges define their procedures and validate their tests in accordance with student access in the programs in which they were placed. Whether the colleges are allowed to select their own instruments, as in California, or uniform tests are administered statewide, as in New Jersey, the IR office has had a portion of its research agenda defined for it. Supplemental state funding for these procedures, if available, is rarely sufficient for the colleges to mount comprehensive programs that integrate findings with practice.

In summation, institutional assessment is a fact of life in contemporary community colleges. Since 1988, the U.S. Education Department has stipulated that for accrediting agencies to be on its approved list, they must require colleges to specify their objectives and conduct studies that determine whether they are meeting their standards. State pressures for assessment date back at least to Florida's College-Level Academic Skills Tests, mandated in 1982. By 1989, half the states required some form of institutional-level assessment (Ewell, 2001). Compliance has been slow. As of 1998, around half the colleges had developed regular assessment routines, the same ratio as in four-year institutions (Peterson, Einarson, Augustine, and Vaughan 1999). But it has accelerated, through several ongoing projects that reach across state lines.

Accountability

A half century ago, the editor of the *Junior College Journal* cautioned the colleges about their mythmaking and marketing enthusiasm. He predicted presciently that "increased sales resistance will bring increased demands for proof—sound proof—to support claims concerning the quality of the [junior college] product." Among the myths for which he found scant evidence were assertions that junior college instruction is superior to lower-division instruction at the universities, smaller classes lead to greater personal attention and improved student outcomes, and the local institution provides greater attention to local educational needs. And he warned that the ever-insistent demands on the public for more money would force the colleges "to translate their folklore into well-authenticated principles" (Reynolds, 1957, pp. 1–2; cited in Meier, 2008).

Accountability has grown since the 1960s as higher education expanded and as trust in and respect for all social institutions declined. The term refers to the responsibility of campus and system administrators to provide reports of their stewardship of public funds and "policy-relevant statistics produced regularly to support overall planning and monitoring at the national, state, or system level" (Leveille, 2006, p. 8). *Performance accountability* has three forms: performance funding, budgeting, and reporting. *Performance funding* connects state funding tightly to institutional performance. *Performance budgeting* means that the links between performance and funds allocated are more contingent. *Performance reporting* involves little or no connection between performance and funding.

Nearly all the states have some form of performance accountability. As of 2003, all but four used performance reporting; twenty-one had performance budgeting; and fifteen had performance funding (Burke and Minassians, 2003). All these systems are based on the same types of measures: remediation success; transfer to four-year institutions; graduation rate; and job placement rate. The performance accountability framework in California includes student progress and achievement in three areas: degree and transfer, occupational and workforce development, and basic skills. A fourth area is participation rates in the system as compared to the state's adult population (Carducci, 2007).

Performance accountability has had varied effects. Where it has been tied to funding, the amount that each college receives has been too small a portion of the college budget to induce the managers to make radical changes, and all but a few states that introduced it subsequently abandoned it. Some practitioners have publicized intra-institutional comparisons, especially when an indicator makes their college look better than others. But comparisons are tenuous at best and essentially useless between colleges in different states because the measures of remedial success and job placement rates usually differ. Overall, accountability's main positive effects have been to focus institutional managers' attention on outcomes and state priorities and to increase their research capabilities. Most of the negative effects have been in the nature of what is called "gaming the system." In order to raise their graduation and retention rates, some colleges have weakened their academic standards by reducing course requirements or by presenting faculty with directives that they submit detailed reports on each student who has dropped their courses (Dougherty and Hong, 2006, p. 74). A social science principle called Campbell's Law holds that "the more that a social indicator is used for social decision making, the more subject it will be to corruption pressures and the more apt it will be to distort and corrupt the social processes it is intended to monitor" (Campbell, 1975). And indeed, the accelerated drive for accountability has yielded some strange fruit.

Problems in Assessment

Consultant: You need to set up an automated process- and outcomes-tracking data system.

President: Would the tables and graphs be useful?

Consultant: Of course. You can refer to them with confidence when you present the decisions you have already made based on institutional politics.

The overarching problem of assessment is that most decision making is based on other realities. Furthermore, whatever the source and the forms it takes, research on the community colleges suffers several limitations stemming from imprecision in the language of the social sciences and from the relationships between researchers and practitioners. Additional difficulties center on the nature of reportage and the way that support for the colleges is generated and sustained. These problems are prevalent in other sectors as well, but here they are related to the literature about the community colleges (further described in Cohen, 2005).

Styles in research in education affect studies about community colleges. The higher education research community is considerably less likely to use psychological measures such as the Omnibus Personality Inventory and the Minnesota Multiphasic Personality Inventory than it was a generation ago. And research adherent to theories of the developing adolescent is also less frequently seen. Still in use are high-powered statistical tests applied to the soft data typical of the social sciences—rather like driving Indianapolis race cars on dirt roads.

Moreover, the recent literature, especially dissertations, displays a drift toward qualitative analysis, reports based often on observations of or interviews with a handful of students, faculty, or staff. Although it is daunting to pick up a three-hundred-page dissertation filled with verbatim transcriptions of commentary by a half-dozen students, the practice suggests a move toward storytelling, a venerable mode of information transmission. Significant differences displayed by subsets of students drawn from large-scale databases provide one way of understanding; interpretations made from conversations with only a few offer another.

The historical and sociological treatises are evidence that there is no such thing as unbiased scholarship. The attempt to link institutional formation and development to sociological theory, the premise that either broad social forces or local initiative gave rise to community colleges, and the conclusion that society is well served or betrayed by the existence of these open-access, postsecondary structures all argue that the term *objective inquiry* is an oxymoron. The findings are as stylized and predictable as those reached by quantitative researchers who discover that only 20 percent of the entering students transfer. (How many transfers would it take for them to remove the qualifier "only"?) The researchers who demonstrate (once again) that students who matriculate at a community college are less likely to obtain the baccalaureate than those who start at a university have offered nothing new. Their conclusions—"The colleges should begin offering the B.A.," or "The colleges should abandon their collegiate function," for example—reveal their prejudgments. Hoos (1972) critiqued the latter types of research, saying that relying on it to make policy decisions is almost always an ex post facto justification of a position already taken.

Survey research, too, has its limitations. Even NCES sometimes provides ambiguous information. For example, the question, "Which of the following services does your institution provide?" addressed to all the colleges, listed services for students with various types of disabilities. It yielded the finding that 837 of the nation's 1,020 public two-year institutions offer "assistance for the visually impaired" (National Center for Education Statistics, 1994b, p. 21). But the reader of the report has no way of telling whether that assistance is a full-scale curriculum or a set of Braille markers on the campus's elevator buttons.

One complication in accountability measurement is in assigning responsibilities for student learning. The directives demanding program review if certain outcomes are not attained bump into this problem. Whose fault is it: the colleges' or the students'? Always an issue, it has become even more unwieldy as many students transfer among institutions several times before completing a degree. When a student matriculates at one college, attends for a term, enrolls concurrently at a second institution in the next term, abandons both of those and takes classes at a third institution in a subsequent term, and eventually completes a degree at yet a fourth institution, which one is most accountable for the student's progress?

The premise that institutional effects can be separated from the students' tendencies is flawed. Some residential colleges may have been able to demonstrate their value to students who enrolled and stayed for four years straight. But such cohorts are in a minority among students in bachelor's degree–granting institutions and practically nonexistent in the associate degree–granting colleges. Stop in, stop out, take classes here or there, amass credits, get a degree eventually; where and how did learning occur? Assessing students at entry and at graduation, the traditional way of estimating the cognitive or affective change, loses its power in an institution where relatively few students graduate; too few of the entrants are there to take both halves of the measurement.

Research on the contemporary colleges confronts the realities of the institutions. On the one hand, teaching and learning are open-ended. We can always do better: graduation rates can be higher; the students can be more satisfied. On the other hand, the professional staff have only limited incentives to improve what they do. Their welfare does not depend on their institution's performance as measured by student outcomes. They do not get paid more when the students learn more, and no one is dismissed if they learn less. Therefore, major gaps appear between goals (however derived), the research that is supposed to measure attainment of the goals, and the extent to which the institution will change according to the findings. Each is a separate event. No externally generated mandate for institutional accountability can create a hyperrational, tightly coupled system.

This disjuncture is revealed in the types of goals that practitioners prefer to set. Because they cannot penetrate the boundaries separating the different roles of the educators, they usually are stated in a way that does not lend itself to straightforward measurement. Admonishing the faculty to set measurable objectives attacks their unwillingness to put forth targets for which they can be held accountable. State-level pressure for outcomes data confronts administrators' need for positive findings exclusively. Because institutional support depends on image, not data, the quest for valid information may be self-defeating.

Therefore, the goals that intrainstitutional committees pronounce usually relate to process ("The computer lab will upgrade its equipment"; "The college will offer more classes in the evening") and only occasionally to outcomes ("Our graduation rates will increase by 5 percent"; "The percentage of area employers who report they are satisfied with our students' job performance will average 80 across all programs"). Process goals are acceptable because they suggest that the staff are trying harder. Product goals are suspect because too many uncontrollable variables may act to diminish the results, and failure to achieve the objective may generate untoward criticism. This is the main reason that college leaders remain suspicious of, if not antagonistic to, performance indicators.

In intramural research, the people studying the phenomenon are included in the complexity being studied. This characteristic sets intrinsic educational research apart from research in other fields. It is the Heisenberg effect squared; examining a phenomenon changes it, and when the analysts are themselves the object of examination, the paradigms of traditional research are hopelessly distorted. Few practitioners dare to organize studies that have the potential of making them look ineffective; they fear being compared with other institutions or losing credibility. And because the colleges and their clients have multiple purposes, they know that no single outcomes measure captures the institution's complexities. Since we cannot account for all the subtleties in everything we do, some say, why measure anything and risk being misunderstood? Ewell (1987) has discussed many such problems, showing that often no one on campus knows what assessment is for or what its consequences will be. He has also noted the organizational problem of assessment, which, like any other innovation, may disturb many long-standing formal and informal relationships. In a later article, Ewell attempted to clarify various forms of assessment, differentiating "student learning outcomes" from institutional "efficiency, productivity, and effectiveness" and program-level "output and productivity" (2001, p. 8). Burke and Minassians extended those differentiations to community colleges, saying that most of the people responsible for policy have little or no familiarity with the performance reports, which thus "have only minimal effect in improving policymaking on campus" (2003, p. 62).

The assessment of institutional productivity has often led to the untoward practice of ranking the colleges, which can have the effect of misleading the public and generating antagonism on the part of practitioners. One example is available from California, where the state chancellor's office released a list of colleges in order of their transfer rates (Hom, 2000). Spokespersons from the colleges toward the bottom of the list reacted angrily, saying that the calculation did not consider their types of students, emphases, or other programs (Weiss, 2000). A group of researchers criticized the report and similar releases that tallied colleges on the basis of number of degrees and certificates awarded, basic skills development, course completion, and workforce development by pointing up the flaws and dangers in college rankings—for example, lack of statistical significance, errors in measurement, and dangers of misinterpretation (RP Group, 2001). College administrators have long been suspicious of the uses to which any types of reported data are put. "If the data are specific and clear, and if they demonstrate differences among universities and colleges, bitter experience teaches that the regulators will praise those whose indicators are high and condemn those whose are low, without paying the slightest attention to purpose, organization, circumstance, or mission of the institutions involved" (Lombardi, 2006, p. 17).

These types of reactions and criticisms have been evident in other states and are certain to appear every time reports are released showing how colleges rank on any variable. No matter how carefully the data are collected and analyzed, the practice of ranking has the inherent flaw of being a zero-sum game; someone has to be on the bottom. And what is the difference between a college with a transfer rate of 36.41 percent and one with a rate of 36.29 percent? The problem is magnified when state funds are allocated or withheld on the basis of a college's position on a list of jobs attained or licensure-pass rates exhibited by its students. Public display of rankings and funding decisions based on them tend to feed the unease that most practitioners have long felt about outcomes studies. Even so, the states' and the federal government's pressure for comparative outcomes data has been increasing and shows no sign of subsiding.

Many nonnormative listings of community colleges are available, such as the state reports showing the variety of programs offered by each college or the proportion of income that each derives from various sources. Two systems for differentiating community colleges along descriptive, not evaluative, dimensions have been publicized recently. In 2001 the U.S. Education Department classified the two-year institutions in seven categories, public divided by size, and other nonprofit and for-profit colleges. In 2004 the Carnegie Classification system, which for decades had named all community colleges as *associates colleges*, was revised and the institutions broken out into fourteen categories, including not only size and control but also locale. Such differentiations follow the even more detailed benchmarking project, described by Seybert (2006), in which researchers can compare colleges with similar institutions along narrowly defined categories.

Many reasons that assessment of student learning has not been widely adopted have been advanced, including the uncertain feasibility of measuring important outcomes, the limited time or money available to implement a testing program, the tendency for the faculty to teach primarily what the test will measure, the risk of outsiders' misusing the information gained, and the students' unwillingness to cooperate in a process that has no relevance to them. But overriding all these objections is the dilemma of research in the social sciences in general. For at least a century, social scientists have sought the predictability and absolute conclusions that they thought marked mathematics and the physical sciences. But that quest leads only to trivial findings or mathematical modeling that few people within the colleges or among their support groups can follow. Banta issued "a warning on measuring learning outcomes," saying that calls for collecting data that would allow for interstate comparison of student learning, such as those made recently by the Spelling Commission, are highly questionable. First, standardized test scores are highly correlated with entering student ability and reflect individual differences among students more accurately than they do differences in the quality of education offered at different institutions. "For nearly fifty years, measurement scholars have warned against pursuing the blind alley of value added assessment. . . . We see no virtue in attempting to compare institutions, since by design they are pursuing diverse missions" (2007, p. 2). Hoos (1979) was skeptical of quantitative approaches to assessing the effectiveness of social institutions and pointed out how seeking only that which can be measured leads to ignoring all else. And as Biesta and Burbules paraphrase from John Dewey: "The idea of 'improving' education practice in any direct way through educational research should be abandoned. . . . Educational problems are always unique and for that reason always require unique responses, tailored as best as possible to the idiosyncrasies of the actual, unique situation" (2003, p. 81). In other words, all findings in educational research are tentative, equivocal, and derivative, and dressing them up with statistics only gives the illusion of precision. McKeachie (1963) put it most succinctly when he concluded that, at bottom, research on teaching can demonstrate only that in *college A, on day B, instructor C used method D to teach concept E to F set of students.* Change any of those variables and the findings shift.

Possibilities in Assessment

Why should the staff members in any colleges measure the learning attained by their students or other institutional outcome? Such measurement in the abstract is an exercise not likely to gain much staff support. Most of a college's funds are calculated according to formulas fixed in a political arena, not assigned on the basis of results attained, and attempts to link a substantial portion of a college's funding to its students' learning (sometimes quaintly called "value added") have so far yielded little more than political uproar. The data can be used for institutional public relations, but only if a skilled leader knows how to spin them into statements of institutional worth. Appeals to professionalism are of little use because the staff perceive information on student learning gathered by outsiders as irrelevant. Information on student outcomes might be used to bolster staff morale, but only if sizable learning gains are demonstrated: like the children of Lake Wobegon, all one's students must be above average. Attempts to feed student learning data back to instructors, so that classroom practices can be improved, usually prove ineffectual because few instructors will accept data about their students from anyone else.

Even so, assessment can be used for several purposes. Students can be tested at entry so that they can be directed into proper courses. The scores can be used to establish a baseline against which students' learning can be measured periodically as they progress through the programs in which they are enrolled. Students' achievement on licensure examinations, their rate of placement in jobs, their graduation success, and their movement into further education can also be measured, along with their satisfaction with their education. Any type of standardized or locally developed instrument may be applied.

Testing individuals, which is familiar to all educators, is done to motivate students, set goals, design and modify media, and estimate learning attained through various interventions. Using the same process to assess group attainment distorts it, especially when it becomes the basis for judging the worth of a program. Because testing individuals to determine their progress is so familiar, it militates against educators using methods that are considerably more reliable and valid for estimating group progress. Multiple matrix sampling, a technique known for decades, serves as an example. The National Assessment of Educational Progress uses it to estimate and publicize how much nine-year-olds, thirteen-year-olds, and seventeen-year-olds know. A sample of items is given to a sample of students in a sample of schools, with the items, students, and schools sampled anew at each biennial iteration.

A longitudinal study can be initiated, with a cohort of students who are entering for the first time as its subjects. However, this procedure, favored by many higher education researchers, stems from a view of college as a place where students develop over years of attendance, clearly not the community college norm. If it is to be used, it works best where a percentage of students is sampled. Each term these students can be asked about their aspirations and course-taking patterns. Different forms of the placement exam or other measures can be used to test the students at entry and at various points along the way. When a small group is sampled, follow-up becomes much more feasible. Although community college-based researchers such as Rasor and Barr (1998) have detailed straightforward ways of sampling, the practice has not been widely adopted.

An alternative form of outcomes assessment is based on a cross-sectional model, where content measures are included along with items asking about student satisfaction, course-taking behavior, use of support services, and other information about intrainstitutional concerns. An item bank can be developed, with items categorized by skills, such as critical thinking, reading, and writing; by content, such as history, chemistry, and mathematics; and by response type, including multiple and free response. The items can be as specific or as general as desired. Tests can be constructed and administered to students in classes, and certain demographic information can be solicited at the same time. After the tests have been taken, groups of students can be classified according to aspiration, number of units taken, prior school experience, or any other measure that seems of interest. This model was used as the basis for the *General Academic Assessment* and the *General Academic Learning Experience*, both described in Chapter Eleven.

The longitudinal model works best in a college where students matriculate with the intention of participating in programs organized sequentially and where the college's processes are designed to ensure that they do. The cross-sectional model should be used if the college leaders are serious about providing an institution where students can drop in and out at will—the lifelong learning ideal. It skirts the problem of student retention and the difficulty of follow-up because it generates new cohorts each time it is administered. The level of knowledge displayed by the students collectively, first at entrance, then after they have completed a certain number of units, and at graduation, can be compared. Any available demographic information can be used to make further differentiations.

The mode of assessment in use for the longest time, however, has been student satisfaction, a concept that fits with the perception that the clients must be pleased with the experience if they are to continue returning. For decades most community colleges have designed and administered surveys asking students if they used services such as counseling, food services, library, job placement, and instruction, and the extent to which they were satisfied with them. Most such surveys were designed at individual colleges, thus between-college comparisons could not be made, and little attention was paid to sampling or response rates. But standardized instruments are available. The *Noel-Levitz Student Satisfaction Inventory* includes a version specific to community colleges and maintains a national comparison group so that staff members may determine whether their students are more or less satisfied with academic services, instruction, concern for the individual, and so on. Between 2004 and 2007, over 220,000 students in 245 colleges participated. In 2006, the *Community College Survey of Student Engagement*, described in Chapter Six, surveyed nearly one-quarter million students in 447 colleges, with class sections sampled randomly. Findings for various subgroups (part-time and older students, women and men, ethnic minorities, and developmental students) are available.

Outcomes Assessment

Community college outcomes refer in the main to licensure-exam pass rates, employment status, transfer rates, and graduation rates. They are related to accountability when they are used to assess institutional effectiveness against preset standards. North Carolina presents one example of such a statewide program. Dating from a legislative mandate of 1989, it includes twelve indicators of student success, along with several in such categories as workforce development (three indicators), resources (seven), technology (five), and learning needs of diverse segments of the population (seven). Data regarding each of these thirty-four indicators are displayed for each college, each year, along with notes showing the number of colleges "meeting standard" (North Carolina Community College System, 2007a, pp. 42–44). Any college not meeting a standard is required to submit an action plan for improving performance to the state board. In 2005–06, all fifty-eight colleges met the standards or "showed significant improvement" on nearly all of the indicators. The success rate for each indicator is based on a definition that is peculiar to the state. For example, the practically 100 percent employment rate for North Carolina associate's degree recipients (noted in Chapter Eight in the section titled Program Success), considerably out of line with other states' averages, is tabulated by adding the locality's unemployment rate to the percentage of job gainers. In other words, if 90 percent of a college's graduates are employed and the college district's unemployment rate is 8 percent, then the college is considered to have a 98 percent success rate. An indicator asking how many students "report that their primary goal in attending has been met" (p. 20) is based on responses to a survey administered by each college. In 2005–06 the colleges averaged 99 percent attainment based on a survey response rate of 8 percent!

The methods that colleges use to verify attainment of performance indicators obviously do not meet standards of academic research. But why should they? If state support depends on successful attainment, then political realities demand that all colleges qualify on practically all criteria. In brief, the research noted in this chapter varies depending on the audience for whom it is intended. For much of the history of community colleges, spokespersons would respond to questions of college value with anecdotes, lauding the progress of individual students: "Do students succeed at our college? Let me tell you about Mildred, a single parent, marginally literate when she came to us. We mentored and encouraged her and now she's a pre-med student at the state university."

Such stories have been superseded by studies using larger numbers but having no greater validity. The researchers who publish in academic journals must adhere to accepted standards of research in the social sciences, and if their reports are for internal college staff, they must provide information on programs within that institution and recognize that faculty prefer using their own instruments or other classroom-based assignments to test particular outcomes. But an audience unknowledgeable about data validity has no problem applauding the Littlefield study summarized in Chapter Five. The similarly designed Christopherson and Robinson studies, also noted in Chapter Five, would gain credibility if they did parallel studies of communities that do not have colleges within their borders or used data on the same communities before the college opened. But their audience is not the researchers concerned with quasi-experimental design, control groups, and validity. It is the people satisfied with brief, easily understood numbers that present favorable information. Not incidentally, the colleges that commission such reports invariably issue press releases sharing the good news (Dembicki, 2007). Few, if any, of the media carrying the stories mention the obvious fact that since the colleges draw most of their funds from outside their service area, whereas most of their beneficiaries reside within the locality, a net cash benefit to the community is guaranteed *a priori*. Similar economic benefits would result if instead of a college the examined entity was a sanitarium, hospital, prison, or asylum. (In the early years of public higher education, communities competing for state colleges were often mollified by legislatures' awarding such institutions to them instead.)

One of the basic problems in assessing learning outcomes is that the "gold standard" for assessing group progress is random assignment (Levin and Calcagno, 2007, p. 11). And random assignment is rarely undertaken in practice. In the case of remedial education, for example, it would demand assessing students at entry, determining which of them need remedial studies, and then randomly assigning a portion of that group to the college's developmental education activities and a different set of the group to the regular collegiate program. This would mitigate the problem defined by Bailey and Alfonso (2005), who said that the issue of how and why students enter remedial programs in the first place is rarely examined. If students could be placed on the basis of random assignment, then evidence of the consequences of various interventions could be brought forward. Otherwise, the question of which students participated in which learning activities and for what reasons always remains open.

In one of the few studies using random assignment, MDRC presented the results of a program in Louisiana "designed to help low-income parents attending community college cover more of their expenses and also provide a financial incentive to make good progress" (Brock and Richburg-Hayes, 2006). Two New Orleans-area colleges offered $1,000 per year scholarships, in addition to any other financial aid for which students qualified. The program was evaluated using a random assignment research design; that is, low-income parents were randomly assigned to two groups, one receiving the scholarships and a control group that received only whatever aid was available to all students. The group receiving the scholarships was more likely to enroll full time, pass more courses, and return for successive semesters. Jaschik (2008) reported a similar study at Kingsborough Community College (New York) where full-time students were assigned at random to learning communities or to a control group. Those in the learning communities took and passed more courses, earned more credit, and showed greater increases in English test scores.

Each area of the college deserves its own set of measurements. For example, an area of inquiry dating to the behavioral objectives movement pioneered by Ralph Tyler in the 1950s has been promoted vigorously in recent years by Angelo and Cross (1993). Each instructor is to set objectives and assess the effects of different techniques, using the findings as the basis for instructional modification. There is no comparing one instructor's outcomes with another; no attempt to relate the outcomes to other college purposes. With intrinsically designed goals, each classroom is its own object of study, each instructor a researcher.

Extending this concept of the self-contained study to other areas is just as feasible. Only a few easily understood principles of research need control the process; for example, where surveys are employed, population sampling and nonrespondent bias checks are basic. Most important is that no comparisons be sought between institutions or between programs in the same institution. Each area is discrete. The presidents should limit their "We're number one!" to their speeches to athletic booster clubs.

Answers to most questions are available through data on community demographics and college enrollment patterns and through follow-up studies of students who matriculated and then dropped out, completed programs, or went on to further pursuits. When a legislator or a newspaper reporter calls and asks, "How many students who entered your college have gained employment?" the researcher should deliver a number based on a valid analysis of the available data. The questioner will not be satisfied by a reference to a lengthy report in which the data are manipulated by an endless array of categories of students and programs, types of jobs sought, student abilities and aspirations, and the like. Difficult for many database managers to realize, some questions deserve straightforward responses even if the database could yield an incredible array of permutations. The analogy is with a parent who, when asked how old the child is, can simply give a number expressed in years (in the case of infants, in months). The number given does not fully describe the child's weight, height, gender, IQ, eating habits, favorite toy, or any of the other characteristics that combine to tell a more complete story of the individual. Although the parent is fully aware of the child's other characteristics, to report them is to miss the essence of the transaction. One number suffices to answer the question, "How old is your child?" just as one number can be given in response to, "How many students gain employment?" even though that number says nothing about the purposes for which students enrolled, their learning of basic skills, and whether they had jobs prior to entry.

Each of the community colleges' main missions of transfer, job entry, career upgrading, literacy and general education development, and personal satisfaction can be assessed separately and regularly, with results communicated routinely. The measurements could yield periodic reports arrayed as follows:

Transfer: "X percent of the students who entered our college with no prior college experience four years ago completed at least four courses here. Of those, Y percent have transferred to an in-state, public university. We anticipate an increase to a Z percent transfer rate within the next two years because of our emphasis on recruiting full-time students and because we have recently concluded new articulation agreements for three of our basic programs with our major receiving university."

Job entry: "X percent of the students who enter with no prior experience in the field and who complete three or more courses in one of our office skills or sales training programs obtain full-time positions in their field of study within one year, and four times that are working part time. This suggests that our clerical and sales programs serve predominantly as a route to part-time employment and hence can be modified to address that clientele more directly. During the coming year, we will organize job placement and training sessions in Y sites to accommodate these job seekers."

Developmental education: "We administered basic-skills tests to all our first-time students and directed X percent of them to our integrated developmental program. Y percent of those who enrolled completed the program and matriculated in collegiate studies. Z percent of that group obtained associate degrees or transferred to universities within four years. We plan on building closer links between our developmental and collegiate programs with the intention of increasing that proportion to Z plus 15 percent within five years."

These examples display how the definitions and methodologies are revealed in the report along with the study's purposes, projections, and actions to be taken based on its findings. This process would also yield the data that state and federal agencies are determined to acquire. Unless each college controls its own research agenda, a mentality of compliance develops in response to these external demands, and research in and about the colleges cannot reach the potential it deserves. Although college leaders rarely use assessment information in making decisions about program maintenance or support, they could well abandon what have been their traditional reactions to it: "The data are flawed, because they didn't consider . . ."; "We may fall short there but look what we are doing over here"; and the ultimate, one-size-fits-all rationalization: "If we had more money we could correct the problem."

In an article commenting on the gap between policymakers and policy scholars, Birnbaum sketches reasons for the disconnection, saying that the nature of policy problems is such that solutions are not apparent through research and "the ways in which policy makers define a problem is often part of the problem" (2000, p. 122). He notes further that "trying to improve research methods is not a solution" (p. 124) because closer adherence to scientific standards only makes the reports less understandable to those outside the research community. But if scholars write in the form of opinion pieces, how is their work more trustworthy than that of journalists in general? He concludes, as did Bowen in 1981, that the cumulative aggregation of many small studies eventually can be used to support such sweeping statements as, "Higher education is a social good and a positive force for economic development."

In summation, the sources and forms of research, the purposes for which it has been conducted, the problems with social science research in general, and above all, the colleges' managers' essential need for findings that in no way can be interpreted as disparaging their institutions, results in widely inconsistent reports. This problem can never be reconciled because of disparities in perspective. From a distance, mountains appear as silhouettes with pointed, rounded, or jagged peaks. Close up, the peaks are not visible and the mountains have become collections of rocks, crevasses, and foliage.

It is gratifying to conclude with Pascarella and Terenzini's view from a distance:

> The post-1990 research . . . paints a more complex and more positive picture than does the pre-1990 research on differences in educational and occupational outcomes associated with two- versus four-year college enrollment. Indeed, studies published since 1990 indicate that in certain outcome areas, community college students derive benefits equal to or even greater than those realized by similar students at four-year colleges or universities. After one year of college, for example, and after adjusting for precollege ability, motivation, and other confounding influences, community college students gain to about the same degree as similar students at four-year institutions on measures of reading comprehension, math skills, and critical thinking skills. After two years, the two groups also showed increases of about the same degree in their science reasoning and writing skills. Moreover, although community college students in general reap these benefits, the gains are greatest among students of color, older students, and less affluent students—in other words, those most likely to attend a community college rather than a four-year institution in the first place. And for similar individuals of equal educational attainment, initial attendance at a two-year college appears to impose no significant penalty on earnings. [2005, p. 639]

Issues

The meager support for research on community colleges is not surprising because research in education does not nearly reflect the importance of schooling in American life. However, research on community colleges has improved, and much information is available, even if it must be sifted from a mass of reportage that includes self-congratulatory commentary, data compiled with little regard for relevance, unwarranted criticism based on selected statistics, and interpretations of stories told by a few people presumptively representative of a group.

Few colleges have developed their own research agendas. Can they continue providing data according to external agency definitions without distorting public views of individual college accomplishments?

Will federal and state agency and accrediting association demands for accountability lead to institutional betterment? For how much longer will the colleges treat them as no more than mandated compliance activities?

Will the colleges of their own volition produce routine data on productivity (degrees awarded, licensure, and job-getting rates), as well as data on student learning outcomes (knowledge gained in humanities, science, math, social science, English usage)?

Can researchers sustain a proper balance between adherence to social science research standards and the need to report in a journalistic style suitable to a broad audience?

More than anything else, answers to these questions rest on the extent to which the college staff themselves become critical consumers of the research that is produced about their institutions.

13

The Social Role

A Response to the Critics

A few scholars in addition to those noted in the previous chapter have been concerned with the community colleges. Their commentary often takes the form of criticizing the institution in its social role or the institution as a school. In the first of these criticisms, the college is often seen in a negative light. It is an agent of capitalism, training workers to fit business and industry; it is a tool of the upper classes, designed to keep the poor, especially minorities, in their place by denying them access to the baccalaureate and, concomitantly, to higher-status positions in society. When it is criticized as a school, questions are raised about its success in teaching: Do these colleges really teach the basic skills that the lower schools failed to impart? Can they provide a foundation for higher learning? Here, too, the answers are usually negative; since the community colleges pass few of their students through to the senior institutions, they are said to have failed the test.

This chapter reviews the allegations made by analysts who contend that the community colleges are negative influences in American society, and it provides a counterpoint to their assertions. It discusses the allocative function, necessary in every educational system, the colleges' real contributions, and possible alternatives to the role that they play.

Criticizing the Role

Several distressingly similar articles have taken community colleges to task for their failure to assist in leveling the social class structure of America. These writings became prominent beginning in the 1970s, when the rapidly expanding institutions brought them to the attention of sociologists. Karabel asserted that they are elements in both educational inflation and the American system of class-based tracking. The massive community college expansion, he said, was due to an increase in the proportion of technical and professional workers in the labor force. This increase caused those who wanted any job other than the lowest paying to seek postsecondary training, thereby contributing to a heightened pressure for admission to higher education in general. Hence educational inflation: an increased percentage of people attending school and staying longer. But the system of social stratification has not changed: "Apparently, the extension of educational opportunity, however much it may have contributed to other spheres such as economic productivity and the general cultural level of the society, has resulted in little or no change in the overall extent of social mobility and economic equality" (1972, pp. 525–526). Students yes, equality no.

Ever class conscious, Karabel cited data showing that community college students were less likely to be from the higher socioeconomic classes than were students at four-year colleges or universities. They were more likely to be from families whose breadwinner was a skilled or semiskilled worker, had not completed grammar school or had not completed high school, and was not a college graduate. (Not incidentally, these facts had been noted by Koos, the first analyst of junior colleges, fifty years earlier.) Some years later, Karabel argued that the research conducted since he put forth his thesis had confirmed his perspective: "With a far greater body of empirical evidence now available, the fundamental argument may be stated again with even greater confidence: Far from embodying the democratization of higher education and a redistribution of opportunity in the wider society, the expansion of the community college instead heralded the arrival in higher education of a form of class-linked tracking that served to reproduce existing social relations. . . . The overall impact of the community college has been to accentuate rather than reduce prevailing patterns of social and class inequality" (1986, p. 18). And he concluded that "the community college has become a vocational-training institution, more and more divorced from the rest of academia, with potentially serious consequences for the life chances of its students" (Brint and Karabel, 1989, pp. 12–13).

Zwerling echoed the thesis that the community college plays an essential role in maintaining the pyramid of American social and economic structure: "It has become just one more barrier put between the poor and the disenfranchised and a decent and respectable stake in the social system which they seek" (1976, p. xvii). The chief function of the community college is to "assist in channeling young people to essentially the same relative positions in the social structure that their parents already occupy" (p. 33). The institution is remarkably effective at controlling mobility between classes because its students come primarily from the lowest socioeconomic classes of college attenders, its dropout rate is the highest in the college population, and dropouts and graduates alike enter lower-level occupations than the equivalent students who attend higher-status colleges. This dropout rate is "related to a rather deliberate process of channeling students to positions in the social order that are deemed appropriate for them" (p. 35).

Pincus, another writer in the same genre, also discussed the community colleges in terms of class conflict, with a particular emphasis on their role in vocational education. He traced the development of the occupational function, showing how it fit everyone's needs exactly: "Corporations get the kind of workers they need; four-year colleges do not waste resources on students who will drop out; students get decent jobs; and the political dangers of an excess of college graduates are avoided" (1980, p. 333). And he alleged that "business and government leaders—those at the top of the heap—regard postsecondary vocational education as a means of solving the political and economic problems created by the rising expectations of the working class" (p. 356).

Pincus deplored the unemployment rates for college graduates, saying that "between one fourth and one half of those graduates who found jobs were 'underemployed'; that is, they held jobs that did not require a college degree" (1980, p. 332). He showed that nonwhite and low-socioeconomic-status students were more likely to attend community colleges than senior institutions and were more likely to be enrolled in the vocational programs than in the transfer programs. In justice to Pincus, he did conclude that "capitalism in the United States cannot always deliver what it promises. There are a limited number of decent, well-paid jobs, and most working-class and nonwhite young people are not destined to get them. Vocational education does not and cannot change this" (pp. 355–356). His argument, then, was less with the schools than with the system itself. In 1994, Pincus again purported that "community colleges are a part of a stratified system of higher education that reproduces the race, class and gender inequalities that are part of the larger society" (pp. 624–625).

Other commentators have also contended that the career programs divert students from lower-class backgrounds away from baccalaureate studies. Levine postulated a cabal, based in the colleges themselves: "Faced with a potential student body increasingly large and diverse in socioeconomic backgrounds and interests, . . . educators encouraged the formation of a new type of postsecondary education devoted to semi-professional vocational training" (1986, p. 183). It was easy for him to conclude, then, that "the interests and needs of the many who attended the junior college to prepare for the university were frustrated by educators' elitist intentions" (p. 184). Richardson and Bender, in their treatise on minority access and achievement, pointed out that despite increased college attendance rates, "there has been little change in economic and social class mobility for minorities because their curriculum choices have been so concentrated in the career and vocational areas" (1987, p. 1). They argued further that "concentrating occupational offerings on campuses serving the highest proportion of minorities while concurrently permitting transfer programs to decline in availability and quality" leads minority students to "become vocational/technical majors because no viable alternatives are provided to them" (pp. 44–45).

Data to support the arguments regarding class-based tracking are easy to find. After examining patterns of college-going in Illinois, Tinto (1973) concluded that low-socioeconomic-status students who go to community colleges are more likely to drop out than their counterparts who attend senior institutions. Dougherty pursued a similar line. He saw the community college as both "democratizing access to higher education" and "hampering attainment of the baccalaureate" (1994, p. 21). He stated that these colleges do allow more students to enjoy the benefits of higher education, but they are not successful at propelling students toward the baccalaureate. Instead, they attract students away from universities because tuition is less, the colleges are often conveniently located to students' homes, and students do not pay for on-campus housing. They accommodate less able students by offering vocational training, but they inherently discriminate against the lower class because community college students tend to drop out of college at a high rate.

Pedersen stated that many "neoconservatives" have helped promote the opinion that community colleges should serve the training and education of potential members of the workforce. Rather than focusing their attention on perceived distractions, such as training students to become culturally aware and prepared for various life opportunities, the community colleges' "real task" is to narrow the curriculum to workforce training only (1994, p. 4).

And last, in their examination of state systems of higher education as they relate to bachelor degree attainment, Orfield and Paul (1992) aligned themselves with those who disparage the community colleges. They concluded that states with a greater commitment to community colleges have lower levels of baccalaureate completion, and neither higher state expenditures per student nor lower tuition increases the completion rates. The institution itself is the stumbling block.

These jeremiads are more politically inspired than empirically founded. At bottom, those who pronounce them are less antagonistic to the community college than they are to what they perceive as a pernicious American social class system, which they wish was more equitable. The arguments are decades old, different now only in that they name the community college as the villain. Schools at all levels have long been criticized for failing to overturn the social class system. In 1944, Warner and his colleagues asserted that Americans were not sufficiently conscious of the class structure and the place of the schools in it. They felt that lack of understanding of the class system would lead eventually to a loss of social solidarity. Their concern was for equality of opportunity, curricular differentiation, and teaching people to accept the idea of social status.

More recently, belief in the inevitability of the class structure has become attenuated, confounded now with social justice, equality of opportunity, cultural deprivation, and a determination to correct the abuses historically heaped onto certain peoples. The fact that African Americans, Hispanics, and Native Americans tend to be overrepresented in the lower socioeconomic classes has contributed to this confusion, but it has provided the protagonists with a cachet. In Gabler's words, "One of the great political achievements of conservatives over the past 30 years or so has been to tie social welfare to race rather than class" (2002, p. M6). The practice is not new; for decades, the labor movement in the South was retarded by industrialists' deliberately pitting whites against blacks every time a union organizer appeared. And, indeed, the polemics directed toward community colleges for their role in perpetrating the structure of social class have now been superseded by contentions that college culture is antagonistic to students (read "minorities") from outside a tradition of rationality and literacy.

London's *The Culture of a Community College* (1978) and Weis's *Between Two Worlds* (1985), early books in this genre, were followed by Rhoads and Valadez's *Democracy, Multiculturalism, and the Community College* (1996) and Shaw, Valadez, and Rhoads's *Community Colleges as Cultural Texts* (1999). These commentators examined college ideology, morale, the messages that students receive, and interactions among faculty, students, policies, and requirements, and then concluded that a vast disjuncture exists between the collegiate form and the students' expectations, aspirations, and abilities. A typical conclusion is that the college culture, with its roots in a language-centered orthodoxy, militates against student progress toward the baccalaureate.

An additional, and larger, set of critics confronts the colleges in terms of their influence on students of color, some using euphemisms such as "nontraditional," "new," or "first-generation" students, others examining the achievements of African Americans or Hispanics specifically. Seeking reasons for the students' uneven progress toward program completion or transfer to four-year institutions, they often blame college staff members' lack of caring, improper institutional policies, inappropriate curriculum, insufficient financial aid, untoward academic standards, or undercurrents of racial bias. In the extreme, they term as racists those who say that the number of people with qualifications for top jobs is quite small and that people are not born equal but instead have diverse potentialities. By extension, an institution that matriculates a high proportion of students of color and passes few through to high-status jobs becomes a racist institution, a tool of the capitalists.

These types of critiques have appeared less frequently in recent years as political leaders and educators alike have come to appreciate the community colleges' role as a viable option to the universities' inability to expand their freshman classes sufficiently to accommodate the greater number of people seeking admission.

This has become apparent also to the lay public who realize that scrambling for a limited number of places in selective universities is a game of musical chairs and many college seekers will be refused admission regardless of their qualifications. Among the applicants to the 2006 entering class rejected by a highly selective liberal arts college in Massachusetts, half had perfect SAT scores (G. Winston, personal communication, February 9, 2007). Furthermore, after several decades of affirmative action and financial aid in all of higher education, the charge that ethnic minorities are deliberately tracked into community colleges has lost its credibility.

The Neo-Marxist contentions still reappear though, but in different guises: *globalization, neoliberalism, new economy*, terms used by various commentators. One example is Dowd: "A capitalist ideology has been forcefully reshaping the community college and its mission. . . . The increase in contract training programs . . . coincides with this shift in focus from students to industries" (2003, pp. 98–99). Ayers provides another: "The community college itself is instrumental in reproducing the class inequalities associated with advanced capitalism" (2005, p. 528). "Learners are reduced to an economic entity designed to please employers so that business and industry may remain competitive in the global economy" (p. 539). And the faculty are displaced by representatives of business in planning educational programs. The arguments are the same: the corporations get the kinds of workers they need; the community colleges are vocational training institutions; and the colleges are complicit with the global reach of the multinational corporations, even to the extent of exploiting their own workers, the part-time instructors. In summation, the issue of community college complicity in a neoliberal agenda has a long history, except that capitalism was the term of choice in earlier decades. But now as then, the core credit programs are holding firm to ensure that their degree requirements include a liberal arts component if a degree is the goal. The issue is actually related to the certificate and contract training programs, along with a portion of the noncredit offerings, that have no degree requirements and where the liberal arts are greatly abbreviated if, indeed, they are at all included.

Criticizing the School

A second set of criticisms pertains to the community colleges as schools. Can they really teach the basic skills that the lower schools failed to impart? Do they provide a foundation for higher learning? Do their students learn the proper skills and attitudes that will enable them to succeed at jobs or in senior institutions? Stripping away the rhetoric and social implications reduces these questions to the following: How many occupational education students obtain jobs in the field for which they were trained? How many students transfer to the senior colleges?

The few large-scale studies that have been conducted provide some clues. After reviewing several comparative studies, Pascarella and Terenzini concluded that "Even when educational attainment is taken into account, initially attending a two-year college appears to have only a modest, negative effect on subsequent occupational status, and for similar individuals of equal educational attainment, initial attendance at a two-year college does not appear to confer a significant earnings penalty." They also found that, "Consistent with pre-1990 estimates, beginning pursuit of a bachelor's degree at a two- rather than a four-year institution reduces the chances of ultimately earning that degree by 15 to 20 percentage points." Part of this may be attributed to the difficulty of transferring. "The difference in bachelor's degree completion rates appears to lie in whether a community college student seeking a bachelor's degree actually transfers to a four-year institution. Once across that bridge, community college transfer students have about the same likelihood of earning a bachelor's degree as do similar students who began at a four-year college or university, although community college students tend to take longer to complete their degrees" (2005, p. 592).

If the analysts would bother to ask the question, *If students are qualified to enter universities why are they enrolling in community colleges?* their conclusions might be different. Since most community college students would not be in higher education if not for the community colleges, "it does not make sense to ask how most students who attended a two-year college would have fared at a four-year college" (Rosenbaum, Redline, and Stephan, 2007, p. 50). Pascarella and Terenzini conclude that community colleges are relatively underfunded but "in some cases having greater impact than four-year institutions. . . . Viewed in such a light, at least one implication is that two-year institutions may well provide students (and taxpayers) with cost-effective routes to the bachelor's degree that do not sacrifice either intellectual rigor or competitiveness in the marketplace" (p. 640).

The U.S. Department of Education's longitudinal study of high school graduates from the class of 1972 reported on the role that the community college had played in their lives (Adelman, 1992, 1994). The findings lent evidence to the contention that this cohort of students used the community college to achieve their own personal goals and not necessarily to earn degrees. Comparing students who attended community colleges, those who attended other educational institutions, and those who did not continue their education after high school, data showed that the community college functioned in a variety of "occasional" roles (p. 152) in the lives of these students; the students could engage in learning on their own terms and in their own time. More students attended community colleges than did students who discontinued their education after high school or who attended only four-year institutions. Community college attendance was more representative of minority students, students who served in the military, and those of moderate to lower socioeconomic backgrounds. Only 20 percent of those who attended a community college earned an associate degree, but earning any kind of degree still made a difference. More students who completed an associate of arts degree earned professional jobs than did students who attended a four-year institution but failed to earn a baccalaureate degree.

What does this information tell us? Adelman suggested that we use postsecondary institutions for "utilitarian purposes"; once school is no longer mandatory, we use it when we want to and on our own terms. In addition, we are more interested in learning, gaining new skills, and completing a basic education than we are in earning more-advanced degrees. Finally, Adelman states that "our youthful aspirations and hopes exceed what actually happens to us, no matter what we do in between." These hopes and aspirations usually translate into effort, which "makes something better than what it otherwise would have been" (1994, p. 167).

Data on the numbers of students who transfer from community colleges to four-year colleges and universities are scattered because the ways of counting transfers vary greatly from system to system and state to state. Patterns of student flow have never been linear; they swirl, with students dropping in and out of both community colleges and universities, taking courses in both types of institutions concurrently, transferring from one to another frequently. Among the students in junior standing at a university, some may be included who took their lower-division work in a community college and in the university concurrently, some who started as freshmen in the university but dropped out to attend a community college and subsequently returned, some who took summer courses at community colleges, some who attended a community college and failed to enroll in the university until several years later, and some who transferred from the community college to the university in mid-year. However, as reported in Chapter Two, when the data are compiled uniformly across the nation, the transfer rates are consistent from year to year. In numerical terms, of the 1.25 million students per year whose initial higher education experience is in a community college, at least 350,000 eventually transfer to universities and they transfer to more selective four-year institutions than they would have attended right out of high school. Whether this rate verifies the community colleges as contributors to social mobility or as agencies displacing the hopes of the underprivileged depends entirely on the viewers' perceptions.

Responding to the Critics

The community colleges are not selective, residential collegiate institutions. The data about their matriculants may be interpreted in various ways, but it is certain that in the aggregate, students prepared in community college vocational programs earn less over a lifetime than those who receive baccalaureate or graduate degrees. It is also certain that in the aggregate, students who begin collegiate studies in community colleges are more likely to drop out or, if they do go on to the baccalaureate, to take longer in obtaining it.

What else can we say to the critics? They are on firm ground when they present data showing that many community college matriculants do not transfer; that the community colleges enroll sizable percentages of minority students and students from a low-socioeconomic-status background; and that of those students who do transfer, the smallest percentage is among students from the minorities and lower-income groups. But their conclusions are not always warranted. Several of the commentators suggest elevating the class consciousness of community college students so that they become aware of the social trap into which they have been led. Zwerling (1976) recommends that students be shown how they are being channeled within the social class structure; they should know that the school is an instrument of power, so that they can act to resist it. Pincus (1980) similarly seeks to elevate class consciousness, saying that community college educators should help working-class and minority students by providing them with a social context from which to understand the dismal choices they face.

They might then begin to question the legitimacy of educational, political, and economic institutions in the United States.

Other critics reach different conclusions. Some want to make the community colleges equal to the universities, so that the low-socioeconomic students who attend them will have an equal chance at obtaining baccalaureate degrees and higher-status positions. Zwerling (1976) suggests converting two-year colleges into four-year institutions, a notion that has gained some support from college leaders recently. Dougherty (1994) also contended that the community colleges should undergo complete organizational reconstruction and become four-year institutions. He would start with the two-year branch campuses that are effective in helping students transfer to the parent four-year institutions.

Astin suggests equating funding so that the community colleges and universities get the same number of dollars per student. He further suggests that "states or municipalities that wish to expand opportunities for such students should consider alternatives to building additional community colleges or expanding existing ones. Although community colleges are generally less expensive to construct and operate than four-year colleges, their 'economy' may be somewhat illusory, particularly when measured in terms of the cost of producing each baccalaureate recipient" (1977, p. 255). Karabel (1972) admits that the colleges are caught in a dilemma. If they increase their occupational offerings, they increase the likelihood that they will track the lower-class students into lower-class occupations, and if they try to maintain comprehensiveness, they magnify the probability that their students will drop out without attaining any degree or certificate.

Clowes and Levin seek a different solution because, as they maintain, the community college is coming close to a position "outside graded education and at the penumbra of higher education" (1989, p. 354). They propose that the colleges should deemphasize baccalaureate education and focus instead on the vocational and career education of their students. In this way, they would be able to offer strong programs leading to immediate employment, and by connecting with university-based programs, they would also maintain their place within higher education. Kinnick and Kempner (1988) reach similar conclusions.

And so the critics skirt the notion of the community college as an agency enhancing equal opportunity. Faced with the unreconcilable problem of social equalization, they present draconian solutions. Suppose all two-year colleges were converted into four-year institutions. Would all colleges and their students then miraculously become equal? There is a pecking order among institutions that even now are ostensibly the same. Neighboring institutions such as Harvard and Northeastern, the University of California at Los Angeles and Pepperdine, the University of Chicago and Loyola all offer the doctorate. But in the eyes of the public, they are not equivalent. Authorizing the community colleges to offer the bachelor's degree, as is happening now in several states, does not change public perceptions of their relative merit; it merely establishes a bottom stratum of former two-year colleges among the senior institutions.

Suppose funding were equalized. Would the colleges then contribute less to the maintenance of a class structure? Perhaps two-year colleges would teach better if sizable funds were diverted from the universities and run to them. Perhaps they would not. But one thing is certain: the major research universities would be crippled. That eventuality might well satisfy those critics who are obsessed with the idea of social class. They would argue that the power of the schools to maintain the social class structure could be reduced quite as effectively by chopping down the top-ranking institutions as by uplifting those serving the lower groups.

As for the centrality of vocational education, all higher education, including graduate and professional school, is career oriented. The poverty-proud scholar, attending college for the joy of pure knowledge, is about as common as the presidential candidate who was born in a log cabin. Both myths deserve decent burials.

The Mythology of Schooling

The truism that the further one goes in school, the greater one's earnings has been modified in favor of a myth: that the type of school that people attend determines their future success.

The various rulings designed to mitigate discrimination based on a person's gender, religion, or ethnic identification were designed to facilitate access. Young people from every social stratum were to enter college and train for lucrative careers. But the more the goal of equal opportunity was approached, the greater the importance of schooling became. The most marked measure of that importance is the gap in earnings between college graduates and people who have not finished high school, something on the order of three to one. Thus, an anomaly: when the standards for who entered college were set on the basis of wealth, race, and intelligence, the arguments for equal opportunity centered on the notion that we were wasting talent by depriving qualified young people of an education. As the doors swung open, as civil rights legislation, state and federal grants for students, and institutions with open-admissions policies became prevalent, issues of segregation within higher education came to the fore. The opportunity to go to college was not enough. Which college was available? Which program? What were the achievement rates for certain members of certain groups? The target kept shifting. Another myth is that equal opportunity to attend school leads to equal outcomes. America is still composed of people with unequal status and income; thus, although the community colleges have equalized access, the colleges must be at fault. As Levin put it, "while individual students may receive some measure of justice, groups of students or classes of students do not" (2007, p. 4).

Jencks (1972) offered one response when he explored the socially constructed notion of inequality and concluded that educators confound equal opportunity for education with equalizing income in the population. Rather than demanding that all persons receive the same education, a better way to decrease the gaps in income is to change such public policies as the tax structure. He believed that even if a college education were as easy to obtain as an elementary education, not everyone would attend and inequalities would persist. People work at different paces; they have different abilities and are of different value to their employers. Chance may propel them toward a field that blossoms or withers over the length of their career. The type of school they attend or the cognitive ability they manifest has little to do with equalizing those traits in the general population. If society really wanted to equalize outcomes, a system would be erected whereby those who attend school and those who do not would receive the same or similar benefits.

More recently Michaels extended Jencks' contentions, saying that what's keeping poor people out of elite colleges "is not their inability to pay but their inability to qualify for admission in the first place" (2006, p. 87). He reproduced a chart prepared by the College Board showing family income and SAT scores rising in tandem (detailed in the Decline in Literacy section in Chapter Nine). And he explained how the correlation arises from the wealthier families' ability to send their children to private schools or to better public schools associated with high-income neighborhoods and to pay for extensive tutoring. He attributed much of the problem of inequity to the public's (or at least the academics') fixation on identity: "We like diversity and we like programs like affirmative action because they tell us that racism is the problem we need to solve and that solving it requires us just to give up our prejudices. (Solving the problem of economic inequality might require something more; it might require us to give up our money)" (p. 89).

Another response might be that the community colleges are no more able to overturn the inequities of the nation than the lower schools have been, that all schools are relatively low-influence environments when compared with other social institutions.

But the critics' fundamental error is that they have attempted to shift the meaning of educational equality from individual to group mobility. If equal opportunity means allowing people from any social, ethnic, or religious group to have the same chance to enter higher education as people from any other group, the goal is both worthy and attainable. And few would question the community colleges' contribution to the breaking down of social, ethnic, financial, and geographical barriers to college attendance. But when that concept is converted to group mobility, its meaning changes, and it is put beyond the reach of the schools. Ben-David put it well: "Higher education can make a real contribution to social justice only by effectively educating properly prepared, able, and motivated individuals from all classes and groups. . . . Higher education appears to have been primarily a channel of individual mobility. . . . It can provide equal opportunities to all, and it may be able to help the disadvantaged to overcome inherited educational disabilities. But it cannot ensure the equal distribution of educational success among classes or other politically active groups" (1977, pp. 158–159). Neither the community colleges nor any other form of school can break down class distinctions. They cannot move entire ethnic groups from one social stratum to another. They cannot ensure the equal distribution of educational results.

Suppose the figures on the percentage of students who transfer to universities were doubled. Would it matter to the critics? The colleges still would not be doing their part in the critics' fanciful dream of class leveling. Warner and his associates said, "The decision to be made by those who disapprove of our present inequality and who wish to change it is not between a system of inequality and equality; the choice is among various systems of rank. Efforts to achieve democratic living by abolishing the social system are utopian and not realistic" (1944, p. 145).

Ordinarily, it serves neither education nor society well when the schools are accused of misleading their clients by making promises they cannot keep. Such charges can have the effect of generating public disaffection, on the one hand, and, on the other, intemperate reactions by educators. Many commentators, past and present, have been guilty of exaggerated claims that the community college would democratize American society if only all geographical, racial, academic, financial, motivational, and institutional barriers to attendance were removed (witness the title of Medsker and Tillery's 1971 book on the community colleges, *Breaking the Access Barriers*). But criticizing the rhetoric is one thing; criticizing the institution itself is quite another. Although there has been no public outcry against the community colleges, should one arise, it will be difficult to tell whether the reaction is directed against the institution itself or toward the image that its advocates have fostered and the claims they have made.

Using data from the National Longitudinal Study (NLS) of the High School Graduating Class of 1972 and subsequent surveys sponsored by the U.S. Education Department, some researchers have found that where a student begins college has an important effect on baccalaureate attainment and that students who reside or have jobs on campus are much more likely to persist. Although the conclusions are logical, the statistics are questionable. Putting variables in a regression equation assumes equivalency at the outset. The NLS analyses assume that all people in the sample had an equivalent chance to enter the university as freshmen, and the universities had classroom space and residence halls available to accommodate everyone, which clearly is not so.

Students who start at a community college instead of a university are less likely to obtain bachelor's degrees. Much of the difference relates not only to the differing environments but also to the logistics of moving from one institution to another. The phenomenon may be similar to that experienced by people who have to change planes en route to a destination, as compared with those who have nonstop accommodations. Those who must change may miss their connection because of flight delays or cancellations, or they might get diverted because they have met friends at the connecting airport. But no one accuses the airlines of attempting to subvert their clients' intentions.

How do the analysts interpret the data regarding the University of California's freshman class? Each year, tens of thousands of qualified applicants cannot be accommodated; many of them have to begin their higher education careers in one of the state's community colleges. Undoubtedly, for them, baccalaureate attainment will be slightly less likely or will take somewhat longer. Is the selection process the result of an elitists' plot, or was it instituted because of lack of space? The critics' conclusions that community colleges evince an insidious conspiracy against the poor are not warranted. Instead, since sizeable percentages of their students are from the lowest income group, the colleges should be applauded for the opportunities they provide.

The Inevitability of the Allocative Function

Granted that the community colleges are part of an educational system within a larger social system in which numerous institutions sort, certify, ticket, and route people to various stations, what are the options? We could say that society should not be structured along class lines, that it should not support institutions that tend to allocate people to status positions. Those who hold to that view would do well to seek to change the social structure by modifying some considerably more powerful influences—the tax structure, for example. But as long as there are hierarchies of social class (and all societies have them), some social institutions will operate as allocative agencies.

Clark analyzed the allocative function in community colleges and in 1960 applied the term *cooling out* to describe it. He showed that the process began with preentrance testing, shunting the lower-ability students to remedial classes and eventually nudging them out of the transfer track into a terminal curriculum. The crucial components of the process were that alternatives to the person's original aspirations were provided; the aspiration was reduced in a consoling way, encouraging gradual disengagement; and the students were not sent away as failures but were shown the relative values of vocational and academic choices short of the baccalaureate degree.

Twenty years later, Clark (1980) reexamined his thesis, asking whether the cooling-out function might be replaced by some other process and whether the roles of community colleges could be altered so that the process would be unnecessary. He named six options: preselection of students, to take place in the secondary schools or at the door of the community college; transfer-track selection, which would bar the students from enrolling in courses offering transfer credit; open failure, whereby students who did not pass the courses would be required to leave the institution; guaranteed graduation, which would have the effect of passing everyone through and depositing the problem at the doorstep of the next institution in line; reduction of the distinction between transfer and terminal programs, which could be done if the community colleges had no concern about the percentages of their students who succeed in universities; and making the structural changes that would eliminate the two-year colleges' transfer function, convert all two-year institutions into four-year ones, or do away with community colleges entirely.

Clark rejected all those alternatives. Preselection "runs against the grain of American populist interpretations of educational justice which equate equity with open doors" (1980, p. 19). Limiting the number of people who can take courses for transfer credit would confirm the beliefs of those who see class-based tracking. Open failure is too public and is becoming less a feature in four-year colleges, as well as in community colleges, because it seems inhumane. The dangers of guaranteed graduation have already been realized in the secondary schools: "Everyone is equally entitled to credentials that have lost their value" (p. 21). Reducing the distinction between transfer and terminal courses "has limits beyond which lies a loss of legitimacy of the community college qua college . . . (auto repairing is not on a par with history or calculus as a college course)" (p. 22). And doing away with the community colleges is unlikely because of the reluctance of senior college faculties to value two-year programs and because of the continued and growing need for short-cycle courses or courses such as those offered in university extension divisions.

Clark concluded, "The problem that causes colleges to respond with the cooling-out effort is not going to go away by moving it inside of other types of colleges. Somebody has to make that effort, or pursue its alternatives" (1980, pp. 23–24). He pointed to examples in other countries, where the longer the higher education system held out against short-cycle institutions and programs, the greater were the problems when educators tried to open the system to wide varieties of students coming for numerous purposes. The trend there is toward greater differentiation of types of institutions and degrees, but "the dilemma is still there: Either you keep some aspirants out by selection or you admit everyone and then take your choice between seeing them all through, or flunking out some, or cooling out some" (p. 28). As he put it, "Any system of higher education that has to reconcile such conflicting values as equity, competence, and individual choice—and the advanced democracies are so committed—has to effect compromise procedures that allow for some of each. The cooling-out process is one of the possible compromises, perhaps even a necessary one" (p. 30). In sum, even if the college only matches people with jobs, providing connections, credentials, and short-term, ad hoc learning experiences—even if it is not the gateway to higher learning for everyone that some commentators wish it were—these functions must be performed by some social agency.

What the Colleges Really Provide

The real benefit of the community college cannot be measured by the extent to which it contributes to the overthrow of the social class system in America. Nor can it be measured by the extent to which the college changes the mores of its community. It is a system for individuals, and it does what the best educational forms have always done: it helps individuals learn what they need to know to be effective, responsible members of their society. The colleges can and do make it easier for people to move between social classes. As long as they maintain their place in the mainstream of graded education, they provide a channel of upward mobility for individuals of any age. Those who deplore the colleges' failure to overturn inequities between classes do a disservice to their main function and tend to confuse the people who have looked on them as the main point of access to, exit from, and reentry into higher education—the lungs of the system.

There is a difference between social equalization and equal access, between overturning the social class structure and enabling people to move from one stratum to another. The college that teaches best uplifts its community most. People must learn in college, or what is its purpose? More learning equals a better college; less learning, a poorer college; no learning, no college. The fact that the community colleges serve minority students, marginally capable students, and other groups never before served by the higher education establishment does not mean they have abandoned their commitment to teach.

A person who receives a degree or certificate and does not work in the field in which that certificate was earned does not represent an institutional indictment unless no other programs were available to the person. If the community college were a participant in an educational system that said to potential matriculants, "You may enter but only if you are particularly qualified and only in this program," subsequent failure to obtain employment in that field might be cause for dismay. But the community college does not operate that way; most of its programs are open to all who present themselves. When programs do have selective admissions, as in dental hygiene, nursing, and some of the higher-level technologies, nearly all the entrants graduate and obtain positions in the fields for which they were trained. When programs are open to everyone, as in most of the less professionalized trades, such as real estate or marketing, the chances that a matriculant will complete the curriculum and begin working in that field are markedly reduced. "Dropout" is a reflection of the structure of a program. An institution, or a program within that institution, that places few barriers to student matriculation cannot expect a high rate of program completion. The students use the collegiate and the career programs alike, as though each were providing a single set of courses that they might take depending on their goals at the time. The elitists and conspirators may have hoped to divert the masses into vocational studies, but the students are remarkably resilient.

Few commentators have mentioned an important social and economic role played by community colleges: their relieving pressure on the universities and their saving money for the states. Both are apparent in the articulation agreements designed to enhance transfer that have become widespread across the nation. Such agreements have been in place for many decades, but until recently they tended to be voluntary compacts agreed on by the public-sector institutions and monitored by state agencies or coordinating boards. Now that many legislatures have mandated them, they have become important politically even though college promises to enhance economic development and relieve unemployment remain the gold standard in state governments. Anderson, Alfonso, and Sun posit a connection between "the dramatic increase in statewide articulation agreements between 1985 and 1995" and "sharp decreases in state appropriations for higher education as a share of expenditures" (2006, p. 431), arguing that they constitute "a new state strategy to cope with . . . the spiraling costs of tuition, and an excess demand for affordable higher education" (p. 422).

What Are the Alternatives to Community Colleges?

It is possible to sketch the outlines of alternative institutions that would perform the tasks now performed by community colleges. Yet there is no point in taking an ahistorical approach to postsecondary education. Tempting as it is, a view of higher education, of what students need, of what would be good for society, without a corresponding view of the institutions in their social context is not very useful. To start with the questions of what individuals need or what society needs is nice, but regardless of the answers, the current institutions will not disappear. Institutional needs are as real as individual and social needs; in fact, they may be more valid as beginning points for analysis because they offer somewhat unified positions that have developed over time, whereas "individual" and "social" needs are as diverse as anyone cares to make them. And despite the rapid growth of the Internet and its counterparts, it is thoroughly out of line to pose a view of society with no educational institutions but with everyone learning through the electronic media. The desire for social interaction is too strong; the demand for institutional certification is too great.

Any imagined institution must be postulated totally. That is, what changes will be made in funding patterns, institutional organization, the role of the professionals within the institution, and people's use of their time? The institution's goals must be stated realistically; for too long we have suffered the open-ended goals of those who would break all access barriers; would see all citizens enrolled successively throughout their lifetime; would envisage the community college taking on functions previously performed not only by the higher and the lower schools but also by welfare agencies, unemployment bureaus, parks and recreation departments, and community help organizations.

Can we develop a learning community? Some evidence suggests we can. People are enrolling in university extensions and taking classes in the community colleges for their own interest.

A sizable cohort will attend school without being compelled. In addition, the ways that individuals gain information and that society stores and transmits it have grown enormously.

On the negative side are the individual needs for structured learning situations, the discipline of learning, the sequence that learning demands. Many forms of learning simply do not lend themselves to instant apprehension and immediate applicability; they build one on the other, and a disciplined situation is necessary to hold the learner in the proper mode until the structure is complete. It would also be difficult to fund the infinite variety of learning situations that would be required. Most of the voluntary learning situations now are funded either by the individuals partaking of them or as adjuncts to more structured institutions.

It is possible to pose alternatives to the community college and stay within the context of existing social institutions. In 1968, Devall offered five such alternatives: proprietary trade schools, on-the-job training, universal national service, university extension divisions, and off-campus courses under expanding divisions of continuing education operated by the universities. However, in the intervening decades, the proprietary trade schools are the only alternatives that have grown extensively. And they do not enjoy a history unmarred by excessive claims, inflated costs, and fraudulent advertising. These schools appear as shining lights only to those who feel that the for-profit sector invariably does a better job than the nonprofit institutions do.

Still, some modifications to traditional practice are suggested by examples from the proprietary schools, which enroll populations similar to those in community college vocational programs. Instead of dozens of options, each has only a few programs built on specific sets of required courses. They guide their clients through compressed exercises, typically shorter in duration than fifteen-week semesters. They mandate soft-skills instruction in dress, demeanor, and punctuality, and they assist their clients in preparing résumés and connecting with employers. They have a paucity of amenities, no campus, libraries, or recreational facilities. Community colleges have broader purposes even though, as Rosenbaum, Redline, and Stephan conclude, their "offering multiple programs may also reduce program coherence and ultimate degree completion" (2007, p. 56).

The other options would also lead to unintended consequences. On-the-job training would narrow educational opportunity by focusing the learner's attention solely on the tasks to be performed, and it would shift the burden of payment to business corporations that might not benefit therefrom if the trained workers chose to take positions with competitors. Universal national service suggests compulsion; it would extend the grip that public agencies have on individuals and, in effect, prolong the period of mandatory school attendance. Expansion of university extension divisions would have the effect of turning program monitoring back to the universities. But it would also place the programs on a self-supporting basis and would thus deny participation to people with limited discretionary funds. And expanding the university divisions of continuing education would place adult basic education, literacy training, and similar lower-school functions under the aegis of an institution that throughout history has attempted to divest itself of them.

The percentage of community college matriculants who go on to the baccalaureate varies greatly between institutions. It depends on the vigor with which students interested in other outcomes are recruited and on an institution's relations with its neighboring secondary schools and universities. Although the colleges provide vocational and community education, they are certainly not going to surrender the university-parallel portion of their curriculum. If they did, they would be denying access to higher education to those of their students who do go on, particularly to the students from families in which college going is not the norm. They would betray their own staff members, who entered the institution with the intent of teaching college courses. They would no longer serve as the safety valve for the universities, which can shunt the poorly prepared petitioners for admission to these alternative colleges and that would otherwise be forced to mount massive remedial programs of their own or face the outrage of people denied access.

Some states have multiple college systems and so separate the collegiate from other functions. The Wisconsin Vocational, Technical, and Adult Education Centers perform all community college functions except for the university lower-division courses; Wisconsin has a university-center system with numerous branch campuses of the state university doing the collegiate work. In South Carolina, state technical colleges coexist with branch campuses of the university. The North Carolina system operates both technical institutes and community colleges. These and other alternative structures can also be found in large community college districts. Coast Community College District (California) has two full-service, comprehensive colleges along with one institution devoted exclusively to short-cycle education, open-circuit broadcasting, and community services. The institutional forms adapt, but all functions are maintained.

We do not necessarily need new structures. Many forms of reorganization can be made to accommodate the changing clientele. Some of the more successful adaptations have been made in vocational programs in which the liaison occasioned by the use of trades advisory councils and other connections between the program and the community have fostered continual modifications in curriculum and instruction. The community service divisions engage in their own forms of modification by slanting their offerings toward areas in which sizable audiences can be found. On-campus media forms are introduced to accommodate the different modes of information-gathering exhibited by new groups of students. The community college baccalaureate and the dual enrollment and early college initiatives both represent vertical expansion within the context of existing institutions. Although neither is in place yet in a majority of colleges, their rapid growth suggests they are more than passing fads. And along with the growth of honors programs, the baccalaureate reveals the colleges' tendencies to respond to a changing clientele, in this case the demographic shift toward greater numbers of eighteen-year-olds. The list could be extended; the point is that adaptations within existing forms are continually occurring.

The list of potential changes can also be extended by accommodations that are rarely made. Long overdue is a reconception of the liberal arts to fit the occupational programs: What portions of traditional liberal arts studies are most useful for students in occupational programs, and how might they best be inserted into those areas? Modular courses have been tried in several institutions, but much more work needs to be done there to build bridges between these two central college functions. Advanced placement for high school students has been authorized in several states. That pattern is growing and could be encouraged through supplemental legislation.

The community colleges' potential is greater than that of any other institution because their concern is with the people most in need of assistance. President Clinton referred to that characteristic when he described the community colleges as functioning on the "fault line" of American education (Bourque, 1995). If the community colleges succeed in moving even a slightly greater proportion of their clients toward what the dominant society regards as achievement, it is as though they changed the world. They are engaged with people on the cusp, people who could enter the mainstream or fall back into a cycle of poverty and welfare. That is why they deserve the support of everyone who values societal cohesion and the opportunity for all people to realize their potential.

Issues

The community college has been criticized for its failure to move sizable proportions of its matriculants to the baccalaureate. But these effects are not uniform. Why do different students go through at different rates? How do institutional and personal factors interact to affect progress?

Although some of the critics have recommended major changes in institutional structure and functioning, few suggest closing the colleges. However, what would happen to a community if its local college's budget were halved?

Nearly everyone has access to the telephone system. It is a passive, instantly responsive tool that allows people to interact with one another at will. What is the value of the human contact fostered by community colleges?

A television network is another form of passive tool. One turns the television on or off at will, seeking entertainment or diversion. How much is the entertainment provided by the colleges worth?

Museums offer both entertainment and education. A museum may be compared with another museum according to the strength of its collection, the appeal of its exhibitions, and the number of people who participate in its programs. What would be the value of assessing the colleges along those dimensions?

Government agencies are social institutions designed to provide services. They are successful to the extent that they enhance the quality of life in a community by maintaining order and providing public places where people may conduct their own affairs. Can the colleges be so assessed?

Because few scholars are concerned with community colleges, there is no true forum. The colleges' own spokespersons do not help much. Either they do not know how to examine their own institutions critically, or they are disinclined to do so. They say the colleges strive to meet everyone's educational needs, but they rarely acknowledge the patent illogic of that premise. They say the colleges provide access for all, but they fail to examine the obvious corollary question: Access to what? The true supporters of the community college, those who believe in its ideals, would consider the institution's role on both educational and philosophical grounds. Democracy's college deserves no less.

14

Toward the Future

Trends, Challenges, and Obligations

Just as historians like to play with the past, educators enjoy speculating on the ways the future will affect their institutions. It is tempting to believe that the future is manageable, that an institution can be set on a course that ensures its efficiency, relevance, and importance for the community it will serve.

A decade or so ago, the imminence of a millennial year stimulated an abundance of commissions organized to assess trends in community college functions and support. State-level groups in Alabama, Connecticut, Maryland, and North Carolina, among others, were active in the 1980s, along with a national Commission on the Future of Community Colleges, empaneled under the auspices of the Carnegie Foundation for the Advancement of Teaching and the AACJC. The flurry continued into the 1990s, with California establishing the Commission on Innovation, designed to advise the community colleges on how to accommodate increasing populations with limited resources. At the national level, the W. K. Kellogg Foundation funded the New Expeditions project, coordinated by American Association of Community Colleges and Association of Community College Trustees, which was supposed to set a strategic direction for the community colleges for the first part of the twenty-first century (AACC, 2000).

The commissions based their studies on apparent population trends, especially age and ethnicity, and on changes in the economy. Predictions were that the growth of the ethnic minority population would accelerate and the proportion of middle-aged workers would decline as the post–World War II baby boomers aged. The economy would continue shifting away from manufacturing and toward service functions as the dominant form for the United States. This postindustrial or information age would require a more literate workforce and fuller participation by groups heretofore excluded or consigned to the no-longer-prevalent assembly line. Competition from newly industrialized countries would force us to take a global perspective toward production. America would remain a dominant force, but only if we worked more intelligently.

Each of the commissions issued reports predicting the need for enhanced educational services and emphasizing the importance of maintaining comprehensive, high-quality community colleges that would serve a broad range of clients. Each was optimistic that these institutions were well suited to act in the best interests of the population. None suggested reducing the scope of the colleges. None suggested major departures from contemporary patterns of service. But all warned that the colleges would be expected to serve more students with fewer resources.

In common with similar studies in prior decades, all reports stressed the importance of vocational education, open access, partnerships with industry, excellence in teaching, and cooperative relationships with other educational sectors. But a new emphasis on outcomes assessment appeared in these commissions' reports. The importance of valid information on college effects had become so evident that the commissions, which might not have been expected to give more than a passing reference to this issue, put it high on their list of essential institutional and state activities.

This chapter merges information from the commission reports with trend data emanating from other literature to yield a picture of what community colleges might look like in the coming years. It deals with the students and the faculty, organization and structure, and curriculum and instruction. The chapter also discusses outcomes assessment, a concept that continues to grow and gain acceptance from educators at all levels of schooling, as well as among the lay public.

The Institutions

Projecting the future for the community colleges of the early twenty-first century involves projecting the future for the nation in general: its demographics, economy, and public attitudes. The demographics are apparent; population trends are predictable and the potential college students are in the lower schools, but the number who will attend community colleges is uncertain. The national economy is even less certain. However, the United States is a great economic engine, with a highly trained cadre of professional practitioners able to adjust to shifting influences in the workplace. Barring a major social upheaval such as an expansion of the expensive, open-ended war that the United States launched in reaction to the atrocious crime of 9/11/2001, a depression, or severe inflation, the nation will be able to continue educating more of its youth and sustaining lifelong learning for its adults. The community colleges will play a role in this process similar to that which they have developed over much of this century: prebaccalaureate, vocational, developmental, and adult education provided to a broad spectrum of the local population.

Public attitude, always mercurial, influences the colleges. Periodic disgruntlement with taxation and the rise of other priorities such as prisons and the criminal justice system sometimes translate into lower support for education. But as long as college degrees are perceived as the route toward personal advancement, people will demand access and will eventually agree to pay for it. None of the fiscal crises in any of the states has led to serious calls to shrink the higher education system severely. And as long as the community colleges remain accessible and relatively inexpensive, they will remain attractive not only to people seeking education but also to corporate managers and industrialists.

The number of public community colleges will hardly change; practically all the colleges necessary had been built by 1975, when a college could be found within commuting distance of nearly all the people in all but a few states. The number has remained constant ever since, reaching stasis at under eleven hundred. Change in this group will occur only as the colleges continue expanding linearly, especially as the number offering the baccalaureate increases.

The business colleges, specialized training institutes, and proprietary trade schools are a different sector entirely. They thrive on public funds administered through state and federal student aid, but their programs, purposes, governance, and decision-making processes set them quite apart. Since nearly one thousand are accredited to award associate degrees, they appear in the tabulations generated by the NCES and the Carnegie Foundation. But several thousand more are in existence, and no one can predict with certainty how many will attain degree accreditation and be classified as two-year colleges in coming years.

The independent or private junior colleges seem destined to cling to a small territory, similar to that held by the four-year private colleges in relation to the massive public universities. Woodroof's analysis found them shouldered aside by the public colleges. His data were sobering: in contrast to NCES, which reported 175 private junior colleges in the late 1980s, he found half that number operating as distinct, separate, liberal arts institutions, with one-third single sex and three-fourths of them east of the Mississippi. But his conclusion was overly somber: "There may come a time in the near future when there are simply too few resources, too few students, and too few faculty members willing to work at poverty income levels" (1990, p. 83). Even so, although the independent nonprofit junior colleges passed their prime decades ago, they will not disappear.

The form of the community college will not change. The institution offering vocational, collegiate, developmental, and community education, with the associate degree as its highest award, has become well accepted by the public and by state-level coordinating and funding agencies. The college staff also are familiar and comfortable with it. Most modifications will be in emphasis, not in kind, although some institutions will drive toward expanded community services—as in contract education, building separately funded and managed programs that may grow to be as large as the traditional college services, while others will blur the community college image even further by offering baccalaureate degrees. However, as long as the accrediting agencies and the major national data compilers continue moving such institutions out of the *community college* category, the definition will remain intact. Where the state universities build numerous branch campuses and otherwise make it easy for students to matriculate, the colleges will emphasize vocational studies and continuing education. Where the colleges serve largely as feeders to the universities, the collegiate function will remain strongest. But all current services will continue to be provided, with growth or shifting emphases depending on funding and different population bases, not on educational philosophy.

Because the community college drive for new markets has become more pronounced than ever, it deserves additional comment. For many decades the colleges have expanded laterally, as in modifying their occupational programs in response to changing workforce demands. The rise of the for-profit sector has brought forth a set of competing institutions, but to date both have been able to coexist. Similarly, the colleges' continuing education and the university extension divisions have each found sectors of the market sufficient to maintain their programs.

Vertical Expansion

The community college's recent foray into early college initiatives and baccalaureate programs is different; a vertical expansion toward grades 10 to 12 on the one hand, and toward grades 15 and 16 on the other. One forces them into linkages with the K–12 sector, where many of them began, whereas the other brings them into an area where few had been previously involved. The rationale differs for each of these moves. *Early college* is similar to dual enrollment programs that can accelerate postsecondary attainment, except that it is directed more toward the low-achieving high school students. By bringing college courses and staff to that group, they are more likely to stay in school and matriculate in college programs, thereby serving to reduce the main leakage point for at-risk youth, the place where most of the dropout from the education system occurs. Preliminary findings are positive, with students showing educational gains in their first year in the program and with those graduating from high school winning college scholarships far in excess of others in their SES group (Jaschik, October 5, 2007).

For many years universities have offered upper-division classes on community college campuses. Why then do the colleges seek to offer bachelor's degrees when they can bring bachelor's level courses to their students with two-plus-two agreements or partnerships with proximate universities? The response presented by devotees of the community college baccalaureate take three forms. First, they say that the universities won't make essential changes unless the legislatures allow competition. Second, where universities do offer courses on community college campuses the university faculty treat such assignments as though they were teaching in university extension; that is, not as a part of their regular program. And third, the uniformity or progress toward a degree in the same institution makes it more likely that students will complete their programs.

Both early college initiatives and the community college baccalaureate are based on sound rationales and both have enjoyed much support: the first from foundations committed to assisting students from low-income families; the second from the legislatures concerned about labor shortages in key areas where the baccalaureate is required for entry. Both will expand unless K–12 reform strengthens the secondary schools so that assistance from community colleges becomes unnecessary, and unless more universities open satellite centers dedicated to preparing teachers and health professions practitioners, and support them vigorously. Neither is likely any time soon. One certainty, though, is that colleges that do make the vertical expansion in either direction (or both) will be changed markedly, both internally and in the eyes of the public.

The Students

Projecting the number of college students in general is precarious because various factors—such as employment possibilities, financial aid availability, and the demands of the military—influence the rate of college going. Estimating the numbers who will attend community colleges is further complicated because of unknowns, such as the attractiveness of competing institutions. Even a seemingly straightforward projection of the magnitude of the population in general is subject to variability because of immigration patterns. One factor is certain: as long as the economic benefit of going to college remains high, there will be a demand for collegiate studies.

There will be plenty of students to share among all postsecondary sectors. The absolute number of eighteen-year-olds in the United States peaked at 4.3 million in 1979, bottomed at 3.3 million in 1992, regained the 1979 level by 2007 (Table 14.1). Anticipating less school dropout, NCES predicted that the number of high school graduates in 2011 would surpass 3 million, the same as the number that graduated when the population of eighteen-year-olds was at its peak in 1979 (Hussar and Bailey, 2006). It seems likely that the high school graduation rates of Anglo students will remain steady over the next several years, whereas those for minorities will rise; the proportion of minorities

Table 14.1. Demographics and Enrollments, 1990–2015

Year (July 1)	Number of Eighteen-Year-Olds (in thousands)	Enrollment in Public Two-Year Degree-Granting Institutions (in thousands)
1979	4,316	4,056
1993	3,455	5,337
1995	3,601	5,278
1997	3,780	5,361
1999	3,993	5,339
2001	4,070	5,997
2003	4,124	6,208
2005	4,157	6,310
2007	4,316	6,450
2009	4,429	6,617
2011	4,293	6,750
2013	4,168	6,901
2015	4,048	7,050

Source: Hussar and Bailey, 2006; NCES, 2006.

in the group comprising all eighteen-year-olds also will rise. Since over half of the Hispanics who enter higher education do so in community colleges, any increase in their rate of high school graduation or college entry will have an accentuated effect on enrollments. Overall, though, as Adelman states, "Neither gender nor race/ethnicity nor second language background nor first generation status ends up playing a statistically significant role in explaining who starts out at a community college but SES . . . does play such a role: the higher the SES quintile, the less likely the student will start in a community college" (2005, p. xvii).

In general, the community colleges will sustain their enrollments because the demand for postsecondary education will remain high. As shown in Table 14.1, by 2015 they will enroll 7.0 million students or nearly 43 percent of all higher education. They will continue to get their share of eighteen-year-olds because of their traditional appeal: easy access, low cost, and part-time-attendance possibilities. They will continue enrolling job seekers because of the high demand for people in occupations for which some postsecondary training but not a bachelor's degree is expected. Of the ten occupations projected to have the largest job growth for the decade subsequent to 2004, six are in fields for which the two-year colleges have training programs: dental hygienist, physical therapy assistant, home health aide, medical assistant, dental assistant, and personal and home care aide (U.S. Bureau of Labor Statistics, 2005). The only caveat is that competition with the proprietary schools will intensify.

Assuming that financial aid availability for middle- and upper-income students does not increase sufficiently so that tuition differentials are offset, the community colleges will get an even greater share of the students as tuition at four-year colleges and universities continues its rapid rise. Assuming that further limitations are not put on Latino and Asian immigration and on international students, college enrollments will benefit from those groups. The students will continue their intermittent attendance patterns; most will continue to be employed, pursuing work and study as parallel activities. The enrollment of part-time students will decrease slightly, from 64 percent to 62 percent by 2011, and the percentage of younger students will increase. In 1997, 39 percent of California's community college students were between the ages of 17 and 20; six years later, 49 percent were in that age group, yet that demographic had changed not at all in terms of its proportion of the state's population. The higher percentage apparently is associated less with the size of the age group than with the availability of the freshman class at four-year colleges and universities (Sengupta and Jepsen, 2006). The number of associate degrees conferred will increase to 665,000 per year. In brief, we will see a mature set of institutions with some gain in full-time student enrollment and in number of degrees awarded, but very little dramatic change.

Pressure to sort students at entry will increase. The matriculation plans that have been in effect for several years reveal the persistence of a trend toward regulations demanding that the colleges guide students into programs consonant with their abilities. It will be difficult for a student anywhere to find an institution that will allow a random walk through the curriculum. Students will be tested, guided, and matriculated into programs that have measurable entry and exit criteria.

Put in broader terms, the community colleges are experiencing a metamorphosis similar in this regard to that which affected the compulsory sector earlier as state-level testing, curriculum standards, and graduation requirements gained prominence. A laissez-faire approach to student attendance had rather generally permeated community college management, leading to the high ratio of students attending intermittently and the presentation of classes as discrete units. Now, the strong moves toward assessment and placement, toward students making steady progress toward completing a program, will change the pattern of attendance in the direction of higher full-time-student equivalent (FTSE) ratios and more rapid progress toward program completion. That is the main reason that the number of associate degrees awarded will increase at a rate greater than the number of students served. The practice of letting everyone in and letting them take what they want is being put to rest rapidly.

The Faculty

Because college enrollments will grow slowly, the number of faculty will show similarly small increases. The ratio of full-timers to part-timers has stabilized at just under 40:60 and will be likely to remain there as administrators' desires to save money by employing part-timers and faculty organizations' ability to protect full-time positions offset one another. A high proportion of full-timers teach additional courses for extra pay, thus making it unnecessary to employ additional staff except in singular areas. Demands that the full-time instructors be awarded rights of first refusal when overload classes are imminent will continue.

Pro rata pay for part-time employment has long been discussed but shows no sign of spreading. As long as full-time faculty are willing to teach extra classes at effectually lower pay rates and as long as administrators need part-time, hourly rate instructors to help balance the budget, pro rata pay will find few champions. Contentions that instructors engage in duplicity when they argue for reduced teaching hours on the grounds that they need more time to prepare for class while simultaneously petitioning to teach overload classes at additional pay will find few ears.

Faculty hiring practices show little sign of change. Affirmative action programs have been in place in all colleges for many years, but progress in employing members of minority groups has been distressingly slow. Nor has there been much progress in preservice preparation for instructors who are inclined to teach across disciplinary lines. The number of career-bound students who take collegiate classes and the number of baccalaureate-bound students in occupational classes seem destined to force some form of faculty crossover to accommodate members of both groups. But the colleges will have to foster their own interdisciplinarians. The greatest need is for faculty who will become leaders in integrating curriculum and assessing outcomes. These will come from within the ranks of the practicing instructors; few people with those skills can be expected to appear as new employees.

Many aspects of instruction will not change. The faculty will continue to hold solo practice as their primary code. The number of hours that a full-time instructor spends in the classroom has not changed for decades. Few sustained innovative practices that would teach more students with fewer instructor-contact hours are being introduced. Instruction is stubbornly labor intensive. As Bok has pointed out, "College instruction remains among the small cluster of human activities that do not grow demonstrably better over time" (1993, p. 170). If the productivity of college instructors does not increase and if everyone in the profession is paid and advanced at the same rate, there will be little room for overall pay increases or for individuals to elevate themselves above their colleagues. Teachers cannot anticipate making more money merely because they work harder or are cleverer than their fellows.

How might the profession become differentiated? One way would be if instead of—or perhaps in addition to—the image of the instructor in the classroom with a group of students, practicing a profession in solo fashion, the instructor at the apex of a pyramid of paraprofessionals—readers, test scorers, peer advisors, and paraprofessional aides—came to the fore. But there have been few efforts to build these types of assistants into the instructional pattern.

Until recently, moves toward professionalization as evidenced by managerial roles or enhanced productivity have been made by those instructors who have taken command of learning resource centers and various curricular projects designed to maximize student learning by combining instructional and student support services. The next professional enhancements will be led by the instructors who build reproducible learning sequences and interactive media. To the extent they can demonstrate that their efforts have effected greater learning opportunities for less money, they will be recognized as instructional leaders. More than managers of paraprofessionals, they will be involved with new sets of colleagues: media technologists, script writers, editors, and production coordinators. This will happen slowly, and only to the extent that the colleges can make funds available for this expensive enterprise.

The road to professionalism is a long one, and although the faculty have made great strides in extricating themselves from the administrator-dominated, paternalistic situation of an earlier time, they have far to go. In some institutions, they may settle in to an untoward model: continuing antagonism between themselves and the administrators, isolation and solo performance in the classroom, and periodic battles for smaller classes, augmented salaries, and more far-reaching fringe benefits. The faculty must take care not to act too much like other public agency workers in their negotiating sessions, in the way they seek redress for grievances through legislative action and the courts, and in their inability to police their own ranks as members of a profession must, lest they be viewed as merely another category of civil servants.

A more desirable model is a faculty involved with curriculum planning in the broadest sense: reading and writing in their disciplines and in the field of education; conducting research on students' exit and entrance abilities; and becoming media production specialists, program directors, laboratory managers, or curriculum coordinators. The actuality will be somewhere between the two extremes. In fact, progress toward both civil service status and professionalism can occur simultaneously. In some districts, the faculty champion both a union speaking for wages and welfare and a vigorous academic senate concerning itself with curricular and instructional issues.

It is possible that the conditions of the workplace will support a return to a time when the faculty within single colleges shared a sense of community. The growing move toward assessing learning outcomes, as differentiated from graduation, transfer, and job-getting rates, could perforce involve the entire faculty in creating and employing student learning measures. The part-timers are the biggest stumbling block. Will they be treated as partners? If the conditions of their employment evolve so that they have rights and status equal to the full-timers, a professional community could arise. If they receive pro rata pay and benefits but are still excluded from the mainstream of faculty functioning, the conditions for community will not follow.

Organization, Governance, and Administration

Few changes in the pattern of organization and governance in community colleges are evident. The number of institutions will change hardly at all; branch campuses, satellite centers, and courses offered off campus in rented quarters will accommodate the need for expanded facilities. Many small, autonomous centers or specialized units within larger districts will be built. Some of these centers will emphasize career studies and recertification for paraprofessionals; others, operating much like university extension divisions, will offer courses in numerous locations and over open-circuit television. These types of instructional centers have accounted for nearly all the institutional expansion that has occurred since the early 1970s. Few of them have grown into full-service colleges.

The trend toward greater state-level coordination will continue at a slow pace. As the states become more involved with college policies, gaps in interinstitutional cooperation will be filled, and criteria for student matriculation and progress will be set. Statewide coordination has also been emphasized as a means of providing proportionate funding, avoiding curriculum duplication, and easing the flow of students from one sector of public postsecondary education to another. The number of states with single governing boards covering all public institutions will increase.

The pressure for state control will result in continued efforts to micromanage the colleges, but it has had minimal effect on instruction and student services. State-level coordination relates more to reporting, compliance with regulations, and accountability for numerous aspects of institutional operations; there is much room for local autonomy within those requirements. Before a major change can be made, the procedure has to be vetted through an incredible array of organizations, especially state-level associations of trustees, deans, presidents, academic senate, humanities faculty, physical education faculty, counselors, librarians, and on and on. Nothing very sudden or dramatic can survive that process. The combination of state and local control is intact.

The federal government will probably continue its efforts to regulate higher education. It has been relentless in pressing accrediting agencies to stiffen their requirements on institutions so that expected completion, placement, and licensure pass rates are established for every program, including vocational education. It has also been attempting to move toward prohibiting institutions from basing the acceptance of transfer credits solely on the type of accreditation manifest by the sending institutions, a change that has been advocated by the for-profit sector. But some of its moves will advantage community colleges; in fall 2007, the College Cost Reduction and Access Act repealed the provisions that reduced Pell Grant eligibility for students attending lower-cost schools, cut the interest rate on student loans, and provided tuition assistance for undergraduates committed to teaching in high-need public schools and debt forgiveness for alumni after ten years of working in certain public sectors.

Administrative patterns will not shift notably. The colleges are public entities, and their support depends on legislative perceptions and available public dollars. Their products are human learning and community uplift. Accordingly, institutional support is sustained in a political arena; it is only tangentially related to outcomes. The administrators work in a milieu of process, not product. They do not give orders to underlings, nor do they sanction subordinates for disobedience. Instead, they attempt to influence behavior by outlining issues and leading by example.

The major changes in local college administration will occur in three areas. The first will be to augment the number of people assigned to collect data and prepare reports showing that the college is in compliance with constantly increasing extramural demands. The second will be in program coordination, with staff members assigned to manage the specially funded programs that the colleges develop to serve new clients and increase budgets. More of this staff differentiation will occur through internal reassignments than through new hires. The third shift will be an increase in campus security. The tragedy at Virginia Polytechnic Institute in April 2007 was a shock to all college presidents, and articles headlined "Colleges Especially Vulnerable to Crime, Terrorism" (Chappell, August 16, 2007) served to accentuate the alarm. The colleges will not erect a multibillion dollar agency dedicated to X-raying shoes and confiscating nail clippers, but the budgets for campus safety and student surveillance will certainly increase.

Finance

Characteristics of financing community colleges will change little in the coming years. Most of the institutions began with substantial funding from their localities but since then, the trend has been toward state-level support. This will not be reversed. The colleges will compete for state funds along with other public agencies, ranging from other sectors of education to state-supported welfare, parks, and prisons.

The community colleges have a decided advantage over other higher education sectors in the cost of instruction. Although the precise amounts allocated to lower-division instruction in the universities are rarely calculated with any reliability, the overall student cost differential is obvious. Community college instruction costs as little as one-half as much as the per-student cost in a comprehensive four-year institution and one-fourth as much as in a public research university.

Enrollment restrictions or caps on growth will continue to be imposed with ever-increasing specificity. As a supplement to funding on an FTSE basis, a greater proportion of operating funds may be allocated according to the number of students making steady progress within programs, graduating, or transferring to four-year institutions. So far, the amounts involved in performance funding are small, but several far-reaching shifts are under way: allocation based in part on performance, as contrasted with entitlements; an acceleration of the move from local to state priorities; different indicators for two-year and four-year colleges; and a turn away from any involvement with lifelong learning that does not contribute to career upgrading, retraining, or occupational entry skills.

The colleges will be asked incessantly to provide evidence of increased productivity and specific programmatic outcomes. Difficult to achieve in a labor-intensive enterprise, one that has been attuned more to process than to product, these demands for data on expenditures relative to outcomes will lead steadily toward greater efficiencies. Cost savings will be sought in many areas, the most obvious in moves toward year-long calendars and eighteen-hour days. These would relieve capital costs but would also increase costs of campus security, energy use, and building maintenance.

Some commentators have anticipated that the retirement of high-cost senior faculty who entered the institutions during their growth years in the 1960s would lead to lower faculty costs. However, to the extent that the senior instructors are replaced with junior full-timers, the cost savings will be short-lived. Most salary schedules award automatic pay increments for years of service, with no proviso for increased productivity, and the number of years between the beginning and the top salaries is few. The savings in instructional expenditures will come primarily in institutions that convert their staff to a higher preponderance of part-time, hourly-rate teachers.

Overall, it is quite unlikely that any state will increase its allocations to its community colleges by more than a couple of percentage points a year. Therefore, the colleges cannot expect to fund wage increases or the costs of new programs, including the widely heralded instructional technology revolution, through traditional budget lines. Similarly, capital funds will be in short supply. Any new construction will have to be supported by special appropriations; the aging buildings will get older.

Because all the community colleges in a state tend to be funded under the same formulas, college budgets will be augmented to the extent that local leaders are entrepreneurial. Seeking grants from philanthropic foundations, finding public agencies with funds for staff training, and acquiring state funds for unique programs will be rewarded. Leasing the open areas on campus to agencies that want to conduct fairs, shows, swap meets, and the like will become increasingly popular, along with long-term leases for projects benefiting the community. College foundations will be pursued with increasing vigor. Contract training has expanded rapidly and bodes to continue as a favorite way of mounting new, specialized programs that benefit local businesses while relieving a portion of the overhead that the college-credit programs bear.

Interestingly, the idea that the colleges should be funded programmatically the way parks, recreation centers, and libraries are funded has made no headway in state capitols, but it will progress nevertheless as each college acquires its own funds for special programs. Using the funds generated by higher tuition to support greater aid to low-income students, a favorite concept of the economists who study higher education, will continue getting lip-service but little tangible support in state legislatures. Instead, the states will use the higher tuition as an excuse to deny requests for increased allocations. Similarly, the contention that two-year college funding should be brought more in line with other public institutions will fall on deaf ears; the colleges' low per-student expenditures are essential for keeping postsecondary costs down. Nor will the frequently raised proposals to make the colleges tuition-free gain any traction.

Instruction and Student Services

Instruction is the process of causing learning. Learning may occur in any setting, but instruction involves arranging conditions so that it is predictable and directed. Those conditions include access to new information, organization of sequence and content, and, not least, whatever else is necessary to keep the learners attendant on the task—a condition that requires traditional instruction. Would that the drive to learn were so powerful that all people engaged themselves individually with learning all they need to know to play valued roles in society. Absent that, instruction remains essential. Regardless of the spread of multimedia, interactive media, and other distance-learning technologies that are currently available, classroom-centered instruction will not only not disappear, it will not even diminish very much as a percentage of instructional effort.

Some of the more sanguine commentators envision instruction as fully learner controlled and totally responsive to individual knowledge seekers. Virtual, online arrangements would enable the faculty and students to change roles, teaching each other at will. Interestingly, although such a pattern has been given impetus by the availability of the Internet, it actually stems from the philosophy undergirding adult education; Ivan Illich wrote about it in *Deschooling Society* in 1972, and the *Learning Annex*, an informal network of education users and providers, affords a contemporary example. However, in an anarchistic information environment, intermediaries are essential, not because they alone possess knowledge, but because the knowledge seeker needs their help in navigating the sea of irrelevant and often inaccurate information available online.

Before distance learning through any medium can become central to community college instruction, the instructors must adopt it as a desirable concept. It is possible for a college to purchase or lease multimedia or interactive instructional programs and present them without involving the instructional staff, but to do so would require a shift in focus from faculty ownership of instruction. Some colleges will do that, leaving the tenured instructors in their classrooms teaching in traditional ways and building massive instructional programs through ancillary organizations. But most will maintain several instructional forms within the parameters of the preexisting college organization.

It is fascinating to reflect on all the media that were supposed to change the conditions of teaching. To the phonograph, telephone, radio, television, and computer have been added the laser-directed disc, satellites and downlinks, and other electronic marvels too numerous to be tabulated. These automated media did indeed change the way that information is transmitted, but not in the way that the educators had hoped. Their primary application has not been in socially valuable directions or even in the schools. It has been in the world of entertainment, where the media have tended to lure audiences away from the imagery occasioned by reading, away from reflectiveness, patience, and perseverance. The dream of students learning on their own while their instructors were freed from information dispensing to engage in creative interaction with them has remained just that—a dream from which visitors to the schools awaken as they walk the corridors and see instructors and students in classrooms acting quite as they did before the microchip or, for that matter, the vacuum tube.

The concept of instructional productivity will be central to moves toward media production and use. Productivity in the university coalesced around ideas of research and scholarship. In the community colleges, productivity has been defined as numbers of students taught per instructional dollar. Unending demands for accountability and measures of productivity will force continuous review of productivity measures. Although telecourses have been widespread for decades, questions about the learning they effect are still open. The number of students exposed to an instructional medium, whether in a classroom or on a television screen or computer terminal elsewhere, is only one among many possible measures of productivity. Few auditors will continue to accept instructional productivity as a measure of the number of students within range of the instructor's voice. Changes in instructional form and in measures of instructional productivity will have to proceed in tandem. Eventually, measures of student learning, achievement, and satisfaction will have to be emphasized.

The development of instruction as a discipline has been retarded by many forces, ranging from preservice faculty preparation that ignores concepts of instruction to institutional funding on the basis of student attendance that pays too little attention to student learning. However, the classification of students into various subgroups is also a rarely acknowledged but powerful limitation. As long as instructors, researchers, and administrators continue subdividing student achievement according to race, gender, and ethnicity, Instruction (deliberately capitalized) as a process leading to measurable student learning cannot progress. The categories afford a too convenient rationalization for variant student attainment: "They didn't learn because they are . . . ," "They achieved good scores because they are. . . ." The acceptance of mastery learning or any similar concept will not suffuse the colleges while characterization of students allows the staff to disclaim responsibility for defining, predicting, and measuring learning across all fields, disciplines, and programs.

Although practitioners of student services have long advocated better integration of their programs with the colleges' instructional efforts, only rarely have strong links been built between the counseling, tutorial, and orientation efforts, on the one hand, and the instructional programs, on the other. More recently, led by managers of instructional resource centers and learning laboratories, student services and instruction have come closer together. As an example, a "student success center," integrating several aspects of student services with instruction, would include computer-based learning for student access to software, tutorial activities, faculty instructional development support, student assessment, and numerous other functions now typically scattered across the campus. The budgetary lines that divide student services from instruction have tended to retard the development of this form of integration. But to the extent its proponents can demonstrate financial savings, it will proceed.

Curriculum

An outline of curriculum classified broadly as vocational, developmental, community, and collegiate studies can be projected.

Vocational Education

Vocational education will remain prominent. There can be no reversing the perception that one of the colleges' prime functions is to train workers, and ample funds are available to support this function. Competition from universities that develop programs in the technologies and from proprietary schools and publicly funded ad hoc job training programs that teach the more specific skills will not change the central tendency. There is enough demand to keep them all occupied, even as programs within the category rise and fall.

Enrollment and funding caps will limit the introduction of new programs. In 1991, the Texas Higher Education Coordinating Board adopted a policy of linking approval of new associate degrees to the college's job-training record: "An institution must show that 85 percent of the students completing existing technical programs over a three-year period are employed or pursuing additional education" (Aumack and Blake, 1992, p. 2). Specifications for the Job Training Partnership Act and in the more recent Welfare-to-Work rules put limits on programs that a community college may offer for adults because educational attainment per se is not considered a successful training outcome. More than in any other area, the specter of institutional accountability looms over the occupational programs. But they are so popular in an era of intense economic competitiveness that modest change in format is about all that will differentiate them from their predecessors.

Developmental Education

Developmental education will also be high on the agenda. It has come to the fore after decades of being treated as an embarrassing secret—as something that the colleges did but that their leaders would rather not publicize. The report of the commission planning for the future of the Alabama college system noted that economic development in the state depends in large measure on the colleges' "establishing innovative solutions to chronic illiteracy" (Alabama State Department of Postsecondary Education, 1987, p. 19). The Commission on the Future of the North Carolina Community College System indicated that the colleges could bring about significant increases in literacy levels by improving the quality of literacy education programs, increasing the number of graduates, and increasing "support among business and government agencies for literacy programs" (1989, p. 20). Both the Maryland State Board for Community Colleges (1986) and the Board of Trustees of Regional Community Colleges (1989) in Connecticut concluded that community colleges have a primary responsibility to provide developmental education. In California, the Joint Committee for Review of the Master Plan for Higher Education (California State Legislature, 1987) elevated remedial education to a priority second only to transfer and occupational studies. Clearly, developmental education has come out of the closet.

Despite all the increases in high school graduation requirements and the apparent increase in the test scores made by prospective college students, developmental education is as big as it ever was. One reason may be that the tests are at variance with the types of learning that the students have attained, a reason implicit in an NCES report on literacy, which states that half the adult students who were tested were reading at the lowest two of the five levels of literacy (Kirsch, Jungeblut, Jenkins, and Kolstad, 1993). Another clue comes from the pattern of students completing high school: graduation requirements increased during the 1980s, but so did the proportion of students completing high school at age twenty-one or older. The rate of high school completion for seventeen-year-olds remained static, averaging 73 percent in the 1960s and 71 percent in the 1990s; in 2004 it was 75 percent. But the rate of high school completion for people in their twenties increased from 83 percent in 1972 to between 85 and 86 percent from the mid-1980s onward (Laird, DeBell, and Chapman, 2004). An even more dramatic increase was seen in high school completion rates for twenty-nine- and thirty-year-olds, from 78 percent in 1972 to 87 percent in the early 1980s and succeeding years. Many of the students who take longer to complete programs, and receive high school diplomas or equivalency certificates when they are in their twenties, either never learned or forgot the dimensions of literacy that the awards purport to certify.

A sizable amount of basic skill development would continue to be necessary for many years merely to accommodate the backlog of functionally illiterate and non-native-English-speaking people in America. No other postsecondary structure is in a position to provide this essential instruction. The community colleges will not only offer it on their own campuses but will also expand their teaching of literacy in universities, lower schools, and business enterprises. Whether developmental education is funded separately or whether its cost is aggregated along with other curricular functions, it will account for one-third of the instructional budget. This amount will vary widely between colleges; it will be highest where the lower schools pass through numbers of marginally literate students, college going and immigration rates are high, and matriculation testing and placement are mandated.

Community Education

Community education expanded dramatically during the 1970s and held its own even in the face of budget reductions in the 1980s. Its proponents have been skilled in effecting cooperative relationships and securing special funds for it. Nonetheless, its future is not assured because questions of intent, quality control, and institutional credibility have not been answered. Funding will continue to be the most difficult problem to resolve. Although community education advocates certainly will not achieve their fanciful dream of serving as the nexus of the region's educational services, their greatest successes will be in rural areas where competing institutions are weakest. Contract training and adult basic education will do well, but personal interest courses will do poorly unless they are presented on a self-supporting basis.

Issues of definition and scope will be no less prominent than they always have been. The notion of community education as "building communities" has never been credible. "Communities" typically were defined as including everyone in the district, which the internationalists extended to the world. Thus, the colleges were supposed to build local, then global communities, a fey concept even before the ugliness of September 11, 2001, forced a reconsideration of the term globalization itself. As Fukuyama explained, "A community is not formed every time a group of people happens to interact with one another; true communities are bound together by the values, norms, and experiences shared among their members." And "geographical proximity remains important—perhaps even more important—than previously" (2000, pp. 14–15).

Colleges could be reorganized to maintain large-scale community education operations. Ideally, community education would be funded programmatically; that is, a college would be awarded a fixed sum each year to provide cultural, occupational upgrade, recreation, personal interest, community health, and semiprofessional retraining programs to the people of its district. Or the colleges could maintain their open-access policies—with students taking courses that may or may not lead to degrees—but would build a transfer or honors college within such a structure. The main funding pattern would be for individuals participating in courses with reimbursement on an attendance basis, but the transfer or honors college would be operated separately, with a variety of specially funded enrichment opportunities and work assistance or scholarship monies made available. A third way of sustaining community education might be to maintain the college's collegiate and vocational functions but to offer all the community education services through an extension division, as many universities have done. This would put all community education on a self-sustaining basis, since those who take the short courses or participate in the activities offered would pay for them ad hoc. Still another way of maintaining the traditional college with a community education component would be to place the community service work, along with the developmental and adult basic education function, in a separate center, where staff members might not have credentials. Unlike the regular faculty, who are paid on a class-hour basis, they would be paid for working a forty-hour week. None of these models is likely to enjoy widespread adoption. Community education will continue as adjunctive, supported by participant fees, contracted services, and special-purpose grants.

Collegiate Education

The prognosis for the collegiate curriculum is good. The linkage aspect of the collegiate function, centering on preparing students to enter junior-level programs leading to the bachelor's degree in health fields, business, technologies, and the professions, will thrive because entrance to those programs depends on students' completing courses in the humanities, sciences, social sciences, mathematics, and English usage. And because of a steady increase in population, the need to maintain access to traditional collegiate studies has become greater than at any other time since the first wave of baby boomers reached age eighteen in the early 1960s. Few universities will expand their freshman classes; distance education will not satisfy the demand. Greater numbers of eighteen-year-olds will find they have no choice but to enroll in a community college, and transfer rates will continue increasing as they have since the late 1990s.

The collegiate function will thrive also as the colleges enroll greater numbers of minority students. Like most students, they want jobs; and like all students, they need a perspective on the culture, a sense of interpersonal relations, and an ability to analyze situations and communicate appropriately. They seek the higher education that they need to progress in society: increased literacy, understanding of ethical issues, and realization of past and present time. Someday, readers of today's education literature will react with emotions ranging from curiosity to indignation and shame as they review the allegations that an influx of minority students rationalizes a curriculum centering on ethnic identity. Racism dies hard, and it is distressing to hear commentators suggesting special curricula for those students they euphemistically call "new" or "untraditional."

Difficult to recall in an era when a preponderance of research in higher education has been devoted to ferreting out and deploring colleges and programs where students are not represented in exact proportion to their numbers in racial subgroups, these categories are not immutable. They are instead linked to political will, and they and the conditions that the analysts complain about mutate continually. As an example, now that women are in a clear majority in the student body and approximate parity in the community college faculty, those who for years lamented their subordinate position are having difficulty finding areas where they are treated unequally (although unrepentant ideology will keep them seeking pockets of discrimination for years to come). Racial categorizations, too, will shift as progress in higher education for each group expands and as different ways of stratifying people gain appeal.

The emphasis on ethnic identity may be shifting gradually toward family income as a way of differentiating among students. A few foundations, including Jack Kent Cooke, Lumina (2007), and Nellie Mae, have focused on assisting low-income students to enter and progress in higher education. The federal Cost Reduction and Access Act, mentioned earlier, is another aid.

Among its provisions is one offering challenge grants—matching funds given to states or organizations providing need-based grants and support services to high school and college students from low-income families or those whose parents had not attended college. The need is tremendous: Fischer noted, "Perhaps as few as 1000 out of the 11,000 community college transfer students who enrolled at selective colleges in 2002 are from low income households . . ." (January 26, 2007, p. 1). Michaels summed the situation saying, ". . . when we focus on globalization as a cultural issue, we're trying to solve a real problem (economic inequality) by working on a false one (cultural identity)" (2006, p. 165). But it may be a long time coming; the poor are not nearly as well organized as the identity groups are.

The continuation of schooling from grades 1–20 reveals some broad patterns of curriculum differentiation. From the beginning of school through grade 8, a rather homogeneous curriculum centering on literacy, numeracy, and acculturation is presented. From grades 15–20, that is, the upper division of college through graduate school, the major emphasis is on professional development and in-depth learning. In grades 9–14, secondary school, and community college, the curriculum is most mixed. Part is directed toward workforce development, and part toward preprofessional education, personal interest studies, and remedial education. Most of the tracking and sorting of people and most of the student attrition occurs in institutions providing this least homogeneous curriculum.

Integrated general education has struggled for decades. Among other forces antagonistic to it, the heavy hand of academic discipline-based distribution requirements maintained in the universities limits college efforts to build interdisciplinary curriculum. Fundamental curricular reform occurs very slowly. The clerically dominated classical curriculum was under attack for at least half of the nineteenth century before a secularized curriculum centering on science became the norm. The twentieth century saw the rise of vocational education and the acceptance of remedial studies as a legitimate collegiate function. A mandated, integrative education through which students gain historical perspective and a sense of the social and environmental trends that affect their future has yet to take center stage. In sum, except in the rare institution, general education will continue being debated in the context of distribution requirements. It is a centripetal idea that is constantly subverted by the centrifugal forces of staff members and students with their own agenda and by universities that have rarely provided it for their own students.

The best prospect for socially desirable general studies in community colleges is to merge two strands of curriculum that have been thriving individually: service-learning (civic engagement) and sustainability. Both relate to the educated person's acting on behalf of the broader community, the general education ideal. Service-learning is well established in most colleges, popular with students who understand they must give something back to their communities. Sustainability, the newer thread, is manifest in the environmental science (technology/management/studies/ stewardship/design) and ecology courses now offered throughout the country. A link between them offers a chance to penetrate the conceptual separation between collegiate studies and community service.

As of 2003, half the colleges involved in service-learning reported linkages with environmental conservation (G. Robinson, e-mail, October 12, 2007). Chandler-Gilbert Community College (Arizona) has an environmental service-learning project for biology majors. Cape Cod Community College (Massachusetts) has sponsored environmental internships with more than fifty partnering agencies. Rowe describes numerous examples of sustainability courses and programs along with studies showing that involved students develop "increased caring about the future of society, and increased belief that they can make a difference" in solving environmental problems (2002, p. 1). The League for Innovation in the Community College and the American Association of Community Colleges have pledged support for these types of programs. It seems likely that students will be required or at least urged to participate in sustainability projects in the community and the colleges will modify general education to better fit their mission.

Research

Research in community colleges should center on assessing institutional outcomes. The classical educational research paradigms apply to the community colleges no less than they do to other forms of schools. Students attend, learn, and move on to other pursuits. Those outcomes can be assessed—as, indeed, they are in many districts and states. More such studies should be done in individual colleges. But too few institutional research officers are available to coordinate them, too few high-level administrators appreciate their importance, and when they are conducted, too many well-meaning but futile attempts are made to relate the findings to particular college practices.

The colleges should be assessed on the basis of their success in promoting individual mobility. How many people used them as a step toward the baccalaureate or higher-status jobs? How many broke out of a cycle of family poverty? How many gained rapid access to society by becoming literate? How many learned to put their own lives together? If the goal of individual mobility is not broad enough for those who seek measures of the colleges' contributions, let them look to measures of what the colleges have done for special populations in the aggregate: the aged, disabled, at-risk youth, or immigrants. How much do the colleges contribute to the solution of perennial social issues, such as homelessness, a balanced economy, energy conservation, and white-collar and street crime? The most likely answer is, very little. The community colleges—all schools—are limited in their ability to take direct action. Staff predilections, the paucity of leadership, and funding priorities internally, along with the externalities of public perceptions, community power bases, and the competing influences of the mass media, ensure that the colleges reflect the times more than they lead them. It would be wonderful if the colleges could reorganize their curriculum and their instructional programs so that they were providing forms of education that had a direct effect on social problems. But that goal is elusive; all that any school can do is to encourage its students to participate in the polity, question their own and the community's values, and consider the consequences of contemporary policies that affect the problems.

An institution whose leaders pride themselves on the number of people attending finds it difficult to provide data in longitudinal format. Furthermore, college leaders have had ceaseless difficulty in explaining how students who attend for not more than one or two classes have benefited. For half the students who enter the community college as their first higher education experience, a course or two before they drop out is the norm. How many of them found what they needed? In an education system designed as a structure to move people from one grade to another, it is difficult to shift the paradigm and argue that successive enrollments in schooling are not the essential outcome but rather that something else—job skills, a sense of well-being, or some other intangible—has been a positive result. As Mellow (2008) summarized, "It does matter if a community college moves an adult from reading at the 5th grade to the 9th grade level, or learns how to compute percentages, or develops the capacity for the intellectual problem solving necessary to get and keep a job" (p. 3).

Who will ask and answer these questions? The coming years will not see augmented institutional research budgets; there is too much competition for discretionary funds. State legislatures have never been inclined to support research categorically, or to suggest overarching research agendas, but they are so interested in outcomes and accountability that they will continue sustaining research on college effects in particular areas. Some of the answers will be provided by the nationally oriented researchers housed in universities and federally sponsored agencies, but progress will be sporadic. Perhaps research in education must proceed that way: uncoordinated, underfunded, dependent on the interests of people concerned with particular questions and with the time and will to pursue them.

Overall, the community college is a stable institution. Its faculty, curriculum, and types of students change little from year to year. Although innovations in remedial education that were forced on the colleges by ill-prepared students were notable and although instruction presented through reproducible media found an early home in these institutions, the most successful experiment that the colleges pursued was open access. To a much greater extent than any other postsecondary structure, the colleges opened their doors to all who wished to participate.

Institutional stability is evidenced indirectly by viewing the environmental scans conducted periodically to alert college leaders to trends that might affect their institutions. Three recent reports issued by the Association of Community College Trustees (2004), the RP Group (2004), and the Colorado Community College System (2003) are illustrative. The first was based on a survey of college trustees and the other two on reviewing the popular press plus professional literature. The reports anticipated the importance of

- Predictable funding
- Collaboration across sectors, including for-profit
- Increased numbers of students
- K–12 weaknesses
- Responding to changing workforce requirements
- Demands for accountability

- Federal influence

- Online instruction

In brief, except for comments regarding the for-profit sector, and the growth of online instruction that poses potential competition from providers worldwide, the scans would have reached the same conclusions had they reviewed the literature of the 1960s.

The Social Role

Social changes affect the way the nation views its social structures. For example, health care reform became a prominent issue in the 1990s as costs of coverage rose and the percentage of people whose employers included health care among their benefits declined. A shift in the direction of contingent, fungible, and part-time workers reduced the likelihood that people could expect their health care costs to be covered by their employers. Accordingly, the burden somehow had to be shifted to the broader community. The magnitude of this change was similar to that which industrial nations faced earlier in the century when the breakdown of the nuclear family meant that the elderly would have to be supported at least in part by a ubiquitous form of old age insurance—hence, the creation of the Social Security Act.

An analogous situation in education has been developing over several decades. As fewer people are prepared for careers that will sustain them throughout their working life, the need for successive retraining experiences becomes apparent. This retraining is more than merely learning to use the latest developments in technology in one's own field; continuing education offered through professional organizations and companies can accommodate most of that. Retraining is for people who are changing careers altogether, going from production jobs to entrepreneurial situations, or from one trade or profession to another. At best, a person's early education will emphasize flexibility, critical thinking, literacy skills, and social awareness, so that a move between endeavors can be undertaken with facility. At least, an easily accessible, low-cost educational structure should be available for the necessary realignment.

These elements of institutional mission are somewhat different from those that guided the community colleges during the 1960s and 1970s. When the colleges were expanding, one contention was that newly emergent populations of college goers needed access to higher education so that the finest minds among them might be nurtured. A widespread myth was that inequality was caused by unequal access to education. Many analysts opined that talent was distributed more or less at random across gender, ethnic, and social class lines; therefore, as access to higher education became available to everyone, new geniuses would emerge. The more sanguine pundits contended that a readily accessible system of postsecondary institutions would lead to a broad-scale increase in general community intelligence, taste, understanding, political will, and so on. The first contention, that everyone should be given an opportunity, has borne fruit as women have entered careers in business, law, and medicine and as greater numbers of people from ethnic minorities have joined the middle class. The increase in general intelligence and participation in the polity has proved considerably more elusive.

The colleges have contributed to the paradoxes that surround the structure of education. For one, they enhance inequality. Since they are avenues of individual mobility, the more successful they are in attracting students, the greater the resultant societal inequities as the brighter, more motivated, more opportunistic people move out of the social strata into which they were born. At the same time, the colleges often attempt direct social action, organizing food banks, conducting workshops on grant-getting and tax-return filing, seeking enhanced levels of student aid, and in general becoming entrepreneurial in finding opportunities to bring funds into the community.

Although these two functions seem complementary, they are in fact in opposition. The first, the college as an agent of individual mobility, forces it to act like a school. The college must teach reading and writing, basic computation, American culture. It must teach job-related generic skills, from the use of office equipment to enhancing students' propensities for dressing appropriately and showing up on time. It must maintain an academic posture, one that says that it is a school, a special environment; it is not a rap session or an extension of the street.

The social service or social welfare agenda, taken to the extreme, can lead to an institution that surrenders many of these elements of schooling. Its leaders can say they do not emphasize the teaching of English because many of their students use another primary language. They can justify preparing students for specific jobs through contract training. They can let health services and other ancillary activities become central. They can cultivate an image as a funding channel by continuously seeking dollars to run directly to the community. Some combination should be recognized, because the community colleges should not function as social welfare agencies to the detriment of their teaching and learning core.

One option or bridge between individual mobility and social welfare may be in helping students develop local businesses and remain in their community. Most colleges have had success in teaching entrepreneurship, business law, small business accounting, and employee relations; over 96,000 associate degrees and half that many certificates in Business Management and Administration are awarded annually. This is much more useful for community development than a continuing drum roll of commentary on race relations, capitalistic systems, and disputes over which group is more victimized than another.

Some unstated but obvious lessons in what happens to an institution that drifts away from its instructional core toward a social service role might be drawn from the experience of the American secondary schools. As they reduced curriculum requirements and attended more directly to student welfare and social or community services, several things happened. They began to employ ill-trained teachers, they began passing marginally literate students through, they effectually put a cap on the percentage of students graduating, and they enlarged the separation between teachers and administrators. Not incidentally, they gained a full share of public opprobrium and consequent support for competing institutions, such as private and charter schools.

Within the context of these philosophical anomalies, the peculiarities of individual colleges are obscured. Legislatures see transfer and developmental and occupational education as top priorities, with all else peripheral. If the colleges try to do too much, they may be accused of doing nothing well. The institutional image contributes to its outcomes. If a college has an exceedingly low transfer rate, the academically inclined students shun it and its transfer rate goes down ever further. Similarly, if a college is dedicated more to contract training than to generic occupational education, the students who seek skills that can be related to a multiplicity of jobs may go elsewhere. If student flow is to be a measure of institutional success, then relationships with the secondary schools and the universities will have to be carefully cultivated and monitored. This demands an association between educational structures that might otherwise be competitive for funding, public support, and students—a very touchy situation, but there is no option.

Another paradox is that distance learning, the reconfiguring of instruction that is supposed to save money, may be directed toward the marginal, nondirected, nonserious, casual students. Why a paradox? Because the young people from families with a high regard for education will find their way to a campus that promises a traditional collegiate experience.

One more paradox is that education tends to increase productivity whereas incarceration decreases productivity; yet the budget for prisons in some states has now grown greater than that for higher education. How legislators can call for increased productivity and competition in the global economy while at the same time appropriating more money for the corrections system at the expense of support for higher education eludes rationality.

Last, despite massive growth in access to schooling and the vastly greater and diverse numbers who have enrolled, the communities from which they come have been little affected. Do the schools not build a better society? The individual mobility that they effect does not translate into reorganized cities, changed working conditions, modified immigration policies, or much of anything else affecting the quality of life across the community.

A view of social conditions in the United States at the turn of the century provides a view of the context for the colleges:

- High immigration, in both absolute numbers and percentages of the American population, along with demands for anti-immigration regulations
- Multilingualism, with scores of foreign-language newspapers and a population housed in ethnic enclaves
- Overcrowded cities, with unclean pavements and parks and intractable homelessness
- For the workforce, practically no fringe benefits and piecework in the workplace and take-home or cottage industries
- Powerful media determining what people think
- A great gap between the rich and the poor
- Producer or assembly jobs that yield wages insufficient to sustain a family above the poverty line
- Weak trade unions, representing a small proportion of the work force
- For the individual, business entrepreneurship as the path to capital formation

- A seeming paucity of civility when compared with an earlier era
- A tendency of youth to form gangs and engage in various criminal activities

At the turn of which century? The twentieth and twenty-first alike. One thousand community colleges have not changed those conditions. But did anyone but the most passionate, self-deceiving institutional advocates ever think that they could?

The college may have no ostensible reason for existence other than to serve its students and the business community, but it also has a life of its own as an intellectual community. It is easy to reduce the institution's value to the increase in its graduates' social mobility and to ignore its position as a center of acculturation and historical continuity. But the institution's traditions act to ensure that these values are not completely set aside. Learning is infinite. We can always teach more, learn more efficiently, do better. Thus, there is continual striving for innovation in education, with the innovators occupying prominent places in the system. Too often overlooked is a view of the staff as models of rational discourse.

Educators do not solve problems or cure ills. But neither do they deliberately sell false dreams or spread bad taste. It is only when they imitate the worst characteristics of business corporations and the mass media that they lose the status the public has granted them. They must not betray the virtues that distinguish the American Community College.

References

National Center for Education Statistics publications are abbreviated in text as NCES. The NCES *Digests*, published annually, are listed here as one entry. Additionally, many of the references can be found using the Education Resources Information Center (ERIC) search engine.

Abraham, A. A., Jr. *A Report on College-Level Remedial Developmental Programs in SREB States.* Atlanta: Southern Regional Education Board, 1987.

Academic Senate for California Community Colleges. *The State of Basic Skills Instruction in California Community Colleges.* Sacramento: Academic Senate for California Community Colleges, 2000.

Academic Senate for California Community Colleges. *Issues in Basic Skills Assessment and Placement in the California Community Colleges.* Sacramento: Academic Senate for California Community Colleges, 2004.

Accrediting Commission for Community and Junior Colleges. *Primary Purposes of ACCJC.* Santa Rosa, Calif.: Accrediting Commission for Community and Junior Colleges, 2001.

Adelman, C. "A Basic Statistical Portrait of American Higher Education." Paper presented at the Second Anglo-American Dialogue on Higher Education, Washington, D.C., 1987.

Adelman, C. *The Way We Are: The American Community College as Thermometer.* Washington, D.C.: U.S. Department of Education, 1992.

Adelman, C. *Lessons of a Generation*. San Francisco: Jossey-Bass, 1994.

Adelman, C. *Moving into Town and Moving On: The Community College in the Lives of Traditional Age Students*. Washington, D.C.: U.S. Department of Education, 2005.

Adelman, C. *The Toolbox Revisited: Paths to Degree Completion from High School Through College*. Washington, D.C.: U.S. Department of Education, 2006a.

Adelman, C. "Additional and Critical Data Points." *Inside Higher Ed*, Dec. 21, 2006b, n. p. http://www.insidehighered.com/news/2006/12/19/bailey. Accessed Oct. 21, 2007.

Adelman, C. "Making Graduation Rates Matter." *Inside Higher Ed*, Mar. 12, 2007 n. p. http://www.insidehighered.com/views/2007/03/12/adelman. Accessed Oct. 10, 2007.

Alabama State Department of Postsecondary Education. *Dimensions 2000: A Strategic Plan for Building Alabama's Future*. Montgomery: Alabama State Department of Postsecondary Education, 1987.

Alfred, R., Ewell, P., Hudgins, J., and McClenney, K. *Core Indicators of Effectiveness for Community Colleges. Toward High Performance*. (2nd ed.). Washington, D.C.: Community College Press, 1999.

Alfred, R., Shults, C., and Seybert, J. *Core Indicators of Effectiveness for Community Colleges*. Toward High Performance. (3rd ed.). Washington, D.C.: American Association of Community Colleges, 2007.

American Association of Community and Junior Colleges. *Building Communities: A Vision for a New Century: A Report of the Commission on the Future of Community Colleges*. Washington, D.C.: American Association of Community and Junior Colleges, 1988a.

American Association of Community Colleges. *Community Colleges: Core Indicators of Effectiveness*. Washington, D.C.: American Association of Community Colleges, 1994.

American Association of Community Colleges. *Charting the Future of Global Education in Community Colleges. New Expeditions: Charting the Second Century of Community Colleges*. Washington, D.C.: American Association of Community Colleges, 2000.

American Association of Community Colleges. *State-by-State Profile of Community Colleges*. (6th ed.). Washington, D.C.: American Association of Community Colleges, 2003.

American Association of Community Colleges. *Faces of the Future: Findings from the 2006 National Comparison Data Report*. Washington, D.C.: American Association of Community Colleges, 2006.

American Association of Community and Junior Colleges. *Community, Junior, and Technical College Directory*. Washington, D.C.: American Association of Community and Junior Colleges, 1992.

American Association of Junior Colleges. *A National Resource for Occupational Education*. Washington, D.C.: American Association of Junior Colleges, 1964.

American Association of University Professors. *Financial Inequality in Higher Education: The Annual Report of the Economic Status of the Profession*. Washington, D.C.: American Association of University Professors, 2007.

American College Testing (ACT). *Reading Between the Lines: What the ACT Reveals About College Readiness in Reading*. Iowa City, Iowa: 2006.

American College Testing. *ACT National Profile Report*. Iowa City, Iowa: ACT, 2007.

Anderson, G., Alfonso, M., and Sun, J. C. "Rethinking Cooling Out at Public Community Colleges: An Examination of Fiscal and Demographic Trends in Higher Education and the Rise of Statewide Articulation Agreements." *Teachers College Record*, 2006, *108*(3), 422–451.

Angelo, T. A., and Cross, K. P. *Classroom Assessment Techniques*. (2nd ed.) San Francisco: Jossey-Bass, 1993.

Arendale, D. R. *Postsecondary Peer Cooperative Learning Programs: Annotated Bibliography*. Minneapolis: University of Minnesota, 2005.

Armstrong, W. B. "The Association Among Student Success in Courses, Placement Test Scores, Student Background Data, and Instructor Grading Practices." *Community College Journal of Research and Practice*, 2000a, *24*(8), 681–695.

Armstrong, W. B. "The Relation Between Placement Testing and Curricular Content in the Community College: Correspondence or Misalignment?" *Journal of Applied Research in the Community College*, 2000b, *7*(1), 33–38.

Ash, B. *Research on Maryland Community College Students with Disabilities for the 2005 Taskforce on Community College Students with Disabilities*. Annapolis: Maryland Association of Community Colleges, 2005.

Ashburn, E. "An Honors Education at a Bargain-Basement Price." *Chronicle of Higher Education*, Oct. 27, 2006, pp. B1–2.

Ashley, H., Barr, R., and Lattuca, L. R. *Report on the Conference: Community College Issues: Issues and Research*. Chicago: Spencer Foundation, Oct. 1999.

Ashworth, P. C., and Vogler, D. E. "Community College Funding Goals: Senate and Presidential Comparison." *Community Services Catalyst*, 1991, *21*(1), 22–26.

Association of Community College Trustees. *Community College Environmental Scanning*. Washington, D.C.: Association of Community College Trustees, 2004.

Astin, A. W. *Four Critical Years: Effects of College on Beliefs, Attitudes, and Knowledge*. San Francisco: Jossey-Bass, 1977.

Astin, A. W. *Minorities in American Higher Education: Recent Trends, Current Prospects, and Recommendations*. San Francisco: Jossey-Bass, 1982.

Astin, A., and Astin, H. (1995). *Social Change Model of Leadership Development*. Los Angeles: Higher Education Leadership Institute, University of California, 1995.

Astin, A. W., Korn, W. S., and Dey, E. L. *The American College Teacher: National Norms for the 1989–90 HERI Faculty Survey*. Los Angeles: Higher Education Research Institute, University of California, 1991.

Astin, H. S., and Leland, C. *Women of Influence, Women of Vision: A Cross-Generational Study of Leaders and Social Change*. San Francisco: Jossey-Bass, 1991.

Attewell, P., Lavin, D., Domina, T., and Levey, T. "New Evidence on College Remediation." *The Journal of Higher Education*, 2006, *77*(5), 887–924.

Augenblick, J. *Issues in Financing Community Colleges*. Denver: Education Finance Center, Education Commission of the States, 1978.

Aumack, B., and Blake, L. J. *Texas State Technical College Review*. Austin: Texas Higher Education Coordinating Board, 1992.

Aviles, C. B. *A Study of Mastery Learning Versus Non-Mastery Learning in an Undergraduate Social Work Policy Class*. Buffalo, N.Y.: Buffalo State College, Social Work Department, 2001.

Ayers, F. A. "A Neoliberal Ideology in Community College Mission Statements: A Critical Discourse Analysis." *Review of Higher Education*, 2005, *28*(4), 527–549.

Bailey, T. "Multiple Missions of Community Colleges." In S. A. Rosenfeld (ed.), *Learning Now*. Washington, D.C.: Community College Press, 2000.

Bailey, T., and Alfonso, M. *Paths to Persistence: An Analysis of Research on Program Effectiveness at Community Colleges*. Indianapolis: Lumina Foundation for Education, 2005.

Bailey, T., Alfonso, M., Scott, M., and Leinbach, T. "Educational Outcomes of Postsecondary Occupational Students." *CCRC Research Brief*, no. 24. New York: Community College Research Center, Teachers College, Columbia University, 2004.

Bailey, T., Crosta, P. M., and Jenkins, D. *The Value of Student Right to Know Data in Assessing Community College Performance*. New York: Community College Research Center, Teachers College, Columbia University, 2007.

Bailey, T. R., Gumport, P. J., and Badway, N. "For-Profit Higher Education and Community Colleges." *CCRC Research Brief*, no. 16. New York: Community College Research Center, Teachers College, Columbia University, 2003.

Bailey, T., Jenkins, D., and Leinbach, T. *Graduation Rates, Student Goals, and Measuring Community College Effectiveness*. New York: Community College Research Center, Teachers College, Columbia University, 2005a.

Bailey, T., Jenkins, D., and Leinbach, T. "Graduation Rates, Students Goals, and Measuring Community College Effectiveness." *CCRC Brief*, no. 28.

New York: Community College Research Center, Teachers College, Columbia University, 2005b.

Bailey, T., and Morest, V. S. (eds.). *Defending the Community College Equity Agenda*. Baltimore: Johns Hopkins University Press, 2006.

Banta, T. W. "A Warning on Measuring Learning Outcomes." *Inside Higher Ed*, Oct. 26, 2007, 1–2.

Barnes, C. A. (ed.). *Critical Thinking: Educational Imperative*. New Directions for Community Colleges, no. 77. San Francisco: Jossey-Bass, 1992.

Barnes, C. A. "Critical Thinking Revisited: Its Past, Present, and Future." In C. M. McMahon (ed.), *Critical Thinking: Unfinished Business*. New Directions for Community Colleges, no. 130. San Francisco: Jossey-Bass, 2005.

Baron, W. *The Problem of Student Retention: The Bronx Community College Solution—The Freshman Year Initiative Program*. New York: Bronx Community College, 1997.

Barr, R. B., and Tagg, J. "From Teaching to Learning: A New Paradigm for Undergraduate Education." *Change*, 1995, *27*(6), 12–25.

Bayer, A. E. "Teaching Faculty in Academe: 1972–73." *ACE Research Reports*, 1973, *8*(2), 1–68.

Ben-David, J. *Centers of Learning: Britain, France, Germany, United States*. New York: McGraw-Hill, 1977.

Bennett, W. J. *To Reclaim a Legacy: A Report on the Humanities in Higher Education*. Washington, D.C.: National Endowment for the Humanities, 1984.

Bensimon, E. M. "Understanding Administrative Work." In A. M. Cohen, F. B. Brawer, and Associates (eds.), *Managing Community Colleges: A Handbook for Effective Practice*. San Francisco: Jossey-Bass, 1994.

Berger, D. M. "Mandatory Assessment and Placement: The View from an English Department." In J. Ignash (ed.), *Implementing Effective Policies for Remedial and Developmental Education*. New Directions for Community Colleges, no. 100. San Francisco: Jossey-Bass, 1997.

Bers, T. "Assessing Critical Thinking in Community Colleges." In C. M. McMahon (ed.), *Critical Thinking: Unfinished Business*. New Directions for Community Colleges, no. 130. San Francisco: Jossey-Bass, 2005.

Biesta, G.J.J., and Burbules, N. C. *Pragmatism and Educational Research*. Lanham, Md.: Rowman and Littlefield, 2003.

Birnbaum, R. "Policy Scholars Are from Venus; Policy Makers Are from Mars." *Review of Higher Education*, 2000, 23(2), 119–132.

Bishop, C. C. *The Community's College: A History of Johnson County Community College 1969–1999*. Overland Park, Kans.: Johnson County Community College, 2002.

Blocker, C. E. "Are Our Faculties Competent?" *Junior College Journal*, 1965–1966, 36, 12–17.

Blocker, C. E., Plummer, W., and Richardson, R. C., Jr. *The Two-Year College: A Social Synthesis*. Upper Saddle River, N.J.: Prentice Hall, 1965.

Bloom, B. S. "Recent Developments in Mastery Learning." *Educational Psychologist*, 1973, 10(2), 53–57.

Blum, D. E. "Seeking to Prepare Global Citizens, Colleges Push More Students to Study Abroad." *Chronicle of Higher Education*, Oct. 27, 2006, p. B10.

Board of Trustees of Regional Community Colleges. *Towards 2000: A Long-Range Plan for the Community Colleges of Connecticut*. Hartford, Conn.: Board of Trustees of Regional Community Colleges, 1989.

Bogart, Q. J., and Galbraith, J. D. "Marketing America's Community Colleges: An Analysis of National Marketing Efforts of Community Colleges. A Final Report on the MECCA Project of the Council of North Central Community and Junior Colleges." Paper presented at the annual convention of the American Association of Community and Junior Colleges, Las Vegas, April 1988.

Bogue, J. P. *The Community College*. New York: McGraw-Hill, 1950.

Bok, D. *The Cost of Talent*. New York: Free Press, 1993.

Boone, E. J., and Associates. *Community Leadership Through Community-Based Programming: The Role of the Community College.* Washington, D.C.: Community College Press, American Association of Community Colleges, 1997.

Boone, E. J., Pettitt, J. M., and Weisman, I. M. (eds.). *Community-Based Programming in Action: The Experiences of Five Community Colleges.* Washington, D.C.: Community College Press, American Association of Community Colleges, 1998.

Borden, V.M.H. "100 Top Degree Producers, 1999–2000. Associate's Degrees: All Disciplines." *Community College Week,* July 10, 2000, p. 7.

Borglum, K., and Kubala, T. "Academic and Social Integration of Community College Students: A Case Study." *Community College Journal of Research and Practice,* 2000, *24*(7), 567–576.

Borquist, B. "The Community College Approach to Serving Business and Industry." *Community Services Catalyst,* 1986, *16*(4), 19–21.

Boulard, G. "Online Education Can Serve Students with Disabilities Better." *Community College Times,* Mar. 2, 2007, p. 4.

Bourque, M. P. "On the Fault Line: President Clinton Salutes Community Colleges." *Community College Journal,* 1995, *65*(6), 38–42.

Bowen, H. R. "Cost Differences: The Amazing Disparity Among Institutions of Higher Education in Educational Costs per Student." *Change,* 1981, *13*(1), 21–27.

Boyer, E. L. *College: The Undergraduate Experience in America.* New York: Harper Collins, 1987.

Bradburn, E. M., and Hurst, D. G. "Community College Transfer Rates to Four-Year Institutions Using Alternative Definitions of Transfer." *Education Statistics Quarterly,* 2001, *3*(3), 119–125.

Brawer, F. B. "The Liberal Arts." In G. Schuyler (ed.), *Community College Curriculum.* New Directions for Community Colleges, no. 108. San Francisco: Jossey-Bass, 1999.

Brawer, F. B., and Friedlander, J. *Science and Social Science in the Two-Year College*. Los Angeles: ERIC Clearinghouse for Junior Colleges, 1979.

Breja, L. M. "A Study of the Academic Performance of Iowa Valley Community College District Transfer Students." Unpublished doctoral dissertation, Iowa State University, 2006.

Breneman, D. W. *Guaranteed Student Loans: Great Success or Dismal Failure?* Fishers, Ind.: United Student Aid Funds, 1991.

Brick, M. *Forum and Focus for the Junior College Movement*. New York: Teachers College Press, 1965.

Brick, M. "Review of Student Development Programs in the Community Junior College." *Journal of Higher Education*, 1972, *43*(98), 675–677.

Brightman, R. W. "Entrepreneurship in the Community College: Revenue Diversification." In J. L. Catanzaro and A. D. Arnold (eds.), *Alternative Funding Sources*. New Directions for Community Colleges, no. 68. San Francisco: Jossey-Bass, 1989.

Brint, S., and Karabel, J. *The Diverted Dream: Community Colleges and the Promise of Educational Opportunity in America, 1900–1985*. New York: Oxford University Press, 1989.

Brock, T., and Richburg-Hayes, L. *Paying for Persistence: Early Results of a Louisiana Scholarship Program for Low-Income Parents Attending Community College*. New York: MDRC, 2006.

Brown, J. R., and others. *Developmental Studies Department Special Services Project*. Suffern, N.Y.: Rockland Community College, 1989.

Burke, J. C., and Minassians, H. *Performance Reporting 'Real' Accountability or Accountability 'Lite' Seventh Annual Survey 2003*. Albany: The Nelson A. Rockefeller Institute of Government, State University of New York, 2003.

Burns, J. M. *Leadership*. New York: HarperCollins, 1978.

Burnstad, H. M. "Part-Time Faculty Development at Johnson County Community College." In G. E. Watts (Ed.), *Enhancing Community Colleges Through Professional Development*. New Directions for Community Colleges, no. 120. San Francisco: Jossey-Bass, 2002.

Bushnell, D. S. *Organizing for Change: New Priorities for Community Colleges.* New York: McGraw-Hill, 1973.

Butte Community College. *Secondary/Postsecondary Articulation: The Partnership Concept, The Partnership in Action, and Highlights of Partnership in Action.* Oroville, Calif.: Butte Community College, 1990.

Byers, D. N. "So Why Use Multimedia, the Internet, and Lotus Notes?" Paper presented at the Technology in Education Conference, San Jose, Calif., April 1997.

Calcagno, J. C., Crosta, P., Bailey, T. R., and Jenkins, D. *Stepping Stones to a Degree: The Impact of Enrollment Pathways and Milestones on Community College Student Outcomes.* New York: Community College Research Center, Teachers College, Columbia University, 2006.

California Community Colleges Chancellor's Office. *Report on Staffing and Salaries, Fall 1998.* Sacramento: California Community Colleges Chancellor's Office, 1999.

California Postsecondary Education Commission. *Student Transfer in California Postsecondary Education.* Sacramento: California Postsecondary Education Commission, 2002.

California State Auditor. *California Community Colleges: Part-Time Faculty Are Compensated Less Than Full-Time Faculty for Teaching Activities.* Sacramento: California State Auditor, 2000.

California State Board of Education, and California Community Colleges. *Noncredit and Adult Education: Challenges, Opportunities, Changes.* Final Report. Sacramento: California State Board of Education and California Community Colleges, 1998.

California State Department of Education. *Summary of Source and Education Background of New Teachers in California Junior Colleges, 1963–64.* Sacramento: California State Department of Education, 1963.

California State Legislature, Joint Committee for Review of the Master Plan for Higher Education. *California Community College Reform: Final Report.* Sacramento: Joint Committee for Review of the Master Plan for Higher Education, 1987.

California State Postsecondary Education Commission. *Comments on the California Community Colleges' Plan for Allocating Board Financial Assistance to Community College Students: A Report to the Fiscal and Educational Policy Committees of the Legislature.* Sacramento: California State Postsecondary Education Commission, 1984.

Campbell, D. T. "Assessing the Impact of Planned Social Change." In G. Lyons (ed.), *Social Research and Public Policies: The Dartmouth/OECD Conference.* Hanover, N.H.: Dartmouth College, 1975.

Carducci, R. Community College Accountability: New Perspectives in the Ongoing Policy Dialogue. *Community College Journal of Research and Practice,* 2007, *31*(2), 167–175.

Carmichael, J. B. "Meeting Small Business Needs Through Small Business Development Centers." In G. Waddell (ed.), *Economic and Work Force Development.* New Directions for Community Colleges, no. 75. San Francisco: Jossey-Bass, 1991.

Carnegie Foundation for the Advancement of Teaching. *Size and Setting Description Classification.* Stanford, Calif.: Carnegie Foundation for the Advancement of Teaching, 2006.

Carvell, J. B. *On Course: A Report to the Legislature on the Employee-Based Training Program, 1987–88.* Sacramento: Office of the Chancellor, California Community Colleges, 1988.

Cataldi, E. F., Bradburn, E. M., and Fahimi, M. *2004 National Study of Postsecondary Faculty: Background Characteristics, Work Activities, and Compensation of Instructional Faculty and Staff.* Washington, D.C.: U.S. Department of Education, 2005.

Center for the Study of Community Colleges. *Community College Involvement in the Education of Adults: Spring 1986 Student Survey—Frequencies.* Los Angeles: Center for the Study of Community Colleges, 1986.

Center for the Study of Community Colleges. *Art Education in American Community Colleges: Final Report.* Los Angeles: Center for the Study of Community Colleges, 1988.

Center for the Study of Community Colleges. *Entrepreneurship Training in American Community Colleges.* Los Angeles: Center for the Study of Community Colleges, 1994.

Cervantes, M. *Don Quixote*. New York: Penguin Books, 2003.

Chaffee, E. E. *Organization/Administration*. Washington, D.C.: Association for the Study of Higher Education, 1986.

Chang, J. C. "Transfer Adjustment Experiences of Underrepresented Students of Color in the Sciences." Unpublished doctoral dissertation, University of California, Los Angeles, 2006.

Chappell, C. "New Jersey Scholarship Triples Recipients." *Community College Times*, Jan. 19, 2007, p. 3.

Chappell, C. "Colleges Especially Vulnerable to Crime, Terrorism." *Community College Times*, Aug. 16, 2007, pp. 3–8.

Christophersen, K. A., and Robison, M. H. *The Socioeconomic Benefits Generated by 58 Community Colleges in North Carolina*. Moscow, Idaho: CC Benefits, 2004a.

Christophersen, K. A, and Robison, M. H. *The Socioeconomic Benefits Generated by Fourteen Community College Districts in Oklahoma*. Oklahoma City: Oklahoma State Regents for Higher Education, 2003b.

Ciardi, J. "Give Us This Day Our Daily Surrealism." *Saturday Review*, 1971, 54(24), 48.

Clark, B. R. "The 'Cooling-Out' Function in Higher Education." *American Journal of Sociology*, 1960, 65(6), 569–576.

Clark, B. R. "The 'Cooling-Out' Function Revisited." In G. B. Vaughan (ed.), *Questioning the Community College Role*. New Directions for Community Colleges, no. 32. San Francisco: Jossey-Bass, 1980.

Clark, B. R. "The Absorbing Errand." Remarks Presented at National Conference of the American Association of Higher Education, Washington, D.C., March 1988.

Clinton, W. J. *Address Before a Joint Session of Congress on the State of the Union*. In *Public Papers of the Presidents of the United States: Vol. 1*. Washington, D.C.: U.S. Government Printing Office, 1998.

Cloud, R. C. (ed.). *Legal Issues in the Community College*. New Directions for Community Colleges, no.125. San Francisco: Jossey-Bass, 2004.

Clowes, D. A., and Levin, B. H. "Community, Technical, and Junior Colleges: Are They Leaving Higher Education?" *Journal of Higher Education*, 1989, 60(3), 346–355. (EJ 390 779)

Cohen, A. M. "Why Practitioners and Researchers Ignore Each Other (Even When They Are the Same Person)." *Community College Review*, 2005, 33(1), 51–62.

Cohen, A. M., and Brawer, F. B. *The Two-Year College Instructor Today*. New York: Praeger, 1977.

Cohen, A. M., and Brawer, F. B. *The Collegiate Function of Community Colleges: Fostering Higher Learning Through Curriculum and Student Transfer*. San Francisco: Jossey-Bass, 1987.

Cohen, A. M., and Brawer, F. B. *Policies and Programs That Effect Transfer*. Washington, D.C.: American Council on Education, 1996.

Cohen, A. M., Brawer, F. B., and Eaton, J. S. "Policies and Programs That Effect Student Transfer." Paper presented to the annual convention of the American Association of Community Colleges, Apr. 24, 1995.

Cohen, A. M., and Ignash, J. M. "Trends in the Liberal Arts Curriculum." *Community College Review*, 1992, 20(2), 54–59.

Cohen, A. M., and Ignash, J. M. "An Overview of the Total Credit Curriculum." In A. M. Cohen (ed.), *Relating Curriculum and Transfer*. New Directions for Community Colleges, no. 86. San Francisco: Jossey-Bass, 1994.

Cohen, A. M., Schuetz, P., Chang, J. C., and Plecha, M. "Assessing Community College Student Knowledge in the Liberal Arts." *Journal of Applied Research in the Community College*, 2003, 11(1), 21–31.

Cohen, M. D., and March, J. G. *Leadership and Ambiguity: The American College President*. (2nd ed.) Boston: Harvard Business School Press, 1986.

Cohen, M. J. "Junior College Growth." *Change*, 1972, 4(9), 32a–32d.

College Board. *College Bound Seniors: The 1994 Profile of SAT and Achievement Test Takers*. Princeton, N.J.: The College Board, 1994.

College Board. *Trends in Student Aid*. Princeton, N.J.: The College Board, 2000.

College Board. *College-Bound Seniors: Total Group Profile Report*. Princeton, N.J.: The College Board, 2005.

College Board. *College-Bound Seniors: Total Group Profile Report*. Princeton, N.J.: The College Board, 2007.

College Board. *Education Pays Second Update: A Supplement to Education Pays 2004: The Benefits of Higher Education for Individuals and Society*. Princeton, N.J.: The College Board, 2006a.

College Board. *Trends in Student Aid*. Princeton, N.J.: The College Board, 2006b.

Collins, C. C. *Junior College Student Personnel Programs: What They Are and What They Should Be*. Washington, D.C.: American Association of Junior Colleges, 1967.

Colorado Community College System. *Environmental Scan for the Colorado Community College System*. Denver: Colorado Community College System, 2003.

Commission on the Future of the North Carolina Community College System. *Gaining the Competitive Edge: The Challenge to North Carolina's Community Colleges*. Chapel Hill, N.C., 1989.

Community College of the Air Force Fact Sheet. Montgomery, Ala.: Maxwell Air Force Base, 2007.

Community College Survey of Student Engagement. *Act on Fact: Using Data to Improve Student Success*. Austin: Community College Survey of Student Engagement, 2006.

Conklin, K. A. Follow-Up of Johnson County Community College Career Program Completers: Class of 1998–99. Overland Park, Kans.: Johnson County Community College, 2000.

Connecticut Department of Higher Education. *Higher Education: Building Connecticut's' Workforce*. Wethersfield: Connecticut Department of Labor, 2006.

Coombs, P. H. *The World Educational Crisis: A System Analysis*. New York: New York University Press, 1968.

Copperman, P. *The Literacy Hoax: The Decline of Reading, Writing, and Learning in the Public Schools and What We Can Do About It*. New York: Morrow, 1978.

Corson, J. J. *The Governance of Colleges and Universities*. New York: McGraw-Hill, 1960.

Council for the Advancement of Adult Literacy. *Adult Basic Education and Community Colleges in Five States: A Report from the Comprehensive Adult Student Assessment System to the Council for Advancement of Adult Literacy*. New York: Council for the Advancement of Adult Literacy, 2003.

Couturier, L. K. *Checks and Balances at Work: The Restructuring of Virginia's Public Higher Education System*. San Jose, Calif.: National Center for Public Policy and Higher Education, 2006.

Cowles, J. R. "Characteristics and Professional Activities of Community College Counselors." Unpublished doctoral dissertation, Southern Illinois University Carbondale, 2002.

Cress, C. M., Astin, H. S., Zimmerman-Oster, K., and Burkhardt, J. C. Developmental Outcomes of College Students' Involvement in Leadership Activities. *Journal of College Student Development*, 2001, 42(1), 15–27.

Cross, K. P. "Access and Accommodation in Higher Education." *Research Reporter*, 1971, 6(2), 6–8.

Cross, K. P. "Toward the Future in Community College Education." Paper Presented at the Conference on Education in the Community College for the Non-Traditional Student, Philadelphia, March 1978.

Cross, K. P. *Adults as Learners: Increasing Participation and Facilitating Learning*. San Francisco: Jossey-Bass, 1981.

Crozer, N. *Individualized Vocabulary Instruction on the Computer*. Los Angeles: Los Angeles Pierce College, 1996.

Cullen, C., and Moed, M. G. "Serving High-Risk Adolescents." In J. E. Lieberman (ed.), *Collaborating with High Schools*. New Directions for Community Colleges, no. 63. San Francisco: Jossey-Bass, 1988.

Cunningham, G. *Annual Report for the Workforce and Community Transition Training for Incarcerated Youth Offenders Program: 2005–2006 Academic Year*. Richmond: Virginia Department of Correctional Education, 2007.

Cvancara, K. J. "In Prison, in College." *Community College Times*, Nov. 1, 1994, pp. 1, 4.

Dallas County Community College District. *ITV Close-Up: The First Six Years*. Dallas: Dallas County Community College District, 1979.

Dallas County Community College District. TeleCollege Home Page, May 2002 [http://telecollege.dccd.edu] (May 28, 2002).

Dassance, C. R. "Student Services." In A. M. Cohen and F. B. Brawer (eds.), *Managing Community Colleges: A Handbook for Effective Practice*. San Francisco: Jossey-Bass, 1994.

Dee, J. R. "Turnover Intent in an Urban Community College: Strategies for Faculty Retention." *Community College Journal of Research and Practice*, 2004, 28(7), 593–607.

Dembicki, M. "Two-Year Colleges Bear the Brunt of Remediation." *Community College Times*, Sept. 12, 2006, p. 1.

Dembicki, M. "A Simple Message Is Critical in Economic Impact Studies." *Community College Times*, June 8, 2007, 1–2.

Dickmeyer, M. *Comparative Financial Statistics for Public Two-Year Colleges: FY 1993 National Sample*. Washington, D.C.: National Association of College and University Business Offices, Apr. 1994.

Diener, T. *Growth of an American Invention: A Documentary History of the Junior and Community College Movement*. Westport, Conn.: Greenwood Press, 1986.

Dillon, T. J. *Writing Across the Curriculum Annual Report 1997–1998*. Monroe, Mich.: Monroe County Community College, 1998.

Doucette, D. *Community College Workforce Training Programs for Employees of Business, Industry, Labor, and Government: A Status Report*. Laguna Hills, Calif.: League for Innovation in the Community College, 1993.

Doucette, D., and Hughes, B. (eds.). *Assessing Institutional Effectiveness in Community Colleges*. Laguna Hills, Calif.: League for Innovation in the Community College, 1990.

Doucette, D. S., and Dayton, L. L. "A Framework for Student Development Practices: A Statement of the League for Innovation in the Community College." In W. L. Deegan and T. O'Banion (eds.), *Perspectives on Student Development*. New Directions for Community Colleges, no. 67. San Francisco: Jossey-Bass, 1989.

Dougherty, K. J. "The Politics of Community College Expansion: Beyond the Functionalist and Class-Reproduction Explanations." *American Journal of Education*, 1988, 96(3), 351–393.

Dougherty, K. J. *The Contradictory College: The Conflicting Origins, Impacts, and Futures of the Community College*. Albany: State University New York Press, 1994.

Dougherty, K. J., and Bakia, M. F. *The New Economic Development Role of the Community College*. New York: Community College Research Center, 1999.

Dougherty, K. J., and Hong, E. "Performance Accountability as Imperfect Panacea: The Community College Experience." In T. Bailey and V. Morest (eds.), *Defending the Community College Equity Agenda*. Baltimore: Johns Hopkins University Press, 2006.

Dougherty, K. J., and Reid, M. *Fifty States of Achieving the Dream: State Policies to Enhance Access to and Success in Community Colleges across the United States*. New York: Community College Research Center, Teachers College, Columbia University, 2007.

Douglas, B., and Harmening, T. *Comparative Financial Statistics for Public Two-Year Colleges: Fiscal Year 1998 National Sample*. Washington, D.C.: National Association of College and University Business Offices, 1999.

Dowd, A. C. "From Access to Outcome Equity: Revitalizing the Democratic Mission of the Community College." *Annals of the American Academy of Political and Social Science*, 2003, 586, 92–119.

Dowdy, H. B. *Manual for Trustees of the North Carolina Community College System*. Raleigh: North Carolina State Department of Community Colleges, 1987.

Doyle, W. R. "Community College Transfers and College Graduation: Whose Choice Matters Most?" *Change*, 2006, 38(3), 56–58.

Drury, R. L., and Mallory, W. D. "Entrepreneurship Education in the Virginia Community College System." *Inquiry*, 2000, 5(1), 45–57.

Dubin, R., and Taveggia, T. C. *The Teaching-Learning Paradox*. Eugene, Ore.: Center for the Advanced Study of Educational Administration, 1968.

Dufresne, R. J., and others. "Classtalk: A Classroom Communication for Active Learning." *Journal of Computing in Higher Education*, 1996, 7(2), 3–47.

Eaton, J. S. *Strengthening Collegiate Education in Community Colleges*. San Francisco: Jossey-Bass, 1994.

Ebersole, T. *A Learning Community for New Faculty*. Phoenix: League for Innovation in the Community Colleges, 2003.

Eddy, P. L. "Faculty Development in Rural Community Colleges." In P. L. Eddy and J. P. Murray (eds.), *Rural Community College: Teaching, Learning, and Leading in the Heartland*. New Directions for Community Colleges, no. 137. San Francisco: Jossey-Bass, 2007.

Education Commission of the States. *State Funding for Community Colleges: A 50-State Survey*. Denver: Education Commission of the States, Center for Community College Policy, 2000.

Educational Testing Service. *The Concern for Writing*. Princeton, N.J.: Educational Testing Service, 1978.

Educational Testing Service. *Measure of Academic Proficiency and Progress Test Overview*. Princeton, N.J.: Educational Testing Service, 2007.

Eells, W. C. *The Junior College*. Boston: Houghton Mifflin, 1931.

Eells, W. C. *Present Status of Junior College Terminal Education*. Washington, D.C.: American Association of Junior Colleges, 1941a.

Eells, W. C. *Why Junior College Terminal Education?* Washington, D.C.: American Association of Junior Colleges, 1941b.

Elder, L. Critical Thinking as the Key to the Learning College: A Professional Development Model. In C. M. McMahon (ed.), *Critical Thinking: Unfinished Business*. New Directions for Community Colleges, no.,130. San Francisco: Jossey-Bass, 2005.

Elder, L., and Paul, R. "Critical Thinking: The Nature of Critical and Creative Thought, Part II." *Journal of Developmental Education*, 2007, 30(3), 36–37.

Elsner, P. A., and Beauchamp, C. J. *Community Building: The Community College as Catalyst*. Washington, D.C.: American Association of Community Colleges, 2002.

ERIC Clearinghouse for Community Colleges. *National Transfer Assembly Results-Update for 1995*. Los Angeles: ERIC Clearinghouse for Community Colleges, 2001.

Erisman, W., and Contardo, J. B. *Learning to Reduce Recidivism: A 50-State Analysis of Postsecondary Correctional Education Policy*. Institute for Higher Education Policy, 2005.

Ernst, R. J. "Collective Bargaining: The Conflict Model as Norm." In W. L. Deegan and J. F. Gollattscheck (eds.), *Enduring Effective Governance*. New Directions for Community Colleges, no. 49. San Francisco: Jossey-Bass, 1985.

Evans, N. D., and Neagley, R. L. *Planning and Developing Innovative Community Colleges*. Upper Saddle River, N.J.: Prentice-Hall, 1973.

Ewell, P., and Boeke, M. *Critical Connections: Linking State's Unit Record Systems to Track Student Progress*. Boulder, Colo.: National Center for Higher Education Management Systems, 2007.

Ewell, P. T. *Implementing Assessment: Some Organizational Issues*. Boulder, Colo.: National Center for Higher Education Management Systems, 1987.

Ewell, P. T. *Accreditation and Student Learning Outcomes: A Proposed Point of Departure.* Washington, D.C.: Council for Higher Education Accreditation, 2001.

Ewens, T. *Think Piece on CBE and Liberal Education.* Bowling Green, Ohio: Bowling Green State University, 1977.

Feldman, K. A., and Newcomb, T. N. *The Impact of College on Students.* San Francisco: Jossey-Bass, 1969.

Fields, R. B. *The Community College Movement.* New York: McGraw-Hill, 1962.

Filipp, L. *Performance of Community College Transfer Students at Maryland Public Four-Year Colleges and Universities.* Annapolis: Maryland Higher Education Commission, 2004.

Finley, C. E. "The Relationship Between Unionization and Job Satisfaction Among Two-Year College Faculty." *Community College Review*, 1991, *19*(2), 53–60. (EJ 436 343)

Fischer, K. "Wanted: Low-Income High Achievers." *The Chronicle of Higher Education*, Jan. 26, 2007, p. A18.

Flanigan, P. K. *California Community Colleges Faculty Role in Shared Governance*, 1994.

"Flexibility Sought in Award of Educational Credit." *Chronicle of Higher Education*, Feb. 6, 1978, p. 9.

Florida Department of Education. *Taking Student Life Skills Course Increases Academic Success, Data Trend no. 31.* Tallahassee, Fla.: Department of Education, 2006.

Florida Department of Education. *The Fact Book: Report for the Florida Community College System.* Tallahassee: Florida Department of Education, 2007.

Florida State Board of Community Colleges. *Florida's Community Colleges: An Information Guide for Trustees.* Tallahassee: Florida State Board of Community Colleges, 1990.

Floyd, D. L., Skolnik, M. L., and Walker, K. P. (eds.). *The Community College Baccalaureate: Emerging Trends and Policy Issues.* Sterling, Va.: Stylus, 2005.

Fossey, R., and Wood, R. C. Academic Freedom and Tenure. In R. C. Cloud (ed.), *Legal Issues in Community Colleges*. New Directions for Community Colleges, no. 125. San Francisco: Jossey-Bass, 2004.

Fredrickson, J. "Today's Transfer Students: Who Are They?" *Community College Review*, 1998, 26(1), 43–51.

Freedman, I., and Freedman, E. "California Court Rules Reorganization is the Right of Administration." *Community College Week*, Apr. 9, 2007, p. 3.

Frye, J. H. *The Vision of the Public Junior College, 1940–1960*. Westport, Conn.: Greenwood Press, 1992.

Fryer, T. W., Jr., and Lovas, J. C. *Leadership in Governance: Creating Conditions for Successful Decision Making in the Community College*. San Francisco: Jossey-Bass, 1991.

Fukuyama, F. *The Great Disruption*. New York: Touchstone, 2000.

Gabler, N. "Class Dismissed." *Los Angeles Times*, Jan. 27, 2002, pp. M1, M6.

Gainous, F., and others. *Kansas Community Colleges Business Industry Relationships Report, 1985–86 School Year*. Topeka: Kansas State Department of Education, 1987.

Gallagher, E. A. *Jordan and Lange: The California Junior College as Protector of Teaching, Working Papers in Education, 94–1*. Palo Alto, Calif.: Hoover Institution, Stanford University, 1994.

Gallegos, M. T. "So Who Are Our Students Anyway? A Report on the Characteristics of Incoming Freshmen." *Research and Teaching in Developmental Education*, 2006, 23(1), 34–63.

Gardenhire-Crooks, A., Collado, H., and Ray, B. *Whole 'Nother World: Students Navigating Community College*. New York: MDRC, 2006.

Gardner, D. P., and others. *A Nation at Risk: The Imperative for Educational Reform. An Open Letter to the American People*. Washington, D.C.: National Commission on Excellence in Education, 1983.

Garmon, J. "Baccalaureate Community Colleges Provide More Opportunities." *Community College Times*, Feb. 2, 2007, p. 9.

Geesaman, J. A., Klassen, P. T., and Watson, R. "Community College Strategies Assessing General Education Using a Standardized Test: Challenges and Successful Solutions." *Assessment Update*, 2000, *12*(6) 8–9.

Geisel, V. *Online Student Support Services: A Best Practices Monograph*. Phoenix: League for Innovation in the Community College, 2006.

Gilder, J., and Rocha, J. "10,000 Cooperative Arrangements Serve 1.5 Million." *Community and Junior College Journal*, 1980, *51*(3), 11–17.

Gillespie, D. A., and Carlson, N. *Trends in Student Aid: 1963 to 1983*. Washington, D.C.: College Entrance Examination Board, 1983, 68 pp.

Girardi, A. G., and Stein, R. B. State Dual Credit Policy and Its Implications for Community Colleges: Lessons from Missouri for the 21st Century. In B. K. Townsend and S. B. Twombly (eds.), *Community Colleges: Policy in the Future Context*. Westport, Conn.: Ablex Publishing, 2001.

Gittell, M. "Reaching the Hard to Reach: The Challenge of Community-Based Colleges." *Change*, 1985, *17*(4), 51–60.

Glass, J. C. Jr., and Harrington, A. R. "Academic Performance of Community College Transfer Students and "Native" Students at a Large State University." *Community College Journal of Research and Practice*, 2002, *26*(5), 415–430.

Gleazer, E. J., Jr. *The Community College: Values, Vision, and Vitality*. Washington, D.C.: American Association of Community and Junior Colleges, 1980.

Gleick, J. *Chaos: Making a New Science*. New York: Penguin Books, 1987.

Goan, S. K., and Cunningham, A. F. *Differential Characteristics of 2-Year Post-secondary Institutions*. Washington, D.C.: U.S. Department of Education, 2007.

Goldman, L. H. *Cultural Affairs: A Vital Phase of Community Services*. Washington, D.C.: U.S. Department of Education, 1969.

Gottschalk, K. "Can Colleges Deal with High-Risk Community Problems?" *Community College Frontiers*, 1978, 6(4), 4–11.

Green, K. C. *Campus Computing, 2001: The Twelfth National Survey of Computing and Information Technology in American Higher Education*. Encino, Calif.: Campus

Computing Project, 2001.

Green, K. C. *Campus Computing 2006: The 17th National Survey of Computing and Information Technology in American Higher Education*. Encino, Calif.: The Campus Computing Project, 2006.

Green, T. F. *Predicting the Behavior of the Educational System*. Syracuse, N.Y.: Syracuse University Press, 1980.

Griffin, K. "Transfer Track Versus Workforce Development: Implication for Policy Changes in Florida Community Colleges." Paper presented at the Annual Conference of the Council for the Study of Community Colleges, Tampa, Fla., April 2007.

Grubb, W. N. "The Economic Benefits of Pre-Baccalaureate Education: Results from State and Local Studies." *CCRC Brief*, no. 3. New York: Community College Research Center, Teachers College, Columbia University, 1999.

Grubb, W. N. *Getting into the World: Guidance and Counseling in Community Colleges*. New York: Community College Research Center, Teachers College, Columbia University, 2001.

Grubb, W. N., and associates. *Honored but Invisible: An Inside Look at Teaching in Community Colleges*. New York: Routledge, 1999.

Grubb, W. N., and Kraskouskas, E. A. *A Time to Every Purpose: Integrating Occupational and Academic in Community Colleges and Technical Institutes*. Berkeley: National Center for Research in Vocational Education, University of California, Berkeley, 1992.

Gruber, D. *Building Community College CBO Partnerships: A Report to the William and Flora Hewlett Foundation*. New York: Workforce Strategy Center, 2004.

Guess, A. "The Yearly Report Card." *Inside Higher Ed*, June 1, 2007, n. p.

Guess, A. "A Community College Grows in Idaho." *Inside Higher Ed*, May 24, 2007, n.p.

Guskey, T. R., and Pigott, T. D. "Research on Group-Based Mastery Learning Programs: A Meta-Analysis." *Journal of Educational Research*, 1988, 80(4), 197–216.

Hagedorn, L. S., and Lee, M. *International Community College Students: The Neglected Minority?* Los Angeles: Center for Higher Education Policy Analysis, Rossier School of Education, University of Southern California, 2005.

Hagedorn, L. S., and Maxwell, B. *Research on Urban Community College Transfer and Retention:* The Los Angeles TRUCCS Project. Los Angeles: University of Southern California, 2002. (JC 020 353)

Hale, E. "Management Perspectives at the State Level." In A. M. Cohen, F. B. Brawer, and Associates (eds.), *Managing Community Colleges: A Handbook for Effective Practice.* San Francisco: Jossey-Bass, 1994.

Hamilton, J. *Relationship of Remedial Reading Needs to First-Attempt Grade Distributions in Introductory College Algebra at a Two-Year College: Fall 1992 to Fall 1997.* Gainesville, Ga.: Gainesville College, 1998.

Hamilton, J. M. *Impact of Georgia's College Preparatory Curriculum on Academic Success at Gainesville College.* Gainesville, Ga.: Gainesville College Office of Institutional Research and Planning, 1992.

Hammons, J. "The Department/Division Chairperson: Educational Leader?" *Community and Junior College Journal,* 1984, *54*(3), 3–7.

Hammons, L. D., and Mathews, J. G. "Characteristics of Students Who Successfully Complete Two-Year Degree Programs at an Urban, Historically Black, Community College." Paper presented at the Annual Meeting of the Mid-South Educational Research Association, Point Clear, Ala., Nov. 1999.

Hansman, C. A., and Wilson, A. L. "Teaching Writing in Community Colleges: A Situated View of How Adults Learn to Write in Computer-Based Writing Classrooms." *Community College Review,* 1998, *26*(1), 21–42.

Harlacher, E. L., and Gollattscheck, J. F. *"Editors' Notes."* In E. L. Harlacher and J. F. Gollattscheck (eds.), *Implementing Community-Based Education.* New Directions for Community Colleges, no. 21. San Francisco: Jossey-Bass, 1978.

Harlacher, E. L., and Ireland, J. "Community Services and Continuing Education: An Information Age Necessity." *Community Services Catalyst,* 1988, *18*(1), 3–5.

Harman, D. *Illiteracy: A National Dilemma.* New York: Cambridge Book Company, 1987.

Harper, H., and others. *Advisement and Graduation Information System*. Miami: Miami Dade Community College, 1981.

Harris, N. C., and Grede, J. F. *Career Education in Colleges: A Guide for Planning Two- and Four-Year Occupational Programs for Successful Employment*. San Francisco: Jossey-Bass, 1977.

Hawken, P. *Blessed Unrest: How the Largest Movement in the World Came into Being and Why No One Saw It Coming*. New York: Viking, 2007.

Haynes, F. T., and Polk, C. H. "Choosing a Rationale for Continuing Education." *Community Services Catalyst*, 1991, *16*(4), 1.

Heard, F. B. "The Development of a Computerized Curriculum Monitoring System to Ensure Student Success." Unpublished doctoral practicum, Nova University, 1987.

Helfgot, S. R. "Counseling at the Center: High Tech, High Touch." In S. R. Helfgot and M. M. Culp (eds.), *Promoting Student Success in the Community College*. New Directions for Student Services, no. 69. San Francisco: Jossey-Bass, 1995.

Hennessy, D., and Evans, R. "Reforming Writing Among Students in Community Colleges." *Community College Journal of Research and Practice*, 2005, *29*(4), 261–275.

Hickman, R. C., and Quinley, J. W. "A Synthesis of Local, State, and National Studies in Work Force Education and Training." Paper presented at the Thirty-Seventh Annual Forum of the Association for Institutional Research, Orlando, Fla., May 1997.

Hirsch, E. D., Jr. *Cultural Literacy*. Boston: Houghton Mifflin, 1987.

Hoachlander, G., Sikora, A. C., and Horn, L. *Community College Students Goals Academic Preparation and Outcomes*. Washington, D.C.: U.S. Department of Education, 2003.

Hobbs, R. L. *Academic and Developmental Services End of Year Status Report, 1987–88: Shelby State Community College*. Memphis, Tenn.: Shelby State Community College, 1988.

Hollinshead, B. S. "The Community College Program." *Junior College Journal*, 1936, *7*, 111–116.

Holton, B., Vaden, K., O'Shea, P., and Williams, J. *Academic Libraries: 2004*. Washington, D.C.: U.S. Department of Education, 2006.

Holton, N. *Service Learning in the Rural Community College*. Roscommon, Mich.: Kirtland Community College, 2003.

Hom, W. *A Statistical Analysis to Define the "Low-Transfer" California Community College*. Sacramento: California Community Colleges, Office of the Chancellor, 2000.

Hoos, I. *Systems Analysis in Public Policy: A Critique*. Berkeley: University of California Press, 1972.

Hoos, I. "Societal Aspects of Technology Assessment." *Technological Forecasting and Social Change*, 1979, *13*, 191–202.

Horn, L., Nevill, S., and Griffith, J. *Profiles of Undergraduates in U.S. Postsecondary Education Institutions, 2003–04: With a Special Analysis of Community College Students*. Washington, D.C.: U.S. Department of Education, 2006.

Howard, A., and others. *Instructional Computing in the Community Colleges of Washington State*. Olympia: Washington State Board for Community College Education, 1978.

Hunter, R., and Sheldon, M. S. *Statewide Longitudinal Study: Report on Academic Year 1979–80. Part 3: Fall Results*. Woodland Hills, Calif.: Los Angeles Pierce College, 1980.

Hussar, W. J., and Bailey, T. M. *Projection of Education Statistics to 2015*. Washington, D.C.: U.S. Department of Education, 2006.

Ignash, J. M. "The Scope and Status of English as a Second Language in U.S. Community Colleges." Unpublished doctoral dissertation, University of California, Los Angeles, 1994.

Ignash, J. M. "Who Should Provide Postsecondary Remedial/Developmental Education?" In J. Ignash (ed.), *Implementing Effective Policies for Remedial and Developmental Education*. New Directions for Community Colleges, no. 100. San Francisco: Jossey-Bass, 1997.

Illich, I. *Deschooling Society*. New York: HarperCollins, 1972.

"Illinois Colleges Sue Over Local Control." *Community College Times*, Oct. 24, 2006, p. 1.

Illinois Community College Board. *Curriculum Enrollment Summary in the Public Community Colleges of Illinois: 1975–76*. Springfield: Illinois Community College Board, 1976.

Illinois Community College Board. *2000 Follow-Up of Fiscal Year 1999 Occupational Program Graduates*. Springfield: Illinois Community College Board, 2000.

Illinois Community College Board. *Data and Characteristics of the Illinois Public Community College System*. Springfield: Illinois Community College Board, 2005.

Indiana Department of Workforce Development. Indiana Workforce Proficiency Panel Annual Report: Indiana Essential Skills and Technical Proficiencies Initiative. Indianapolis: Indiana Department of Workforce Development, 1996. 21 pp.

"Ivy Tech CC System Assesses General Education Outcomes with CAAP." *Activity*, 2007, 45(1), 6.

Ivy Tech Community College. *2005–06 Graduate Profile and Trend Report*. Indianapolis, Ind.: Ivy Tech Community College, 2007.

Jaschik, S. "Adjuncts and Graduation Rates." *Inside Higher Ed*, Oct. 16, 2006, n.p.

Jaschik, S. "Surge in Distance Ed at Community Colleges." *Inside Higher Ed*, Apr. 16, 2007, n.p.

Jaschik, S. "Early (Encouraging) Data on Early Colleges." *Inside Higher Ed*, Oct. 5, 2007, n.p.

Jaschik, S. "Promising Path on Remediation." *Inside Higher Ed*, Mar. 11, 2008, n.p.

Jencks, C. *Inequality*. New York: Basic Books, 1972.

Jencks, C., and Riesman, D. *The Academic Revolution*. New York: Doubleday, 1968.

Jenkins, D. *What Community College Policies and Practices Are Effective in Promoting Student Success? A Study of High and Low Impact Institutions*. New York: Community College Research Center, Teachers College, Columbia University, 2006.

Johnson, B. L. *General Education in Action*. Washington, D.C.: American Council on Education, 1952.

Johnson, D. C. "Managing Non-Profit Marketing." In R. E. Lahti (ed.), *Managing in a New Era*. New Directions for Community Colleges, no. 28. San Francisco: Jossey-Bass, 1979.

Joliet Junior College. *ACT Non-Returning Student Survey 2004–2005*. Joliet, Ill.: Joliet Junior College, 2005.

Kahlenberg, R. D. *Left Behind: Unequal Opportunity in Higher Education*. New York: Century Foundation, 2004.

Kane, H. R. "Honors Programs: A Case Study of Transfer Preparation. In F. S. Laanan (ed.), *Transfer Students: Trends and Issues*. New Directions for Community Colleges, no. 114. San Francisco: Jossey-Bass, 2001.

Kane, T. J., and Rouse, C. E. "The Community College: Educating Students at the Margin Between College and Work." *Journal of Economic Perspectives*, 1999, *13*(1), 63–84.

Kangas, J. *San Jose City College Withdrawing Students Study*. San Jose, Calif.: San Jose Evergreen Community College District, 1991.

Kansas Board of Regents. *Kansas Community Colleges Enrollment and Financial Statistics*. Topeka: Kansas Board of Regents, 2005.

Kaplin, W. A. *The Law of Higher Education: A Comprehensive Guide to Legal Implications of Administrative Decision Making*. (2nd ed.) San Francisco: Jossey-Bass, 1985.

Karabel, J. "Community Colleges and Social Stratification." *Harvard Educational Review*, 1972, *41*, 521–562.

Karabel, J. "Community Colleges and Social Stratification in the 1980s." In L. S. Zwerling (ed.), *The Community College and Its Critics*. New Directions for Community Colleges, no. 54. San Francisco: Jossey-Bass, 1986.

Karp, M. M., Bailey, T. R., Hughes, K. L., and Fermin, B. I. "State Dual Enrollment Policies: Addressing Access and Quality." *CCRC Brief, no. 25*. New York: Community College Research Center, Teachers College, Columbia University, 2005.

Kearney, R.C. *Labor Relations in the Public Sector*. Boca Raton, Fla.: CRC Press, 2001.

Kemerer, F. R., and Baldridge, J. V. *Unions on Campus: A National Study of the Consequences of Faculty Bargaining*. San Francisco: Jossey-Bass, 1975.

Kentucky Developmental Education Task Force. *Securing Kentucky's Future: A Plan for Improving College Readiness and Success*. Frankfort, Ky.: Council on Postsecondary Education, 2007.

Kinnick, M. K., and Kempner, K. "Beyond the Front Door Access: Attaining the Bachelor's Degree." *Research in Higher Education*, 1988, *29*(4), 299–318.

Kintzer, F. C. *Organization and Leadership of Two-Year Colleges: Preparing for the Eighties*. Gainesville: Institute of Higher Education, University of Florida, 1980a.

Kintzer, F. C. *Proposition 13: Implications for Community Colleges*. Los Angeles: ERIC Clearinghouse for Junior Colleges, 1980b.

Kintzer, F. C., Jensen, A., and Hansen, J. *The Multi-Institution Junior College District*. Los Angeles: ERIC Clearinghouse for Junior Colleges; Washington, D.C.: American Association of Junior Colleges, 1969.

Kintzer, F. C., and Wattenbarger, J. L. *The Articulation/Transfer Phenomenon: Patterns and Directions*. Washington, D.C.: Council of Universities and Colleges, American Association of Community and Junior Colleges, 1985.

Kirsch, I., Braun, H., Yamamoto, K., and Sum, A. *America's Perfect Storm: Three Forces Changing Our Nation's Future*. Princeton, N.J.: Educational Testing Service, 2007.

Kirsch, I. S., and Jungeblut, A. *Literacy: Profiles of America's Young Adults*. Princeton, N.J.: National Assessment of Education Progress, 1986.

Kirsch, I. S., Jungeblut, A., Jenkins, L., and Kolstad, A. *Adult Literacy in America: A First Look at the Results of the National Adult Literacy Survey.* Washington, D.C.: National Center for Education Statistics, U.S. Department of Education, 1993.

Kirst, M. "Who Needs It? Identifying the Proportion of Students Who Require Postsecondary Remedial Education is Virtually Impossible." *National Cross Talk,* 2007, *15*(1), 11–12.

Kisker, C. B. "Key Resources for Student Affairs Professionals in Learning-Centered Community Colleges." In S. R. Helfgot and M. M. Culp (eds.), *Community College Student Affairs: What Really Matters.* New Directions for Community Colleges, no. 131. San Francisco: Jossey-Bass, 2005.

Kisker, C. B. *Integrating High School and Community College: A Historical Policy Analysis.* Unpublished doctoral dissertation, University of California, Los Angeles, 2006.

Klemm, W. R. "Using Computer Conferencing in Teaching." *Community College Journal of Research and Practice,* 1998, *22*(5), 507–518.

Knapp, L. G., and others. *Trends in Student Aid: 1983 to 1993.* Update. New York: College Board, 1993.

Knapp, M. S. "Factors Contributing to the Development of Institutional Research and Planning Units in Community Colleges: A Review of the Empirical Evidence." Paper presented at the annual meeting of the American Educational Research Association, San Francisco, November 1979.

Koehler, G., and Burke, A. *Transforming the Treadmill into a Staircase: Preparing Nontraditional First-Generation College Attenders for Success.* Champaign, Ill.: Parkland College, 1998.

Koos, L. "Rise of the People's College." *The School Review,* 1947, *55*(3), 138–149.

Koos, L. V. *The Junior College.* Minneapolis: University of Minnesota Press, 1924.

Kulik, C.J.C., and others. "Effectiveness of Mastery Learning Programs: A Meta-Analysis." *Review of Educational Research,* 1990, *60*(2), 265–299.

Kuttner, B. "The Declining Middle." *Atlantic*, 1983, *252*(1), 60–64, 66–67, 69–72.

Laanan, F. S. Accountability in Community Colleges: Looking Forward Toward the 21st Century. In B. K. Townsend and S. B. Twombly (eds.), *Community Colleges: Policy in the Future Context*. Westport, Conn.: Ablex, 2001.

Lail, A. A. "Early Career Faculty Perceptions of their Teaching Preparedness and Professional Development in the North Carolina Community College System." Unpublished doctoral dissertation, The University of North Carolina at Greensboro, 2005.

Laird, J., DeBell, M., and Chapman, C. *Dropout Rates in the United States: 2004*. Washington, D.C.: National Center for Education Statistics, 2006.

Lander, V. L. "The Significance of Structure in Arizona Community College Districts: A Limited Study." Graduate seminar paper. University of Arizona, 1977.

Landsberg, M. "Grades Rising as Learning Is Lagging, Reports Finding." *Los Angeles Times*, Feb. 23, 2007, p. A14.

Lane Community College. *Workplace Training Project. Final Report for the National Workplace Literacy Program*. Eugene, Ore.: Lane Community College, 1998.

Lange, A. F. *The Lange Book: The Collected Writings of a Great Educational Philosopher*. San Francisco: Trade Publishing Company, 1927.

Lanham, R. A. *The Electronic World: Democracy, Technology and the Arts*. Chicago: University of Chicago Press, 1993.

Larson, R., King, L., McGee, M., and Shea, B. "Making Entrepreneurship Education Work: The REAL Enterprises Model." In Connecting Learning and Work: The Rural Experience: Proceedings of the School-to-Work in Rural Communities, Northeast Technical Assistance Conference, Saratoga Springs, N.Y., Nov. 1997.

Lederman, D. "Campus Accountability Proposals Evolve." *Inside Higher Ed*, June 26, 2006, n.p.

Lederman, D. "Anti-Lobbying Fever? Not in Higher Education." *Inside Higher Ed*, Dec. 21, 2006, n.p.

Lederman, D. "Taming the Student Loan Wild West." *Inside Higher Ed*, Jun. 7, 2007, n.p.

Lee, C. C., and Ramsey, C. J. "Multicultural Counseling: A New Paradigm for a New Century." In C. C. Lee (ed.), *Multicultural Issues in Counseling: New Approaches to Diversity*. (3rd ed.) Alexandria, Va.: American Counseling Association, 2006.

Lestina, R., and Curry, B. A. "Alternative Education/Alternative Revenue. A. Contract Training: Public and Private Sector Models." In J. L. Catanzaro and A. D. Arnold (eds.), *Alternative Funding Sources*. New Directions for Community Colleges, no. 68. San Francisco: Jossey-Bass, 1989.

Leveille, D. *Accountability in Higher Education: A Public Agenda for Trust and Cultural Change*. Berkeley: Center for Studies in Higher Education, University of California Berkeley, 2006.

Levin, H., and Calcagno, J. C. *Remediation in the Community College: An Evaluator's Perspective*. New York: Community College Research Center, Teachers College, Columbia University, 2007.

Levin, J. S. *Globalizing the Community College: Strategies for Change in the Twenty-First Century*. New York: Palgrave, 2001.

Levin, J. S. *Nontraditional Students and Community Colleges. The Conflict of Justice and Neoliberalism*. New York: Palgrave, 2007.

Levin, J. S., Kater, S., and Wagoner, R. L. *Community College Faculty: At Work in the New Economy*. New York: Palgrave, 2006.

Levine, D. O. *The American College and the Culture of Aspiration, 1915–40*. Ithaca, N.Y.: Cornell University Press, 1986.

Lewis, G., and Merisotis, J. P. *Trends in Student Aid: 1980 to 1987: Update*. Washington, D.C.: College Entrance Examination Board, 1987.

Lichtenberger, E. J., and Onyewu, N. *Virginia Department of Correctional Education's Incarcerated Youth Offender Program: A Historical Analysis*. Richmond: Virginia Department of Corrections, 2005.

Littlefield, W. N. *The Economic Impact of the Long Beach Community College District*. Long Beach, Calif.: Long Beach Community College District, 1982.

Lombardi, J. *Managing Finances in Community Colleges*. San Francisco: Jossey-Bass, 1973.

Lombardi, J. *The Duties and Responsibilities of the Department/Division Chairman in Community Colleges*. Los Angeles: ERIC Clearinghouse for Junior Colleges, 1974.

Lombardi, J. *Riding the Wave of New Enrollments*. Los Angeles: ERIC Clearinghouse for Junior Colleges, 1975.

Lombardi, J. *No or Low Tuition: A Lost Cause*. Los Angeles: ERIC Clearinghouse for Junior Colleges, 1976.

Lombardi, J. *Changing Administrative Relations Under Collective Bargaining*. Los Angeles: ERIC Clearinghouse for Junior Colleges, 1979.

Lombardi, J. V. "Regulating the New Consumerism." *Inside Higher Ed*, Sep. 26, 2006, pp. 15–17.

London, H. B. *The Culture of a Community College*. New York: Praeger, 1978.

Lucas, J. A., and Meltesen, C. *Study of Students Who Withdrew from Courses, Summer 1988–Spring 1990*. Palatine, Ill.: William Rainey Harper College, 1991.

Lukenbill, J. D. *Tuition Scholarship Program*. Unpublished memorandum. Miami: Miami-Dade College, 2004.

"Lumina Renews Commitment to Achieving the Dream." *Community College Times*, Mar. 16, 2007, pp. 5, 9

Lynch, R., and others. *Community College Involvement in Contract Training and Other Economic Development Activities*. Washington, D.C.: American Association of Community and Junior Colleges, 1991.

Marashio, P. *Pedagogy Journal*, 1999, 6. Concord: New Hampshire Community Technical Colleges, 1999.

March, J. G., and Weiner, S. S. "Leadership Blues." In W. E. Piland and D. B. Wolf (eds.), *Help Wanted: Preparing Community College Leaders in a New Century*. New Directions for Community Colleges, no. 123. San Francisco: Jossey-Bass, 2003.

Martorana, S. V., and Piland, W. E. "Promises and Pitfalls in Serving Organized Community-Based Group Interests." In S. V. Martorana and W. E. Piland (eds.), *Designing Programs for Community Groups*. New Directions for Community Colleges, no. 45. San Francisco: Jossey-Bass, 1984.

Maryland State Board for Community Colleges. *Statewide Master Plan for Community Colleges in Maryland, Fiscal Years 1978–1987*. Annapolis: Maryland State Board for Community Colleges, 1977.

Maryland State Board for Community Colleges. *The Role of Community Colleges in Preparing Students for Transfer to Four-Year Colleges and Universities: The Maryland Experience*. Annapolis: Maryland State Board for Community Colleges, 1983.

Maryland State Board for Community Colleges. *Blueprint for Quality: Final Report of the Committee on the Future of Maryland Community Colleges*. Annapolis: Maryland State Board for Community Colleges, 1986.

Maryland State Board for Community Colleges. *Maryland Community Colleges: 1987 Program Evaluations*. Annapolis: Maryland State Board for Community Colleges, 1988.

Massachusetts Community College Development Education Committee. *Access and Quality: Improving the Performance of Massachusetts Community College Developmental Education Programs*. Boston: Massachusetts Community College Development Education Committee, 1998.

Mawdsley, R. D. Student Rights, Safety, and Codes of Conduct. In R. C. Cloud (ed.), *Legal Issues in Community Colleges*. New Directions for Community Colleges, no. 125. San Francisco: Jossey-Bass, 2004.

McCabe, R. H. (ed.). *The American Community Colleges: Nexus for Workforce Development*. Mission Viejo, Calif.: League Publications, 1997.

McCabe, R. H. *No One to Waste: A Report to Public Decision-Makers and Community College Leaders*. Washington, D.C.: American Association of Community Colleges, 2000.

McDonough, M. L. "A New Degree for the Community College: The Associate of Arts in Teaching. In B. K. Townsend and J. M. Ignash (eds.), *The Role of the Community College in Teacher Education*. New Directions for Community Colleges, no. 121. San Francisco: Jossey-Bass, 2003.

McGee, E. A. "The Role of the President in Supporting the College's Foundation." In M. D. Milliron, G. E. De Los Santos, and B. Browning (eds.), *Successful Approaches to Fundraising and Development*. New Directions for Community Colleges, no. 124, San Francisco: Jossey-Bass, 2003.

McGuire, K. B. *State of the Art in Community-Based Education in the American Community College*. Washington, D.C.: Association of American Community and Junior Colleges, 1988.

McIntyre, J. F. "Individualized Mastery, the Adaptable, Efficient, and Economical Link to the Future." *Education-Canada*, 1991, *31*(4), 36–40, 47.

McKeachie, W. J. "Research on Teaching at the College and University Level." In N. Gage (ed.), *Handbook of Research on Teaching*. Skokie, Ill.: Rand McNally, 1963.

McMahon, C. M. (ed.). *Critical Thinking: Unfinished Business*. New Directions for Community Colleges, no. 130. San Francisco: Jossey-Bass, 2005.

Medsker, L. L. *The Junior College: Progress and Prospect*. New York: McGraw-Hill, 1960.

Medsker, L. L., and Tillery, D. *Breaking the Access Barriers: A Profile of Two-Year Colleges*. New York: McGraw-Hill, 1971.

Meier, K. "The Community College Mission: History and Theory, 1930–2000." Unpublished doctoral dissertation, University of Arizona, 2008.

Mellow, G. "Call for Equity for Community Colleges" *Inside Higher Ed*, Feb. 11, 2008, n.p.

Miami Dade College. *About the Honors College*. Miami: Miami Dade College, 2007. http://www.mdc.edu/honorscollege/. Accessed Oct. 1, 2007.

Michaels, W. B. *The Trouble with Diversity: How We Learned to Love Identity and Ignore Inequality*. New York: Metropolitan, 2006.

Michigan State Board for Public Community Colleges. *Michigan Community Colleges Activities Classification Structure (ACS) 1997–98 Data Book*. Lansing: Michigan State Board for Public Community Colleges, 1999.

Middleton, L. "Emphasis on Standards at Miami-Dade Leads to 8,000 Dismissals and Suspensions in Three Years." *Chronicle of Higher Education*, Feb. 3, 1981, pp. A3–A4.

Monroe, C. R. *Profile of the Community College: A Handbook*. San Francisco: Jossey-Bass, 1972.

Morest, V. S., and Jenkins, D. *Institutional Research and the Culture of Evidence at Community Colleges*. New York: Community College Research Center, Teachers College, Columbia University, 2007.

Moriarty, D. F. "The President's Office." In A. M. Cohen, F. B. Brawer, and Associates (eds.), *Managing Community Colleges: A Handbook for Effective Practice*. San Francisco: Jossey-Bass, 1994.

Moriarty, J., and Savarese, M. *Directory of Faculty Contracts and Bargaining Agents in Institutions of Higher Education*. New York: National Center for Study of Collective Bargaining in Higher Education and the Professions, 2006.

Morrison, D. G., and Martorana, S. V. *Criteria for the Establishment of 2-Year*. Washington, D.C.: U.S. Department of Health, Education and Welfare, 1961.

Mounfield L. A. "Activities Used by Community College Faculty to Maintain Discipline Currency: Identification and Influencing Factors." Unpublished doctoral dissertation, University of South Carolina, 2005.

Mundt, J. C. "State vs. Local Control: Reality and Myth over Concern for Local Autonomy." In S. F. Charles (ed.), *Balancing State and Local Control*. New Directions for Community Colleges, no. 23. San Francisco: Jossey-Bass, 1978.

Murray, J. P. "The Genesis of the Community College." *Community College Review*, 1988–89, 9(1–2), 25–34.

Myran, G. A. "Antecedents: Evolution of the Community-Based College." In E. L. Harlacher and J. F. Gollattscheck (eds.), *Implementing Community-Based Education*. New Directions for Community Colleges, no. 21. San Francisco: Jossey-Bass, 1969.

National Center for Education Statistics (NCES). *Opening Fall Enrollments in Higher Education*. Washington, D.C.: U.S. Department of Education, 1963–1975.

National Center for Education Statistics. *Digest of Education Statistics*. Washington, D.C.: U.S. Department of Education, 1970–2006.

National Center for Education Statistics. *Scholarship and Fellowship Expenditures*. Washington, D.C.: U.S. Department of Education, 1986.

National Center for Education Statistics. *Characteristics of the Nation's Postsecondary Institutions: Academic Year 1993–94*. Washington, D.C.: U.S. Department of Education, 1994a.

National Center for Education Statistics. *Descriptive Summary of 1989–90 Beginning Postsecondary Students: Two Years Later*. Washington, D.C.: U.S. Department of Education, 1994b.

National Center for Education Statistics. *Faculty and Instructional Staff: Who Are They and What Do They Do?* Washington, D.C.: U.S. Department of Education, 1994c.

National Center for Education Statistics. *Vocational Education in G-7 Countries: Profiles and Data*. Washington, D.C.: U.S. Department of Education, 1994d.

National Center for Education Statistics. *Degrees and Other Awards Conferred by Institutions of Higher Education: 1991–1992*. Washington, D.C.: National Center for Education Statistics, 1994e.

National Center for Education Statistics. *Descriptive Summary of 1995–96 Beginning Postsecondary Students with Profiles of Students Entering Two- and Four-Year Institutions*. Washington, D.C.: National Center for Education Statistics, 1998.

National Center for Education Statistics. Projection of Education Statistics to 2011. Washington, D.C.: National Center for Education Statistics, 2001.

National Center for Education Statistics. Projections of Education Statistics to 2014. Washington, D.C.: National Center for Education Statistics, 2004.

National Center for Education Statistics. Condition of Education. Washington D.C.: U.S. Department of Education, 2007.

National Center for the Study of Collective Bargaining in Higher Education and the Professions. Directory of Faculty Contracts and Bargaining Agents in Institutions of Higher Education. New York: National Center for the Study of Collective Bargaining in Higher Education and the Professions, 1974–1994.

New Jersey State Department of Higher Education. Fall 1993 Basic Skills Test Results: Update and Special Analysis. Trenton: New Jersey State Department of Higher Education, 1994.

Nickens, J. M. "Who Takes Community Service Courses and Why." Community/ Junior College Research Quarterly, 1977, 2(1), 11–19.

Nitzke, J., and Wacker, M. E. Dropping Out at Western Iowa Tech Community College: A Report Summarizing Focus Group Interviews. Sioux City, Iowa: Western Iowa Tech Community College, 2001.

North Carolina Community College System. Data Trends and Briefings. Raleigh: North Carolina Community College System, 2006.

North Carolina Community College System. A Matter of Facts: The North Carolina Community College System Fact Book. Raleigh: North Carolina Community College System, 2007a.

North Carolina Community College System. 2007 Critical Success Factors. Raleigh: North Carolina Community College System, 2007b.

Northern Virginia Community College. NVCC Non-returning Student Survey Report. Annandale, Va. Northern Virginia Community College, 2000.

Nunes, M. "Humanities on (the) Line: Classrooms, Space, and the Supplement." Paper presented at the annual conference of the League for Innovation in Community College, Nov. 1996, Phoenix, Ariz.

O'Banion, T. New Directions in Community College Student Personnel Programs. Washington, D.C.: American College Personnel Association, 1971.

O'Banion, T. "A Learning College for the 21st Century." *Community College Journal*. 1996, 66(3), 18–23.

O'Banion, T. *Creating More Learning-Centered Community Colleges*. Mission Viejo, Calif.: League for Innovation in the Community College, 1997.

O'Banion, T. *An Inventory for Learning-Centered Colleges*. Laguna Hills, Calif.: League for Innovation in the Community College, 1999.

O'Brien, T. P. "Application of the DACUM Occupational Analysis Methodology to Health Occupations Education." *Journal of Health Occupations Education*, 1989, 4(2), 52–71.

Oliver, R. Moving *Beyond Instructional Comfort Zones with Online Courses*. Perth, Western Australia: Murdoch University, 2004.

Organization for Economic Co-operation and Development. *Education at a Glance*. Paris: Organization for Economic Co-Operation and Development, 2006.

Orfield, G., and Paul, F. G. *State Higher Education Systems and College Competition*. Ford Foundation, 1992.

Orr, M. T., and Bragg, D. D. *"Policy Directions for K-14 Education—Looking to the Future."* In B. K. Townsend and S. B. Twombly (eds.), *Community Colleges: Policy in the Future Context*. Westport, Conn.: Ablex, 2001.

Ottinger, C. A. *Fact Book on Higher Education*. Washington, D.C.: American Council on Education, 1987.

Outcalt, C. L. "A Profile of the Community College Professoriate, 1975–2000." Unpublished doctoral dissertation, University of California, Los Angeles, 2002.

Outcault, C. L. (Ed.). *Community College Faculty: Characteristics, Practices, and Challenges*. New Directions for Community Colleges, no. 118. San Francisco: Jossey-Bass, 2002.

Outcalt, C. L., and Kisker, C. B. "The Nexus of Access and Curriculum: Analyzing the Teaching of Developmental and Honors Courses within Community

Colleges." Paper presented at the Annual Conference of the Association of Higher Education, Portland, Oregon, November 2003.

Oxford, L., Proctor, K., and Slate, J. R. "Computer-based Instruction and Achievement of Adult Learners." *Michigan Community College Journal: Research and Practice,* 1998, 4(2), 77–84. (EJ 575 956)

Pace, C. R. *Measuring Outcomes of College: Fifty Years of Findings and Recommendations for the Future.* San Francisco: Jossey-Bass, 1979.

Palmer, J. "The Characteristics and Educational Objectives of Students Serviced by Community College Vocational Curricula." Unpublished doctoral dissertation, University of California at Los Angeles, 1987a.

Palmer, J. *Community, Technical, and Junior Colleges: A Summary of Selected National Data.* Washington, D.C.: American Association of Community and Junior Colleges, 1987b.

Palmer, J. C. "Institutional Accreditation, Student Outcomes Assessment, and the Open-Ended Institution." In C. Prager (ed.), *Accreditation of the Two-Year College.* New Directions for Community Colleges, no. 83. San Francisco: Jossey-Bass, 1993.

Palmer, J. C. (ed.), *How Community Colleges Can Create Productive Collaborations with Local Schools.* New Directions for Community Colleges, no. 111. San Francisco: Jossey-Bass, 2000.

Palmer, J. C. "Disciplinary Variations in the Work of Full-time Faculty Members." In C. L. Outcault (ed.), *Community College Faculty: Characteristics, Practices, and Challenges.* New Directions for Community Colleges, no. 118. San Francisco: Jossey-Bass, 2002.

Palmer, J. C., and Gillilan, S. H. *"State Appropriations for Higher Education, 2000–1."* *Chronicle of Higher Education,* Dec. 15, 2000, n.p.

Pankuch, B. J. *Multimedia in Lectures on the World Wide Web.* Princeton, N.J.: Princeton University, Mid-Career Fellowship Program, 1998.

Park, R. "Proffered Advice: Three Presidential Reports." *UCLA Educator,* 1977, 19(3), 53–59.

Parkman, F. "The Tale of the Ripe Scholar." *Nation*, 1869, 9, 559–560.

Parnell, D. *Associate Degree Preferred*. Washington, D.C.: American Association of Community and Junior Colleges, 1985.

Pascarella, E. T., and Terenzini, P. T. *How College Affects Students: Findings and Insights from Twenty Years of Research*. San Francisco: Jossey-Bass, 1991.

Pascarella, E. T., and Terenzini, P. T. *How College Affects Students: A Third Decade of Research*. (2nd ed.) San Francisco: Jossey-Bass, 2005.

Patton, M. "Data Don't Sit on a Shelf in Washington State." *Community College Times*, Jan. 7, 2007, p. 3.

Paul, R. The State of Critical Thinking Today. In C. M. McMahon (ed.), *Critical Thinking: Unfinished Business*. New Directions for Community Colleges, no. 130. San Francisco: Jossey-Bass, 2005.

Pedersen, R. "State Government and the Junior College, 1901–1946." *Community College Review*, 1987, *14*(4), pp. 48–52.

Pedersen, R. "Small Business and the Early Public Junior College." *Community, Technical, and Junior College Journal*, 1988, 59(1), pp. 44–46.

Pedersen, R. "Workforce Education Too Narrowly Focused." *Community College Week*, Mar. 1994, p. 4.

Pedersen, R. P. "The Origins and Development of the Early Public Junior College: 1900–1940." Unpublished doctoral dissertation, Columbia University, 2000.

Percy, W. *The Moviegoer*. New York: Avon Books, 1980.

Perryman, G. *Using Multimedia for Teaching Analysis in History of Modern Architecture. Issues of Education at Community Colleges*. Princeton, N.J.: Princeton University, Mid-Career Fellowship Program, 1998.

Peterson, M. W., Einarson, M. K., Augustine, C. H., and Vaughan, D. S. *Institutional Support for Student Assessment: Methodology and Results of a National Survey*. Palo Alto, Calif.: National Center for Postsecondary Improvement, 1999.

Peterson, M. W., and Mets, L. A. "An Evolutionary Perspective on Academic Governance, Management, and Leadership." In M. W. Peterson and L. A. Mets (eds.), *Key Resources on Higher Education Governance, Management, and Leadership: A Guide to the Literature*. San Francisco: Jossey-Bass, 1987.

Peterson's Guide to Two-Year Colleges, 1995. Princeton, N.J.: Peterson's, 1994.

Philips, J. *Institutions Providing Community College Functions in Other Countries: A Survey of Web Listings*. Los Angeles: UCLA Community College Studies, 2007.

Phillippe, K. Student Financial Aid in Community Colleges. Washington D.C.: American Association of Community Colleges, 1994.

Piland, W. E. "The Governing Board." In A. M. Cohen, F. B. Brawer, and Associates (eds.), *Managing Community Colleges: A Handbook for Effective Practice*. San Francisco: Jossey-Bass, 1994.

Piland, W. E., McFarlin, A., and Murillo, L. "Internship Program Seeks to Increase Diversity Among College Faculty." *Community College Journal*, 1999, 69(3), 30–37.

Pincus, F. L. "The False Promise of Community Colleges: Class Conflict and Vocational Education." *Harvard Educational Review*, 1980, 50(3), 332–361.

Plucker, F. E. "A Developmental Model for the Community/Junior College." *Community College Review*, 1987, 15(3), 26–32.

Portolan, J. S. "Developing Statewide Organization and Exploring a Redefined Role for Instructional Administrators in California Community Colleges." Unpublished doctoral dissertation, University of California, Los Angeles, 1992.

Potter, G. E. "The Law and the Board." In V. Dziuba and W. Meardy (eds.), *Enhancing Trustee Effectiveness*. New Directions for Community Colleges, no. 15. San Francisco: Jossey-Bass, 1976.

Prentice, M., Robinson, G., and McPhee, S. *Service Learning in Community Colleges: 2003 National Survey Results*. Washington, D.C.: American Association of Community Colleges, 2003.

Prince George's Community College. *Underprepared Students: Placement, Enrollment, and Achievement. Enrollment Analysis*. Largo, Md.: Prince George's Community College, Office of Institutional Research and Analysis, 1999.

Prince, D., and Jenkins, D. *Building Pathways to Success for Low-Skill Adult Students: Lessons for Community College Policy and Practice From a Statewide Longitudinal Tracking Study*. New York: Community College Research Center, Teachers College, Columbia University, 2005.

Prince, H. *Money on the Table: State Initiatives to Improve Financial Aid Participation. An Achieving the Dream Policy Brief*. Boston: Jobs for the Future, 2006.

Purnell, R., and Blank, S. *Support Success: Services That May Help Low-Income Students Succeed in Community College*. New York: MDRC, 2004.

Quinley, J. W., and Cantrell, J. E. *Preparing the Work Force for the 21st Century*. Spartanburg, S.C.: Spartanburg Technical College, 1998.

Rasor, R. E., and Barr, J. *Survey Sampling of Community College Students: For Better or for Worse*. Sacramento, Calif.: American River College, 1998.

Ravitch, D. "Curriculum in Crisis: Connections Between Past and Present." In J. H. Burzell (ed.), *Challenge to American Schools: The Case for Standards and Values*. New York: Oxford University Press, 1985.

Redden, E. "'Branding' Community Colleges Abroad." *Inside Higher Ed*, July, 26, 2007, n.p. www.insidehighered.com/news/2007/07/26/ccabroad. Accessed Oct. 1, 2007.

Reed, C. "The Silicon Ceiling: Technology, Literacy, and the Community College Student." Paper presented at the Forty-Seventh Annual Meeting of the Conference on College Composition and Communication, Milwaukee, Wis., Mar. 1996.

Reiss, D. *From WAC to CCCAC: Writing Across the Curriculum Becomes Communication, Collaboration, and Critical Thinking (and Computers) Across the Curriculum at Tidewater Community College*. Virginia Beach, Va.: Tidewater Community College, 1996.

Rhoads, R. A., and Valadez, J. R. *Democracy, Multiculturalism, and the Community College: A Critical Perspective*. New York: Garland, 1996.

Richardson, R. C., Jr. (ed.) *Reforming College Governance*. New Directions for Community Colleges, no. 10. San Francisco: Jossey-Bass, 1975.

Richardson, R. C., Jr., and Bender, L. W. *Fostering Minority Access and Achievement in Higher Education: The Role of Urban Community Colleges and Universities.* San Francisco: Jossey-Bass, 1987.

Richardson, R. C., Jr., and de los Santos, G. E. "Statewide Governance Structures and Two-Year Colleges." In B. K. Townsend and S. B. Twombly (eds.), *Community Colleges: Policy in the Future Context.* Westport, Conn.: Ablex, 2001.

Richardson, R. C., Jr., Fisk, E. C., and Okun, M. A. *Literacy in the Open-Access College.* San Francisco: Jossey-Bass, 1983.

Richardson, R. C., Jr., and Leslie, L. L. *The Impossible Dream? Financing Community College's Evolving Mission.* Washington, D.C.: American Association of Community and Junior Colleges, 1980.

Richardson, R. C., Jr., and Wolverton, M. "Leadership Strategies." In A. M. Cohen, F. B. Brawer, and Associates (eds.), *Managing Community Colleges: A Handbook for Effective Practice.* San Francisco: Jossey-Bass, 1994.

Riley, M. *The Community College General Academic Assessment: Combined Districts, 1983–84.* Los Angeles: Center for the Study of Community Colleges, 1984.

Robinson, G. Community Colleges Broadening Horizons Through Service Learning, 1997–2000. Washington, D.C. American Association of Community Colleges, 1999.

Robinson, G. "Service Learning." *Community College Times*, Jan. 5, 2007, p. 3.

Roessler, B. C. "A Quantitative Study of Revenue and Expenditures at United States Public Community Colleges, 1980–2001." Unpublished doctoral dissertation, University of North Texas, 2006.

Rosberg, W. H. *American Government: An Introduction Using Microcase with Distance Learners.* Cedar Rapids, Iowa: Kirkwood Community College, 1997.

Rosenbaum, J. R., Redline, J., and Stephan, J. L. "Community College: The Unfinished Revolution." *Issues in Science and Technology*, 2007, *23*(4), 49–56.

Rosenfeld, S. A. *Community College/Cluster Connections: Specialization and Competitiveness in the U.S. and Europe.* New York: Community College Research Center, 1998.

Roueche, J. E., and Boggs, J. R. *Junior College Institutional Research: The State of the Art.* Los Angeles: ERIC Clearinghouse for Junior Colleges, and Washington, D.C.: American Association of Junior Colleges, 1968.

Roueche, J. E., Kemper, C. S., and Roueche, S. D. Learning Colleges: Looking for Revolution But Remembering Evolution." *Community College Journal,* 2006–07, *77*(3), 29–33.

Roueche, J. E., and Roueche, S. D. *High Stakes, High Performance: Making Remedial Education Work.* Washington, D.C.: American Association of Community Colleges, 1999.

Roueche, J. E., Taber, L. S., and Roueche, S. D. *The Company We Keep.* Washington, D.C.: American Association of Community Colleges, 1995.

Rouseff-Baker, F., and Holm, A. "Engaging Faculty and Students in Classroom Assessment of Learning." In A. M. Serban and J. Friendlander (eds.), *Developing and Implementing Assessment of Student Learning Outcomes.* New Directions for Community Colleges, no. 126. San Francisco: Jossey-Bass, 2004.

Rowe, D. "Environmental Literacy and Sustainability as Core Requirements: Success Stories and Models." In W. L Filho (ed.), *Teaching Sustainability at Universities.* New York: Peter Lang, 2002.

Rowh, M. C. "Job Duties of Institutional Researchers in Two-Year Colleges." *Community College Quarterly of Research and Practice,* 1990, *14*(1), 35–44.

RP Group for California Community Colleges. *Partnership for Excellence (PFE) Evaluation Project. Summary of Peer Review Teams for PFE Evaluation Project.* Sacramento: RP Group for California Community Colleges, 2001.

RP Group for California Community Colleges. *The Research and Planning Prospectus for California Community Colleges.* Sacramento: RP Group for California Community Colleges, 2004.

RP Group for California Community Colleges. *Basic Skills as a Foundation for Student Success in California Community Colleges*. Sacramento: RP Group for California Community Colleges, 2007.

Rubinson, R. "Class Formation, Politics, and Institutions: Schooling in the United States." *American Journal of Sociology*, 1986, 92(3), 519–548.

Rudolph, F. *Curriculum: A History of the American Undergraduate Course of Study Since 1636*. San Francisco: Jossey-Bass, 1977.

Salt Lake Community College. *Non-Returning Student Follow-Up Survey Report*. Salt Lake, Utah: Salt Lake Community College, 2006.

Salzman, H., Moss, P., and Tilly, C. *The New Corporate Landscape and Workforce Skills*. Palo Alto, Calif.: National Center for Postsecondary Improvement, Stanford University, School of Education, 1998.

Sanchez, J. R., and Laanan, F. S. (eds.), *Determining the Economic Benefits of Attending Community College*. New Directions for Community Colleges, no. 104. San Francisco: Jossey-Bass, 1998.

Sandeen, A. "Educating the Whole Student: The Growing Importance of Student Affairs." *Change*, 2004, 36(3), 28–33.

Santa Monica College. *Learning Communities*. Santa Monica, Calif.: Santa Monica College, 2007.

Schneider, B. L., and Stevenson, D. *The Ambitious Generation: America's Teenagers, Motivated But Directionless*. New Haven, Conn.: Yale University Press, 1999.

Schuetz, P. *Shared Governance in Community Colleges*. Los Angeles: ERIC Clearinghouse for Community Colleges, 1999.

Schuyler, G. "ERIC Review: The Assessment of Community College Economic Impact on the Local Community or State." *Community College Review*, 1997, 25(2).

Schuyler, G. "A Historical and Contemporary View of the Community College Curriculum." In G. Schuyler (ed.), *Trends in Community College Curriculum*.

New Directions for Community Colleges, no. 108. San Francisco: Jossey-Bass, 1999a.

Schuyler, G. (ed.). *Trends in Community College Curriculum.* New Directions for Community Colleges, no. 108. San Francisco: Jossey-Bass, 1999b.

Scoggin, D., and Styron, R. A. "Factors Associated with Student Withdrawal from Community College." *Community College Enterprise*, 2006, Spring, 1–7.

Scrivener, S., Wavelet, M., and Sagness, J. *Early Assessment of Opening Doors Enhanced Services.* New York: MDRC, 2003.

Seidman, E. *In the Words of the Faculty: Perspectives on Improving Teaching and Educational Quality in Community Colleges.* San Francisco: Jossey-Bass, 1985.

Sengupta, R., and Jepsen, C. "California's Community College Students." *California Counts: Populations Trends and Profiles*, 2006, 8(2) 1–24.

Seybert, J. A. (ed.). *Benchmarking: An Essential Tool for Assessment, Improvement, and Accountability.* New Directions for Community Colleges, no. 134. San Francisco: Jossey-Bass, 2006.

Shaw, K. M., Valadez, J. R., and Rhoads, R. A. (eds.). *Community Colleges as Cultural Texts: Qualitative Explorations of Organizational and Student Culture.* Albany: State University of New York Press, 1999.

Sinclair, U. B. *Goose-Step: A Study of American Education.* New York: AMS Press, 1976. (Originally published 1923)

Slavin, R. E. "Mastery Learning Reconsidered." *Review of Educational Research*, 1990, 60(2), 300–302.

Smith, G., and Pather, J. E. "SACS' Effectiveness Criterion: A Self-Analysis Based upon the 'Must' Statements." Paper presented at the annual meeting of the Southern Association for Institutional Research and the Society for College and University Planning, Southern Regions, Pipestem, W. Va., October 1986.

Snow, C. P. *The Two Cultures and the Scientific Revolution.* New York: Cambridge University Press, 1959.

Solmon, L. C. "The Problems of Incentives." In H. F. Silberman and M. B. Ginsburg (eds.), *Easing the Transition from Schooling to Work*. New Directions for Community Colleges, no. 16. San Francisco: Jossey-Bass, 1976.

Solmon, L. C. "Rethinking the Relationship Between Education and Work." *UCLA Educator*, 1977, *19*(3), 18–31.

South Carolina Technical College System. *South Carolina Technical Education System. Program Evaluation Report*. Columbia: South Carolina Technical College System, 1997.

Spurling, S. *Progress and Success of English, ESL and Mathematics Students at City College of San Francisco*. San Francisco: City College of San Francisco, 1998.

Stanley, L., and Ambron, J. (eds.). *Writing Across the Curriculum in Community Colleges*. New Directions for Community Colleges, no. 73. San Francisco: Jossey-Bass, 1991.

Starrak, J. A., and Hughes, R. M. *The Community College in the United States*. Ames: Iowa State College Press, 1954.

Stone, I. F. *The Trial of Socrates*. Boston: Little, Brown, 1987.

Striplin, J. C. "ERIC Review: An Examination of Non-Liberal Arts Course Transferability in California." *Community College Review*, 2000, *28*(1), 67–78.

Sullivan, P. "What Is College-Level Writing?" *Teaching English in the Two Year College*, 2003, *30*(4), 374–90.

Study Group on the Conditions of Excellence in American Higher Education. *Involvement in Learning: Realizing the Potential of American Higher Education*. Washington, D.C.: National Institute of Education, 1984. (ED 246 833)

Talbott, L. H. "Community Problem Solving." In H. M. Holcomb (ed.), *Reaching Out Through Community Service*. New Directions for Community Colleges, no. 14. San Francisco: Jossey-Bass, 1976.

Tennessee Higher Education Commission. *Employer Satisfaction Project 2002–2003: 2000–2005 Performance Funding Cycle, 2003*. Nashville: Tennessee Higher Education Commission, 2003.

Terry, S. L., Hardy, D. E., and Katsinas, S. G. "Classifying Community Colleges: How Rural Community Colleges Fit." In P. Eddy and J. Murray (eds.), *Rural Community Colleges: Teaching, Learning, and Leading in the Heartland*. New Directions for Community Colleges, no. 137. San Francisco: Jossey-Bass, 2007.

Texas Higher Education Coordinating Board. *Institutional Developmental Education Plans and the Texas Success Initiative*. Austin: Texas Higher Education Coordinating Board, 2004.

Thornton, J. W., Jr. *The Community Junior College*. (2nd ed.). New York: Wiley, 1966.

Thornton, J. W., Jr. *The Community Junior College*. (3rd ed.). New York: Wiley, 1972.

Tidewater Community College. *Biennial Transfer Student Report: 2001–02 and 2002–03 Academic Years*. Norfolk, Va.: Tidewater Community College, 2005.

Tinto, V. "College Proximity and Rates of College Attendance." *American Educational Research Journal*, 1973, *10*(4), 277–293.

Tinto, V. "Dropout from Higher Education: A Theoretical Synthesis of Recent Research." *Review of Educational Research*, 1975, *45*(1), 89–125.

Tollefson, T. A., Garrett, R. L., and Ingram, W. G. *Fifty State Systems of Community Colleges: Mission, Governance, Funding and Accountability*. Johnson City, Tenn.: Overmountain Press, 1999.

Tovar, E., and Simon, M. A. *Facilitating Student Success for Entering California Community College Students: How One Institution Can Make an Impact*. Santa Monica, Calif.: Santa Monica College, 2003.

Townsend, B. K. *"Transfer Rates: A Problematic Criterion for Measuring the Community College."* In T. H. Bers and H. D. Calhoun (eds.), *Next Steps for the Community College*. New Directions for Community Colleges, no. 117. San Francisco: Jossey-Bass, 2002.

Townsend, B. K., *"A Cautionary View."* In D. L. Floyd, M. L. Skolnik, and D. P. Walker (eds.), *The Community College Baccalaureate: Emerging Trends & Policy Issues*. Sterling, Va.: Stylus, 2005.

Townsend, B. K., and Ignash, J. M. "Community College Roles in Teacher Education: Current Approaches and Future Possibilities." In B. K. Townsend and J. M. Ignash (eds.), *The Role of the Community College in Teacher Education*. New Directions for Community Colleges, no 121. San Francisco: Jossey-Bass, 2003.

Townsend, B. K., and Wilson, K. "A Hand Hold for a Little Bit: Factors Facilitating the Success of Community College Transfer Students to a Large Research University." *Journal of College Student Development*, 2006, *47*(4), 439–456.

Troller, K. T. College of DuPage Teaching and Learning Center: A Comprehensive Professional Development Program. In G. E. Watts (ed.), *Enhancing Community Colleges Through Professional Development*. New Directions for Community Colleges, no. 120. San Francisco: Jossey-Bass, 2002.

University of Hawaii. *Transfer, Enrollment and Performance of UH Community College Associate in Arts Graduates at UH Manoa*. Honolulu: University of Hawaii, 2005.

Updike, K. M. *A Comparative Study of Contract Training in Select Community Colleges*. Phoenix, Ariz.: Office of Corporate Training and Development, Maricopa County Community College District, 1991.

U.S. Bureau of Labor Statistics. *BLS Releases 2004–14 Employment Projections*. Washington, D.C.: U.S. Department of Labor, 2005.

U.S. Department of Education. *Schools Subject to Loss of Eligibility to Participate in the Federal Family Education Loan Program (FFELP) and/or Federal Direct Student Loan Program (FDSLP) Due to FY 1994, FY 1995, and FY 1996 Cohort Default Rates of 25.0% or Greater*. Washington, D.C.: U.S. Department of Education, Office of Student Financial Assistance, 1998.

Van der Werf, M. "For Community Colleges, Fund Raising Has Become Serious and Successful." *Chronicle of Higher Education*, Apr. 9, 1999, pp. A42–A43.

Van Middlesworth, C. L. "Assessing Learning Communities." In T. W. Banta (ed.), *Community College Assessment: Assessment Update Collections*. San Francisco: Jossey-Bass, 2004.

Vaughan, G. B. (ed.). *Questioning the Community College Role*. New Directions for Community Colleges, no. 32. San Francisco: Jossey-Bass, 1980.

Vaughan, G. B. "Effective Presidential Leadership: Twelve Areas of Focus." In A. M. Cohen, F. B. Brawer, and Associates (eds.), *Managing Community Colleges: A Handbook for Effective Practice*. San Francisco: Jossey-Bass, 1994.

Vaughan, G. B., and Weisman, I. M. *Community College Trustees: Leading on Behalf of Their Communities*. Washington, D.C.: Association of Community College Trustees, 1997.

Vaughan, G. B., and Weisman, I. M. *The Community College Presidency at the Millennium*. Washington, D.C.: Community College Press, 1998.

Veblen, T. The *Higher Learning in America: A Memorandum on the Conduct of Universities by Business Men*. New York: B. W. Huebsch, 1918.

Vocational Education: Status in Two-Year Colleges in 1990–91 and Early Signs of Change. Washington, D.C.: U.S. General Accounting Office, 1993.

Voorhees, R. A., and Zhou, D. "Intentions and Goals at the Community College: Associating Student Perceptions and Demographics." *Community College Journal of Research and Practice*, 2000, *24*(3), 219–232.

Wagoner, J. L. "The Search for Mission and Integrity: A Retrospective View." In D. E. Puyear and G. B. Vaughan (eds.), *Maintaining Institutional Integrity*. New Directions for Community Colleges, no. 52. San Francisco: Jossey-Bass, 1985.

Walker, D. E. *The Effective Administrator: A Practical Approach to Problem Solving, Decision Making, and Campus Leadership*. San Francisco: Jossey-Bass, 1979.

Wallin, D. C. "Motivation and Faculty Development: A Three State Study of Presidential Perceptions of Faculty Professional Development Needs. *Community College Journal of Research and Practice*, 2003, *27*(4), 317–335.

Walters, J., and Shymoniak, L. *The Effectiveness of California Community Colleges on Selected Performance Measures*, October 1996. Sacramento: California Community Colleges, Office of the Chancellor, 1996.

Warner, W. L., and others. *Who Shall Be Educated? The Challenge of Unequal Opportunities*. New York: HarperCollins, 1944.

Washington State Board for Community and Technical Colleges. *Academic Year Report 2005–06*. Olympia: State Board for Community and Technical Colleges, 2006.

Wattenbarger, J. L., and Starnes, P. M. *Financial Support Patterns for Community Colleges, 1976*. Gainesville: University of Florida, 1976.

Waukesha County Technical College. *Waukesha County Technical College Graduate Follow-Up Report, 1999*. Pewaukee, Wis.: Waukesha County Technical College, 1999. 18 pp.

Weeks, A. A. *CSS One-Hour Content-Correlated Courses*. Poughkeepsie, N.Y.: Dutchess Community College, 1987. 35 pp.

Weick, K. E. "Educational Organizations as Loosely Coupled Systems." *Administrative Science Quarterly*, 1976, *21*(1), 1–19.

Weis, L. Between *Two Worlds: Black Students in an Urban Community College*. Boston: Routledge and Kegan Paul, 1985.

Weisman, I. M, and Vaughan, G. B. *The Community College Presidency 2006*. Washington D.C.: American Association of Community Colleges, 2007.

Weiss, K. R. "Transfer Rankings Anger Two-Year Colleges." *Los Angeles Times*, Nov. 24, 2000, Part A, Part 1, p. 3.

Welch, G. F. A New Faculty Orientation Program: Building a Core of New Faculty to Shape the Future of the College. In G. E. Watts (Ed.), *Enhancing Community Colleges Through Professional Development*. New Directions for Community Colleges, no. 120. San Francisco: Jossey-Bass, 2002.

White, J. F. "Honors in North Central Association Community Colleges." Paper presented at the annual meeting of the American Association of Community and Junior Colleges, Seattle, Apr. 1975.

Wilcox, S. A. *Directory of Southern California Community College Researchers*. Los Angeles: Southern California Community College Institutional Research Association, 1987.

Wiley, C. "The Effect of Unionization on Community College Faculty Remuneration: An Overview." *Community College Review*, 1993, *21*(1), 48–57.

Wills, G. "What Makes a Good Leader?" *Atlantic Monthly*, 1994, *273*(4), 63–64, 67–71, 74–76, 79–80.

Windham, P. *Florida Vocational Graduates' Follow-Up Outcomes*. Tallahassee: Florida State Board of Community Colleges, 1996.

Winner, C. N. "The Role and Function of the Departmental Chairperson at Delaware Technical and Community College." Three executive position papers submitted as doctoral requirements, University of Delaware, 1989.

Winter, C. G. *History of the Junior College Movement in California*. Sacramento: Bureau of Junior College Education, California State Department of Education, 1964.

Wisconsin Technical College System. *WTCS Graduate Follow Up Report 2005–2006*. Madison: Wisconsin Technical College System, 2006.

Wisconsin Technical College System Board. Graduate Follow-up Report, 1998–99. Madison: Wisconsin Technical College System Board, 1999.

Witt, A. A., Wattenbarger, J. L., Gollattscheck, J. F., and Suppiger, J. E. *America's Community Colleges: The First Century*. Washington, D.C.: Community College Press, 1994.

Woodroof, R. H. "Doubts About the Future of the Private Liberal Arts Junior College." In R. H. Woodroof (ed.), *The Viability of the Private Junior College*. New Directions for Community Colleges, no. 69. San Francisco: Jossey-Bass, 1990.

Woods, J. E. *Status of Testing Practices at Two-Year Postsecondary Institutions*. Washington, D.C.: American Association of Community and Junior Colleges, 1985.

Wyner, J. "Educational Equity and the Transfer Student." *Chronicle of Higher Education*, Feb. 10, 2006, p. B6.

Wyoming Community College Commission. *Wyoming Community Colleges Annual Performance Report: Core Indicators of Effectiveness*. Cheyenne, Wyo.: Wyoming Community College Commission, 2004.

Zhai, L., and Monzon, R. "Community College Student Retention: Student Characteristics and Withdrawal Reasons." Paper presented at the Annual Meeting of the California Association for Institutional Research, Sacramento, Nov. 2001.

Zimbler, L. J. *Background Characteristics, Work Activities, and Compensation of Faculty and Instructional Staff in Postsecondary Institutions, Fall 1998*. Washington, D.C.: National Center for Education Statistics, 2001.

Zumeta, W., and Frankle, D. *California Community Colleges Making Them Stronger and More Affordable*. San Jose, Calif.: The National Center for Public Policy and Higher Education, 2007.

Zwerling, L. S. *Second Best: The Crisis of the Community College*. New York: McGraw-Hill, 1976.

Name Index

Subject Index

A

Academic departments, 145–147

Academic disciplines, 361–365

Academic freedom, 362

Academic Senate for California Community Colleges, 291, 298, 302–303

Academic standards. *See* Standards

Academic transfer function. *See* Transfer function

Academy for Community College Leadership Advancement, 327

Academy for Leadership Training and Development, 147

Access to Better Jobs program, 227

Access to community colleges, 35, 171–172. *See also* Admissions

Accountability: effects of, 396; and funding, 157, 176; history of, 395; problems with, 397–404. *See also* Accreditation; Assessment

Accreditation, 131–134, 386

Accrediting Commission for Community and Junior Colleges, 375

Activism, student, 234–235

Administration: division of labor within, 144, 146; ethnic minority members of, 138, 142; and faculty members, 104, 459; future of, 461; history of, 141–142;

leadership styles in, 151–154; patterns of, 143–144; president's role in, 142–143; and secondary schools, 142; and student services, 223. *See also* Governance

Admissions: to four-year institutions, 424; history of, 288–289; open, 71, 176–177, 289, 306–310; philosophies of, 50–51; procedures of, 71; selective, 36, 306–308

Adult education, 49; and basic skills, 324; and community education, 321; definition of, 318–319; enrollment in, 322; funding of, 334

Adults as Learners (Cross), 315

Advanced placement (AP), 45, 224, 444

Advanced Technical Education program, 254

Advertising, 70, 339

Advising. *See* Counseling

Affirmative action, 131, 155, 391, 424, 432, 457

African American students. *See* Students, ethnic minority

Alabama State Department of Postsecondary Education, 469

Allocative function, 435–437. *See also* Cooling out function

Alternatives to community colleges, 440–444

547

Placement testing. *See* Testing,
  placement
Planning, future, 449–451
Policies for Lifelong Education
  project, 326
Political model of governance, 115
Politics of college mission, 422
Portland Community College, 226
Practical experience, 363
Preparation of faculty, 85–91
Preparatory education. *See*
  Developmental education function
Presidents of community colleges,
  142–143
Prestige: and community education,
  340; and developmental education,
  302–304; historical aspects of, 301;
  and rankings, 430; and student
  ability, 305; and vocational educa-
  tion, 252
Prince George's Community
  College, 291
Prisons, 331–332
Private community colleges: and
  community service, 25; curriculum
  at, 23, 348–349; development of,
  6, 15–20; future growth of, 450;
  governance of, 116–117; *versus*
  public institutions, 15–22, 168,
  270; tuition and loans at, 169; and
  vocational education, 270, 273.
  See also Proprietary trade schools
Productivity, 401–402, 466
Professional development.
  See In-service faculty training
Professionalization of faculty,
  106–110, 458–459
Professionalization of student
  services, 298
*Profile of the Community College
  Professoriate, 1975–2000*
  (Outcalt), 81
Proposition 13 (California), 22,
  158–160, 322, 336
Proprietary trade schools, 441–443;
  classification of, 49; development

of, 117, 273; financial issues at,
  168–170, 273; public perceptions
  of, 441; standards at, 133; and
  vocational education, 273. *See also*
  Private community colleges
Public community colleges: curriculum at, 23, 24, 256; enrollment
  in, 45–47, 453–454; faculty issues
  at, 85, 91, 95, 147–148; financial
  issues of, 172, 239–240, 357
  (*See also* Funding); governance of,
  116–117, 460 (*See also* State-level
  governance); growth of, 16–17,
  450; mission of, 25–26, 321; *versus*
  private, 15–22; relationship of, to
  secondary schools, 82; scrutiny of,
  157, 301; student issues at, 63, 69,
  223, 289–293, 398; and technology
  usage, 190–191, 208
Public relations, 409
Puente Project, 227
Purpose of community colleges.
  See Mission

Q

Qualitative research, 397
Quinebaug Valley Community
  College, 331

R

Race. *See* Ethnic minority adminis-
  trators; Ethnic minority faculty;
  Students, ethnic minority
Rankings, 401–402, 430. *See also*
  Competition among institutions;
  Prestige
Recruiting: of faculty members,
  88, 101, 142; of nontraditional
  students, 53, 56, 77; and open
  admissions, 45, 70–71; oversight of,
  121, 243; scope of, 223–225, 303
Reform, educational, 287
Remedial education. *See*
  Developmental education
  function
Remediation, 290